The writer of the Gospel of Luke is a Hellenistic writer who uses conventional modes of narration, characterization and argumentation to present Jesus in the manner of the familiar figure of the dinner sage. In this original and thought-provoking study, Willi Braun draws both on social and literary evidence regarding the Greco-Roman élite banquet scene and on ancient prescribed methods of rhetorical composition to argue that the Pharisaic dinner episode in Luke 14 is a skilfully crafted rhetorical unit in which Jesus presents an argument for Luke's vision of Christian society. His contention that the point of the episode is directed primarily at the wealthy urban élite, who stand in most need of transformation of character and values to fit them for membership of this society, points up the way in which gospel writers manipulated the inherited Jesus traditions for the purposes of ideological and social formation of Christian communities.

D1518346

SOCIETY FOR NEW TESTAMENT STUDIES

*MONOGRAPH SERIES*

General editor: Margaret E. Thrall

**85**

FEASTING AND SOCIAL RHETORIC IN LUKE 14

# Feasting and social rhetoric in Luke 14

**WILLI BRAUN**

*Assistant Professor, Department of Religion,
Bishop's University, Lennoxville, Quebec*

CAMBRIDGE
UNIVERSITY PRESS

CAMBRIDGE UNIVERSITY PRESS
Cambridge, New York, Melbourne, Madrid, Cape Town, Singapore, São Paulo

Cambridge University Press
The Edinburgh Building, Cambridge CB2 2RU, UK

Published in the United States of America by Cambridge University Press, New York

www.cambridge.org
Information on this title: www.cambridge.org/9780521495530

First published 1995
This digitally printed first paperback version 2005

A catalogue record for this publication is available from the British Library

Library of Congress Cataloguing in Publication data

Braun, Willi, 1954–,
Feasting and social rhetoric in Luke 14 / Willi Braun.
    p.    cm. – (Society for New Testament Studies Monograph series; 85)
Includes bibliographical references and index.
ISBN 0 521 49553 9 (hardback)
1. Bible. N.T. Luke XIV, 1–24 – Criticism, interpretation, etc.
2. Dinners and dining in the Bible.
I. Title. II. Series:
Monograph series (Society for New Testament Studies); 85.
BS2595.6.D56B73    1995
226.4'066 – dc20    95–42704 CIP

ISBN-13 978-0-521-49553-0 hardback
ISBN-10 0-521-49553-9 hardback

ISBN-13 978-0-521-01885-2 paperback
ISBN-10 0-521-01885-4 paperback

*For Brenda, Naomi, Anita*

# CONTENTS

# ACKNOWLEDGEMENTS AND
# NOTE ON ABBREVIATIONS

I am grateful to Margaret Thrall, editor of the fine SNTS Monograph Series, Alex Wright, theology editor, and the Syndicate of Cambridge University Press for granting what once appeared as a doctoral dissertation (Braun 1993) a second, more public life.

All stages and dimensions of the making of this book have been affected deeply and positively by others who participated in the project with interest and precious criticism. Heinz Guenther indelibly shaped my understanding of early Christianity and its literature as a datum of Hellenistic religion. John Kloppenborg's unfailingly good advice, unnerving erudition and insightful work on Luke's gospel were offered to me as a benefit package of such value that it is repayable only with an expression of gratitude. Vernon Robbins read my work with amazing attention, understanding and respect; I am deeply grateful to him for sharing his deep and precise knowledge of ancient rhetorical patterns of composition. Peter Richardson, has left his stamp on these pages as a scholar, critic and editor, and on me as a teacher and friend. To Paul Gooch I owe much gratitude for his many kindnesses, both scholarly and personal. Meg Miller, with her expertise in the classical texts and ancient symposia, saved me from as many amateurish infelicities in these areas as she could. Margaret Thrall and F. Gerald Downing greatly assisted the task of revision with their counsel on substantive and editorial matters.

I cannot imagine surviving, much less enjoying, this 'diet of words' without the cheer and generosity of friends and colleagues: Muna Salloum's tireless encouragement, timely cajoling and formidable knowledge of the ancient and modern Mediterranean world, often shared in what turned out to be 'table talk' at sumptuous Mediterranean feasts in the Salloum dining room; William Arnal's countless hours of company in a lesser-known Toronto café and the enormous benefit of his incisive criticism of inarticulate, pre-textual versions of almost every paragraph of this work; Ann Baranowski, Darlene Juschka, Arthur McCalla and Russell McCutcheon, members of the editorial collective of the journal, *Method and Theory in the Study of Religion*, and their generous easing of my editorial duties at crucial times. Herbert Berg, Ed Bergen, Judy Bergen, Marion Boulby, Frieda Braun, Heinz Braun, Michel Desjardins, Robert Forrest, Ernest Janzen, Angela Kalinowski, Jane McAuliffe, Leif Vaage, Bill Vanderburg, Harvey White, Donald Wiebe: they and I know why their names are here.

Above all, I am speechlessly indebted to three women with whom I live and share my life. I dedicate this book to them.

I am pleased to acknowledge generous research funding and support by the Social Sciences and Humanities Research Council of Canada, the Ontario Ministry of Colleges and Universities, the University of Toronto and Bishop's University.

Abbreviations of ancient sources follow the standard of *The Oxford Classical Dictionary* or, where necessary, that of Liddell, Scott and Jones, *A Greek-English Lexicon* and, of Jewish and early Christian texts, the 'Instructions for Contributors' of the *Journal of Biblical Literature*.

Department of Religion
Bishop's University
Lennoxville, Quebec, Canada

# 1

## INTRODUCTION: HOW TO READ LUKE 14?

And they explained what had happened on the road (ἐν τῇ ὁδῷ) and how he became known to them in the breaking of the bread (κλάσει τοῦ ἄρτου). (Luke 24.35).

This clause with its references to travel and eating from the coda of Luke's gospel, though infused here with the numinous and liturgical nuances that colour the coda itself,[1] nonetheless accurately echoes the gospel writer's twin devices for advancing the narrative in its lengthy central section and for portraying its principal figure, Jesus, as a travelling benefactor and banqueter.[2] Typically, it is at these frequent prandial pauses, either explicitly within the socially significant confines of the *klinium* (dining room) or within spatially unspecified dining situations that clearly evoke the *klinium* setting, that Luke shows himself to be a master of narrative evocation of the Greco-Roman social dining scene, of adjusting older Jesus traditions towards his narrative aims, and of characterizing Jesus as a kind of δειπνοσοφιστής (dinner sage), a recognizable and credible figure to first-century Mediterranean readers,[3] who expounds for

---

[1] The event 'on the road' is an encounter with the risen Jesus; κλάσις τοῦ ἄρτου is a central ritual of Luke's paradigmatic Jerusalem church; see Acts 2.42–7; Horn, 1983, pp. 36–49.
[2] On the travel motif see Acts 10.38 (Luke's summary of Jesus' career as it has been described in the gospel): διῆλθεν εὐεργετῶν καὶ ἰώμενος πάντας τοὺς καταδυναστευομένος ὑπὸ τοῦ διαβόλου, 'he wandered about doing good and curing all who were overpowered by the devil'. On Luke's portrayal of Jesus as a 'benefactor' within a benefaction-oriented culture see Danker, 1982, p. 395; 1988, pp. 2–10; cf. ch. 6, pp. 116–20 below. On the 'wandering guest' motif in Luke see especially Grundmann, 1959; and Moessner, 1989, whose view of this motif (a midrashic replication of Deuteronomy) I do not share.
[3] The display of sagacity at symposia was a Greek social and literary tradition; hence the 'dinner sage', often an intellectual retainer in wealthy households, was a popular figure who became immortalized in the literary symposia. The late Hellenistic figure of the *deipnosophist* is most aptly illustrated in Athenaeus' *Deipnosophistae*.

*1*

Luke's audience an exemplary commensality – an ideal social dining arrangement – by means of provocative actions and explicating orations.

Among the many dinner stops in Luke's narrative, the one recorded in 14.1–24 stands out in the alignment of its setting (an upper-class dinner party), with Jesus as the featured guest, and a discourse appropriate to the setting in that it consists mostly of *quaestiones convivales*, topics related to banquets and proper dinner behaviour. Why this dinner episode, evidently rather coherent on the face of it, not an obvious unsolved problem in Lukan studies, nor short of studies devoted to it, should receive the lengthy attention I have given it needs a brief explanation.

This study was to be a brief chapter and several scattered footnotes in an analysis of the origin, transmission and literary functions of the parable of the great banquet whose three extant versions are entombed in Luke 14.16–24, Matthew 22.1–14 and *Gospel of Thomas* 64. The need to expand one chapter into a work in its own right was forced upon me by the realization that retold parables 'can be a very tricky thing' (Mack, 1988, p. 150) and, more specifically, that the recovery of the 'parabolic' function of the banquet story in Luke's narrative would be trickier than I had anticipated.

Difficulties lurked on several sides. The first inhered in the notion of 'parable' itself. Luke does not call the dinner story a 'parable' and in 14.7 and elsewhere uses the term to designate material that does not fall into any form-critical category of *Gleichnisrede*. The traditional form-critical supposition that 'forms can tell us much about functions' (Sider, 1981, p. 453) thus would not be very useful. Rather, it would prove to be necessary to go back to Aristotle, the Greek tradition generally, and to a neglected insight in Adolf Jülicher's monumental work on *Die Gleichnisreden Jesu* (1910), where parables are treated not as formal entities but as 'proofs' (πίστεις) for the production of 'conviction' (πίστις) in argumentation.[4]

Second, though not called a parable, the story is evidently an invented narrative and, as others have noted and I point out later, it

---

[4] Aristotle, *Rhet.* 2.20.1–9; on ancient theories of comparison see McCall, 1969; Jülicher, 1910, vol. I, pp. 96, 105; see also ch. 4. n. 4. Jülicher's point, learnt from Aristotle, that parables are 'Beglaubigungsmittel' was subordinated to his larger argument for the distinction between parable and allegory. Since, moreover, his entire work was driven by his famous polemic against an allegorizing parable hermeneutic, the idea that parables are 'proofs' was not fully developed, much less exegetically worked out, even by him.

is thoroughly linked to a larger textual unit that can be shown to consist of 14.1–24 on literary evidence (ch. 2) and rhetorical sense (ch. 8). Hence the Lukan function of the householder story would need to be explicated contextually – in relation to the point of the dinner episode (14.1–24) as a whole – much more rigorously and specifically than had been done before.[5]

The vast literature[6] on the banquet parable demonstrates that the dominant tendency has been towards a figurative and allegorical interpretation in which the narrative context as a hermeneutic guide is largely suppressed.[7] Rather, typically the parable is viewed as half narrative metaphor, standing for the divine realm (βασιλεία τοῦ θεοῦ), and 'half allegory' (Jülicher, 1910, vol. II, p. 416), to be read either as an eschatological story of divine admission to and exclusion from the βασιλεία (symbolized in the mythic messianic meal), hence disclosing Luke's 'ethic of election' (Sanders, 1974; cf. Bacon, 1922–3), or to be viewed as a coded Lukan retrospective on the history of divine election passing from the aristocratic Jewish custodians of the official religious apparatus (refused first invitation) to marginal Jews (second invitation to urban poor) and Gentiles (supplementary invitation to those outside the city), much like the expanding Christian mission pattern depicted in Acts.[8]

How all this could be embedded in a story so explicitly reliant on the vocabulary of wealth and poverty, and which quite evidently has been located within a narrative context where these issues appear only fuzzily, if at all, turned out to be a question demanding another look at the banquet parable and its point and function within the banquet episode. To be sure, I am not the first to point out the problem of an overly imaginative interpretation of Luke's banquet story, nor the first to press for an adjusted appraisal of its meaning and use. Others, upon noting that Luke accentuates socio-economic issues in the parable, have suggested that the point of the story has to do with these issues and that its function was to stand as a fictional model for the Lukan community's orientation towards

[5] Cf. Frankemölle's argument for appraising parables embedded in larger texts with reference to their *Sitz in der Literatur* (Frankemölle, 1981–2, pp. 69–70).

[6] See the entries in Kissinger, 1979; and the 'bibliografia recente' (1960–74) in J. Dupont, 1978a, pp. 331–4.

[7] Dschulnigg, 1989, pp. 335–51, charts the main lines of parable interpretation, using the banquet parable as the illustration; cf. the typology of hermeneutical options by Fabris, 1978, pp. 150–5.

[8] E.g., Manson, 1949, p. 130. This interpretive model is further discussed and criticized in ch. 5, pp. 84–6.

wealth and social relations.[9] These scholars would provide generally compatible company for me in the appraisal of Luke's re-presentation (redaction) of the banquet parable itself, although I would end up stating the socio-economic issues presumed and addressed by the parable more sharply (ch. 5), and identifying its primary point and how it is conveyed more specifically (ch. 6).

Since the parable delivers its message as part of a longer speech in a dinner setting, the point of the parable would need to be tested and clarified with reference to this larger narrative and speech setting. And herein would lie the third and most difficult problem: how to determine what the entire episode was about. Wherein, if anywhere, lay its thematic centre of gravity? Did the unit have an identifiable representational or argumentative function? That is, did it intend to exert a specific influence upon its audience? How could one account for the selection and sequence of all the sub-units of the episode? Most perplexingly, why had the author of the episode elected to introduce a speech, otherwise entirely made up of 'table talk', with a healing scene featuring a person afflicted with dropsy? What, after all, did dropsies have to do with dinners?

Much clarity could be gained on these questions, I thought, if the compositional logic, the design that generated the literary existence of this episode, could be uncovered. In the traditional view, generated by the force of source, form and redaction criticism, the episode consists of thematically related units collected from several pre-Lukan sources which Luke has redactionally adjusted more or less substantially and collated according to a catchword method, using 'banquet' as the catchword. This view is not adequate, however, for it pre-empts a deeper comprehension of the cohesiveness of the dinner episode. It presupposes a highly unliterary author and legitimates an exegetical method, amply reflected in the scholarly commentary traditions, that treats the constituent *pericopae* in isolation from each other. Others have argued that Luke composed the episode along lines suggested by the classical Greek *symposion*, a literary form, popular at least from the time of Plato to the end of antiquity, for depicting philosophers at dinner or drinking party and presenting their opinions and arguments as dinner or drinking talk. But this too would prove to be a hypothesis that either cannot or, in application, does not deal with the combination

[9] Dormeyer, 1974, pp. 211–16, 219; Fabris, 1978, pp. 154–65; Horn, 1983, pp. 184–6; Moxnes, 1986–7, pp. 162–3; Rohrbaugh, 1991, pp. 137–47; cf. passing references to 14.16–24 in the same vein in Elliott, 1991a and 1991b.

of questions the dinner episode raises (see ch. 7; Braun, 1992, pp. 73–5). The challenge thus would be to develop a comprehensive, coherent and historically plausible proposal – i.e., a proposal appropriate to a first-century author and audience – for the interpretation of Luke 14.1–24. The proposal would need to account for the narrative setting (dinner party), the selection, literary characteristics and sequence of all the episode's constituent periods (including the scene of healing a person with dropsy, an apparently odd formal and thematic 'wild card' in the dinner episode), as well as the *dramatis personae* and the contrasted characterization on which the episode depends so heavily. This multi-dimensional challenge, encountered in the pursuit of the point and function of the banquet parable in Luke, would become the central preoccupation in this work.

After outlining several standard assumptions on Luke as an author and providing an initial reading of 14.1–24 (ch. 2), the response to the challenge consists of two major related components. The first, mostly located in chapters 3–6, consists of the demonstration that an historical understanding of the issues upon which the episode focuses depends heavily on appreciating central cultural values, common social and economic realities and popular moral views and traditions by which first-century Mediterranean people ordered and estimated their lives. A milieu analysis[10] reveals that the text takes for granted the audience's familiarity with the values of honour and shame as the controlling and motivating forces in virtually every domain of social interaction; it not only presumes, but, by the selection of its vocabulary and manipulation of the topic of contrast for the purpose of characterization and argumentation, it exaggerates a social system marked by enforced boundaries between rich and poor, noble and ignoble, the élite and the lowly classes; more specifically, it implies a high degree of familiarity with the élite Greco-Roman symposia and dinner-party scene and the symbolic value attached to dining room gatherings. A milieu analysis also indicates that Luke not only relied upon a great deal of traditional and social knowledge on the part of his first-century readers; he also took a critical stance towards conventional values and social patterns that were reflected in and symbolically celebra-

---

[10] The term is derived from Pax, 1975, although I do not accept his restriction of milieu to the Palestinian Jewish social world. Cf. Hock's objections to so narrow a conception of an interpretive milieu and his argument for casting 'the comparative net' widely into the Greco-Roman world (Hock, 1987, pp. 455–6).

ted in the ancient élite symposia, a stance that can be clarified against the back-drop of the Cynic 'anti-sympotic' *repas ridicule* tradition which came to particularly clear expression in the writings of Lucian of Samosata. It is in fact within this tradition that I found the hitherto missing key for specifying the value of dropsy and the aptness of locating and healing a dropsical figure within an élite dinner party whose underlying values and governing rules Luke uses as a negative foil against which to promote an alternative dining ethic.

While this analysis generates a consistent general picture of what the point of the entire episode is, a second component, most sharply articulated in chapters 8 and 9, focuses on the manner in which the point is delivered. Here the analysis turns more explicitly to the question of the composition of the episode. My proposal will be that Luke 14.1–24 consists of a narrative argument that resembles a pattern of argumentation worked out by ancient rhetoricians and widely used in the Greco-Roman educational system as an exercise in literary criticism and rhetorical training, namely the exercise of 'working out' (ἐργασία) a brief attributed saying or action known as a *chreia* (χρεία). Using the *chreia* elaboration exercise described by Hermogenes of Tarsus and other ancient teachers of rhetoric as an analytic guide brings into view a narrative episode in which all its individual sub-units can be shown to contribute thematically and argumentatively to a specific issue addressed by the episode as a whole.

It should be noted, in all fairness, that whatever success or persuasion inheres in this bifocal analysis – if pressed to name it I would call it 'socio-rhetorical', a term Vernon Robbins used to describe his study of the gospel of Mark[11] – as a way of meeting the interpretive challenge presented by Luke 14.1–24 is due to lights switched on for me by several key works of other scholars. Ronald Hock's article on Luke 16.19–31 (Hock, 1987) helped me to understand the similar language of social and economic polarity and reversal in Luke 14 and, insofar as that article steered me towards Cynic or Cynic-influenced sources in my search for analogies that could clarify the use of banquet traditions in Luke 14, Hock deserves acknowledgement for helping me to stumble upon the

[11] In general, a socio-rhetorical analysis links the reconstruction of the cultural norms and pattern implied in and presumed by a text and the analysis of how these cultural items come to literary expression which, too, is governed by conventions (see Robbins, 1984, pp. 1–6).

metaphorical dropsy which, as it turns out, is the pivotal figure in the dinner episode. Richard Rohrbaugh's study of the ancient urban social and economic realities presupposed in Luke 14.16–24 (Rohrbaugh, 1991) appeared after I had begun my own attempt to reinterpret the banquet parable with reference to the rules governing the élite dinner party scene and to ancient views on the rich and the poor and the values and norms that governed their interaction. His article confirmed my investigative direction and helped in the articulation of my hunches. Readers should also recognize in my argument that the banquet parable is a story about the 'conversion' of a wealthy urban householder-host, rather than a story primarily about guests (ch. 6), the conceptual and lectional influence of John Kloppenborg's analogous analysis of Luke 16.1–8a (Kloppenborg, 1989). Finally, I doubt that the final section (ch. 8), containing the 'hard core' of my claims, would have been written without the aid of Burton Mack's and Vernon Robbins's *Patterns of Persuasion in the Gospels* (1989), an exemplary 'grammar' of *chreia* composition in the synoptic gospels.

# 2

## ASSUMPTIONS AND PRELIMINARY READING

A detailed analysis of Luke 14.1–24 in later chapters begs for treatment of some preliminary matters. First, it is appropriate to outline several elements of a canopy of assumptions concerning the characteristics of Lukan authorship and manner of composition in whose shade I plan to work.

Second, as a matter of strategy, I use the banquet parable (14.16–24) as a launching point for sketching the most obvious lines along which the parable has been integrated into the larger textual unit of 14.1–24. In part, the use of the parable as the vantage point from which to survey the narrative episode in which it resides is an expedient means of demonstrating the thematic unity of 14.1–24. Additionally, the move from parable to context helps to justify my resistance (see ch. 1) to studying parables *in vacuo*, and to illustrate, rather, what might be gained by assigning procedural priority to the banquet story's *Sitz in der Literatur* as a path towards discovering the particularly Lukan dimensions of the story and the role that it plays in the thematic and argumentative structure of the sabbath dinner episode.[1]

The most recent decades have been a productive period of research on the nature of Lukan authorship and the literary and generic characteristics of Luke-Acts. I draw from it the following assumptions whose importance for the study of the banquet story will become apparent.

### Luke as Hellenistic author

Among the leading trends in 'a new age of Lucan study' is a shift of comparative vision from the source-redaction method of discerning

---

[1] This approach follows pointers given by Frankemölle, 1981–2, pp. 69–70. In later chapters I will expand the 'parables in context' approach to include the wider

the thought of the third evangelist to 'a comparison of Lucan forms and techniques of composition with those of the Mediterranean milieu'.[2] The results may not be entirely coherent, but they are sufficient to place the author of Luke-Acts firmly within the roster of first-century Greco-Roman *littérateurs*,[3] writers of 'popular' literature destined for the consumption of a rather literate audience worthy to be called κράτιστος (most excellent). This, an item in the formal dedication of the work to a patron, may not by itself accurately disclose the literary sophistication and social standing of Luke's audience,[4] but it supports other indicators that have led scholars to envision a reading clientele drawn from the ranks of the cultured and relatively wealthy urban élite.[5] If we do not demand a rigid, mechanical adherence to generic, formal and stylistic conventions,[6] but expect to see an authorial χαρακτὴρ ὁ ἴδιος (style proper to a person),[7] it is hardly disputable that Luke-Acts is an

Mediterranean literary and social traditions which provide much extra-textual illumination of Luke's text.

2  Talbert, 1989, pp. 297–320 (citations p. 309); cf. Bovon, 1979, pp. 161–90; and Downing, 1982, pp. 546–59. Recently Mealand argued 'that Acts is closer to major Hellenistic historians such as Polybius than has often been granted' (Mealand, 1991, p. 42).

3  Fitzmyer echoes the common opinion when he calls Luke 'a conscious littérateur of the Greco-Roman period' (Fitzmyer, 1964, p. 92). Cadbury's *The Making of Luke-Acts* (1927) is still the most lucid and wide-ranging expression of this view.

4  Alexander (1986, pp. 48–74; 1993, pp. 168–200) makes a convincing case for caution in drawing conclusions about the social position of author and readers on the basis of the Lukan preface and its formal address (κράτιστε Θεόφιλε, Luke 1.3). Cf. Cadbury, 1927, p. 194: Luke's 'preface is one of the most evident marks of the littérateur.'

5  Most recently, Robbins, 1991b; see also Downing 1982, pp. 557–8, who imagines a 'sophisticated reader' or 'high-minded pagans', and the hypothetical reconstruction of Luke's readers (urban merchant class) by Kany, 1986, pp. 75–90. That Luke seems to represent an urban viewpoint was suggested already by Cadbury (1926, p. 309; 1927, pp. 245–53) followed by many others. For a recent analysis of Luke's knowledge of Mediterranean urban life see Rohrbaugh, 1991.

6  Although Luke wrote in a time whose literature is stamped by what van Groningen (1965, p. 55) calls 'veneration for form', a manifestation of the archaizing, imitative proclivities of the age, some allowance for the flouting of forms should be made. This, too, is characteristic of the popular literature of Luke's time. On this see, e.g., Pervo, 1987, p. 11; on the subject of imitation (μίμησις) see Brodie, 1984, pp. 17–46, and the literature he cites.

7  Apollonius of Tyana illustrates this concern for balancing authorial integrity with the value of imitation in his letter to Scopelian the sophist, where, after listing five styles of discourse, he advises that 'despite this orderly array of styles, first in rank is the style that is proper to a person because it is in accordance with his innate capacity or nature, and second in rank is the style that seeks to imitate the best, in cases where a person is lacking natural endowments' (trans. Penella, 1979, pp. 44–5). Brodie (1984, p. 38) adduces a similar notice from Dionysius of Halicar-

example of its contemporary Hellenistic literary culture with which it converges at points on the generic plane,[8] in its use of forms and literary devices,[9] in its familiarity with the 'art of rhetoric', (Kurz, 1980; ch. 8 below) even in its archaizing style and its techniques of characterization.[10]

If Luke thus appears to place his work on the popular book shelves in the library of his Greco-Roman contemporaries,[11] it naturally suggests that we should look out for common Hellenistic

nassus: 'each author's mode of composition is as unique as one's personal appearance'; cf. Cadbury, 1927, pp. 213–14.

[8] The debate on the genre of Luke-Acts is not closed, not least because Acts and Luke pull towards different generic affiliations, as is recognized by Barr and Wentling, 1984. This makes for a less than happy placement within the *bios*-literature. Cf. Talbert, 1974, pp. 125–40. Among the genre-studies of the Acts Plümacher (1972; 1974) sees the closest parallels in the *Roman Antiquities* of Dionysius of Halicarnassus and Livy's historical writings. Pervo links Acts with the ancient historical novels and suggests that Luke might be characterized as a 'biographical novel' (Pervo, 1987, p. 185 n. 5). A reliable summary and evaluation of scholarship on the genre of Luke-Acts is in Thibeaux, 1990, pp. 61–88. The body of genre scholarship makes it clear that Luke-Acts belongs within the matrix of popular Hellenistic writings, which, though they admit of various categories (biographies, histories, novels), nonetheless share many narrative and rhetorical features.

[9] See the general treatment of Cadbury, 1927, especially pp. 127–54 and 194–209 (on Luke's *prooemium*).

[10] Remarks on Luke's LXX-mimesis are commonplace; it perhaps is best explained with reference to the atticistic enthusiasm in the contemporary literary culture (see Cadbury, 1927, pp. 122–3, and Plümacher, 1972, pp. 38–79). On the 'atticistic fanaticism' of Hellenistic authors see van Groningen, 1965, p. 49, and the overview of the various manifestations of archaism in the late first to early third centuries CE (the second sophistic) by Bowie, 1970, and C. Baldwin, 1928, pp. 9–23. Similarly, Luke's fondness for portraying his characters through their speeches is conventional and illustrative of his familiarity with the techniques of προσωποποιΐα and ἠθοποιΐα, standard headings in the *progymnasmata* (Penndorf, 1911). Little noticed is Luke's frequent employment of the technique of competitive comparison (σύγκρισις) of narrative *dramatis personae*, reminiscent of the *vitae parallelae* of, say, Plutarch or Sallust; the standard treatment of *synkrisis* is Focke, 1923, but see also Hense, 1893, pp. 4–40; on *synkrisis* in the third gospel see Vielhauer's comments on Luke's comparison of Jesus and John (Vielhauer, 1975, p. 372) and Hock, 1987, pp. 456–7; cf. additional comments in chapters 4 and 5 below.

[11] In 1899 P. Corssen already emphasized Luke as 'Hochliteratur' or 'belles-lettres' and wrote: 'Mit dem Evangelium des Lukas ist das Evangelium aus dem Dunkel der Conventikel auf den Büchermarkt hinausgetreten' (*Göttingische gelehrte Anzeigen*, 1899, p. 305; cited by Alexander, 1986, p. 48). Corssen's remark does raise important issues that impinge on the question of the socio-economic position of author and readers of Luke. These concern the cost (research expenses [see Luke 1.1–4], papyrus, copying, etc.), circulation and consumption of books in the first century. Evidently books were expensive to produce and therefore purchased primarily by the wealthy sectors (see Wesseling, 1988, p. 72, and the literature cited there). I leave these questions as *desiderata*.

forms and techniques of narration in the composition of the discrete episodes of the gospel. Luke 14.1–24 does indeed consist of rhetorically useful *Gattungen* that were widely employed by Greek and Roman writers. *Chreiai* (14.1–6), 'concise statement(s) or action(s)...attributed to a definite character',[12] may become the basis for an expanded narrative argument.[13] *Parabolai* (14.7–11, 12–14, 16–24 [*paradeigma*]), species of analogous forms of speech (ὁμοίωσις) and techniques of comparison were stock subjects for ancient rhetorical theorists and writers of textbooks from Aristotle to Quintilian and beyond, and constituted part of the basic training of orators and writers alike.[14] How much Luke relies on Greco-Roman literary customs, rhetorical techniques and the 'everyday' kind of social knowledge will become evident in subsequent chapters.

## Dramatic episodes in Luke's central section

The episode on Jesus at dinner in the house of a ruler is located virtually in the middle of Luke's 'central section', the so-called 'travel narrative' (*Reisebericht*) or 'great insertion' (*grosse Einschaltung*).[15] Although one should think that the placement of the dinner story within this section should be of significance for determining Luke's interest in the story, it is difficult to define that significance, for Luke's central section has proved notoriously uncooperative in disclosing a compositional design or a thematic organizing principle that lends coherence to the section and tells of its purpose. Central to this problem is the disagreement between ostensible form (travel

---

12 Aelius Theon, Περὶ Χρείας 2–4 (Hock and O'Neil, 1986, p. 82).
13 In general see Hock and O'Neil, 1986; Robbins, 1988b; Robbins in Mack and Robbins, 1989, pp. 1–29; note also Kennedy, 1984, p. 23: a *chreia* involves 'telling an anecdote about what someone did or said and then explaining its meaning and amplifying it'. See the detailed discussion in chapters 7 and 8.
14 E.g., the treatise Περὶ τρόπων of Trypho Grammaticus (late first century BCE.), under the heading περὶ ὁμοιώσεως deals at some length with forms of comparison. The section begins thus: Ὁμοίωσίς ἐστι ῥῆσις, καθ᾽ ἣν ἕτερον ἑτέρῳ παραβάλλομεν, εἴδη δὲ αὐτῆς εἰσι τρία, εἰκών, παράδειγμα, παραβολή. Detailed treatment of the tradition of comparative speech is McCall, 1969. The instructions for the elaboration (ἐργασία) of the *chreia* in the *progymnasmata* typically provide for a statement from analogy (ἐκ παραβολῆς). See Hock and O'Neil, 1986, pp. 35, 176–7 (Hermogenes), pp. 196–7 (Priscian), pp. 224–35 (Aphthonius), pp. 260–1 (Nicolaus).
15 The varied nomenclature has the support of long tradition; first use has been credited to Streeter ('central section'), Schleiermacher ('travel narrative') and De Wette ('great insertion'). For a survey of various attempts to name this section see Egelkraut, 1976, pp. 3–11.

narrative) and the content and placement of the individual *pericopae*
which neither need nor, indeed, *are* tied to an itinerary. Whatever
significance Luke attached to the journey,[16] no one has been able to
demonstrate to a consensus-forging degree that it functions as a
compositional framework nor that it is the dominant symbolic motif
with the power to unify the central section and to unlock the
meaning of its smaller portions.[17]

The failure to detect a clear correlation between an overarching
narrative framework, whether a real journey or a symbolic one
(ἀνάλημψις, 9.51), and the concatenation of the smaller units that
make up the central section opens the way for the thought that
Luke's presentation of the material in this section does not follow
the rules of a logically, chronologically and geographically linear
narrative. Rather, the compositional mode appears to be similar to
Eckhard Plümacher's description of the style that marks the presentation of Acts, namely the technique of dramatic scene-writing
(*dramatische Episodenstil*) that characterizes the Hellenistic style of
tragic-pathetic historiography, that is, the production of historical
narratives to influence and guide life in the present.[18] Among its
most noteworthy features are the following: (a) the absence of a
continuous, even flow of narrative; (b) the presentation of the story
to be told in a series of discrete episodes which, though they are
linked together, typically with an ἐγένετο-phrase, but also with
various meaningless chronological indicators, are independent of
each other and so can be understood and appreciated on their own;
(c) vivid scenes that emphasize a visual, theatrical style;[19] (d) the

---

16  See Egelkraut, 1976, pp. 30–61, for a synopsis of various scholarly views.
17  The latest attempt is by Moessner, 1989. He argues that Luke's central section
    depicts Jesus as a 'journeying guest-prophet' like Moses, using a literary-theologi-
    cal framework that merges portraits of Moses of Deuteronomy with features of
    the Deuteronomistic view of history. For a review of older claims that Luke's
    central section is a 'Christian Deuteronomy' see Egelkraut, 1976, pp. 55–8.
18  Plümacher, 1972, pp. 80–111; and more concisely, Plümacher, 1974, pp. 255–7.
    The phrase itself is credited to Haenchen, 1965, p. 107 n. 1, who also uses the
    phrase 'dramatische Szenentechnik' (p. 96). Similarly Hengel, 1979, p. 52: 'Lukas
    stand ... mit seinem "dramatischen Episodenstil" (Haenchen) in einer breiten
    Tradition hellenistischer Geschichtsschreibung, die durch die Konzentration auf
    bestimmte paradigmatische Ereignisse dem Leser die geschichtliche Wirklichkeit
    lebendig vor Augen führen wollte.' Note also Aune, 1987, p. 90; and Goulder,
    1989, pp. 453, 455: 'block method' or 'block policy' of composition.
19  Plümacher, 1974, p. 257: 'Was Lukas wichtig erscheint, das teilt er dem Leser
    nicht in trockenem Referat mit, sondern setzt es in das Geschehen lebendiger
    Einzelszenen um, deren dramatischer Handlung der Leser alles wesentliche gleich-
    sam *mit eigenen Augen* entnehmen kann' (emphasis added). Visually-oriented
    oratory and writing was a general cultural ideal. Lucian, for example, speaks of

transposition of abstract ideas or themes into direct speech to heighten the appeal to the reader. It is true, of course, that Plümacher treats only the compositional style of Acts, but the narrative design in the gospel's central section consists of a remarkably similar line-up of episodic divisions.[20] Here, too, it is hardly possible to speak of a continuous flow of narrative. Rather, the larger thematic units in this section are demonstrably presented as dramatic episodes[21] superficially linked with καὶ ἐγένετο (11.1, 14.1, 17.11) or without narrative connection altogether.[22] Luke's *Episodenstil* comes to expression also in 14.1–24, a scene with a clearly marked beginning and end, with enough descriptive details to let readers visualize the setting and circumstances and identify character types, and with the bulk of its narrative in *oratio recta*.[23] Not only does this help in identifying this unit as a discrete episode, but it also provides an initial clue about its function. As

wanting to 'paint word-pictures' ('Εθέλω δέ σοι ... εἰκόνα γραψάμενος τῷ λόγῳ, *Rhet. Praec.* 6). This ideal, formalized in instructions on vividness (ἐνάργεια) and the exercise of ἔκφρασις (description), is discussed in the rhetorical handbooks. On the former, see Thibeaux, 1990, p. 80 and the literature cited there. On the latter, note Theon's definition: ἔκφρασις ἐστι λόγος περιηγηματικὸς ἐναργῶς ὑπ' ὄψιν ἀγὼν τὸ δηλούμενον (*ekphrasis* is a descriptive account vividly bringing before one's sight what is illustrated); later he explains that the virtue of *ekphrasis* is ὁρᾶσθαι τὰ ἀπαγγελλόμενα (to see what is narrated; *Rhetores Graeci*, Spengel, vol. II, pp. 118–19). On this topic generally see Bartsch, 1989, pp. 3–39, and Kennedy, 1984, p. 23.

20 This similarity has been noted and briefly shown by Horn, 1983, pp. 247–51; his summary comment (p. 359 n. 15) bears repeating: 'Die von Plümacher ... genannten Kriterien des dramatischen Episodenstils finden sich sämtlich auch im Reisebericht wieder. Forschungsgeschichtlich verwundert, dass der Reisebericht literaturgeschichtlich bisher kaum Beachtung gefunden hat.'

21 E.g., 11.1–13 (on prayer); 12.13–34 (on possessions); 14.1–24 (dining rules); 15.1–32 (on repentance); 16.1–31 (on possessions); 17.1–10 (on community rules). 'In diesen Einheiten entwickelt der komponierende Evangelist eine dramatische Episode. Er schafft ein Szenarium: Jesus, Zwölf, Jünger, Volk, bisweilen Anwesenheit der Pharisäer und Sadduzäer. Die Darsteller stehen in Interaktion ... Allen Gesprächsteilnehmern ist die wörtliche Rede eigen. So ensteht der Eindruck einer wirklichen, anschaulichen Szene' (Horn, 1983, p. 250).

22 Among the most instructive studies of Luke's *Perikopenpraxis* in the central section, including a detailed inventory of the various techniques of transition from unit to unit, is still Schmidt, *Der Rahmen der Geschichte Jesu*, 1919, pp. 246–73. His summary statement is noteworthy: 'Eine Fülle von Perikopen hat weder eine topographische, noch eine chronologische, noch eine sachlich nach rückwärts verbindende Angabe, sondern skizziert ganz kurz eine neue Situation und hängt dann die eigentliche Erzählung one jegliche Klammer an die vorhergehende an. Diese Situationsangabe ist dabei verschieden gestaltet' (p. 249).

23 Interestingly, Flusser, who makes no reference to the characteristics of the 'Episodenstil', noted them in Luke 14. Nuanced characterization, various descriptive details and the 'plauderhafte Vortragsweise' belong 'zum Gebiet der Ästhetik' or 'ästhetische Verwirklichung' (Flusser, 1981, pp. 284–99).

Wilhelm Horn has noted, this manner of narration 'always aims towards moral edification and transformation of the audience, never towards the historicizing of specific facts' (Horn, 1983, p. 251); it is a style of narrative that functions as a 'representative anecdote' (Burke, 1945, pp. 59–61).[24] It offers a representative (typical) 'slice of life' from an authoritative past as a protreptic representation of a desired, if not an ideal, moral and social state of affairs in the present.

In the course of this study, I will allow the idea of Luke's dramatic *Episodenstil* to intrude on (but not dominate) my analysis as a working assumption in two primary ways. It partially warrants the rather limited textual focus of this work and, more importantly, it broadly directs my interpretive focus towards the social and moral ideals that this text represented and espoused for its early Christian readers.

## Luke 14.1–24 as a unified episode

That Luke 14.1–24 is a discrete literary unit within the gospel's central section is easily spotted and needs hardly to be argued. 14.1 marks its beginning with the typically Lukan formula for introducing a new episode: καὶ ἐγένετο + ἐν τῷ + articular infinitive (ἐλθεῖν).[25] Circumstantial indicators of time (sabbath), place (house of a ruler) and occasion (meal) confirm the opening of a new scene. 14.24 concludes this section, for in 14.25 Jesus obviously has left the dinner party to take to the road once more (implied in συνεπορεύοντο) and to speak to a different audience (ὄχλοι πολλοί).[26]

The episode itself is made up of four sub-units:

(1)    14.1–6. Introductory pronouncement story (*chreia*) featur-

---

[24] Although Burke is not discussing Greco-Roman historical writing, his description of the representational anecdote as a 'paradigm or prototype of action' (p. 61) clarifies how many ancient writers narrated an ideal past with hortatory and/or deterrent aims for the writer's present; cf. Alpers, 1990, p. 36. I am aware of an apparently similar designation of Luke 14.1–24 as a 'type-scene' (McMahan, 1987, pp. 48–69, 183–91), but here the term refers to those recurring similar literary scenes in a larger narrative work as an aid to reading.

[25] This phrase 'occurs so often [in Lucan Greek] as to be monotonous' (Fitzmyer, 1964, p. 119); usually it signals a transition to a new episode. For an inventory and analysis of this phrase, a Lukan Septuagintism, see Johannessohn, 1926; Fitzmyer, 1964, pp. 118–19; Delebecque, 1976, pp. 123–65; Sellin, 1978, especially n. 7.

[26] Schleiermacher is an early example of a major commentary tradition: '... our narrative extends only to verse 24. For the words Συνεπορεύοντο δε αὐτῷ ὄχλοι πολλοί could not have been written in the same context with the preceding passage' (Schleiermacher, 1825, p. 208).

ing Jesus at dinner in a ruler's house and using a livestock saying and a healing demonstration involving a man with dropsy. (2) 14.7–11. Antithetically parallel sayings (given as a παρα-βολή) on the conduct of invited guests in claiming their reclining positions at a wedding banquet (γάμος), followed by a maxim on the reversal of those in low and high positions. (3) 14.8–14. Antithetically parallel sayings on who should be invited to ἄριστον ἢ δεῖπνον, followed by a beatitude concerning rewards for unreciprocated generosity. (4) 14.15–24. A transitional verse (14.15), a macarism on eating in the kingdom of God, sets up and links to the preceding discourse a tale about a householder who prepared a banquet and invited guests.

Scholars have often noted that the material of Luke 14.1–24 is thematically roughly homogeneous, even though its sub-units may have come to their present place from various pre-Lukan depositories of Jesus traditions and though they belong to diverse formal categories. All its sub-units but the apparently anomalous sabbath controversy story (14.1–6) deal with dinners, hosts, guests and behaviour centring around the table. The following section provides additional substance to this notice. I proceed to show this by the expedient means of tracing the lines of integration between dinner parable (14.16–24) and dinner episode.

'Luke normally circumscribes the meaning for his performance [of parables] by contextualization' (Scott, 1989, p. 163; cf. p. 28). Brandon Scott's observation with its important methodological implications for the study of parables in larger narrative contexts holds true also for the presentation of the banquet story – true at least to the extent that there is a connection between parable and literary context. Whether context serves the performance of the parable or whether, conversely, the parable is put in the employ of its context need to remain open options for the moment (see ch. 8). Determining the situational function of the parable first awaits a demonstration of the story's integration into its context.

The parable is not closed in upon itself; it reaches out to its context by means of a series of narrative bridges, verbal and thematic links.

(1) Narrative bridges. The actual story is introduced with the brief phrase ὁ δὲ εἶπεν αὐτῷ (but he said to him, 14.16a). It is a retro-flexive narrative link whose pronominal references to speaker and auditor depend on the preceding context for full identifica-

tion.[27] The most immediately prior reference to the auditor is τις τῶν συνανακειμένων (someone of those who reclined at table, 14.15) where, on the narrative level, he serves as a double-agent in a transitional verse: as listener-responder to what was said before (ἀκούσας ... ταῦτα εἶπεν) and as *provocateur* of the parable that follows. Although the diner's response, formally a beatitude, is most apparently evoked by the association of blessing and the eschatological age in 14.14,[28] ταῦτα must include at least 14.12–14, for 14.14 concludes a dinner-table saying that begins in 14.12. To be sure, this saying is not specifically addressed to the 'someone' of 14.15 and 14.16; it is directed τῷ κεκληκότι αὐτόν (to the one who had invited him, 14.12a).[29] But there are several indications that 14.12–14 should not be isolated from its preceding saying (14.7–11). The adjunctive καί in 14.12a hearkens back to what has already been said 'to those who were invited' (πρὸς τοὺς κεκλημένους, 14.7a; cf. λέγων πρὸς αὐτούς, 14.7c). The symmetrically parallel construction of the two sentences respectively addressed to invited and inviter further speaks for purposeful narrative collation.[30] Lastly, the unnamed diner of 14.15 is implicitly introduced as an auditor of the dinner-table sayings in 14.7a. Thus he functions as an externally unifying frame around the double-panelled set of instructions concerning dinner-party behaviour (14.8–14).

We may go further. 14.7 also is a retro-flexive introduction. It links the table instructions to the preceding scene where the unnamed κεκλημένοι are first identified as lawyers and Pharisees

---

[27] K. Schmidt, 1919, pp. 249, 259, describes this type of introductory formula as one which effects a 'sachlichen Anschluß nach rückwärts'; it is typically Lukan ('typisch lukanische Eigenheit'). See also Fabris, 1978, p. 128: 'Il soggetto innominato ὁ δέ del verbo εἶπεν e il destinatario o interlocutore sottinteso nel promome αὐτῷ, rimandano a un contesto precedente.'

[28] 14.14: μακάριος ... ἐν τῇ ἀναστάσει τῶν δικαίων
   14.15: μακάριος ... ἐν τῇ βασιλείᾳ τοῦ θεοῦ

[29] The proliferate use of second person singular pronouns might reinforce the impression that this sentence is a private aside to the host, but this may not be the case, given the same pronominal syntax in the previous sentence which is addressed to a plurality of hearers.

[30] The parallel structure is easily seen in the following synoptic figure:

| 14:7–11 | 14:12–14 |
|---|---|
| ἔλεγεν δέ ... | ἔλεγεν δέ ... |
| ὅταν ... | ὅταν ... |
| μὴ ... | μὴ ... |
| μήποτε ... | μήποτε ... |
| ἀλλ᾽ ὅταν ... | ἀλλ᾽ ὅταν ... |
| τότε ἔσται ... δόξα ... ὅτι ... | καὶ μακάριος ἔσῃ ὅτι ... |

(14.3) gathered for a sabbath dinner at the house of a leading Pharisee (14.1). Luke's way of identifying the interlocutors, naming them once and then using pronominal or participial tags in hook and clasp fashion, achieves an internal bond between 'parable' and context which is itself a series of discrete, compact passages similarly held together.

(2)   Verbal manipulation of scenario. The internal cohesiveness of the episode in which the dinner parable is embedded is enhanced by an hypnotic use of word groups that conscript the reader to attend to the setting and ambience in which the conversation plays itself out. First, dining-room terminology abounds from beginning to end:

14.1   Jesus goes to dine (literally, 'eat bread'; φαγεῖν ἄρτον) at the house of a leader (ἀρχόντων) of the Pharisees.

14.7   He sees the other invited guests vying for the prestigious reclining places (τὰς πρωτοκλισίας).

14.8   Promptly he proceeds to give the assembled diners a brief lecture (παραβολή!) on their concern with seating arrangements when invited to wedding banquets (γάμοι): 'do not recline (κατακλιθῇς) in the prestigious reclining place (14.8) ... but ... recline (ἀνάπεσε) in the lowest place (ἔσχατον τόπον) ... then you will have honour in the presence of all those sitting at table with you (πάντων τῶν συνανακειμένων σοι)'.

14.12   Then Jesus turns to the host with advice on drawing up guest lists for breakfast or dinner (ἄριστον ἢ δεῖπνον) or a reception (δοχή, 14.13).

14.15   The eschatological beatitude savours the prospects of the one who will eat bread (φάγεται ἄρτον) in the kingdom of God.

14.16   This evokes the story of the man who prepared a large dinner (δεῖπνον μέγα) and invited guests at the time of the dinner (τῇ ὥρᾳ τοῦ δείπνου).

14.24   The story and the dinner episode end with the solemn lesson that 'none of those men who were invited shall taste my dinner' (οὐδεὶς ... γεύσεταί μου τοῦ δείπνου).

From the meal in the οἶκος of the ἄρχοντες in 14.1 to the dinner in the οἶκος of the κύριος in 14.23, from episode's start to finish, the train of convivial vocabulary smoothly taxies the reader across the terrain of the text.[31] Of course, the 'ride' from the real meal to the fictitious dinner demands interpretation.[32] Here I simply point out that dining-room language is another indication of how parable and its hosting context embrace each other.

A second lexical unifying thread is provided by the καλεῖν (to invite) group of words.[33] In its various forms the verb is used twelve times in 14.7–24; the monotony of the καλεῖν-string is interrupted only once by φωνεῖν (to call, 14.12b), a word rarely used for invitations (Plummer, 1914, p. 358). Add to this from the same semantic orbit παραιτεῖσθαι (to beg off, 14.18,19; cf. οὐ δύναμαι ἐλθεῖν, I cannot come, 14.20) and the scenic coherence of the episode is further enhanced.

(3) *Thematic integration*. The most obvious bond between parable and preceding context is the reintroduction in 14.21c of the second of the two contrasted quartets of potential dinner guests in 14.12–13:

| 14.12 | 14.13 | 14.21 |
|---|---|---|
| μὴ φώνει | κάλει | —— |
| τοὺς φίλους | πτωχούς | πτωχούς |
| τοὺς ἀδελφούς | ἀναπείρους | ἀναπείρους |
| τοὺς συγγενεῖς | χωλούς | τυφλούς |
| γείτονας πλουσίους | τυφλούς | χωλούς |
| —— | —— | εἰσάγαγε ὧδε |

This twice-appearing foursome in but slightly varied order not only fuses the parable with the preceding saying on proper guest lists, but also serves to table a thematic centre piece in the entire δεῖπνον episode: an inversion of the taken-for-granted pattern of hospitality so as to deny it to the expected and expecting folk and to offer it to the unexpected and unexpecting. Not merely juxtaposition of opposites or the dissimilar, but a tension of opposites made to cohere in relation to Jesus (who, his mere status as guest notwithstanding, is the chief and paradigmatic figure in the dramatic episode) stamps the polymorphous periods of the episode with an unmistakable

---

31 Cf. de Meeûs, 1961, p. 861: 'Le lecteur entraîné par le récit, passe de l'une à l'autre sans s'en apercevoir.'

32 'Real' is not equivalent to 'historically factual', for the entire episode is a Lukan literary creation. Rather, 'real' indicates the realistic narrative depiction of the sabbath meal in contrast to the fictitious supper story embedded within the dinner episode. Cf. Scott, 1989, p.163, and Fabris, 1978, pp. 133–4.

33 See Fabris, 1978, pp. 134–5, for a detailed analysis; cf. Gaeta, 1978, p. 118.

thematic homogeneity. The great banquet story shares in this, extends it and sharpens its clarity.

This tensive relation of opposites, dramatized as an inversive movement from a meal shared among well-to-do peers (14.1) to a banquet house filled with the ne'er-do-well poor (14.23),³⁴ even embraces the sabbath-healing controversy story (14.2–6), *prima facie* (but only *prima facie*, as we shall see) an anomaly within the dinner episode. As a 'literary device to provide a setting fòr the [dinner-table] sayings'³⁵ the controversy story concerning the ἄνθ-ρωπός τις ἦν ὑδρωπικός (a certain man who had dropsy) makes no sense; rather, as Sjef van Tilborg has shown, the healing scene follows a script that is echoed in the dinner parable so that the former helps to coordinate the audition (reading) of the latter (van Tilborg, 1987, pp. 146–7). Thus, first, Jesus' attempt to win Pharisees and lawyers over to his point of view, using question (14.3), demonstrative action (14.4) and wisdom saying (14.5), has an affinity with the fictional host's triple effort to procure guests for his dinner by issuing an initial invitation to many of his friends (ἐκάλεσεν πολλούς, 14.16), then by sending a servant to issue the call to table (14.17) to two sets of alternative guests (14.18–20). Second, the grudging, implicitly resistant silence of those addressed in 14.4,6 is matched by the snubbing excuses of the invited in 14.18–20. Third, Jesus' controversial attention to the sick guest (14.2–4) parallels the fictional householder's angry (ὀργισθείς) turn to the poor and sick for table companions (14.21). Last, both stories end similarly, the first with impotent interlocutors, the second with impertinent dinner guests. The inability of the Pharisees and lawyers to find a reply to Jesus (οὐκ ἴσχυσαν ἀνταποκριθῆναι, 14.6) finds its counterpart in the moral of the parable where the anticipated bliss of participating in the eschatological banquet (14.15) is categorically denied (οὐδεὶς τῶν ἀνδρῶν ἐκείνων τῶν κεκλημένων γεύσεταί μου τοῦ δείπνου, 14.24). The symmetry may not be flawless, and the analysis somewhat superficial, but the similarity in the internal logic of healing story and parable is visible enough to suspect prelimina-

---

³⁴ Both ends of this movement are marked by an *inclusio*: εἰς οἶκόν τινος κτλ. (14.1); μου ὁ οἶκος (14.23).
³⁵ Creed, 1930, p. 188; similarly Fitzmyer, 1985, p. 1038: 'a means to introduce the following episodes of Jesus' dinner-table discourses'. This is not to say, of course, that 14.1–6 does not introduce the episode, but it goes much beyond providing a literary setting. A setting is clearly and sufficiently provided in 14.1 upon which 14.7 and the following sayings follow logically and smoothly. The dropsy anecdote plays a much more important role in the episode (see chs. 3 and 8).

rily that dramatic action and fictional story stand in some kind of mutually illustrating or interpreting relationship to each other. This will be confirmed when the rhetoric in the dinner story is examined (ch. 8).

In sum, there are enough narrative clasps, lexical links and thematic lines of cohesion in 14.1–24 to consider it as a unitary episode. While this initial observation is sufficient for the standard commentary notices (see ch. 7, pp. 132–3) that Luke has placed heterogeneous bits of 'table talk' within the literary framework of a meal scene, this is not a satisfactory conclusion. My intention is to follow the impression gained by a quick first reading with a reach for a deeper comprehension of the dinner episode in order to determine if the cohesiveness is indicative of a more studied compositional strategy than mere collation of topically related *pericopae* within an appropriate narrative setting. What is the significance of the narrative setting? Why introduce a discourse on hosts, guests, rules of invitation and dining-room etiquette with what ostensibly is a controversy over the legality of healing a sick man on a sabbath? On what logic, if any, does the order of the constituent *pericopae* ride? How extensively is the episode a product of Lukan composition? To what extent does not only this composition but also its interpretability depend on familiarity with first-century Mediterranean practices of narrative rhetoric?

Beyond literary form and rhetorical dynamics within the text itself, does the intelligibility of the episode, including its choice of vocabulary, contrastive characterization and heavy reliance on a sympotic setting and imagery, hinge on extra-textual knowledge and experience of the intellectual and social traditions shared and in force in the urban Mediterranean world of Luke's time? What, finally, is the rhetorical (persuasive) point of the episode?

These questions indicate the issues on which I shall focus. In chapters 3–6, I examine in succession the individual units that make up the dinner episode. Each is studied from three vantage points: (a) a brief formal analysis draws on traditional form-critical scholarship and ancient rhetorical instructions in an attempt to identify the speech form to which the unit is related; (b) a source analysis deals with the source-redaction question, but with a primary focus on determining the extent of Luke's authorial imprint on each unit;[36]

---

[36] For the most part, the redaction issue is treated in familiar terms, following and depending upon the distinction of, say, Fitzmyer, 1964, p. 83, between tradition (a

(c) in a milieu or comparative tradition analysis, each unit is set afloat, as it were, on the sea of Greco-Roman intellectual and social traditions in an attempt to observe its drift towards idioms, literary *topoi*, common social realities and moral(izing) views that offer themselves as clarifying analogies. The double-panelled sayings complex (14.7–11, 12–15) will be treated in a single chapter (4) on Luke's *nomoi sympotikoi*. In the case of the so-called banquet parable (14.16–24), the opacity of the story and the volume and complexity of scholarship lead me to expand this three-point analysis into two chapters (5 and 6). This analysis yields preliminary insights on the rhetorical (argumentative) usefulness of each unit and identifies the moral and social ideals which are promoted or censured in it. I will return to the episode as a whole in chapter 8 and try to demonstrate there that Luke 14.1–24 displays an overarching logic in its composition and an identifiable claim in its narrative argument.

more or less unaltered insertion of an item from the pre-Lukan inventory of Jesus traditions), redaction (modification of something inherited from a source, written or oral) and composition (creativity without depending on a known literary source). This method, however, does presuppose a rather limited view of authorship in the first century. To compensate, I tend to be generous in crediting Luke as author (1) if a source cannot be clearly identified and (2) if the material in question is either formally or topically commonplace enough in the traditional or contemporary culture of Luke's world to make such a 'source' unnecessary (cf. ch. 7).

# 3

## JESUS AS A HEALER OF CRAVING DESIRE (14.1–6)

Luke 14.1–6 is a single unit where 14.1 bears the double duty of introducing both the healing scene and the dinner episode as a whole. Several commentators consider 14.1 to be a complete sentence and so posit a division between 14.1 and 14.2 (e.g., Plummer, 1914, p. 354; Marshall, 1978, p. 578; RSV). This is doubtful. The entire first verse is merely the protasis; the apodosis begins with καὶ ἰδού (14.2) and not with καὶ αὐτοί (14.1b), a paratactic element of the protasis. As Fitzmyer points out, 'unstressed *kai autos* functions in a special way in the *kai egeneto* construction in some instances. There Luke uses it to continue a paratactic, epexegetical description which is at times parallel to the temporal clause.'[1] Hence I would translate the first sentence thus: 'And it happened, after he went into the house of a certain ruler of the Pharisees one sabbath to eat bread, and they were watching him, that (καί), behold, a certain man who had dropsy was before him.'

Despite the fact that this passage recounts a healing miracle it is not formally a miracle story.[2] The therapeutic action is neither the focal point of the story nor important in itself. Rather, it is a practical action (which *happens* to be a miracle) that sets the stage for the proverbial saying which follows (14.5) so that 14.4 and 14.5 together form an action-saying response to a challenging and controversial situation, namely whether it is 'lawful to heal on the sabbath or not'

[1] Fitzmyer, 1964, p. 121; similarly, Delebecque, 1976, p. 139; cf. Luke 5.1,17; 8.1,22; 9.51; 17.11.

[2] Theissen, 1974, p. 120, discusses 14.1–6 as a miracle story, but notices the lack of fit in that he classifies it as a 'rule miracle' with an 'exposition-stressed structure' where the characteristic elements of a miracle story – account of the sick person's medical history, details of the therapeutic action, proofs for the success of the therapy, etc. – are missing. The miracle itself is overshadowed by the expositional argument. Note, as a comparison, Luke 13.10–17, an analogous story, but where the malady, treatment and acclamation combine to accentuate the healing in a way that differs from the dropsy story (see O'Toole, 1992, pp. 84–107).

(14.3b, cf. 14.1b). The therapeutic action thus is characterized as an element of the response (ἀπόκρισις, 14.3a) to an implicit challenging question. This is not without form-critical significance. Luke uses ἀποκρίνομαι frequently (22 times), both redactionally *contra Marcum* (5.22, 5.31, 6.3, 20.3, cf. 20.26), in *Sondergut* passages (7.40, 10.41, 13.2, 13.15, 14.3, 17.17, 17.20, 19.40), and more often than not (14 times) in passages that commonly are defined as pronouncement stories or *chreiai* (Schneider, 1983). Luke 14.1–6 belongs to this form-critical class, as many have recognized.[3] Its peculiarities identify 14.1–6 as a *chreia*,[4] or, more specifically, as a mixed, responsive *chreia*, mixed because its character (Jesus) combines action and saying to make a didactic point,[5] responsive because his audio-visual remark is a reply (ἀπόκρισις)[6] to an accusing question, here verbalized by Jesus himself on behalf of his audience, and to the inquisition-like situation in general[7].

3 Dibelius, 1933, p. 55: 'paradigm'; Bultmann, 1964, p. 12: 'conflict saying'; Hultgren, 1979, pp. 26, 190–3: 'conflict story'; V. Taylor reckoned it among the 'pronouncement stories' (1933, pp. 53, 55), but later discussed it in connection with Luke 13.10–17 as a 'story about Jesus' (p. 155); Roloff, 1970, p. 66, sums up the form-critical verdict: 'Das klar gegliederte Apophthegma hat die Form eines Streitgespräches'.
4 According to Aelius Theon (first century CE), χρεία ἐστι σύντομος ἀπόφασις ἢ πρᾶξις μετ' εὐστοχίας ἀναφερομένη εἴς τι ὡρισμένον πρόσωπον ἢ ἀναλογοῦν προσώπῳ, 'a chreia is a concise statement or action with apt pointedness attributed to a definite character or something analogous to a character' (Περὶ Χρείας 2–4; Hock and O'Neil, 1986, pp. 82–3). The most economical and precise definition is given by Aphthonius of Antioch (late fourth century CE), but he relied on the earlier handbooks on rhetoric: χρεία ἐστὶν ἀπομνημόνευμα σύντομον εὐστόχως ἐπί τι πρόσωπον ἀναφέρουσα, 'a chreia is a concise reminiscence aptly attributed to some character' (Περὶ Χρείας 2–3; Hock and O'Neil, 1986, pp. 224–5). A full discussion of the definition of the *chreia* in the handbooks on rhetoric is provided by Hock in Hock and O'Neil, 1986, pp. 23–7, but see also the very useful discussion by Kindstrand, 1986. The requirement of conciseness, a staple element in the handbook definitions and which theoretically distinguishes the *chreiai* from the reminiscences (ἀπομνημονεύματα; see Theon, Περὶ Χρείας, 25–8; Hock and O'Neil, 1986, p. 83) was probably heeded only by pupils in the classroom (Hock and O'Neil, 1986, p. 27). Its lack in Luke 14.1–6 is not unusual in the actual literary world.
5 The textbooks commonly classify the *chreiai* into sayings, action and mixed types. The mixed *chreiai* combine saying and action to make their point. For an overview and discussion of the handbooks' classification see Hock and O'Neil, 1986, pp. 27–35.
6 The formula καὶ ἀποκριθεὶς ... εἶπεν is an element of Lukan style, as Trautmann, 1980, p. 288, has shown.
7 Theon mentions four species of responsive (ἀποκριτικόν) *chreiai* (Hock and O'Neil, 1986, pp. 84–7). The first three are interrogative types with a standard structure: ἐρωτηθεὶς ... εἶπεν or πυθομένου τινός followed by a longer answer (πύσμα). The last is a non-interrogative responsive type in which the character's response is evoked by a variety of situations rather than by a formal question. Luke

Despite numerous efforts to settle the question whether 14.1–6 is a traditional story or an anecdote composed by the third evangelist, the source problem remains. The evidence for a pre-Lukan existence of 14.1–6 is scarce and indecisive.[8] It appears only in the third gospel and, excepting 14.5 which has a remote parallel in Matthew 12.11, the story would seem to leave us with little vocabulary or grammatical basis for attributing it to anyone but the author of Luke (Jeremias, 1980, pp. 235–6).

Arguments to the contrary are not lacking, but they are notable primarily for the interpretive ingenuity and methodological bias of their sponsors. Bultmann considered Luke 14.1–6 a 'variant' of Mark 3.1–6; the former is composed 'on the analogy' of the latter. Probing for how he knows this leads to his familiar theory of the dynamism of the tradition: the variation is due to 'the generating power of the apophthegm' (Bultmann, 1964, pp. 12, 62). Mark 3.1–6 and Luke 14.1–6 (cf. 13.10–17) are indeed form-critical and thematic relatives, but postulating a genetic link or even a literary relationship between the two passages on the basis of their formal kinship and similarity of subject alone is not justifiable. It is Luke 6.6–11 that is 'generated' by the Markan story; 14.1–6 evinces too many differences in structure and detail to be a demonstrable derivation of the Markan sabbath conflict story.[9]

Other commentators, noting the similarity between Luke 14.5 and Matthew 12.11 and Luke's immediately previous use of the sayings gospel Q (13.34–5), toy with the possibility that the Lukan *chreia* has an origin in Q.[10] Objections, however, are not difficult to identify (Kloppenborg, 1988, p. 160; Kosch, 1989, pp. 201–4). The point of contact between Luke 14.5 and Matthew 12.11 cannot be denied but the significant differences between them are hardly

---

14.1–6 does not strictly adhere to the form of any of Theon's four types, yet clearly shares features of the interrogative and the non-interrogative species. This need not be surprising, for Theon himself has trouble illustrating his fourfold classification with clear examples.

[8] For convenient summaries of the various solutions to the source question see Busse, 1977, pp. 305–6, and Trautmann, 1980, p. 287. The three options usually considered are (a) a variant of Mark 3.1–6; (b) a variant of Luke 6:6–11 (par. Mark 3.1–6); a Lukan composition based on some other pre-Lukan version.

[9] See especially Klein, 1987, pp. 24–5, and Trautmann, 1980, pp. 287–9, for a description of the differences. Cf. Easton, 1926, p. 225: '[T]he logion in Mark has little in common with those in L', that is, Luke 13.10–17, 14.1–6.

[10] E.g., Hirsch, 1941, pp. 134–6; Schürmann, 1968, p. 213: 'von Matthäus ausgelassenes Q-Gut'; Schneider, 1977, p. 312; Marshall, 1978, p. 578; Ernst, 1979, p. 64; Turner, 1982, p. 107. For the most recent detailed assessment of Q provenance, but without decisive results, see Kosch, 1989, pp. 200–6.

explained with an appeal to different redactions of a common Q saying.[11] Even if the saying had been in Q, for which no compelling proof can be adduced,[12] Luke's version is so integral to 14.1–6 that we must reckon with the possibility that the entire story was in Q, from which Matthew cleanly excised and perhaps reworded the livestock saying in order to make use of it in his redaction of a Markan story. But this is conjecture without restraint, for we have no way of knowing whether the entire story was in Q.[13] The plain evidence is that the story is an item of exclusively Lukan material which contains one saying (14.5) that may have had a prior life (cf. Matthew 12.11). Marking the sacredness of sabbath time with the aid of livestock metaphors is in any case a traditional technique[14] and, therefore, its appearance is hardly startling enough to warrant a search for a source. Thus, unless we speculatively insist on assigning 14.1–6 to L,[15] that marvellous catch-all for the Lukan source critics' left-overs, nothing prevents us from concluding that Luke wrote the story.[16]

The compositional and rhetorical motives for opening the dinner episode with this *chreia* still need to be explicated (see ch. 8, pp. 162–8). To prepare for that, it will prove useful to examine the most

---

11 Cf. the differing grammatical constructions and especially the remarkable variation in choice of words: πρόβατον ἕν (Matt.) = υἱὸς ἢ βοῦς (Luke); βόθυνον (Matt.) = φρέαρ (Luke); κρατήσει ... καὶ ἐγερεῖ (Matt.) = εὐθέως ἀνασπάσει (Luke). Those who suggest a Q origin 'solve' the remarkable variation by taking recourse to the notion that Matthew and Luke drew on different recensions of Q. Thus, typically, Hübner, 1973, p. 137: 'Die Möglichkeit, daß Mt 12,11 ein Einzellogion aus Q vorliegt, besteht durchaus, zumal ja Matthäus wahrscheinlich eine andere Q-Ausgabe benutzte als Lukas.' Cf. Turner, 1982, p. 107.

12 Rightly Klein, 1987, p. 26, who concludes: 'Bloß soviel kann gesagt werden: Lk hat die Perikope ... kaum aus Q übernommen.'

13 In agreement with Kosch, 1989, p. 201: 'Die Q-Zugehörigkeit von Lk 14,1–6 lässt sich aber nicht wahrscheinlich machen, zumal Q keine Texte mit ähnlicher Gattung (Streitgespräch) oder gleicher Thematik (Sabbat) enthielt, und der Abschnitt stark lk geprägt ist.'

14 See Str-B, vol. I, pp. 629–30 and vol. II, p. 199 for numerous rabbinic parallels; also Roloff, 1970, p. 67 and n. 59. In addition to Matt. 12:11 and Luke 14:5 note also Luke 13:15.

15 The best, though not convincing, argument for L provenance of 14.1–6 is found in Klein, 1987, pp. 25–8: 'Die aramäisch sprechende Gemeinde des SLk konzipiert auf das Jesuswort 14,5 hin eine Heilungsgeschichte, die relativ farblos bleibt' (p. 28). According to Klein's reconstruction the L story consisted of a setting (14.1), introduction of the man with dropsy (14.2), description of the healing (14.4b) and a question to others present to verify the healing (14.5).

16 In agreement with Neirynck, 1975, p. 230: 'almost completely due to Lukan redaction'; and Trautmann, 1980, p. 289: 'eine genuin lk Komposition', 'bewußt

important features of this pericope in a larger context, including its native literary context (Luke) and its wider cultural milieu. The latter, especially, provides us with several literary *topoi* and features of social interaction of which knowledge may well have been assumed in the writing of this passage as well as in its reading by the first Mediterranean Christians. What follows will underline further the probability that we are dealing with a Lukan composition virtually in its entirety.

## Accounting for the dropsical guest

The most immediately noticeable feature of the anecdote on the dropsy at dinner is its controversial nature. Apparently it is somehow to serve in the depiction and evaluation of Jesus' conflict with the Pharisees over sabbath proprieties. Yet, the question, ἔξεστιν τῷ σαββάτῳ θεραπεῦσαι, 'Is it legal to heal on the sabbath?', is perplexing. Contrary to the view of some interpreters, it appears to be not so much a genuinely legal question, a matter of sabbath *halakah*,[17] as a more general moral question, a matter of the virtuous thing to do.[18] What the 'lawful' ( = morally proper) thing to do on a sabbath is, Luke happily had learnt from Mark's Jesus in terms that the third evangelist could hardly have improved: sabbath time is the time 'to do good' (ἀγαθοποιῆσαι) and 'to save life' (ψυχὴν σῶσαι),[19] that is, to act benevolently and compassionately towards

redaktionelle Bildung'. Similarly Busse, 1977, pp. 306–7; Fitzmyer, 1985, pp. 1038–9; Klinghardt, 1988, pp. 232–3.

17 J. T. Sanders argues that the third gospel features a contest between Pharisaic 'Torah-strict *halakah*' (1987, p. 110) and the (Lukan) Christian '*halakah* of salvation' (p. 112). 'In Luke 14.1–6 the issue is again *halakah* ... [T]he halachic discussion: to heal or not to heal on the Sabbath' (p. 107). Similarly, though critical of some aspects of Sanders' views, also Brawley, 1987, p.102.

18 What Roloff (1970, p. 71) says about 'die Sabbatkonflikte Jesu' generally is apropos here: they are not 'Proteste gegen die pharisäische Gesetzlichkeit'. Similar views are expresssed by Wilson, 1983, pp. 31–9: 'Ultimately the debates do not turn on disputed points of sabbath halakah ...' (p. 38); Horn, 1983, p. 71; Klein, 1987, pp. 24–5; most recently Klumbies (1989, pp. 173–7) has convincingly argued that Luke is not concerned over 'die Sabbatproblematik'; rather he uses the sabbath conflict tradition, known to him from Mark, because it is a 'konfliktträchtiges Thema' suitable for conveying the superiority of Jesus.

19 Luke 6.9 par. Mark 3.4 (with a stylistic improvement of Mark's ἀγαθὸν ποιῆσαι). Wilson, 1983, p. 36, has noted that the principle of saving life on a sabbath would have been acceptable to rabbinic lawyers, but that they would have had trouble with the first principle as too uncontrollable, as 'far too broad to be an acceptable understanding of the law'. This is undoubtedly correct as an historical assessment of rabbinic views on how to keep the sabbath, but not likely the point at issue for Luke, who, echoing Cynic-Stoic sensibilities, seems to advocate the priority of

the marginal and disprivileged in accordance with the hard core of Luke's practical, virtue-oriented piety.[20] This is how 'sabbath' is regularly presented in Luke; it is the time of divine benefaction (4.16–22) that bestows privilege on those who cannot expect to benefit by relying on the existing mechanisms of religious and social patronage, a privilege that is just as regularly opposed by Pharisees and legal or scribal functionaries on supposedly 'legal' grounds (4.31–5; 6.1–5, 6–10; 13.10–17; 14.1–6). The sabbath controversies in Luke thus are not truly halakhic disputes as one might encounter them in Matthew's gospel, but a means of exposing the issue of privilege and of pleading for a model of sabbath piety that stresses benefaction over one that, in Luke's view, opposes benefaction on specious 'legal' grounds.[21]

Another reason for suggesting that an interpretive focus on the legality issue is inapt lies in the observation that if the sabbath healing is presented as a legal issue, it is interjected *in vacuo*. The 'legality' issue is rhetorically forcefully abbreviated in 14.1–6 (see ch. 8, pp. 164–8), then not pursued in the rest of chapter 14. After 14.1–6 the argument moves to the topic of the renunciation of status and honour for the sake of benevolent behaviour towards and association with those who have neither.

The presence of the Pharisees as the ostensible opponents in the 'debate' is also significant. Elsewhere the lack of the quality of generosity and inclusive sociability is the major character flaw of the Pharisees, whom Luke characterizes as self-justifying and self-exalting money lovers (φιλάργυροι, 16.14–15), a standard term of slander used by Hellenistic polemicists against the haughty and avaricious rich person.[22] As such, the Pharisees in Luke are not legal

---

virtue over legal correctness and adhering to patterns of piety hallowed by tradition.

[20] Horn, 1983, pp. 239–43. Cf. other terms that Luke has taken from Hellenism (Greek and Jewish) to characterize Christian piety as practical virtue: the idea of a good conscience (συνείδησις ἀγαθή, Acts 23.1; cf. συνείδησις ἀπρόσκοπη); the καλὸς καί ἀγαθός ideal (Luke 8.15; on this ideal in the Greco-Roman world see Wankel, 1961); the rationalized conception of the divine message as the βουλὴ τοῦ θεοῦ consisting of τὰ συμφέροντα (Acts 20.27).

[21] That Luke uses the sabbath as a way of exposing key elements in his views on privilege, patronage and divine benefaction was pointed out to me by John Kloppenborg in his reading of an earlier version of this chapter.

[22] The best discussion of Luke's depiction of the Pharisees as lovers of money is in Moxnes, 1989, pp. 1–9; 1991b, pp. 58–9; see also Brawley, 1987, p. 86, and Horn, 1983, pp. 225–6. For a more general overview of Lukan characterization of the Pharisees see Carroll, 1988; Denaux, 1989; Gowler, 1991, pp. 297–319; and the large body of additional literature discussed in these works.

adversaries nor, more generally, figures who represent 'a serious sketch of the Pharisaic ethos within Judaism' (Downing, 1992, p. 84), but 'literary stereotypes' who represent a configuration of what Luke thinks to be objectionable moral and social values;[23] they are simply 'fools' (ἄφρονες, 11.40),[24] but whose foolishness, when combined with their role and power as religious patrons, imperils the flow of divine benefaction to those most in need of it. It needs to be stressed, however, that this Pharisaic ethos is Luke's literary creation for rhetorical purposes (see ch. 8, pp. 164–75). Indeed, a reading of Luke's sabbath-controversy stories, together with his representation of the Pharisees as embodiments of haughty social self-display (11.43 [Q]), 14.7, cf. 20.46–7), ἁρπαγή and πονηρία (11.39 [Q]), πλεονεξία (implied in 12.13–34; see Horn, 1983, pp. 58–68), φιλαργυρία (16.14) and ὑπόκρισις (12.1), provides little ground for believing that Luke had anything more than a vague, second-hand knowledge of Pharisees or sabbath *halakah*. Any Greek or Roman would know that the sabbath day was a Jewish sacred day.[25] From the Jesus traditions, common familiar stereotypes and (perhaps) some supplementary research, Luke knew that the Pharisees were among the custodians of the religious apparatus of Judaism and, more importantly, opponents of Jesus. What else but a bit of imagination and literary technique is needed to come up with what we read in Luke 14? The Pharisees are here useful literary figures and this provides further cause for arguing that a focus on the sacrality of sabbath-time as a rabbinic legal issue misses Luke's interest in the story and its function within the banquet episode.

That the sick person who is the beneficiary of the action in the *chreia* is specifically 'dropsical' (ὑδρωπικός, *hapax leg.* in the New Testament), and not suffering from some other malady, is perhaps the

---

23 D. Smith, 1987, p. 637 n. 58; cf. Hintzen, 1991, p. 353: 'literarische Adressaten'; Horn, 1983, pp. 225–6; Moxnes, 1989, p. 19: 'With Luke's use of "typical figures," we can assume that the description of the Pharisee who was a rich ruler functions as a *topos.*'

24 This does not imply mere intellectual dim-wittedness, but failure to discern the wise pursuit of practical piety in Lukan terms that have affinities with Stoic and Cynic conceptions of the wise person (see Vorster, 1990; Downing, 1984, pp. 587–8). In Luke the only other use of 'fool' is applied to a farmer devoted to πλεονεξία (12.16–21) in a context that suggests application of the term to the Pharisees (see McMahan, 1987, p. 195 and n. 103).

25 See Wilson, 1983, p. 37: 'As one of the most clearly visible signs of Jewish allegiance, sabbath observance became one the hallmarks of Judaism in the Hellenistic era. It was one of the features most frequently noted by pagan writers often for the purpose of ridicule ...'

most interesting and telling detail in the anecdote and therefore worthy of a longer comment.

Few interpreters have commented on it beyond giving a brief medical dictionary description of the disease (see most major commentaries), or hastily drawing a vague moral lesson from the pericope for which the specific malady is quite incidental and irrelevant.[26] Those who have attended to the ἄνθρωπος ὑδρωπικός at some length record suggestions that do not hold quite as much water as the man with the water disease. F. Farrar (1887, p. 294), for example, apparently reading the passage as a description of an actual incident, thought that the ἄνθρωπος ὑδρωπικος was part of an astute 'Pharisaic plot' against Jesus to plant before him someone with an 'unsightly' and 'incurable' ailment in the hope 'that perhaps He might fail in the cure of a disease exceptionally inveterate'. H. Klein (1987, pp. 28–9) offers literary and moralizing motives for the selection of the disease. On the literary level, the narrator had a saying containing the image ('Bild') of a son or an ox that has fallen into the water (εἰς φρέαρ!). The narrator wanted to match the action ('Tat') sponsored by the image and cleverly thought of the water disease as most appropriate. Hence there is a neat correspondence between a wet image (son or ox drowning in water) and a wet action (healing a man drowning in his own water). The same image-action correspondence sharpens the moral imperative contained in the incident. Just as someone would feel obliged to rescue a drowning child or animal, so it is permitted to save a man who is drowning in his own water. On whether this interpretation can stay afloat, Klein himself offers this admission and plea: 'This conclusion actually is not stated in Luke 14, but it is intended' (p. 28).

But the most entertaining explanation of ὑδρωπικός results from Michael Goulder's shoe-horn method of accommodating Luke 14.1–6 to his synoptic source theory. Hypothesizing that Luke rewrote Matthew (see Goulder, 1989, pp. 22–6), he explains the dropsical person in Luke as follows:

> For the dropsy, Luke is probably developing themes in Matthew 12. He knows that Jesus healed every disease (Mt. 9.35), and the man with the dry (ξηράν) hand suggests as his antithesis the man with the water disease (ὑδρωπικός).

---

[26] E.g., Trautmann, 1980, p. 290: 'Der Evangelist will positiv am Beispiel der Sabbatheilung die Barmherzigkeit Jesu auf die Folie eines jüdischen Sabbatrigorismus illustrieren.'

Greek medicine from Hippocrates on ... worked on the
theory of the humours, and excessive dryness and wetness
were believed to underlie much disease ... Further, Jesus'
comment on the pit [βόθυνος, Matt. 12.11] is likely to have
been pointed, for a pit is normally dry, and so suited to
compare with a dry hand: if then Jesus was faced with a
man whose body was inflated with water, he will have asked
his opponents if they would not rescue an animal from
water, i.e. a well.                                    (1989, p. 584)

Klein's idea of correspondence is here taken a step further. Not only
does a wet hole require a wet disease, as Klein thinks, but this
parallelism was suggested to Luke by its opposite pair in Matthew
who matches a dry hole with a dry disease. Quite apart from the
suspicious linearity and symmetry of this reasoning,[27] one should
note Goulder's sleight-of-hand. Even if Luke had read Matthew
9.35, the notice there that Jesus healed 'every sickness' (πᾶσαν
νόσον) does not account for the mention of dropsy over some other
illness in 14.2. Actually, Goulder does not explain the presence of
the dropsy in the Lukan scene at all; Jesus simply 'was faced' with
one and this, says Goulder, prompted Luke to change Matthew's
βόθυνος to φρέαρ in the livestock saying. One dares to wonder
whether Matthew and Luke (or Klein and Goulder) knew of the
ancient paradoxical proverb, οὐδὲν ξηρότερον ὑδρωπικοῦ)
'nothing is as dry as a person with dropsy')[28] or, if they did, whether
they considered exchanging holes or sick people with each other. I
should prefer to look for another explanation of the dropsical guest
at Luke's Pharisaic dinner party.

**Dropsy as a Cynic metaphor for consuming passion**

One might begin by noting that a sick person, symbolizing
stigmatized and socio-economically marginalized people gener-

---

[27] It may be too restrictive to take βόθυνος in Matt. 12.11 as a dry pit. It simply
means a hole or trough of any kind. According to LSJ (s.v. βόθρος) the term may
be used to denote 'a natural trough for washing clothes'; see Homer, *Od.* 6.92.
[28] Ps-Longinus, *Subl.* 3.4. The saying – and Longinus does proffer it as a traditional
saying, but without attribution – is found only here, as far as I know, and
therefore may not have enjoyed a great currency, even though the artificial thirst
(implying dryness) of dropsical people was a frequent subject for comment and
even riddles. On the latter see Diogenes Laertius 9.3: Heraclitus 'put this riddle to
the doctors, whether they were able to create a drought after heavy rain'.

ally,[29] hovering in the vicinity of a richly set table of the elevated classes,[30] is an image that Luke likes to employ.[31] It is, moreover, an image that would have been familiar to Greco-Roman ears as a rhetorical commonplace and to Greco-Roman eyes as a feature of everyday life.[32] On the one hand, this *topos* suggests itself as part of the essential interpretive background because it is explicitly drawn into the banquet episode later (14.13, 21). On the other hand, though the social fringe type loitering near élite banquets undoubtedly is to be part of the visualized scene in Luke 14, it does not explain why the sufferer's illness is specified as dropsy. What is the reason for dropsy as the narrator's choice of disease?

My proposal is that Luke placed the ὑδρωπικός before Jesus not to show that he could master even the most 'inveterate' diseases, much less because he wanted a water disease to match the son or ox in the water of the cistern, but to exploit the symbolic and rhetorical value

[29] It was an ancient cliché freely to associate paupers, sick people and invalids, allowing each to stand for the other. The commonplace appears explicitly later in the same Lukan dinner episode (14.13, 21; cf. Plato, *Cri.* 53a, for almost identical associations) and probably reflects the widespread view, not to speak of social reality, that sickness and poverty belonged together. Thus, Sophocles: 'Nobody who is poor seems to be without sickness, but always to be ill' (*TrGF*, fr. 354, Nauck); cf. ch. 5, pp. 181–4.

[30] The observation that the hosting Pharisee is an ἄρχων assures that 'the social class is highlighted in 14.1–24' (Gowler, 1991, p. 243). See also Plummer, 1914, p. 354: 'Sabbath banqueting was common, and became proverbial for luxury'.

[31] This is evident most graphically in 16.19–31 and its sharply contrasted πλούσιος ... εὐφραινόμενος καθ' ἡμέραν λαμπρῶς and πτωχὸς ... ἐβέβλητο πρὸς τὸν πυλῶνα αὐτοῦ εἰλκωμένος (social-historical analysis in Hock, 1987). See also 5.17 where the saying that the sick, not the well need a physician is said in the context of Levi's 'great feast' (δοχή). Not from the ranks of the physically sick, but from the same social fringe is the γυνὴ ἁμαρτωλός at the Pharisee's dinner in 7.36–54. See Derrett, 1970a, for the suggestion that the risqué action of the woman suggests that she was a prostitute, hence unclean. Hamel (1990, pp. 55–6) rightly intimates that hunger or malnutrition, ritual impurity and illness are interrelated dimensions of poverty. These same elements are combined in another Lukan dinner episode (11.37–54): unwashed hands (impurity), call to give alms (implying the presence of the poor at least in the narrative world).

[32] Bolkestein, 1939, p. 209, points out that 'bei häuslichen Festen zeigten sich gerne Leute [i.e., beggars], die hofften, dass in der heiteren Stimmung etwas von dem Überfluss für sie abfallen werde ... So ist es auch zu erklären, dass allgemein für Betteln Wendungen wie ἐπὶ τὰς θύρας ἰέναι u.d. gebräuchlich waren.' This is richly illustrated in Lucian's *Gallus* and *Cataplus*, dialogues that I will find useful for illuminating Luke's dinner episode later (ch. 4, pp. 58–60; cf. Braun, 1992, pp. 76–8). The same phenomenon is familiar from Jewish texts (e.g., *Abot* 1.1,5; see Koenig, 1985, pp. 16–17, and Plummer, 1914, p. 354). The image of the sick beggar near the banquet hall perhaps should be seen as a variation of the even more frequent literary *topos* of the pathetic client hoping for a dinner invitation (e.g., Juvenal, *Sat.* 5.19–23; see Bobertz, 1993, p. 173).

of the disease's paradoxical symptom, namely the unquenchable craving for drink though the body is inflated with fluid, a craving which, when indulged, serves not to ease but to feed the disease. To cast this proposal into the realm of the credible requires us to go beyond the text of the third gospel (or other early Christian sources) to the Cynics and Stoics as well as to other writers influenced by or making use of Cynic traditions.[33]

Hellenistic popular philosophers, notably the Cynics, were fond of metaphors and comparisons from medicine, a field that, in the age and *belles lettres* of the Second Sophistic (see Bowersock, 1969), had become 'a fashionable literary affectation for rhetor and philosopher alike' (Anderson, 1986, p. 139). Lucian's description of Demonax provides a starting illustration. 'Though he assailed sins, he forgave sinners, thinking that one should pattern after doctors (τὸ παράδειγμα παρὰ τῶν ἰατρῶν), who heal sicknesses but feel no anger at the sick' (*Demonax* 7). Or, to offer one more example, Dio Chrysostom describes Diogenes' reason for moving from Athens to Corinth after the death of Antisthenes thus:

> For he observed that large numbers gathered at Corinth on account of the harbours and the hetaerae, and because the city was situated as it were at the cross-roads of Greece. Accordingly, just as the good physician (ἀγαθὸν ἰατρόν) should go and offer his services where the sick are most numerous, so, said he, the man of wisdom (τὸν φρόνιμον ἄνδρα) should take up his abode where fools (ἄφρονες) are thickest in order to convict them of their folly and reprove them.     (*Orations* 8.5; trans. Cohoon, LCL)

This image of Demonax and Diogenes as Cynic 'iatrosophists' (Anderson, 1986, p. 139) is typical of a wider tendency of philosophers to compare themselves to a 'physician administering medi-

---

[33] The relevance of Cynic sources for the study of Luke's gospel hardly needs elaborate justification. Its author wrote perhaps at the height of the revival of Cynicism (see Dudley, 1937, pp. 125–201) whose influence extended much beyond those properly known as Cynics (O'Neil, 1978, p. 301; cf. Fischel, 1968, esp. pp. 372–6). Affinity between early Christians and Cynics was early recognized by Cynics (Lucian, *Peregr.*) and Christians alike (e.g., Tertullian, *De Pallio* 6; see Sayre, 1948, p. 27; Downing, 1984, pp. 590–1). On the influence of Cynic modes of conduct, speech and views on the formulation of the Jesus traditions see, *inter alia*, Wechssler, 1947, pp. 227–50, p. 243: 'Wie nahe ... Jesus den Kynikern kam, bedarf keiner Worte' (!); Downing, 1984; 1987, pp. 51–160; 1988, pp. v–xiii, 1–5; Vaage, 1987; Mack, 1988, pp. 66–9 (esp. n. 11), 73–4, 179–86; Mack and Robbins, 1989, pp. 45–51.

cine' (ἰατροῦ ... νόσον ... φαρμακεύοντος; Bion *ap.*
Plutarch, *Moralia* 561C),³⁴ vices and ignorance with disease (νόσος)³⁵ which
only philosophy could cure,³⁶ and, of course, their own classrooms
with hospitals³⁷ and their lectures (λεγόμενα) with medicines
(φάρμακα).³⁸ Within this larger field of medical analogies, sprouts a comparison, especially popular in Cynic circles, of the illness of dropsy
with the vice of avarice.³⁹ The comparison may go back as far as
Antisthenes, but since attribution is an unsettled issue and since
Antisthenes merely implies the dropsy-avarice analogy,⁴⁰ it is best

³⁴ On the popularity of the ἰατρός as a figure of comparison for the work of the
Cynic (and other) philosophers, see Bernays, 1879, pp. 24, 92 n. 10; Höistad, 1948,
pp. 118–9; Kindstrand, 1976, pp. 31, 228, 241; Nachov, 1976, p. 366; Malherbe,
1980, pp. 24–5, 33 n. 21; Moles, 1983, p. 112, n. 73 for references; Downing, 1987,
pp. 59, 119, cf. p. 143 (on Jesus as a Cynic-like physician); Mack, 1988, pp. 183,
184 n. 8. Cf. the following Cynic sources: Antisthenes *ap.* Diogenes Laertius 6.6;
Diogenes *ap.* Diogenes Laertius 6.36; Lucian, *Demon.* 7; Lucian, *Vit. auct.* 8 (on
Diogenes as ἰατρός τῶν παθῶν; additional citations of Cynic fragments in
Paquet, 1975, s.v. 'médecine' (index); and Downing, 1988, section 159 (pp. 122–3).
That the figure was not restricted to Cynics is shown by Musonius Rufus (1.6–13;
Lutz, 1947, p. 33) and his similar comparison between the ἰατρός who prescribes
φάρμακα and the φιλόσοφος ... διδάσκων τοὺς ἀκούοντες.
³⁵ This may go back as far as Antisthenes, the founder of the Cynic School in Athens,
who is said to have spoken of the greed of tyrants as a 'severe, grievous disease'
(τῆς ἄγαν χαλεπῆς νόσου; Xenophon, *Symp.* 4.37).
³⁶ E.g., Plutarch (*Mor.* 7D-E) approvingly quotes Bion: οἱ φιλοσοφίας μὴ δυνάμενοι
κατατυχεῖν ... ἑαυτοὺς κατασκελετεύουσι, 'those unable to attain philosophy
... emaciate themselves'. Plutarch himself adds that τῶν δὲ τῆς ψυχῆς ἀρρω-
στημάτων καὶ παθῶν ἡ φιλοσοφία μόνη φάρμακόν ἐστι, 'for the sicknesses and
passions of the soul philosophy is the only remedy'. Note also the Stoic, Marcus
Aurelius, speaking of his conversion to philosophy in medical terms; he became
convinced τοῦ χρῄζειν διορθώσεως καὶ θεραπείας τοῦ ἤθους, 'of need for
reform and treatment of character' (1.7).
³⁷ Epictetus, (Arrian) *Epict. Diss.* 3.23.30: Ἰατρεῖόν ἐστιν, ἄνδρες, τὸ τοῦ φιλοσό-
φου σχολεῖον, 'Men, the philosopher's classroom is a hospital.'
³⁸ An example of the λεγόμενα-φάρμακα link is found in the enigmatic *chreia* of
Bion, *Gnom. Vat.* 157 (ed. Sternbach, p. 66; slightly emended by Kindstrand, 1976,
p. 129): Ὁ αὐτὸς ἐρωτηθεὶς ὑπό τινος διὰ τί αὐτὸν οὐκ ὠφελεῖ τὰ ὑπ' αὐτοῦ
λεγόμενα, οὐδὲ γὰρ αἱ πυξίδες, εἶπεν, αἱ τά χρηστότατα φάρμακα ἔχουσαι ἀπ'
αὐτῶν ὠφελοῦνται; 'Being asked by somebody why he did not profit by his
lectures, he said, Neither do the medicine boxes that contain the most useful
remedies profit by them.' See Kindstrand, 1976, p. 292, for useful commentary.
³⁹ See the references compiled by Hense in the apparatus *ad loc.* Stobaeus, *Flor.*
3.10.45, and by Kindstrand, 1976, p. 241; cf. Billerbeck, 1979, p. 25 n. 48: 'Der
Gedanke (sc. *avaritia*) wird veranschaulicht durch den in der [Cynic-Stoic] Dia-
tribenliteratur *heimischen Vergleich* des Habsüchtigen mit einem Wassersüchtigen'
(emphasis added).
⁴⁰ 'I am told of certain despots ... who have such a greedy appetite for riches that
they commit much more dreadful crimes than they who are afflicted with the direst
poverty ... As for such men, I pity them deeply for their malignant disease; for in

to credit Diogenes with first using dropsy and its symptoms as an analogy for insatiable greed:

Διογένης ὡμοίου τοὺς φιλαργύρους τοῖς ὑδρωπικοῖς· ἐκείνους μὲν γὰρ πλήρεις ὄντας ὑδροῦ ἐπιθυμεῖν ποτοῦ τοὺς τε φιλαργύρους πλήρεις ὄντας ἀργυρίου ἐπιθυμεῖν πλείονος, ἀμφοτέρους δὲ πρὸς κακοῦ. ἐπιτείνεσθαι γὰρ μᾶλλον τὰ πάθη, ὅσῳ τὰ ἐπιθυμούμενα πορίζεται.

Diogenes compared money-lovers to dropsies: as dropsies, though filled with fluid crave drink, so money-lovers, though loaded with money, crave more of it, yet both to their demise (κακοῦ). For, their desires increase the more they acquire the objects of their cravings.

(Stobaeus, *Florilegium* 3.10.45; Hense, 1893, p. 419)

Bion of Borythenes, perhaps dependent on Diogenes, also knew the dropsy illustration, although the full comparison between dropsy and greed is drawn only by Teles, who cites Bion's ὕδρωψ-saying and expands upon it:

Καὶ εἴ τις βούλεται ἢ αὐτὸς ἐνδείας καὶ σπάνεως ἀπολυθῆναι ἢ ἄλλον ἀπολῦσαι, μὴ χρήματα αὐτῷ ζητείτω. ὅμοιον γάρ, φησὶν ὁ Βίων, ὡς εἴ τις τὸν ὑδρωπικὸν βουλόμενος παῦσαι τοῦ δίψους, τὸν μὲν ὕδρωπα μὴ θεραπεύοι, κρήνας δὲ καὶ ποταμοὺς αὐτῷ παρασκευάξοι. ἐκεῖνός τε γὰρ ἂν πρότερον πίνων διαρραγείη ἢ παύσαιτο τοῦ δίψους, οὗτός τε οὐκ ἄν ποθ' ἱκανωθείη, ὅταν ᾖ ἄπληστος καὶ δοξοκόπος καὶ δεισιδαίμων.

And if anyone wants either to have himself freed from want and scarcity or to free someone else, let him not seek money for him. For it is, says Bion, as if someone who wants to relieve the thirst of a man suffering from dropsy would not treat the dropsy but would supply him with springs and rivers. For the sufferer would sooner burst with drinking than be cured of thirst. And this man could never be satisfied, since he is insatiable, thirsting for fame and superstitious.

(Teles *ap.* Stobaeus, *Florilegium* 4.33.31 = Kindstrand, 1976, F34; trans. O'Neil, 1977, p. 41)

my eyes their malady resembles that of a person who possessed abundance but through continually eating could never be satisfied' (Xenophon, *Symp.* 4.36–7, trans. Todd, LCL). Had Antisthenes substituted 'drinking' for 'eating' the comparison would have been unmistakable.

In a treatise appropriately titled Περὶ φιλοπλουτίας ('On the love of wealth') Plutarch, Luke's contemporary, uses a similar comparison, although citing Aristippus the Cyrenaic, to excoriate 'the irrational desire to possess great wealth' (O'Neil, 1978, p. 299):

> Those ... who part with nothing, though they have great possessions, but always want greater, would strike one who remembered what Aristippus said as even more absurd. 'If a man eats and drinks a great deal', he used to say, 'but is never filled, he sees a physician, inquires what ails him, what is wrong with his system, and how to rid himself of the disorder; but if the owner of five couches goes looking for ten, and the owner of ten tables buys up as many again, and though he has lands and money in plenty is not satisfied but bent on more, losing sleep and never sated by any amount, does he imagine that he does not need someone who will prescribe for him and point out the cause of his distress'? ... [We] assume that the one who drinks on and on without stopping needs to relieve, not stuff, himself ... So too with money-getters ... [H]e who has more than enough and yet hungers for still more will find no remedy in gold and silver [etc.] ... but in casting out the source of mischief and being purged. For his ailment is not poverty, but insatiability (ἀπληστία) and avarice (φιλοπλουτία) ... and unless someone removes this, like a tapeworm, from his mind, he will never cease to need superfluities – that is, to want what he does not need.
>
> (*Moralia* 524A-D; trans. De Lacy and Einarson, LCL)

One might dispute whether Plutarch does indeed have dropsy in mind in his commentary on the craving for wealth, for he does not actually use the word ὕδρωψ and, moreover, refers also to eating before he thoroughly mixes his metaphors by throwing in the simile of the tapeworm. But within the mix of figures used to characterize avaricious desires, the image of the person whose unquenchable thirst is a symptom of a sickness in need of a physician's treatment seems to describe dropsy without using the term.[41]

In the Roman Stoic, Seneca, the dropsy-greed comparison once

---

[41] The editors and translators of the Loeb text, De Lacy and Einarson, also suggest this in a note on this text.

more is made without naming the disease, but here the condition is described so as to help us to identify the illness without difficulty.

> [I]f [someone] desires tables that gleam with vessels of gold, and silver plate that boasts the names of ancient artists, bronze made costly by the crazy fad of a few [etc.] ...[42] though he should amass all these, they will no more be able to satisfy his insatiable soul than any amount of drink will ever suffice to quench the thirst of a man whose desire arises, not from need, but from the fire that burns in his vitals; for this is not thirst but disease [i.e. dropsy]. Nor is this true only in respect to money or food. Every want that springs, not from any need, but from vice is of a like character; however much you gather for it will serve, not to end, but to advance the disease.
>
> (Ad *Helviam* 11.3; trans. Basore, LCL)

The comparison may be of Cynic origin and perhaps have found its most avid usage in Cynic circles, but references to it are not limited to Cynic texts (or Stoic sources, for that matter). We find it clearly lodged also in Polybius, Horace and Ovid.

> [Scopas, the strategus of the Aetolians] was unaware that as in the case of a dropsy (τῶν ὑδρωπικῶν) the thirst of the sufferer never ceases and is never allayed by the administration of liquids from without, unless we cure the morbid condition of the body itself, so it is impossible to satiate the greed for gain, unless we correct by reasoning the vice inherent in the soul. (Polybius 13.2.2; trans. Paton, LCL)

> If you were troubled by thirst that no water could quench, you would tell your doctor about it; then if, with possessions amassed you feel only cravings for more, would you fail to take counsel with someone about it?
>
> (Horace, *Epode* 2.2.146–9; trans. Passage; cf. *Odes* 2.2.13).[43]

---

[42] A lengthy inventory of luxuries follows; it illustrates a recurring *topos* in popular philosophical diatribes against the unbridled pursuit of wealth. Thus, Billerbeck, 1979, p. 7: 'Die Aufzählung kostbarer Gegenstände und exotischer Schätze ... ist ein fester Bestandteil der Tiraden gegen den Luxus.'

[43] Horace was opposed to the Cynics, but as Moles has shown, he was interested in exploring the relationship between philosophy and practical living and on this question 'the claims of Cynicism at least deserve a hearing, for of all ancient

So he whose belly swells with dropsy, the more he drinks,
the thirstier he grows. Nowadays nothing but money
counts: fortune brings honours, friendships; the poor man
everywhere lies low.

(Ovid, *Fasti* 1.215–16; in the context of a complaint on the
'frantic lust for wealth'; trans. Frazer, LCL)

The comparison seems to have been common enough to become
proverbial.[44] Much later the compiler of the *Gnomologium Vaticanum* attributed it even to Plato.[45] We are thus allowed to assume
an everyday familiarity with the comparison, a familiarity which
made it possible for writers of popular narratives to play with the
double meaning of the term. An episode in Philostratus' *Life of
Apollonius* illustrates the possibility, for here, not unlike what we
shall argue for Luke's case, the healing of a dropsy is rhetorically
exploited in support of Apollonius' Pythagorean asceticism.
Finding himself in the temple of Asclepius, Apollonius encountered
an Assyrian youth who suffered from dropsy, a condition explicitly
linked to his 'life of luxury' and 'pleasure in drunkenness'. Asclepius, either unable or unwilling to cure the sick client, referred the
youth to Apollonius in order to appeal to his healing wisdom
(σοφία). Apollonius advised him to give up doing the 'things that
irritate and aggravate your disease, for you give yourself up to
luxury, and you accumulate delicate viands upon your water-logged
and worn-out stomach, and as it were, choke water with a flood of
mud' (*Life of Apollonius* 1.9). Philostratus stresses that the prescription for the cure of dropsy amounted to an adjustment of moral
character and that it was effected by a clear interpretation of a wise
saw of Heraclitus (τὰ σοφὰ σαφῶς ἑρμηνεύσας) who is said to have
said cryptically that what a dropsical person needs is for someone
'to substitute a drought for his rainy weather' (*Life of Apollonius*
1.9). In brief, Philostratus abundantly clarifies without ever
explicitly citing the common dropsy-greed comparison that the
disease that consumes, though very physical, has its causes in

philosophies Cynicism most nearly brought philosophy and life together. From
that point of view, if from no other, the Cynics are worthy opponents and Horace
is right to take them seriously, even though in the end he condemns them' (Moles,
1985, p. 53).
44 See Kindstrand, 1976, p. 241, for additional references including to Maximus of
Tyre and Lucilius.
45 Πλάτων τοὺς πλουσίους καὶ ἀπλήστους ὑδρωπιῶσιν ἐοικέναι ἔλεγεν· οἱ μὲν
γὰρ πεπλησμένοι ὑδάτων διψῶσιν, οἱ δὲ χρημάτων (*Gnom. Vat.* 434). Sternbach,
p. 162, expresses doubt about the authenticity of the attribution.

consuming passions. Dropsy is a symptom of the addiction to luxury.

## The metaphorical value of dropsy in Luke

Just as in Philostratus, Luke's knowledge of the ὕδρωψ analogy is not self-evident from the text; this has to be admitted, for he makes no explicit comparison between dropsy and avarice. I would contend, nevertheless, that an allusion to the comparison ought to be entertained. The longevity[46] and popularity of the dropsy figure and the stable analogical value of that figure, i.e., the almost unfailing consistency of the *Bild* (dropsy)-*Sache* (avarice) equation in Greco-Roman literature,[47] let us reasonably assume that it was familiar both to the author and to the readers of Luke's gospel. Luke, therefore, could afford to draw the comparison obliquely and elliptically. The literary setting and thematic context of the figure in Luke 14 alone, and together with Luke as a whole and the assumable knowledge of the Greco-Roman literary and social *topos* of the élite dinner scene, could be expected to ignite the reader's imaginative spark and direct it to leap across the gap from ὑδρωπικός to its corresponding pole of self-indulgent gluttony and greed. The setting evokes the Greco-Roman 'big dinner' (cf. 14.16, δεῖπνον μέγα), a chief trademark and status symbol of Greek and Roman rich,[48] and one which Hellenistic polemicists, satirists and moralists frequently exploited in their tirades against and parodies of the

---

[46] The wide range of dates for the dropsy illustrations (from Diogenes to the *Gnomologium Vaticanum*) would be a problem only if it were argued that Luke knew of a particular literary instance of the dropsy comparison. My suggestion, however, is that Luke could be expected to count on his readers' general familiarity with that figure of comparison. For this to be plausible, we need attestation that the figure was in the public domain. The chronological range of the literary evidence strengthens the case.

[47] Of course, one finds numerous references to and discussions of dropsy, especially in the medical writers, without any indication that it stands for greed (cf. n. 28 above). My argument is simply that when dropsy *does* stand for something, it almost always represents unrestrained socio-economic cravings. To my knowledge, Ps-Longinus (*Subl.* 3.4; quoted above) contains the only instance where the dropsy is used analogically for something other than avarice; Ps-Longinus uses it to illustrate and censure a turgid, inflated style of composition.

[48] A fuller discussion of the large banquet as a literary commonplace and as an important institution in the Greek and Roman social worlds is in chapter 6. See Murray, 1981; 1983a; 1983b; 1990; Slater, 1991a; Gowers, 1993. Luke's familiarity with and varied use of the Greco-Roman dinner and symposium traditions, literary and social, has often been noted; see, e.g., de Meeûs, 1961; Grundmann, 1961; Delobel, 1966; Ernst, 1979; Steele, 1981; 1984; D. Smith, 1987.

ostentatious behaviour and gluttonous consumption of the wealthy élite.[49] The host, a ruler (social élite), is identified as belonging to a group already noted for its fondness for dinner parties (7.36–50, 11.37–54) marked by insulting behaviour (7.44), and characterized before and after Luke 14 by means of a barrage of reproachful terms that reads like a Hellenistic thesaurus of slurs. Among these, ἁρπαγή (11.39 [Q], 'extortion'), πλεονεξία (12.15, 'greed')[50] and φιλαργυρία (16.14, 'love of money'; cf. 16.13, δουλεύειν μαμωνᾷ) are precisely the moral pathologies and preying social behaviour which dropsy signifies for the Cynics and other Greek and Roman writers.

Greco-Roman readers could have made the connection between signifier (dropsy) and signified (greed) from another, related angle. One of the stock criticisms by Cynics and others against the Greco-Roman rich was aimed at their extravagant *deipna* and *symposia* and the participants' lack of self-control (ἀκρασία) exhibited in the excessive consumption of luxurious food, wine and other pleasures.[51] As a deterrent against hedonistic intemperance the moralists argued that gluttony is physically harmful. In most exaggerated form, gastronomic excess is said to lead to death, a consequence often illustrated with the 'death by dinner' figure (see Hudson, 1989, pp. 85–6), the comically grotesque image of an overstuffed diner stumbling to the bath where he dies in his own vomit.[52] But more commonly convivial intemperance is linked to all kinds of ills.[53]

---

[49] See esp. Gowers, 1993, and Hudson, 1989 (discussing Juvenal, Horace and Persius and their dependence on the extravagant dinner for hortatory and deterrent ends). Many of Lucian's writings largely depend on the 'much-talked-about dinner' (*Nigr.* 23) image for their satirical punches. On Luke's familiarity with and use of these moralizing traditions see Hock, 1987, and chapter 4 below; cf. Braun, 1992, for Luke's 'anti-sympotic' sympathies.

[50] Πλεονεξία is not a term that is directly attached to the Pharisees, but it is the subject of a speech (12.13–34) within earshot of them (11.53 makes clear that the Pharisees are among the audience) and coherent with the explicit accusations against them.

[51] See Hock, 1987, pp. 457–62; Hudson, 1989, and Booth's detailed tracing of 'the convivial path to perdition' in 'the age for reclining and its attendant perils' (Booth, 1991).

[52] *Locus classicus* in Persius, *Sat.* 3.98–103: 'Bloated with food and queasy in the stomach our friend goes off to his bath, with long sulphurous belches issuing from his throat. As he drinks his wine, a fit of shakes comes over him, knocking the warm tumbler from his fingers; his bared teeth chatter; suddenly greasy savouries come slithering from loose lips. The sequel is funeral march and candles' (trans. Jenkinson). Cf. Juvenal, *Sat.* i.143–6.

[53] Of course, the contrary is that simple living and eating leads to robust health, mental sharpness and moral virtue. References in Hudson, 1989, and Booth, 1991.

Lucian, whose writings I will put to productive use in the next chapter, provides a particularly apt example. In his *Gallus*, the poor cobbler Micyllus asks the Cock (Pythagoras) to describe for him the life of the rich and that of the poor for the purpose of determining if the former are happier than the latter (*Gallus* 21). The answer concerning the rich contains this statement: 'But the rich, unhappy that they are – what ills (κακῶν) are they not subject to through lack of self-control (ἀκρασία)? Gout and consumption and pneumonia and dropsy (ὑδέρους) are the consequences of those extravagant dinners (τῶν πολυτελῶν ἐκείνων δείπνων ἀπόγονοι)' (*Gallus* 23). By contrast, the cobbler, dining on sprats and onions, is said to 'have no use for doctors' visits' (*Gallus* 22–3). This combination of splendid dinners, dropsy and the need for doctors seems to work along conventional metaphorical lines; it clarifies, I think, the similar combination in Luke 14.1–6 (cf. additional 'proof' in the rhetorical analysis, ch. 8).

Added motivation for stressing Luke's interest in the malady of dropsy is gained by comparing 14.1–6 to 13.10–17, another Lukan healing story. Robert O'Toole (1992) recently pointed out the significant differences in the admittedly similar stories. In the latter, the length and severity of the stooped woman's illness is given considerable attention; Jesus addresses her directly; her immediate cure is explicitly noted and emphasized; her response of glorifying God is noted. In a side glance to 14.1–6 for comparative purposes, O'Toole rightly observed that none of these features come to expression in the dropsy story and concluded: 'The woman bent double definitely plays a more significant role in her pericope than does the man with dropsy in his' (p. 104). On this basis he opts for 13.10–17 as the 'better story' (p. 105). The value judgments ('more significant', 'better') do not illuminate anything for me, but the observation on the comparatively diminished role of the dropsy in 14.1–6 is important. I cannot think of a better accounting of its significance than to propose that Luke looks past the ἄνθρωπός τις who is sick to the sickness that happens to inflict an ἄνθρωπός τις. It may be because Luke is not offering 14.1–6 as a 'model' response of a sick person to Jesus' beneficent action, as O'Toole plausibly interprets 13.10–17, that he could not only afford, but needed to efface the man behind the malady in order to focus sharply on the latter as a vehicle for evoking issues that have little to do with physical diseases and cures.

All this raises the question whether the narrator of this episode was encouraging readers to conclude from the presence of the dropsical man at the Pharisaic banquet something about the moral character of the Pharisees and lawyers at dinner. It is unlikely that we are to think of the person with dropsy himself as a real Pharisee,[54] but it is difficult to resist toying with the thought that Luke is insinuating an identification of the guest's illness with the Pharisaic moral character, given his tendency to distort the historical Pharisaic ethos generally. The metaphorical value of dropsy coheres tightly with the 'dropsical' characterization of the Pharisees we have noted. Dropsy as a consequence of sumptuous dining belongs to the conventional criticisms of the extravagant banquet of the upper classes. The stand-in of the dropsical man for the Pharisaic ethos would also help to explain to readers the sufferer's presence at the dinner, a matter that has baffled modern commentators.[55] He just happens to be in front of Jesus (ἔμπροσθεν αὐτοῦ), who heals him without ado, then dismisses him (ἀπέλυσεν).[56] He appears to be there neither as an 'uninvited guest' (ἄκλητος), a stock figure in ancient literary symposia,[57] nor only to evoke the 'beggar near the banquet' image, though he helpfully does that, but as a hapless literary figure whose brief cameo role is to be a physical, visual representation of an ethos of craving desire.

I summarize. 14.1–6 is best regarded as a mixed *chreia* entirely composed by the third evangelist, although he used a version of a traditional saying (14.5) and undoubtedly relied on his familiarity with the standard sabbath healing controversies. The milieu analysis revealed that the *chreia* depends on readers to draw upon know-

54 The rabbinical writings identify dropsy with immorality; see Str-B, vol. II, pp. 203–4; Grundmann, 1961, p. 291. But this evidence all belongs to the third century CE and later (Marshall, 1978, p. 579). Plummer (1914, p. 354) notes that Num. 5.21–2 and Ps. 109.18 indicate dropsy as a curse, but it is not clear that the water spoken of in these texts refers to dropsy.

55 Explanations vary. Farrar (1887, p. 294; cf. Plummer, 1914, p. 354) thought he was planted there as a Pharisaic plot of entrapment. Others think that he was an intruder, hoping for a healing (e.g., Fitzmyer, 1985, p. 1041, who toys also with other speculative explanations).

56 Fitzmyer's claim that the verb implies that the man was sent away, home (1985, p. 1041) is not convincing. Why this particular meaning of all the other possibilities, including simple dismissal or even release from illness? See LSJ, s.v. ἀπολύω, A.II.2.

57 Contra Ernst, 1979, p. 64. The dropsy does not play the role, uniformly assigned to the ἄκλητος in the symposia, of disruptively intruding in the sympotic dialogue. See J. Martin, 1931, pp. 64–79, note p. 68: 'Der ungebetene Gast hat ... durch sein Eingreifen in die Unterhaltung eine Aufgabe in die Ökonomie des Dialogs erhalten, und das ist bedeutsam für seine Person überhaupt und für die Rolle, die er im Symposium nach Platon zu spielen hat.'

ledge provided by Luke's wider narrative and upon familiarity with popular Greco-Roman literary and social customs to visualize the setting as a typical Hellenistic 'big dinner' hosted by a member of the ruling class and attended by others of similar positions whom Luke has portrayed in terms signifying an ethos of exclusive sociability and material greed. That these seem to be the moral issues that make up the central problematic in the anecdote is suggested by the fact that the story focuses on the malady of dropsy, one which in Cynic circles and beyond was used as a metaphor for insatiable greed and, relatedly, as a consequence of gluttonous sympotic behaviour. Thus the ἔξεστιν question turns out to be a question concerning the proper response to a person suffering not only from a physical illness but from a 'disease' symbolized by the malady of dropsy. The protreptic answer (in deed and word in the form of a rhetorical question) of Jesus, appearing not unlike a Cynic 'iatrosophist', a philosopher-medic specializing in the cure of 'diseased' characters and their dropsical cravings, is clear: the thing to do on a sabbath (sacred time) is to heal, an activity that is a sub-category of doing good (ἀγαθοποίησις, Luke 6.9). This cure or transformation of character from greed to generosity, defined as both the disposition of wealth and the renunciation of an ethos of exclusive social interaction, is of course the thematic centre of the remainder of the dinner episode for which 14.1–6 appears to be a tricky but apt introduction.

# 4

## UNCOMMON 'SYMPOSIUM RULES' (14.7–11, 12–14)

The instructions on reclining places (14.7–11) and on whom to invite to a social dining affair (14.12–14) immediately draw attention to themselves by their symmetrically parallel construction (see the figure in ch. 2, n. 30). This parallelism extends beyond literary structure. Both panels almost banally evoke taken-for-granted customs and values that governed the properly conducted *deipnon* or *symposion* in the Mediterranean world of Luke's time. Both panels make reference to reigning symposium rules (νόμοι συμποτικοί) only to deny them and to supplant them with rules rooted in a different sympotic ethos.[1] Finally, the rejection-replacement pattern is supported in each case with a rationale (ὅτι), once in the form of a maxim (14.11), then in that of a macarism (14.14). Formal similarity, topical affinity and commonality in moral outlook allow me to treat these twin instructional panels together in a single chapter.

### Promotion and demotion (14.7–11)

Luke 14.7–11 consists of three distinct elements: a transitional introduction (14.7), the saying on first and last places at a wedding meal (14.8–10), an appended rationale in the form of a saying on the reversal of the lowly and exalted (14.11).

14.7 is an editorial link that connects the following saying with the preceding *chreia*. In this verse Luke describes the saying on seating arrangements as a παραβολή, but this has influenced few modern form critics. It lacks the formal characteristics of any of Jülicher's *Gleichnisreden* (simile, parable, example story; 1910, vol. II, pp. 25–118) nor are its stylistic features accounted for in other

---

[1] Note the clarity of the rejection-replacement pattern in each panel of instructions: (a) ὅταν ... μὴ ... μήποτε, (b) ἀλλ᾿ ὅταν.

modern definitions of a parable.[2] Formally the saying is a neatly balanced, antithetical conditional sentence where the protasis is a tripartite prohibitive injunction, the apodosis a matching, tripartite imperative injunction (Zeller, 1977, p. 67). Both form and subject identify the saying as a 'piece of worldly wisdom advising subtlety rather than effrontery in pursuit of kudos'.[3]

When Luke nonetheless calls this sapiential sentence a parable it does not mean that he knows more (or less) about form criticism than, say, Jülicher or Bultmann. Rather, it indicates that for the author of the third gospel, in keeping with ancient Greek and Roman usage of terms of comparison, παραβολή is not a strictly formal term.[4] The attempt by many scholars to squeeze from Luke 14.8–10 some metaphorical juice, either by construing it as a 'parable in hortatory form' (Plummer, 1914, p. 356), or to see in it a pointer 'to the attitude demanded by the Kingdom of God' (Creed, 1930, p. 190), or to 'how men should behave over against God' (Marshall, 1978, p. 581), is lured along by an understanding of παραβολή that is not contained in the use of the term in 14.7 nor in the saying on prudent posturing for places. The question of what Luke means when he calls the prudential saying a parable will need to be examined later when we consider the compositional pattern of the dinner episode (ch. 8, pp. 169–71).

---

[2] E.g., Scott, 1989, p. 8: 'A parable is a mashal that employs a short narrative fiction to reference a transcendent symbol.'

[3] Goulder, 1989, p. 585; similarly, Jülicher, 1910, vol. II, p. 253: 'sittliche Regel'; Bultmann, 1964, p. 104: 'secular ... rule of prudence'; Zeller, 1977, p. 67: 'weisheitliche Regel'; Fitzmyer, 1985, p. 1044: 'a bit of secular, prudential wisdom'. Crossan correctly advises that the saying goes beyond prudence in the pursuit of recognition; it 'could be described at its most positive as utterly banal and more accurately as rather immoral' (1971–2, p. 301). Apropos is the humorous anecdote recorded by Athenaeus, *Deipnos.* 6.245: 'As for the parasite [a professional τρεχεδείπνος, 'dinner-chaser'] Chaerephon, he says that once he went into a wedding-party uninvited (εἰς γάμον ἄκλητος) and reclined in the last place (ἔσχατος) and when the commissioners on laws for women counted the guests they told him to leave because he exceeded the legal limit of thirty guests. Well, then, he replied, count them again, but begin with me.'

[4] Cf. the use of παραβολή in 4.23 (proverb); 5.36 (proverb); 6.39 (proverb); 12.16–21 (example story); 12.41 (blanket term for sayings on watchfulness); 13.6 (example story); 18.2–8 (example story); 18.10–14 (example story); 19.12–27 (illustration of point given in advance [19.11]). See Scott, 1989, pp. 27–30; Fitzmyer, 1964, pp. 599–601; and Farmer, 1962, p. 306 n. 1: 'Luke uses the term "parable" very loosely.' McCall summarizes the use of terms of comparison among Greek and Roman critics: 'the critics indiscriminately apply the various terms [εἰκών, παραβολή, *imago, similitudo*] to all forms of comparison, and in no treatise does a shift in use from one to another necessarily involve a shift from one form to another' (1969, p. 258).

The saying on the reversal of the exalted and the humbled (14.11) is a common proverb, structured as an 'antithetical aphorism' (Tannehill, 1986, p. 183; cf. 1975, pp. 88–101) chiastically asserting a 'bi-polar reversal' (York, 1991, pp. 78–80). It is able to stand independent of its present context (cf. Luke 18.14b) to which it has been added secondarily for a rhetorical purpose (note ὅτι).

What about the source-critical issues? The transitional verse (14.7) has little that is not characteristic of Luke's editorial style. The λέγειν-παραβολήν formula, πρός + accusative after a verb of speaking (twice), the intransitive use of ἐπέχω are all among favourite Lukanisms (Jeremias, 1980, p. 237). The circumstantial details (ἐπέχων πῶς τὰς πρωτοκλισίας ἐξελέγοντο, 'attending to how they were picking the first places') were furnished by the saying that this verse introduces.

The saying on positions at the dinner table (14:8–10) evidently is Luke's own version of a recurrent *topos* that is deeply rooted, even if in a variety of versions, in literature ranging widely in time and type.[5] It reflects the inter-connection between seating order and social rank in ancient Near Eastern, Greek and Roman sympotic customs and social relationships.[6] As Plutarch, Luke's contempo-

---

[5] The following is a partial listing of thematic parallels: (1) Near Eastern Wisdom: Prov. 23.1; 25.6–7 (formal parallel); Sir. 3.17–20; 7.4; 13.8–10; 29.27; 32.1–2; Zeller (1977, p. 67 n. 95) adduces passages from Ptah-hotep 7 and Kagemni 2 and 3; (2) Jewish writings: Josephus, *Ant.* 12.4.9.210; *LevR.* 1; *Abot R. Nat.* 25; *Ep. Arist.* 263; cf. Philo, *Cont.* 67–8 (ranking at the meals of the therapeutae) and 1QS 2.11–22 (ranking at the meals of the Qumran sectarians); (3) Greek authors: Plato, *Symp.* 177D-E, 212C-213B; Theophrastus, *Charact.* 21.2 (Theophrastus uses shameless clamouring for prestigious places to illustrate the vice of μικροφιλοτιμία. Hence ὁ ... μικροφιλότιμος τοιοῦτός τις οἷος σπουδάσαι ἐπὶ δεῖπνον κληθεὶς παρ' αὐτὸν τὸν καλέσαντα κατακείμενος δειπνῆσαι, 'the *mikrophilotimos* is someone of a kind that when he is invited to dine must find a place to dine next to the host'); Lucian, *Symp.* 9; Plutarch, *Quaest.conv.* 1.2 (= *Mor.* 615D-619) is entirely devoted to the question of the placement of dinner guests; cf. Plutarch, *Mor.* 149B; 219E; Epictetus, *Dissert.* 4.1, 105; Dio Chrysosthom, *Or.* 30.29; Athenaeus, *Deipnos.* 2.47e, 4.44d, 7.245 (concerning Chaerephon: ὁ παράσιτος εἰς γάμον ἄκλητος εἰσελθὼν καὶ κατακλιθεὶς ἔσχατος, 'the parasite went into a wedding-party uninvited and reclined in the last place'); Diogenes Laertius 2.73; cf. citations in Robbins, 1989, pp. 21–2; York, 1991, p. 91 n. 3; (4) Latin authors: Horace, *Sat.* 2.8; Pliny, *Ep.* 2.6; Juvenal, *Sat.* 8.177–178; Petronius (*Sat.* 38.14) refers to the *locus libertinus*, 'the bottom of the end sofa' assigned to a freedman invited to dine with free men, and to be distinguished from the *locus consularis*, the most prestigious position at dinner (see Plutarch, *Mor.* 619B-F, for a discussion of this Roman habit and other people's customs of assigning honour to dining places).

[6] See Jülicher, 1910, vol. II, p. 247: 'Die Platzfrage war bei den auf Korrektheit im Zeremoniell bedachten Orientalen eine sehr wichtige.' Cf. J. Martin, 1931,

rary, shows, the question was a current topic worthy of treatment by the moralists. Thus Plutarch evinces both the moralist's disdain for rank and privilege at the dining table and an aristocratic desire for good order (εὐταξία), which means insisting on correct reclining arrangements. To illustrate, first Plutarch's Thales:

> When we have taken our places ... we ought not to try to discover who has been placed above us, but rather how we may be thoroughly agreeable to those placed with us, by trying at once to discover in them something that may serve to initiate and keep up friendship ... For, in every case, a man that objects to his place at table is objecting to his neighbour rather than to his host, and he makes himself hateful to both.
>
> (*Septem sapientium convivium* [*Moralia*] 149A-B; trans. Babbit, LCL)

And, Plutarch's father to his son:

> It is ridiculous for our cooks and waiters to be greatly concerned about what they shall bring first, or what second or middle or last ... if those invited to the feast are to be fed at places randomly determined: this arrangement gives neither to age, nor to rank, nor to any other distinction the position that suits it; it does no honour to the outstanding man ... For the man of quality does not have his status and station [in the world], yet fails to receive recognition in the place he occupies at dinner.
>
> (*Quaestiones convivales* [*Moralia*] 616B; trans. Clement, LCL, slightly altered)

The subject that Plutarch takes on from opposite points of view is quite familiar to Luke; he 'knows the world of middle-class dinner-parties' (Goulder, 1989, p. 589), as many others have demonstrated.[7] One might therefore consider the subject of the admonition to be an item of traditional convention, but only in a most general sense. There is no convincing reason to regard it as a pre-Lukan saying (or even a Christian statement for that matter),[8] as is some-

pp. 101–4, 135–6. The complex relationship between Roman ideals of equality and convivial customs, including seating order, is discussed by D'Arms, 1990.

[7] See de Meeûs, 1961; Delobel, 1966; Aune, 1978, pp. 88–9; Ernst, 1979; Steele, 1981, pp. 55–90; 1984; Karris, 1985, pp. 62–3; D. Smith, 1987; D. Smith and Taussig, 1990; Braun, 1992, pp. 75–7.

[8] Rightly Horn, 1983, p. 210: 'Die Gastregel selber enhält keine christlichen Züge.'

times done by arguing that the Western interpolation of a similar saying after Matthew 20.28 (D Φ it sy$^c$) is an older translation-variant of the same Aramaic original from which Luke's version also derives (Jeremias, 1963, pp. 25–6, 191–2; Black, 1967, pp. 171–5). Even if one should be favourably inclined towards the view that behind some gospel sayings lie Aramaic originals, in this instance the retranslation fails, as Goulder points out (1989, p. 587). To be sure, neither is it plainly evident that 'the D verse is a later Greek paraphrase of Luke' (Goulder, 1989, p. 587; cf. Streeter, 1924, p. 241). But why go on this kind of chase for a genetic link between Bezae's and Luke's saying at all? We are dealing with an 'utterly banal' topic (Crossan, 1971–2, p. 301) known to any early Christian writer from everyday life (cf. James 2.1–7; Matthew 23.6–11) and, if the writer is even marginally erudite, also from Hellenistic literature, both Jewish and Greek. It does not take a master *littérateur* to compose something like Luke 14.8–10 without the aid of a source. Taking Luke to be the author appeals to me as the least strenuous option even if it is not entirely foolproof.[9] Crossan, for example, suggests that if the saying is original to Luke it 'would hardly have specified only εἰς γάμους but would surely have referred to any meal' (1971, p. 301). Perhaps this speaks against an overly confident judgment on the provenance of the saying, but I would not make too much of the feast vocabulary at any one point in the episode for source-critical purposes. The rather extensive variation in naming dining occasions (φαγεῖν ἄρτον [twice], γάμος, ἄριστον, δεῖπνον [three times], δοχή) covers enough entertainments to give the impression that any and all social meals are under review.

As for Luke 14.11, this bi-polar aphorism concerning the reversed fortunes of the exalted and the humble articulates a sensibility that floats around in the Near Eastern wisdom tradition,[10] and enter-tains a notion familiar to Greeks and Romans.[11] Naturally, it also

---

[9] So also Goulder, 1989, p. 585: 'So the theme is Lukan, and so are the structure and the worldly wisdom ... The language in general is congenial to Luke, and ... it seems clear that Luke has composed the piece.' One does not even need to suppose, as Goulder does, that Luke was here inspired by having Matt. 22 and 23 'to hand'!

[10] For the most detailed discussion of this *logion* and an impressive collection of parallels in the sapiential tradition see Hoffmann and Eid, 1975, pp. 208–11; York, 1991, pp. 78–80; cf. Grundmann, 1969, pp. 6–15; Wengst, 1987, pp. 35–67; the literature cited in the next note.

[11] The closest verbal, thematic and formal parallel is the saying attributed to Aesop in which the activity of Zeus is described as τὰ μὲν ὑψηλὰ ταπεινῶν, τὰ δὲ ταπεινὰ ὑψῶν, 'humbling the exalted and exalting the humble' (*Gnom. Vat.* 553; also *ap.* Diogenes Laertius, 1.69); cf. Polybius 5.26.12; *POxy.* 2554.I.2.5–11. In Euripides,

found its way into Christian texts (Luke 18.14b; Matthew 23.12; cf. Matthew 18.4; James 4.10; 1 Peter 5.5–6; 1 Clement 59.3; Barnabas 3.3). At least on one other occasion this conventional antithesis is found also within a literary symposium.[12] Whether Luke received this from Q or some other (oral?) source is difficult to say and of little matter.[13] What seems clear is that Luke has placed the saying here.[14]

Less clear but more crucial is its meaning and function within Luke 14. Although I will return to this question in chapter 8, a few preparatory comments on the evocative potential of ταπεινός (and its derivatives) for first century Mediterranean readers are appropriate here in order to lay the groundwork for my later remarks.

The ταπεινός-motif in early Christian literature has greatly interested scholars because, one suspects, of the later emergence of *humilitas* as one of the Christian virtues, indeed as a rather early Christian *nova lex* to be acted out in rituals of penitence and fasting.[15] Hence the attention to this motif is implicitly riding on

*Troiades* 612–3, Hecuba issues a saying materially and formally similar, but using different vocabulary: ὁρῶ τὰ τῶν θεῶν, ὡς τὰ μὲν πυργοῦσ᾽ ἄνω τὰ μηδὲν ὄντα, τὰ δὲ δοκοῦντ᾽ ἀπώλεσαν, 'I see the gods' work, who exalt high what was nothing and bring the proud names low.' Note also the same idea expressed in a *chreia* attributed to Diogenes on why he wanted to be buried face down. 'Because after a little time down will be converted into up' (τὰ κάτω ἄνω στρέφεσθαι; Diogenes Laertius 6.32). In light of these sayings there is no need to insist, as Grundmann does, that Luke 14.11 'is a two-membered mashal whose very form betrays its Jewish origin' (1969, p. 16). 'Antithesis was a much-prized device in Graeco-Roman rhetoric' (Beavis, 1990a, p. 138; see also Scaglione, 1972, p. 22). The best treatments of ταπεινός (*humilis*) in Greco-Roman literature and society are Dihle, 1957; Rehrl, 1961; den Boer, 1983; pp. 143–55, 158–62; Wengst, 1987, pp. 15–34; cf. Leivestad, 1966; and Grundmann, 1969.
12  *Ep. Arist.* 262–3: ὁ θεὸς τοὺς ὑπερηφάνους καθαιρεῖ, τοὺς δὲ ἐπιεικεῖς καὶ ταπεινοὺς ὑψοῖ, 'God puts down the proud, but the modest and lowly he exalts.' Cf. *Ep. Arist.* 257.
13  See Kloppenborg, 1988, p. 162, and Arnal, 1991, for surveys of scholarly opinions. Streeter's hunch (1924, p. 285) that Luke himself could have formed the saying is probably right. The notion of ταπείνωσις is among Luke's characteristic interests; e.g., of Mary it is said that the Lord ἐπέβλεψεν ἐπὶ τὴν ταπείνωσιν τῆς δούλης αὐτοῦ (1.48); ὕψωσεν ταπεινούς (1.52); see the analyses of Schottroff, 1978; Wengst, 1987, pp. 77–9.
14  Zeller, 1977, p. 68. The majority of scholars would dissent and argue on the basis of Luke's so-called 'fear of doublets' that 14.11 had already been attached to the preceding saying prior to Luke's redaction of the material. E.g., Sato, 1988, p. 21: 'Lukas bildet von sich aus wohl keine Dublette. Daher muß man annehmen, daß er diesen gleichen Spruch [18.14b] ... schon jeweils mit der Parabel verbunden vorfand.'
15  Grundmann locates this shift in the Christian usage of the ταπειν- words with 1 Clem. and Hermas. 'In 1 Cl. and Herm. humility as penitence and fasting has an established place in Christianity understood as *nova lex*' (1969, pp. 25–6).

theological interests which are best served by defining humility in terms of the paradigmatic σχῆμα ταπεινόν of Jesus himself,[16] and with reference to Jesus as a teacher of ταπείνωσις rather selectively conceived as a childlike religious attitude.[17] That is, to be ταπεινός is to have a morally right and a piously correct attitude; 'humble', therefore, has positive connotations.

But this view, though not entirely inaccurate, is misleading and sustainable only upon the acceptance of questionable suppositions. One is what R. Leivestad has called the 'ineradicable dogma' that the meaning of ταπεινός in biblical usage differs sharply from its meaning in non-biblical literature. A word that Greeks and Romans generally used as a contemptuous appellation supposedly takes on the opposite signification in Christian usage (Leivestad, 1966, p. 36; cf. Wengst, 1987, pp. 12–13). This claim of an anomalous Christian usage of ταπεινός has the marks of being another manifestation of the 'fiction of Biblical Greek' (Horsley, 1989), as A. Dihle and others after him have demonstrated,[18] and thus should not be employed as the prism through which to spot either the redactor's usage in Luke 14.11 or the associative meanings it might have evoked for Mediterranean readers. A related misleading supposition is that ταπεινός is in the first place a term from the sphere of personal morality, signifying unassuming deference or modesty.[19] It

---

16 *Locus classicus* is Phil. 2.5–11 where the antithesis is the framework for the Pauline Christ myth: ἐταπείνωσεν ἑαυτόν ... καὶ ὁ θεὸς αὐτὸν ὑπερύψωσεν. See den Boer, 1983, pp. 154–5.

17 The paradigmatic passage is Matt. 18.1–5 where ὁ μείζων ἐν τῇ βασιλείᾳ τῶν οὐρανῶν is whoever ταπεινώσει ἑαυτὸν ὡς τὸ παιδίον τοῦτο.

18 Dihle notes that ταπεινός and *humilis* eventually *became* 'die bevorzugten Ausdrücke für "demütig" im christlichen Sinn' (1957, p. 740). Leivestad convincingly demolishes the ταπεινός 'dogma' in a detailed survey of the usage of the term in LXX and NT: 'Es is überhaupt zweifelhaft, ob die LXX jemals ταπεινός gebraucht in der bewussten Absicht, eine positive moralische Handlung (Demut) auszudrücken ... Doch wird ταπεινός ... im spätjüdischen und christlichem Sprachgebrauch nur sehr selten positiv angewandt' (1966, p. 40). Cf. his concluding sentence: 'Die Bedeutung "demütig" ist für ταπεινός niemals idiomatisch geworden' (p. 47). Den Boer acknowledges that '*tapeinos* etc ... had a surplus value for Christians' but states that 'there is a far closer analogy between Christian and pagan usage than is often permitted by modern scholars' (1983, pp. 154–5). Wengst, 1987, pp. 12–13, accepts the traditional demarcation between Greco-Roman and Jewish/Christian usage, but by adding important qualifiers – discriminating between various 'Traditionsbereiche' within the literature generally and attending to who calls whom ταπεινός in the texts – he actually paints a much more polychromatic picture.

19 Thus especially Rehrl, 1961, pp. 196–203; see Wengst, 1987, p. 15 n. 1, for criticism of Rehrl.

is used in this way on rare occasions,[20] but most frequently it is a term not so much advocating the virtue of self-restraint ('die Tugend der Selbstbescheidung'; Rehrl, 1961, p. 201), or describing a servile tactic by which to obtain what is not easily had by aggressive force (e.g., someone's affection),[21] as it is a call to stay within the limits of one's social position ('sich selbst und seine Grenzen zu erkennen').[22] A ταπεινός social position within Mediterranean society, however, was severely reprobative. Several examples from ancient authors are sufficient to illustrate this. Pollux (second century CE), though no social commentator, nonetheless illustrates the value of ταπεινός when he includes this term in his lengthy catalogue of adjectives and slurs by which to characterize the good-for-nothing: slavish (ἀνδραποδώδης), neglected (ἀπερριμμένος), insignificant (ἄσημος), anonymous (ἀνώνυμος), inconspicuous (ἀφανής), obscure (ἄδηλος), disreputable (ἄδοξος), wretched (ἄθλιος, cf. δύστηνος), purposeless (εἰκαῖος), without means (ἄπορος), evil-spirited (κακοδαίμων), vulgar, one of the rabble (συρφετός), a fool (ὁ ἀνόητος), a sickly one (ὁ νοσῶν), to be thrown out on the dung-heap (κοπρίων ἐκβλητότερος) or refuse to be cast out at the crossroads (τῶν ἐν ταῖς τριόδοις καθαρμάτων ἐκβλητότερος), presumably near the statutes of Hecate, a gathering place for vagrants and beggars.[23] Another revealing window to Hellenistic sensibilities on what it meant to be ταπεινός is provided by Lucian's *Somnium* (Dream) where he describes his choice of a career with the aid of the analogy of two mistresses (Sculpture and Education) vying for his allegiance. If you go with Sculpture, Paideia warns Lucian,

> you will be nothing but a labourer (ἐργάτης), toiling with your body and putting in it your entire hope of a livelihood, personally inconspicuous (ἀφανής), getting meagre and illiberal returns, lowly in disposition [ambition?] (ταπεινὸς

---

[20] See especially den Boer's attempt (1983) to adduce evidence for the use of ταπεινός in *bonam partem*. Wengst also notes some examples of ταπεινός as a positive counterpart to an arrogant or haughty attitude, but against den Boer adds that 'das Gesamtbild kann der gelegentlich positive Gebrauch nicht grundlegend verändern' (1987, p. 33 n. 82).

[21] E.g., Propertius 1.10.27–28: 'The more modest (*humilis*) you are and subservient to the Amor, the more you will achieve the desired effect.' Cited by Wengst, 1987, p. 34.

[22] Dihle, 1957, p. 738. Wengst, 1987, p. 15 n. 1, rightly stresses the social over the moral dimensions of the word 'Grenze'.

[23] *Onomasticon* 5.162–4. The list is much longer and seems to be driven by a love of synonyms.

τὴν γνώμην),[24] an insignificant figure in public, neither sought by your friends nor feared by your enemies nor envied by your fellow-citizens, nothing but just a labourer, one of the swarming rabble, ever cringing to the man above you and courting the man who can use his tongue, leading a hare's life, and counting as an unexpected bit of luck [i.e. a 'door mat'] to anyone stronger.

(*Somnium* 9; trans. Harmon, LCL, slightly altered)

Paideia promises Lucian to transform him from the poor son of a nobody (ὁ πένης ὁ τοῦ δεῖνος; a reference to Lucian's sculptor father) into someone who will move in the circle of the educated (τοῖς πεπαιδευμένοις) and eminent (τοῖς ἀρίστοις), men such as Demosthenes, Aeschines and Socrates, all of lowly origin whom Paideia made great (*Somnium* 11–12). Paideia continues with the other option:

On the other hand, if you turn your back upon these men so great and noble, upon glorious deeds and sublime words, upon a dignified appearance (σχῆμα εὐπρεπές), upon honour, esteem, praise, precedence, power and offices, upon fame for eloquence and felicitations for wit, then you will put on a filthy tunic, assume a servile appearance (σχῆμα δουλοπρεπές) ... with your back bent over your work; you will be a groundling, with groundling ambitions, lowly in every manner (πάντα τρόπον ταπεινός) ... you will make yourself a thing of less value (ἀτιμότερον ποιῶν σεαυτόν) than a block of stone.

(*Somnium* 13; trans. Harmon, LCL, slightly altered)

As Klaus Wengst has noted (1987, p. 21), Lucian's description of lowliness is richly revealing, because it is drawn with reference to its opposite (ἄριστος). Paideia's speech in Lucian's *Dream* is a rhetorical argument that heavily relies on the technique of competitive comparison (σύγκρισις) to persuade the young (οἱ νέοι) that παιδεία is a way out of poverty and its detrimental effects (*Somnium*

---

24 Harmon (LCL) translates this phrase as 'humble-witted'. This may be appropriate in the context of Παιδεία's speech where ταπεινός τὴν γνώμην may stand opposite to τὸν λέγειν δυνάμενον in the same passage. But γνώμη also carries the value of disposition, inclination, resolve, ambition (see LSJ, s.v. γνώμη). What Lucian seems to suggest is that a lowly status in life is not merely an external social reality but something that worms its way into a person's disposition, lowering resolve and ambition.

18).[25] Certainly some exaggeration and stereotyping of opposites inheres in this kind of rhetorical exercise, but for it to be convincing, it needs also to represent and work with recognized social contrasts and the values attached to these contrasts. Herein lies the illustrative capacity of Lucian's characterization of the person whose life is 'lowly in every manner'. This life is the direct antithesis of the ἄριστος, the cultural ideal for those who are eminent and those who can only dream of being among the eminent élite.

Lucian's Dream is significant also in that it uses ταπεινός language in proximity to and within the signifying orbit of poverty language. This further calls for the recognition of lowliness as a social locus and, correspondingly, of lowly traits, whether thought of as a worthless self-definition, servile disposition or lethargic ambition, as the internalized counterpart of the social situation.[26] Situated at the very bottom of the verticalized social order (see Alföldy, 1985, pp. 94–156, especially the pyramid diagram on p. 146), the lot of the ταπεινοί (humiliores) was relatively fixed. Generally they could not obtain the necessary combination of social, economic and political resources to enable them to move upward across strata boundaries.[27] Hence their options were contained within a range bounded by fatalistic resignation, on one side, and hopeful aspirations and/or fantasies, on the other.[28] The latter could itself admit to a variety of forms, including a determined effort through hard work to live out a 'rags to riches' story,[29]

---

[25] Wengst, 1987, pp. 22–6. Wengst's interest in Lucian's Dream differs from mine in that he cites it as evidence for the possibilities of upward mobility for those in the low classes.

[26] This correspondence between one's place in the social hierarchy and one's disposition is recognized by Dihle (1957, pp. 740–1). Ταπεινός thus denotes both a social lowliness, 'die gedrückte, vielleicht erbarmenswürdige Situation' and 'die dementsprechende Haltung' or 'Gesinnung'. Wengst similarly speaks of 'einen engen Zusammenhang zwischen niedriger sozialer Stellung und niedriger Gesinnung' (1987, pp. 17–22, 26).

[27] Alföldy, 1985, p. 151, summing up his views on social mobility during the early empire: '[S]ocial mobility is not to be over-estimated as a relatively positive factor ... Thus in the Early Empire, by contrast with modern industrial society, it was only seldom possible and in any event atypical for a man to work his way up from the very base to the very heights of the social pyramid.' See also MacMullen, 1974, pp. 88–120; Wengst, 1987, pp. 22–6.

[28] Kloft, 1988a, p. 96: 'Was dem Ptochós [= ταπεινός] blieb, war, sich mit seiner Lage abzufinden oder vielfach die Hoffnung auf Besserung in einer ungewissen Zukunft.'

[29] Lucian is an example of someone who escaped the lowly artisan class through education. Limited chances for upward mobility were indeed available (see esp. Wengst, 1987, pp. 22–6). A wide-spread Aufsteigermentalität, to use Wengst's term, is evinced in proverbial material that compares the shame of poverty to the

uprisings or revolts if the pressures became unbearable,[30] and, perhaps most typically, protesting oppressive lowliness in terms of a utopian (this worldly or eschatological), divinely-effected reversal scheme. Although this utopian reversal perhaps is most programmatic within the Jewish-Christian apocalyptic tradition (e.g., 1 Enoch 92–105; Luke 1.52–3; see Nickelsburg, 1979), it appears also outside of these traditions (see York, 1991, pp. 173–82). The *locus classicus* is an amulet (third century CE) on which an astrological prediction for the next year contains the following notice: 'For the rich it will go badly' (τοῖς πλουσίοις κακῶς ἔσται); 'a great man (μέγας ἄνηρ) will be ruined'; 'and the poor will be exalted, and the rich will be lowered' (καὶ οἱ πτωχοὶ ὑψωθήσονται, καὶ οἱ πλούσιοι ταπεινωθήσονται).[31]

All that I have said concerning lowliness clearly cannot straightforwardly be read into or out of Luke 14.11 which, at its simplest level, merely states a bit of tactical wisdom on how to avoid embarrassment at a dinner party. But its vocabulary, antithetical form and theme of reversal, not to speak of its thematic context (14.1–24), is highly evocative of the social experience of lowliness and a certain kind of response to it. The trite face-saving instructions on how not to be seen or to feel a fool at dinner parties may well play an analogical function in an argument for a reward system that could motivate the high to step down from their exalted positions in support of and conformity with Luke's community ideals in which 'lowliness' is on the way to being redeemed or, at least, 'dressed up' to make it less appalling to the élite for whose patronage and affiliation Luke seems to be campaigning. That is, we

greater shame of not actively seeking to escape it (Thucydides 2.40.1: τὸ πένεσθαι οὐχ ὁμολογεῖν τινι αἰσχρόν, ἀλλὰ μὴ διαφεύγειν ἔργῳ αἴσχιον [cited by Kloft, 1988a, p. 94]); they were fuelled by fantasies and popular success stories. 'Rags to riches' successes, typified by Petronius' Trimalchio, a *nouveau riche* (from frog to king, *Sat.* 77) and the famous case of the poor rustic who went from being a farm labourer to owning large estates and into the magistrate's office (third-century inscription from Mactar; *ILS* 7457), were more due to 'luck' than 'institutionalized paths for upwards mobility' (Alföldy, 1985, p. 152), but they undoubtedly generated some kind of ancient version of modern lottery fever.

30 First- and second-century revolts largely inspired by economic pressures are catalogued by Alföldy, 1985, pp. 154–6. See also Fuks, 1974, pp. 71–9, for a typology of ancient socio-economic conflicts.

31 *POxy.* 2554.I.2.5–11; see the commentary on this text by Kloft, 1988a, p. 96; and MacMullen, 1971, p. 110, and the entire article on the empirical picture of the poor in the ancient astrological treatises. That Luke is quite familiar with Greek socio-economic utopian hopes, in which the ταπεινός saying probably has its *Sitz im Leben*, has recently been affirmed by Bartchy, 1991; and York, 1991; cf. Johnson, 1986, pp. 119–32.

should expect that Luke might exploit the saying's evocative power for a rhetorical purpose (see ch. 8, pp. 169–70).

## Usual and unusual guests (14.12–14)

Like the preceding passage, Luke 14.12–14 is a composite, consisting of a saying on inviting the right guests (14.12–13) to which another *logion* (14.14) has been added. The first saying is structurally identical to the one on dining places. The only formal difference in this passage is that the concluding saying is a macarism instead of an antithetical aphorism (see, in general, Cavallin, 1985).

When answering the source question, the admonition on whom to invite to ἄριστον ἢ δεῖπνον ('breakfast or dinner') coupled with the idea of an eschatological reward is usually taken as an adaptation of a Jewish hospitality rule variously stated in rabbinical, sapiential and apocalyptic texts.[32] That especially 14.15 takes up well-known terms from Jewish and early Christian thought on *post-mortem* fortunes is clear,[33] but in Luke this traditional Jewish/Christian language has been converted to convey an eschatological (utopian) vantage point capable of sponsoring a moral exhortation; it is indeed the moral issue, designed to influence the temporal Lukan community, that is the stressed didactic point.[34] Hence, though the view that we are dealing with a pre-Lukan eschatological hospitality complex has had a tenacious life, I consider it to be restrictive because it has prematurely bracketed out consideration of far more illuminating and compelling parallels in Greco-Roman literature, especially those in the Cynic moralizing tradition.

[32] E.g., Jose b. Johanan: 'Let thy house be opened wide and let the needy be members of thy household' (*Abot* 1.5a). See the citations from ancient Near Eastern wisdom texts given by Zeller, 1977, p. 70, in support of this claim: 'Der Gedanke, daß es sich lohnt, den Niedrigen aufzunehmen, weil Gott vergeltend einspringt, wo dieser eine Wohltat nicht entlohnen kann, ist in der Weisheit nicht neu.' For other (late) rabbinic parallels see especially Gruenewald, 1961, pp. 47–8. For Bultmann the Lukan saying is 'akin to the grudging spirit of the last chapter [108] of Eth[iopic] Enoch' (1964, p. 103).

[33] See Cavallin, 1985, and Fitzmyer, 1985, p. 1048; cf. Luke 20.35, 17.32, 23.6, 24.15; and Luke 13.29–30 (redacted Q material).

[34] See Horn, 1983, e.g. pp. 182, 186; note esp. p. 194 where Horn calls 14.14 a 'moral macarism'. The frequent claim that the primary point of the macarism is to signal a 'spiritual' or 'eschatological' reward schema (for example, most recently York, 1991, pp. 137–9) does not take into account the trope of using an ideal (including a *post-mortem* utopia) to criticize and amend current social arrangements and moral attitudes.

The saying on proper guests takes a Lukan tack on a familiar, traditional Greco-Roman subject which continued to be current in Luke's time.[35] From the Greek and Latin literature one gathers that the dominant etiquette of issuing and accepting dinner invitations adhered to a strict sense of social gradation and segregation; dinner invitations were currency in a sympotic culture where 'snobbery, sycophancy, and humiliation ... lurk menacingly in the background'.[36] Hence, as Lucian advises, οὐδεὶς ἐχθρὸν ἢ ἀγνῶτα ἄνθρωπον ἀλλ᾽ οὐδὲ συνήθη μετρίως ἐπὶ δεῖπνον καλεῖ, 'nobody invites an enemy or an unknown person nor even a slight acquaintance to dinner' (*de Parasito* 22).[37] Plutarch devotes an entire chapter of his 'table talk' (*Moralia* 706F-10A) to the subject of invitations and not surprisingly, given his aristocratic social position and preferences (C. P. Jones, 1971), he criticizes the Roman custom of allowing invited guests to bring along an uninvited 'shadow' (σκιά, *umbra*), fearing that this practice will lead to dinner company of 'different and incompatible types' (ἀσυμφύλους καὶ ἀσυναρμόστους; *Moralia* 709B) and so threaten the feelings of congenial fellowship within the exclusive circle of σύνδειπνοι. A variety of metaphors help Plutarch make his point:

> To have the company of others forced upon one on a voyage, in the family, or in legal business, is not so unpleasant as at dinner ... A dinner party (συμπόσιον) is a sharing (κοινωνία) of earnest and jest, of words and deeds; so the diners must not be left to chance, but must be intimates of one another who will enjoy being together. Cooks make up their dishes of a variety of flavours, blending the sour, the oily, the sweet, and the pungent, but you

---

35 See Murray, 1983b, pp. 196–8, on the Homeric feast and its function in the Archaic period of Greek society. He argues that Homeric Greece consisted neither of a feudal-type nor a kinship-type society, but of a sympotic society in which 'peasantry and aristocracy are relatively independent of each other' (p. 196). Its central structural element was the feast or *symposion*, its focal point the 'great hall' (see *Od.* 17.264–71) where τιμή and influence were acquired, displayed and exercised. Hence dinners were hardly the means for dispensing unconditional charity, but highly competitive affairs conducted under the rule of reciprocity designed for net gain in social prestige. See also Fisher, 1988a.

36 D'Arms, 1990, pp. 314–5. D'Arms remarks on the 'harsher social realities implicit in *clientela*' (p. 314) that governed Roman convivial patterns, but his assessment applies to the Hellenistic sympotic hospitality in general.

37 If this describes the real custom, Lucian's Cynic sympathies are better expressed in the νόμοι συμποτικοί ('symposium rules') of the *Saturnalia*: 'Each one shall recline where he happens to be. Rank, family or wealth shall have little influence on privilege' (*Sat.* 17).

could not get good and agreeable company at dinner by throwing together men who are not similar in their associations and sympathies (ἀνθρώπων μὴ ὁμοφύλων μηδ' ὁμοιοπαθῶν).[38]

Of course, Plutarch also speaks of the συμποτικὸν τέλος ('symposium's aim') as the 'the heightening of friendship or creating it' (*Moralia* 621C), but it should be noted that his ideal, elsewhere aptly described as τὸ φιλοποιὸν τῆς τραπέζης ('the friend-making [power] of the table'; *Moralia* 612D), is unashamedly utilitarian.[39] It applies only to τοῖς παροῦσιν ('those who are present'; *Moralia* 621C), presumably in response to the exclusively defined rules of invitation implicit in the passage cited above.

Plutarch's picture of sympotic hospitality and its implicit definition of generosity as a prudent investment[40] that will bring sure returns – the ἀνταπόδοσις ('repayment') may be a reciprocal invitation or some other benefit, whether honour, influence or profitable political and social connections solidified or newly gained – is evidently reflected and pointedly censured in the protasis of Luke's saying on proper guests (Braun, 1992, p. 75). A narrowly defined list of potential dinner guests, drawn up according to bonds of friend-

---

38  *Quaest.conv.* [*Mor.*] 708D; trans. Minar, LCL, slightly altered. Note also 709A-B where the rule of compatibility is stressed for those who insist on bringing uninvited guests to a symposium: 'if the host is a good fellow, choosing good fellows, if a scholar, scholars, if a man of influence, other men of influence' and not, 'for example, heavy drinkers to an abstemious host, or intemperate and extravagant people to a man of simple life; or ... a young man, fond of wine and gaiety [to] gloomy old men or sophists talking solemnly through their beards'.

39  Plutarch is typical in this regard. On 'the twin poles of idealism and instrumentality' that governed φιλία and ξενία in the Greek world see Herman, 1987, esp. pp. 121–3. Sometime later Lucian (speaking through his character Pythagoras incarnated as a cock) cynically would say 'you must be particularly suspicious of your dearest friends and always be expecting some harm to come from them' (*Somn.* 26). Cf. Mayer, 1989, and Seager, 1977, on Juvenal and Tacitus bemoaning the decline of friendship in their age.

40  I am alluding to Rathje's claim that sympotic 'generosity is an investment' (1983, p. 23). She refers specifically to the Homeric banquet and the early Roman *convivium*, but she might as well have spoken of convivial generosity in Plutarch's and Luke's time. Thus Fisher, 1988b, p. 1205, on the dinner clubs at the time of Cicero: 'The social and political functions of these convivialities and exchanges of hospitality were very great. They developed and cemented reciprocal and equal friendships among the top elite in Rome and in other oligarchies.' That dinner invitations were a means of seeking someone's patronage and support is shown in some of the convivial epigrams. See esp. *Anth. Pal.* 9.92 and 11.44 and the discussion in Giangrande, 1967, pp. 140–3. Horace's poems of invitation (see esp. *Od.* 3.29), dealing with patron-client relationships in relation to a symposium, are perceptively analysed by Murray, 1985.

ship (φίλος), familial ties (ἀδελφός), similar affiliations (συγγενής) or economic status (πλούσιος), but all capable of reciprocating in kind (ἀνταπόδομα, three times!):[41] the language is standard and typical and the dinner-invitation etiquette reflected in it represents a social commonplace. The rejection of this cultural commonplace is the thematic climax of the saying on proper guests. This, too, is not unusual, although the criticism of reciprocal hospitality is a less accentuated motif in the *deipnon*-literature proper. This, of course, is hardly surprising, for the literary symposia generally reflect élite dining culture. Nonetheless, some examples of unease with the rule of balanced reciprocity that governed upper-class dinner invitations can be found. An early example is Xenophon's depiction of the precarious profession of the jester (γελωτοποιός) whose livelihood depended on being able to amuse symposium guests. Philip, unable to draw guffaws at Callias' dinner party, falls into a fit of despair. As he says,

> in times past, the reason why I got invitations to dinner was that I might stir up laughter among the guests and make them merry; but now what will induce anyone to invite me? For I could no more turn serious than I could become immortal; and certainly no one will invite me in the hope that there is a return invitation, as every one knows that there is not a vestige of tradition of bringing dinner into my house. (*Symposium* 1.15; trans. Todd, LCL)

Even Plutarch, whose élitism and sense of proper dinner decorum we have noted, toys with the thought that the dinner table should be an antidote to the 'ambitious rivalry' that obtains at the market-place, theatre or other public places: 'dinner is a democratic occasion' (δημοκρατικὸν ἐστι τὸ δεῖπνον) where the barriers between the 'rich person' (πλούσιος) and the 'person of lesser means' (εὐτελεστέρος) should not be invoked.[42] A similar idea

---

[41] Reciprocity was a central 'law' of Greco-Roman social interactions. With regard to meals it was simply expected in Luke's culture (Rohrbaugh, 1991, p. 141). See, in general, Mott, 1975, and the additional discussion of reciprocity in the Greco-Roman élite symposium scene in chapters 5 and 6.

[42] D. Smith, 1987, p. 635, rightly points out Plutarch is not advocating that people of inferior status should be invited to dinners of the privileged class. He is merely acknowledging that even within the same class some folks are richer than others. Our interest is in pointing out that the distinction between rich and poor in connection with putting on dinners does occasionally find its way even into literature that represents rather than criticizes élite sensibilities.

appears in some of the Cynic-coloured Alexandrian epigrams as the 'anti-sympotic' motif of poverty, typically in the form of a 'eulogy of the frugal life' and a yearning for plain and simple sympotic affairs.[43]

It is indeed within the Cynic sophist tradition where we find a reservoir of comparative material that far exceeds the offerings contained in the symposium literature, for it is in the Cynic material that the theme of wealth and poverty is a frequent subject for rhetorical declamations.[44] Furthermore, these moralizing declamations could make most effective use of the rhetorical exercises of competitive comparison (σύγκρισις) of two persons or groups for the purpose of panning one and praising the other.[45] It is also typical of the sophists to characterize the rich and poor with the aid of banquet motifs and symbols. Nowhere is all this clearer than in some of the satirical dialogues of Lucian (cf. Hock, 1987; B. Baldwin, 1961). From the *Downward Journey* (*Cataplus*), *The Cock* (*Gallus*), the *Saturnalia* and *Dialogues of the Dead* (*Dialogi Mortuorum*) the following thought-structure, with striking resemblance to the broad logic of Luke's dinner-hospitality rule, may be drawn.[46]

(1)  Characterization of the poor. The poor are described as utterly destitute (ὑπερβολὴν πτωχός), lame and half blind (χωλὸς καὶ ἀμυδρὸν βλέπων; *Dialogi Mortuorum* 22).[47] They dream of getting 'four obols to be able to sleep after a fill of bread or barley' (*Saturnalia* 21), but their lot is 'shivering in ... extreme cold and

---

43  See Giangrande, 1967, pp. 140–6. The best example is Nicaenetus (cited by Athenaeus, *Deipnos.* 15.673b).

44  The biographer of the sophists, Philostratus, already contrasted the 'ancient sophistic' with the 'second sophistic' by noting that the former discoursed on 'philosophical themes' while the latter were typically concerned 'with definite and special themes' among which he lists first that 'they depict the types of the poor and the rich' (τοὺς πένητας ὑπετυπώσατο καὶ τοὺς πλουσίους; *Vit.Soph.* 481); similarly Cicero, *Tusc.* 5.10; cf. Petronius, *Sat.* 48.5, where, in response to Trimalchio's question as to what subject he had declaimed at school that day, the sophist Agamemnon says 'pauper et dives inimici erant'. See Hall, 1981, pp. 221–51, for a broad survey of this 'one of the most popular subjects in the rhetorician's repertoire' (p. 225).

45  *Inter alia*, Hermogenes, *Prog.* 8; Theon, *Prog.* 1, 9; discussed by Hock, 1987, pp. 456–7. For literature on the theory and practice of *synkrisis* see chapter 2, n. 10.

46  This section appeared in briefer, but similar form in my article for the Heinz O. Guenther FS (Braun, 1992, pp. 76–8, 83–4).

47  We have here a literary cliché. Cf. Plato, *Cri.* 53a: οἱ χωλοὶ δὲ καὶ οἱ τυφλοὶ καὶ οἱ ἄλλοι ἀνάπηροι, 'the lame and the blind and the other crippled'. See also the additional discussion of 14.21 in chapter 5, pp. 81–8.

[being] in the grip of famine' (*Saturnalia* 31). They accuse the rich of 'gorging alone behind closed doors' (*Saturnalia*. 32) and if, on rare occasions, they do get invited to the feasts of the rich, the poor are humiliated with inferior wine and smaller portions of meat (*Saturnalia* 32) so that they remain as inferior partners in a vertical social relationship.[48]

(2) Characterization of the rich. Since Lucian is by no means neutrally disposed towards the rich he tends to characterize them in harshly negative terms, as those, for example, ἁρπάζοντες καὶ βιαζόμενοι καὶ πάντα τρόπον τῶν πενήτων καταφρονοῦντες, 'who plunder and violate and in every way humiliate the poor' (*Necyomantia* 21). When he portrays their life he speaks with monotonous regularity of their banquets. The rich person is one who 'gorge[s] himself on all these good things, belching, receiving his guest's congratulations and feasting without a break' (*Saturnalia* 21; see also 26: the rich 'can have expensive dinners, get drunk on sweet wine …'). This feasting happens 'alone behind closed doors' (*Saturnalia* 32) so as to deny access to the poor. To be rich means to have exclusive enjoyment of life's blessings. The moralist's judgment on this state of affairs is stated in Lucian's letter to Cronos (*Saturnalia* 21) where he tells the patron of the Saturnalia κελεύειν τοὺς πλουσίους μὴ μόνους ἀπολαύειν τῶν ἀγαθῶν, 'to urge the rich not to have exclusive benefit of the good things'.

(3) Comparison of Micyllus and Megapenthes/Eucrates. The *Gallus* and *Cataplus* constitute in their entirety a rhetorical comparison of a destitute (πτωχός) cobbler, Micyllus, and a rich man (πλούσιος), either Eucrates (*Gallus*) or the wealthy tyrant Megapenthes (*Cataplus*). In his contrastive characterization Lucian relies heavily on food and dinner imagery: the rich enjoy sumptuous feasts (see especially *Gallus* 12) while Micyllus goes about 'hungry from morning to night' (*Cataplus* 20). Οὐ πρότερον … παρὰ πλουτίῳ τινὶ δειπνήσας ἐν ἅπαντι τῷ βίῳ, 'Never before in all my life

---

48 A vertical relationship between superior and inferior partners is one of the defining characteristics of patronage. The complaint of the poor in the *Saturnalia* thus uses *deipnon*-language to protest against a social and economic system that functions to keep the poor in their place. Plutarch (*Quaest. Graec.* 18) describes the revolt of the poor Megarians in similar terms: 'Among the shocking acts of misconduct against the wealthy, the poor [Megarians] would enter their homes and *insist on being entertained and banqueted sumptuously*. But if they did not receive what they demanded, they would treat all the household with violence and insult' (emphasis added); cited and discussed by Millet, 1989, pp. 21–3. On Luke and patronage, see now the excellent article by Moxnes, 1991a, note esp. the definition on p. 242.

have I dined with a rich person' (*Gallus* 9). When by chance he is invited to dine with Eucrates his frantic preparation is a comic expression of his desire to participate in a banquet of the rich. (4) 'Invite the poor'. This contrastive characterization has a moral purpose. In the *Saturnalia* Lucian states that it is 'most irrational' (ἀλογώτατον) for some to be 'super-rich' (ὑπερπλουτεῖν) while others are 'dying of hunger'. He urges Cronos to abolish this inequality and to make life's 'good things' (τὰ ἀγαθά) available to everyone (19). On the basis of a doctrine of a post-mortem egalitarian society (ἰσοτιμία)⁴⁹ Lucian bids Cronos to tell the rich 'to invite the poor to dinner' (22). For, Cronos' νόμοι συμποτικοί ('symposium rules') require, among other things, that 'rich shall not send for rich nor shall the rich entertain anyone of equal standing at Cronos' feast' (15).⁵⁰

(5) Post-mortem punishment and reward. Lucian makes extensive use of the mythological constitution of life in Hades to criticize the cleavage between rich and poor on earth. For the exemplary figures we go again to Micyllus and Megapenthes and the fates assigned to them by Rhadamanthus, the judge of Hades. Megapenthes' earthly excesses are punished with an after-life of remembering his life of luxury (ἀναπεμπαζόμενος τὴν τρυφήν) in a state of constant thirst (*Cataplus* 28). Micyllus, the poor cobbler, is sent to the Isles of the Blessed, there to be together with the good (τοῖς ἀρίστοις συνεσόμενος; *Cataplus* 25), or, to fill out the image from elsewhere in Lucian's writings (*Juppiter Confutatus* 17), there 'to drink, reclining among the heroes' (πίνειν μετὰ τῶν ἡρώων ... κατακείμενος).⁵¹

⁴⁹ This doctrine is most clearly stated by Menippus (evidently speaking for Lucian) in *DMort.* 30: ἰσοτιμία γὰρ ἐν ᾅδου καὶ ὅμοιοι ἅπαντες, 'In Hades is equality and all are alike.' See B. Baldwin, 1961, for a discussion of ἰσοτιμία in Lucian.
⁵⁰ The letters that make up most of the *Saturnalia* reflect the Roman Saturnalia, an occasion when the rich traditionally fêted the slaves and the poor. B. Baldwin argues that the Saturnalia festivities 'served only to emphasize the injustice and inequality of "normal" conditions' and that Lucian shrewdly exploited this incongruity in his critique of normal conditions (1961, p. 203).
⁵¹ The depiction of both the good life and the good after-life as a 'reclining' exploits the symbolic value of the κλίνη. Murray, 1981, argues that as banqueting couch the κλίνη attracted to itself the power to symbolize life's blessings, but as bier the κλίνη represents the pleasures of earthly feasting carried over into death. He draws attention to the Tomb of the Diver at Paestum where the dead man is depicted as feasting among his companions. Note also the fragment, cited by Murray, of an anonymous sepulchral epigram in which the dead remembers the earthly symposium:

Then he will lie in the deep-rooted earth
sharing no more in the *symposia*,

Although there is neither a formal nor (obviously) a literary connection between Lucian and Luke 14.12–14 and thus no precise correspondence, a dense solidarity nevertheless is unmistakable: similarly juxtaposed social roles, shared authorial views on these roles, corresponding flagging of *deipnon*-invitation conventions, tapping into a common hoard of terms and themes, analogous moralizing from the vantage point of a normative social order depicted in a mythic (or eschatological) key, the *isotimia* of Hades (Lucian) or the 'the uprising of the just' (Luke 14.14; cf. ἡ βασιλεία τοῦ θεοῦ; 14.15).[52] There is no need to deny that Luke's hospitality rule alludes to motifs related to the Jewish messianic banquet (cf. 14.15), but its formulation is more patently a synecdoche of Greco-Roman conventions and their critique in the Cynic sources of which Lucian's dialogues are the most instructive examples.[53]

What Ronald Hock has said of the value of Lucian's writings, standing in for the Cynic critique of ancient élite dining culture, for the study of Lazarus and Dives, applies here as well: they 'clarify the *Mentalität*, the social and intellectual conventions, which [the Lukan text] assumes of its readers and hearers' (1987, p. 463). These conventions and 'everyday' kind of social knowledge also seem to drive the Lukan retelling of the traditional story of a host who gave a dinner, to which I now turn.

> and the lyre,
> or the sweet cry of flutes.

On the implicit link between dining couch and death see also Lucian, *DMort.* 16: 'Foolish man, what advantage do you think there is in life that we shall never again partake of? You will say drinking parties (πότους), no doubt, and dinners (δεῖπνα) ...'

52 The term ἀνάστασις (14.14) is usually taken to speak of the resurrection of the dead, but this may be too limiting; as in Luke 2.34 (where ἀνάστασις is defined as the opposite of πτῶσις; see York, 1991, p. 114), in 14.14 'rising' is best seen in juxtaposition with 'lowliness'.

53 Jülicher, 1910, vol II, pp. 253–4 rightly called this Lukan passage 'eine Art von Synekdoche' of a common complex of social wisdom, but wrongly looked to Proverbs and Sirach for the most illuminating parallels.

# 5

## THE BIG DINNER (14.15–24): ASPECTS OF LUKAN PERFORMANCE

The so-called parable of the great banquet is the final unit in the dinner episode. It also presents the greatest challenge for the interpreter. Although usually reckoned among the parables, it is not so designated in the text. Evidently it is a pre-Lukan story, but the recovery of the antecedent version is as treacherous as it is necessary for estimating what Luke has done with it. The voluminous scholarly commentary tradition devoted to this story contains mixed blessings. On the one hand, the quest for sources and pristine originals that has driven parable study has generated sophisticated reconstructive efforts on which I do not presume to improve. On the other, appraisals of the significance of Luke's performance of the story, though remarkably unified, are, to speak in dangerously general terms here, heavily taken by the view that the story is at least a 'half-allegory' (Jülicher, 1910, vol. II, p. 416) whose meaning must be unlocked with extra-textual hermeneutic keys.

Engaging these views critically and constructively, the latter in the form of a counter-reading, makes for a rather lengthy treatment. In this chapter, I deal first with formal and source-critical issues and then devote the remainder to an assessment of Luke's retelling of the story. The results are then used as a base with which to support an interpretation of the story as a fictional but paradigmatic tale about the 'conversion' of a rich, dishonoured householder (ch. 6).

### Dining in the kingdom of God (14.15)

Evidently a macarism (14.15b) has been utilized to make the narrative transition from the guest rule to the banquet story (note a similar use of a macarism in 11.27). The attribution of the beatitude to a definite even if impersonal 'someone' (τις τῶν συναvακειμένων; 14.15a) gives the entire verse a *chreia*-like impression (Dibelius, 1933, p. 161). But not every attributed saying is a *chreia*.

In this case the attribution appears to serve a subordinate narrative and argumentative function within a larger argument in Luke 14, although this still needs to be confirmed by an analysis of the pattern of argumentation in the dinner episode as a whole. Luke has no particular interest in the speaker; he is merely a convenient τις – contextual verisimilitude demands a fellow diner, a Pharisee – required by Luke's choice to advance the story through direct speech. To be sure, the banquet story appears to be directed at τις (14.16), but at the end of the story (14.24) the third person plural ὑμῖν, a conventional form of extra-narrative audience address, indicates that a larger audience is intended.[1]

On the origin of the eschatological beatitude one cannot be certain. The transitional function of this verse obviously called for some degree of redactional formulation on Luke's part. This is most easily spotted in 14.15a where the vocabulary is largely taken from the context (τις τῶν συνανακειμένων points to 14.10) and augmented with lexical and grammatical features characteristic of Luke.[2] Despite the Lukan patina, the saying's banally conventional ring cannot be missed; the messianic feast is a familiar image of eschatological salvation in the Hebrew scriptures and in rabbinic sources.[3] Many commentators thus identify the beatitude of 14.15b as a pre-Lukan saying (e.g., Bultmann, 1964, p. 109; Marshall, 1978, p. 587). The implied logic is neat, but it works only if one is happily confident that Luke could not or would not draw on a traditional *topos* to form his own saying. In this case he likely did. One interpreter recently pointed out that '[b]y his additional material and redactional alterations Luke exhibits an interest in the Messianic Banquet which is quite unique in the New Testament' (Esler, 1987, p. 192).[4]

---

[1] The λέγω ὑμῖν formula represents an interpretive problem that I will discuss more fully in the next chapter (see pp. 121–6). On the change in intended audience see Jülicher, 1910, vol. II, p. 409; Linnemann, 1960, p. 248. Note Bain, 1977, p. 192: 'Second person plurals and references to ἄνδρες are obvious pointers to audience address.'

[2] Ταῦτα in the introduction of a new pericope is favoured by Luke (see esp. 16.14; 19.11,28; 24.36 which share with 14.15 a similar grammatical structure: participle + ταῦτα + aorist infinitive). The ἀκούω + ταῦτα is Lukan, as is the use of post-positive δέ and the τις τῶν phrase. For detailed presentation of evidence see Schulz, 1972, p. 391 n. 107; Pesce, 1978, pp. 174–5; Steele, 1981, pp. 19, 26.

[3] Str-B, vol. I, pp. 180–1; this image found its way into Christian texts where it is sometimes blended with eucharistic overtones, e.g., Rev. 19.9: μακάριοι οἱ εἰς τὸ δεῖπνον τοῦ γάμου τοῦ ἀρνίου κεκλημένοι. On the messianic meal see E. Davis, 1967, ch. 1; and D. Smith, 1991.

[4] See, e.g., Luke's redaction of a Q saying (13.29; by adding 'and from north and south') to underline the universal participation in the eschatological feast; only

Not so unique but nonetheless characteristic of Luke is his fondness
for the use of macarisms which he uses elsewhere as a means for
stereotypically depicting flawed forms of piety as a foil for Jesus'
corrective teaching (cf. 11.27).[5] Thus theme, form and tone combine
to make us lean if not fall towards the third evangelist as the author
of 14.15 in its entirety.[6]

## The big dinner (14.16–24)

To call this story a parable is to bow to convention more than to
make a precise form-critical judgment,[7] which seems to me not only
impossible but also unnecessary. First, as already noted, Luke does
not use the term παραβολή in a modern form-critical sense; rather it
designates an elastic range of illustrative or analogous speech forms.
In this case (14.16–24) a patently fictive story is identified neither
directly by the term 'parable' (cf. Matthew 22.1; εἶπεν ἐν
παραβολαῖς),[8] nor indirectly by means of a term of comparison to
an abstract *Sache* (cf. Matthew 22.1; ὡμοιώθη ἡ βασιλεία τῶν
οὐρανῶν)[9] or to a moral imperative (cf. Luke 10.37; πορεύου

Luke augments the Markan Jesus *logion* (14.25) on not drinking wine again until he
does so in the Kingdom of God with a similar remark on eating (Luke 22.16);
similarly, in Luke alone Jesus promises his disciples at the last supper they will
'eat and drink at my table in my kingdom' (22.30); cf. Luke 1.53; 6.21; 16.22.

5   Goulder, 1989, p. 589, calculates that 'outside the Beatitudes he has eleven, where
    Matthew has four and Mark none'. Cf. Schulz, 1972, pp. 391–2: 'V.15b ... dürfte
    wohl nicht von Lk stammen, da er kaum selbst Makarismen bildet.'
6   So also, *inter alia*, Jülicher, 1910, vol. II, p. 409 (with hesitation); Easton, 1926,
    p. 230; Haenchen, 1968, p. 140; Pesce, 1978, pp. 175–6; Ernst, 1979, p. 63 n. 38;
    Fitzmyer, 1985, p. 1052; Goulder, 1989, p. 589.
7   In Jülicher's classification of Jesus' *Gleichnisreden* this story is sorted among the
    *Parabeln* (1910, vol. I, pp. 92–111; vol. II, pp. 407–33) whose formal difference
    over against the 'pure similitudes' (reine Gleichnisse) is the 'story-telling form' (die
    erzählende Form). His terminology continues to be widely used even though his
    parable theory has been subject to criticism.
8   This rather obvious point is not often recognized even though it does have some
    significance for the interpretation of the dinner story. See esp. Glombitza for
    cogent objections against the habit 'die lukanische Fassung als ein Gleichnis zu
    behandeln' (1962, p. 10). Cf. p. 11: 'Es wird zuerst zu beachten sein, dass der Text
    by Lukas im Unterschied zu Matthäus nicht als ein Gleichnis bezeichnet wird.'
9   Linnemann is quite right in the observation that '[d]ie Parabel vom großen
    Abendmahl, wie sie bei Lukas vorliegt, stellt das merkwürdige Problem, daß sich
    hier Bildhälfte und Sachhälfte nicht zu entsprechen ... scheinen' (1960, p. 246). I
    am even more pessimistic: what is the extra-narrative *Sachhälfte* and how are we to
    apprehend it? Linnemann's solution is to posit the 'thing/subject' (an invitation to
    the meal that is inclusive without being exclusive) that the 'image' (parabel) *should*
    illustrate and then to prune the dinner story to make sure it does. In my view, the
    *Sache* for which the story is an analogy is to be looked for in the argumentative
    point of the entire dinner episode.

καὶ σὺ ποίει ὁμοίως). The fictive character of the dinner story is given away by the indefinite main character, 'a certain man' (ἄνθρωπός τις), a narrating formula typical in Luke's parables,[10] but not one from which any formal inferences can be drawn.

Second, even if formal inferences could be drawn from the Lukan parable, classifying it by means of a taxonomy of forms, typically Jülicher's threefold classification (similitude, narrative parable, example-story), is not helpful in determining its function within the dramatic episode (Luke 14.1–24). In the case of parables, especially retold parables contained in secondary or tertiary literary contexts, clear recognition of form is no sure clue to its meaning nor to its function in context.[11]

Third, a shift of emphasis from form to function is sponsored not only by our earlier notice of the cohesion between parable and the Lukan episodic context but also by the role that analogies played in Greco-Roman patterns of argumentation.[12] Aristotle is an influential example. At the core of his *Rhetoric* stands his instruction on the 'common proofs' (κοιναὶ πίστεις) basic to all forms of

[10] The formula is unique to Luke's writings in the NT. Seven out of nine times it occurs in parables (10.30; 12.16; 14.16; 15.11; 16.1,19; 19.12), once in a *chreia* (14.2), once in a miracle story (Acts 9.33). Alternately and almost as often Luke uses ἀνήρ τις, also unique to Luke in the NT. Jeremias claims that the former is traditional and the latter redactional (1980, p. 191). Why this should be so is not made clear; 'both should be reckoned as part of [Luke's] own style' (Fitzmyer, 1985, p. 886). The formula is a common figure for initiating a fictional story. See Berger, 1984a, pp. 53–4; and Hintzen, 1991, pp. 336–7.
[11] An example of overworking the truism that 'forms can tell us much about functions' in relation to parables is Sider, 1981, p. 453. He argues that παραβολή has a 'normative value for genre' (p. 454), but in the course of his deliberation 'form' is redefined to mean 'form of thought' (p. 459) and is hardly distinguished from 'function' which he rightly identifies as that of providing an 'analogy'. But as a vehicle for 'analogy' παραβολή is not functionally different from other forms of ὁμοίωσις (comparison), such as the παράδειγμα (historical example) or αἶνος/μῦθος/λόγος (fable), which, in the Greek rhetorical tradition, are differentiated not on the basis of form or function, but content. See McCall, 1969, p. 27 (commenting on Aristotle): 'Form ... is a relatively interchangeable feature of historical example, παραβολή, and fable: all serve as means of persuasion and differ not so much in form as in content.' On the functional affinity between parable and fable see Beavis, 1990b; and Jülicher, 1910, vol. I, pp. 94–102, esp. p. 98: 'Die Mehrzahl der παραβολαί Jesu, die erzählende Form tragen, sind Fabeln wie die des Stesichoros und des Aesop.'
[12] The development of analogical (inductive, inferential) argumentation in Greek thought up to and including Aristotle is charted by Lloyd, 1966, pp. 172–420. The use of analogies in argumentation continued to be indispensable in the Hellenistic period although the use of analogy shifted from being an aide in speculative reasoning to being a rhetorical (persuasive) device.

rhetoric.[13] One major division of these πίστεις is said to be the proof by example (παράδειγμα), a category which Aristotle further divides into two: the historical example (also called παράδειγμα) and the invented one, the latter of which might be either an analogy drawn from everyday life (παραβολή) or a story of pure fiction (λόγος, 'fable').

Aristotle's understanding of parable as a *Funktionsbegriff* ('designation of function') rather than as a *Gattungsbegriff* ('designation of genre')[14] becomes the most important operative principle for the later, more technically oriented Hellenistic *rhetores*. Here parable 'theory' recedes and what we might call considerations of parable 'pragmatics', or the function of παραβολή in argumentative performance, moves prominently to the fore. Given that this rhetorical use of analogy (παραβολή) was disseminated in the Hellenistic school system and, to the uneducated classes, by means of a variety of public declamations,[15] the familiarity with parable as proof can be assumed. One should entertain the possibility that the recitation of a fictive story in Luke 24 has an argumentative purpose. That is, rather than deriving meaning from a form-critical unit called parable, it is worth asking how the fictive dinner story works in making, illustrating or analogously supporting an argument.[16] Further reason for this pursuit is given by the

---

13 See *Rhet.* 2.20.1–9 for a discussion of the κοιναὶ πίστεις. Solmsen maintains that '[t]he system of "proofs" (πίστεις) may be called the core of Aristotle's *Rhetoric*' (1941, p. 39).

14 These terms are used by Baasland, 1986, who urges a method of parable classification based on function rather than form.

15 Farmer thinks that 'Hellenistic rhetoric probably exerted an influence even beyond the educated classes' (1962, p. 312). He adduces a statement of Tacitus: 'But now all of these rules of rhetoricians ... are common property and there is scarcely a bystander in the throng but who, if not fully instructed, has at least been initiated into the rudiments of culture' (*Dialogue* 19). See also Kennedy, 1984, pp. 8–12.

16 The rhetorical function of parables has long been recognized within biblical scholarship, although this recognition has not been overly consequential in modern parable research. Already B. Weiss (1861) stated: 'Die Parabel will beweisen' (cited by Jülicher, 1910, vol. I, p. 105). Jülicher himself, following Aristotle, stressed the persuasive function of the parable: 'Sie ist ein Beglaubigungsmittel (zu den κοιναὶ πίστεις gerechnet), sie will bei dem Hörer etwas erreichen, was der Redende ohne diese Hülfe nicht erreichen zu können fürchtet' (p. 96); see also R. Taylor, 1946, pp. 80–1, 88–90. The recent renewal of interest in the influence of ancient rhetoric in the composition of the gospels has brought into sharper focus the prominent place of παραβολή in ancient rhetorical argumentation, especially in the elaboration (ἐργασία) of *chreiai*. See Hock and O'Neil, 1986; Mack and Robbins, 1989, esp. chapters 2 and 6; Mack, 1988, pp. 157–65; and Berger, 1984b, pp. 1110–24, esp. p. 1115, where he states that the parable is a 'Teil der Überzeugungsstrategie oder Argumentation im weiteren

apparently declamatory character of the dinner episode. The introduction of a moral *crux* in the opening scene (ἔξεστιν τῷ σαββάτῳ θεραπεῦσαι ἢ οὔ) and the contrastive comparison of rich and poor by means of a feast-famine motif are conventions of Greco-Roman declamations (ὑπόθεσις, μελέτη) in which a fictive story stands as a 'model case' ('Modellfall'; Berger, 1984b, pp. 1120–3) of the attitude or action urged for imitation in the deliberative speech or declamation.[17] Within the context of declamatory speech,

> invented cases are not in themselves parables. They receive their parable-like character first and foremost because they are told within a specific (pragmatic or literary) context . . . These texts thus present us with the remarkable situation where it is not so much the literary structure of the text itself but much more its role and function within the context that determine whether it is a 'parable'.
>
> (Berger, 1984b, p. 1122).

Unlike the other segments in the dinner episode the banquet parable cannot be suspected as a Lukan invention *ex nihilo*. It is a traditional story. The decisive evidence for this is the existence of structurally similar versions in Matthew 22.1–14 and *Gospel of Thomas* 64. Since neither of these is literarily dependent on Luke 14.16–24,[18] some form of the banquet story existed independently of and probably prior to Luke's performance of it.[19]

Sinne'. For a general orientation to the theory and practice of ancient rhetorical argumentation see Mack, 1990.

[17] For a general overview of Greco-Roman declamation and its types see D. Clark, 1957, pp. 213–61. References to 'rich man, poor man' stories in Greek declamations are amply found in Russell, 1983, pp. 27–30; cf. pp. 14, 19, 21–2.

[18] As far as I know nobody has ever argued that Matt. 22.1–14 is a redaction of Luke 14.16–24. *G. Thom.* 64 is a different matter. Quite apart from how one answers the larger question whether or not Thomas used the synoptics as sources, I know of no convincing demonstration that *G.Thom.* 64 is dependent upon its synoptic parallels. Even Schrage, 1964, pp. 133–7, whom one would not expect to overlook evidence that could support his thesis that Thomas is dependent upon the synoptic tradition, found virtually no decisive points of contact to warrant the view that *G.Thom.* 64 is a reworking of one of its synoptic parallels. For the independence of *G.Thom.* 64 see the arguments of Hunzinger, 1960; Montefiori, 1960–1; Hahn, 1970, pp. 60–3; Beatrice, 1978, esp. pp. 265–74; Crossan, 1985, pp. 39–52; Patterson, 1988, pp. 124–5, whose brief observations are all the more weighty owing to the methodological sophistication with which he treats the tradition-historical problem of *G.Thom.*. For the view that *G.Thom.* 64 is derivative of its synoptic parallels see, for example, Schürmann, 1963, esp. pp. 246–7; Sevrin, 1989, pp. 429–32.

[19] The *Vorleben*, including provenance and transmission history, of the dinner story has not yet been described in all its complexity. The issue is on the fringe of my

A reliable measure of Luke's redaction of the received story is that story itself. But this can be pulled into view only as a 'skeleton outline'[20] or 'gist'[21] and even that only by means of 'daring hypotheses', as Adolf Jülicher recognized long ago.[22] Although a conjectured *Vorlage* presents difficulties for the interpretation of an original story, it does not hinder our effort to appreciate the features of Luke's retelling, provided we are allowed to credit the Lukan redactor with those aspects of the story that cannot be assigned to the received story by any other than speculative means. On the basis of vocabulary and plot elements shared by the extant versions we are able to wring out a bare pre-Lukan story[23] that approximated the following structure and vocabulary.[24]

### The 'gist' of the pre-Lukan story

(1)   Attribution. 'Jesus said' (εἶπεν). Whether or not the pre-Lukan attribution identified the story as a παραβολή (Matthew 22.1) of the βασιλεία (Matthew 22.2; cf. Luke 14.15) is a disputed question, owing to inconclusive evidence. Matthew 22.1–2 and Luke

concerns and hence need not be considered here. The most important discussions are Trilling, 1960; and Dillon, 1966, pp. 8–12; cf. Vögtle, 1971; Dormeyer, 1974, pp. 208–11; Lemico, 1986; the essays in J. Dupont, 1978a; and J. Dupont, 1978b.

[20]   Manson, 1931, p. 84, relies on 'points of contact' between Luke 14.16–24 and Matt. 22.1–14 to arrive at the 'skeleton outline' of the pre-synoptic story.

[21]   Funk, 1992, uses the term to refer to traditional narrative material that migrated along lines of transmission in vague, general form, allowing later story-tellers to retell the material in their own words. In this case we likely have to do with a story that Luke encountered in a verbally fixed (i.e. textual) form, but he might have treated it as he would have traditional oral 'gists'.

[22]   'Es ist ein trauriges Schicksal, dass wir auch bei dieser Parabel...nur durch kühne Hypothesen uns der Form ... und also ihrem ursprünglichen Grundgedanken zu nähern vermögen' (1910, vol. II, p. 430). Of course, Jülicher was daring enough 'aus Mt und Lc den Wortlaut der "Quelle" zurechtzukomponieren oder *gar den Buchstaben der von Jesus gesprochenen Parabel*' (p. 420; emphasis added).

[23]   The method, a 'paring knife' approach, which Eichholz calls 'Subtraktionsverfahren' (1984, p. 145), may be too mechanical and thus dubious. Yet if the aim is not to reclaim and appraise an 'original' story but to measure creativity in the retelling of that story, the 'featureless rump' (Goulder, 1989, p. 592) gained by this method is a useful foil against which to highlight Lukan redaction.

[24]   Cf. previous reconstructions: Harnack, 1908, pp. 119–22; Jülicher, 1910, vol. II, pp. 407–33; Bacon, 1922–3, pp. 341–8; Manson, 1931, pp. 83–6; Hirsch, 1941, pp. 138–9; Jeremias, 1963, pp. 63–9, cf. pp. 176–80; Hahn, 1970, pp. 51–60; Schulz, 1972, pp. 391–8; Pesce, 1978, pp. 167–236; Weder, 1978, pp. 177–85; Polag, 1979, p. 70; Schenk, 1981, p. 108; Breech, 1983, pp. 114–23; Zeller, 1984, pp. 87–8; Crossan, 1985, pp. 39–42; Schottroff, 1987, pp. 192–5; Scott, 1989, pp. 166–8. Among these some concentrate on the original (Jesus') story while others are content to pry out the pre-synoptic (Q) version.

14.15–16a are patently redactional (Schulz, 1972, pp. 392–3; Pesce, 1978, pp. 170–6; see also Pesce's detailed argument, pp. 176–82, for excluding the βασιλεία theme from Luke's *Vorlage*).

(2) Introduction. 'A person prepared a dinner' (ἄνθρωπος [ποιεῖν] δεῖπνον [ἄριστον?]). Matthew's aorist ἐποίησεν is likely original. Luke's ἐποίει-ἐκάλεσεν is an example of the imperfect-aorist verb sequence that typically initiates the narration of his ἄνθρωπός τις parables (cf. 10.30, 12.17, 15.11, 16.1). Pesce rightly states that 'è più probabile nell'archetipo l'aoristo ἐποίησεν che non l'imperfetto' 'it is most likely that the original was the aorist ἐποίησεν, and not the imperfect' (1978, pp. 184–5). That the meal was a δεῖπνον is probable (Luke 14.16; *Gospel of Thomas* 64.1) and certainly preferable to Matthew's γάμος. But could it have been an ἄριστον? The term turns up in Matthew 22.4 (*hapax leg.* in the first gospel) as a puzzling substitute for γάμος and in Luke 14.12, where it seems to indicate editorial indecision (ἄριστον ἢ δεῖπνον). Both may be due to the residual effect of a common source. Luke's notice that the banquet was of μέγα size is a Lukan 'escalation of situation' (Crossan, 1985, p. 47) required by the fact that 'many' (πολλούς) were invited. Pesce again provides good reason to conclude that 'La correlazione μέγα-πολλούς è lucana', 'the μέγα-πολλούς correlation is Lukan' (1978, p. 194; see already Jülicher, 1910, vol. II, p. 409.

(3) Invitation (καὶ ἐκάλεσεν) of (an unspecified number of) first-choice guests. Luke's πολλούς is redactional; it is descriptively connected to the 'large' dinner but functions also as an advance indication of the need for a large number of replacement guests to be rounded up upon two successive invitations (see especially Haenchen, 1968, p. 147, and Schulz, 1972, p. 393).

In the *Gospel of Thomas* the preparation-invitation sequence is not clear. Crossan notes that the *Gospel of Thomas* 'seems to envisage a situation where the arrival of unexpected visitors necessitates the sudden arrangement of a dinner for their entertainment and thus the unwarned invitation of others' (1985, pp. 39–40). The ambiguity is partially cleared up when the imperfect tense of the Coptic verb *ney^entaf* (64.1a) is recognized. I would translate, 'a person was (used to) having guests'. Rendered thus, the introduction speaks of the host's habitual practice of which the reported dinner is a particular instance, rather than of the unexpected arrival of guests and an impromptu dinner followed by an odd invitation of yet more guests.

(4)   Sending of a servant to deliver the invitation by means of *oratio recta* (καὶ ἀπέστειλεν τὸν δοῦλον αὐτοῦ εἰπεῖν τοῖς κεκλημένοις) which cannot be reconstructed *verbatim*, but probably included a reference to things being 'ready' (ἕτοιμος) and perhaps a request to 'come' (δεῦτε or ἔρχεσθε).

(5)   Refusal by first-choice guests to accept the invitation (παραιτεῖσθαι [Luke, *Gospel of Thomas*] along with examples of excuses, likely having to do with ἀγρόν, ἐμπορία and γάμος affairs, to legitimate their refusal. All versions cite exemplary excuses, but difference in number and kind effectively hides the Lukan *Vorlage*. The excuses may be tabulated thus:

| Matthew | Luke | Thomas |
|---|---|---|
| 1. ἀγρόν | ἀγρόν | ἔμπορος owes money |
| 2. ἐμπορία | five yoke of oxen | house |
| 3. οἱ λοιποί wantonly vent their ὕβρις | γυναῖκα ἔγημα | duties at wedding δεῖπνον |
| 4. —— | —— | κώμη |

There are some common traces: Matthew (1) and Luke (1) share ἀγρόν to which the κώμη of the *Gospel of Thomas* (4) is thematically related. Matthew (2) and the *Gospel of Thomas* (1) cite 'business' (ἐμπορία/ἔμπορος) transactions to which Luke's oxen purchase (2) has a vague connection (Schulz, 1972, p. 395). Luke (3) and the *Gospel of Thomas* (3) have a common marriage motif which, if present in the original story, might have been what prompted Matthew to recast the entire story as a wedding banquet. As for relative faithfulness to the excuses in the source story, earlier commentators (e.g., Harnack, 1908, p. 121; Jülicher, 1910, vol. II, p. 420) preferred Matthew's version because of its brevity, simplicity and lack of typically Matthean redactional language (see Schulz, 1972, p. 395). But this is effectively refuted by Hahn (1970, pp. 55–6) who, noting that Matthew's interest is squarely focused on the ὕβρις of οἱ λοιποί (22.6), argues that 'V. 5 ist im Interesse von V. 6 umgestaltet'. The major commentary tradition considers Luke's excuses to be closest to the source story, although 14.20 (excuse 3) is sometimes excised on stylistic grounds (lack of ἔχε με παρῃτημένον; Linnemann, 1960, p. 250). Yet an abundance of Lukan vocabulary (see Jeremias, 1980, pp. 239–40; Pesce, 1978, pp. 199–209; Schulz, 1972, p. 395 n. 139) renders this view problematic as well. An original narration of the excuses cannot be recovered; Luke's version hence must be considered a rather free composition, though possibly riding on traditional motifs. Linnemann suggests: 'Man muß ja bedenken, daß der Erzähler freie Wahl unter allen nur möglichen Entschuldigungen hatte' (Linnemann, 1960, p. 250). Indeed, it is the failure to consider Linnemann's caveat that might account for stressed source-critical observations on the excuses frequently found in the literature.

(6) Report of the messenger and the angry reaction of the host (ὀργισθεὶς ὁ [ἄνθρωπος]). the *Gospel of Thomas* is silent on the host's anger. Since there is no apparent reason for the *Gospel of Thomas* redactor to eliminate this motif, one is entitled to suspect that it was not in the originally told story (Scott, 1989, p. 168; *contra* Breech, 1983, p. 119). There is, however, some cause for thinking that the motif was present in the Q story (Schulz, 1972, pp. 395, 402; Pesce, 1978, pp. 209–11) from whence it came to Matthew and Luke. On the other hand, Matthew needs an angry host to bend the story to his purposes and Luke could have added the same motif, as I will argue later. An irritated host is, in any case, a recurrent *topos* in the narration of snubbed dinner invitations (see Xenophon, *Symposium* 1.7; Plutarch, *Moralia* 511D-E; Pliny's effusive excuse letter, *epistulae* 9.37; cf. *epistulae* 1.15).

It should be noted that the original story probably spoke of the host simply as an ἄνθρωπος. In 14.21 Luke has enhanced his status by referring to him as κύριος and οἰκοδεσπότης (see Fabris, 1978, p. 148) for reasons that will occupy us later (see pp. 73–4).

(7) Dispatch of a servant (εἶπεν τῷ δούλῳ αὐτοῦ) to go (ἐξελθεῖν) into the streets (εἰς τὰς ὁδούς) (indiscriminately) to gather in (συνάγειν, Matthew; εἰσάγειν, Luke) replacement dinner guests to fill (πιμπλάναι, Matthew; γεμίξειν, Luke) the banquet room (μου ὁ οἶκος). The command to go into the streets is in all three versions and hence undoubtedly pre-Lukan. In the Lukan *Vorlage* the replacement guests likely were indiscriminately chosen. Matthew and the *Gospel of Thomas* have retained this detail explicitly, although they do not agree with each other in the phrasing of this motif. Luke's reference to the poor, the injured, the lame and the blind (14.21) is a redactional specification of this general motif; he simply uses a slightly rearranged version of the quartet mentioned in 14.13. The motif of a filled banquet hall is absent in the *Gospel of Thomas*, but possibly it was in the Q parable. If it was, Luke's οἶκος is preferable to Matthew's νυμφών, because the latter vocabular

choice is determined by Matthew's decision to construe the parable as a royal wedding reception (see Pesce, 1978, pp. 209–24, for the most considered reconstruction of the substitute guest element).

(8)   An *epilogion*, probably beginning with λέγω ὑμῖν ὅτι, to the effect that none of the first κεκλημένοι will participate in the δεῖπνον. The original parable probably ended with the second invitation (Scott, 1989, p. 168; Bultmann, 1964, p. 175) to which each evangelist has added a different saying to lift out the moral of the story. Was such a saying already attached to the Q version on which Luke 14.24 depends? Lack of a common text base precludes a sure answer, but several considerations tilt towards a 'yes'. First, Luke's dual secondary invitations, and indeed the story as a whole, put the redactional accent on the formation of a new social grouping intiated by the effort of a rich householder, rather than on the *exclusion* of the originally preferred guests (Schottroff, 1987, p. 209; *contra* Hahn, 1970, p. 57 n. 26; see ch. 6). The exclusionary tone echoing in 14.24 strains against this accent somewhat, a stress that may be due to an original *epilogion* which Luke has not quite successfully re-aimed to serve the point of his story. Second, the parallel phrases μου ὁ οἶκος (14.23) and μου τοῦ δείπνου (14.24), the causal γάρ and the ὑμῖν (addressing hearers outside the story world) are sometimes taken as indicators of a secondary attempt to link 14.23 with 14.24 (Jülicher, 1910, vol. II, p. 416; Jeremias, 1963, p. 178; Linnemann, 1960, p. 248; Schulz, 1972, pp. 397–8; Pesce, 1978, pp. 224–34, most convincingly). Pesce (p. 225) plausibly opines that 14.23, especially the phrase μου ὁ οἶκος, was created by Luke in anticipation of 14.24 in the source, not the other way around. Third, the exclusionary saying coheres with Q's theme of judgment on unresponsive Israel (Zeller, 1984, p. 88; cf. Schottroff, 1987, pp. 204–5) and it may have been added to the parable in the redaction of Q. Fourth, the bare λέγω ὑμῖν formula is a securely established Q idiom (Schulz, 1972, pp. 397–400; Pesce, 1978, pp. 225–33; see Kloppenborg's tabulation of its usage in Q in 1988, p. 237), while in Luke it is merely one of seventeen variations of the 'I say to you' formula (Dawsey, 1986, pp. 16–17). Hence it likely is a phrase taken from Q (*contra* Scott, 1989, p. 257 n. 10; Jeremias, 1963, p. 45). On the other hand, the evidence is inconclusive enough for some scholars to make a case for 14.24 as Lukan redaction, perhaps even composition (e.g., Easton, 1926, p. 230; Fitzmyer, 1985, p. 1052).

The reconstructed pre-Lukan banquet story allows us to spot the main features that characterize Luke's retelling of the banquet story. We should identify them first separately, then attempt to discern if they share a common aim (ch. 6). First, Luke's story 'escalates' the situation (Crossan, 1985, p. 47). What is simply a dinner in the received story has become a mega-dinner. Μέγα is used explicitly as a signifier of the scale of the invited dinner company (πολλούς), but it also may be suggestive of the abundance and lavishness of the festal spread, of the social importance of the event and, by implication, of the high social position of its host. The escalation of scale is carried through to the end of the story where the double secondary invitation in order to fill the dining room contributes to the impression that the dinner is a sizeable affair that is reminiscent of a Hellenistic literary *topos* and social commonplace, i.e., the conspicuous, 'much-talked-about dinner' (Lucian, *Nigrinus* 23) as an identifying mark of the wealthy.[25]

Second, Luke has sharpened the profiles of the characters in the retold story. His characterization is extreme and appears to be quite tendentious. It takes place on two fronts: on the one, there is a promotion in economic status and social rank of some of the *dramatis personae*; on the other, there is a corresponding demotion of others on the economic and social scale. The well-to-do are accentuated as such while the poor are characterized as destitute, as physically and, undoubtedly, socially disabled. Since an accurate appraisal of characterization will become important in our interpretation of the parable, each of Luke's moves needs a fuller description.

### First invitation: a banquet of the élite

The dinner host, an undifferentiated 'someone' in 14.16 (*ad verbum* Q; cf. *Gospel of Thomas* 64.1), is re-identified later in the story as 'master' (κύριος; 14.21,22,23) and 'householder' (οἰκοδεσπότης; 14.21) – appellations for a person of means and rank and quite

---

[25] I will continue to evoke the Greco-Roman élite party scene as an important element of the social knowledge which the banquet parable assumes. See, for now, Hintzen, 1991, pp. 199–200: 'Das üppige Mahl der Reichen, worauf Lk 6,25; 12,19; 14,1–14; 16,19.21 anspielen weist auf das sozial-wirtschaftliche Bezugsfeld des antiken Lebens...Wenn im lukanischen Doppelwerk immer wieder das Mahl begegnet, so steht sicherlich auch dieses bekannte Bild der Reichen dahinter.'

appropriately aligned with the enlarged dinner setting.[26] There is no need to regard these terms as cryptic guises for characters in a theological or christological drama, to look *per allegoriam* beyond a 'big dinner' host, well known as a Greco-Roman literary character and prosperous social type, to spiritual *personae*.[27] The most significant aspect of the term 'master' is a relational one that reflects the host's socio-economic position over against others whose position is lower and hence inferior.οἰκοδεσπότης underscores this. The host is the owner of a household, probably a large one, judging from the size of his dining room (implied in 14.23).[28] The narrative clues suggest that he is a landowner living in the city (14.21),[29] judging especially from the company that he invites.[30]

The profile of the preferred, first-invited guests follows suit, perhaps inspired by the source, but likely accentuated by Luke. The trio which typifies the 'many' original guests are all *Oberschichtmänner* ('upper-class men'), as Schottroff calls them (1987, p. 206). All are severely characterized as having a single, compelling interest in the acquisition of property or, more particularly, as being preoccupied with taking possession of a purchase or acquisition. This is especially evident in the case of the first two men where a motif of quasi-legal necessity (ἀνάγκην ἰδεῖν; πορεύομαι δοκιμάσαι) related to the transfer of ownership of things appears in the telling of their

---

[26] Fabris, 1978, p. 148: 'Le designazione successive del personaggio come οἰκοδεσπότης, una volta, ὁ κύριος, tre volte corrispondono allo sviluppo della vicenda.'

[27] Κύριος is often taken as an allegorical term, signifying the risen Christ calling his own to the eschatological feast (Jülicher, 1910, vol. II, pp. 413, 416; Marshall, 1978, p. 591). Dillon nicely phrases a popular view: 'It is instructive concerning the evangelist's understanding of the meal scenes that in the middle of the sequence in Lk 14, the Lord, who is *table guest* at 14,1 suddenly becomes *host* of the 'great banquet,' according to 14,22' (1978, p. 202 n. 133).

[28] The reference in the Lukan story to a single slave does not imply that the householder owned merely one slave and, therefore, that he was a rather modest householder. The slave we meet in the story is not the only slave the owner has, but the one slave whose duty is to be the dispenser of dinner invitations. On the figure of the κλητήρ (*vocator*) see the literature cited in ch. 6 n. 9.

[29] This use of οἰκοδεσπότης to refer to a landowner is adduced by LSJ, s.v. οἰκοδεσπότης.

[30] Jülicher correctly noted that the host belongs to 'den wohlhabenden Ständen' (1910, vol. II, p. 409). Among recent interpreters Schottroff and Stegemann (1986, pp. 100–2) and Rohrbaugh (1991, pp. 137–47) stand out in their stress on the prosperity and position of the dinner host. Cf. Crossan's notice that the host eventually engages in an act of benefaction, presupposing a person of means and rank (1991, p. 12). Although the householder as 'benefactor' needs to be qualified (see ch. 6, pp. 116–19), Crossan's point is appropriate here.

excuses.[31] If we can infer from the story that it is set in a city,[32] the purchasers of land and draft animals 'are prosperous landowners who are able to live in a city'[33] while attending to their agri-business in the country. They are absentee landlords. That the one was able to purchase (ἀγοράξειν) land at all is a further indication of his wealth;[34] that the second was able to buy (ἀγοράξειν) ten draft animals in a single transaction hardly suggests that he was merely 'a peasant with yokes of oxen' (Fitzmyer, 1985, p. 1056).[35]

It remains to be seen if the third man, the newly-wed, is an anomaly in Luke's pattern of accentuating the business-minded character and wealth of the original guests. First impressions suggest so. While the first two excuses clearly concern purchases made and the need to inspect them to complete the transactions, the third appears to belong to the sphere of familial duties (or sexual pleasures) rather than to the domain of economic enterprise.[36] First

31 That 14.18–19 allude to legal procedures regulating 'transfer of ownership' (Besitzübernahme) is suggested by Schottroff, 1987, p. 208 and n. 36. Kaser, 1980, section 20.I.1 (pp. 108–9) describes Roman procedures. See, e.g., *Dig.* 41.2.18.2 on the taking-over of land.

32 Such is suggested in 14.21 (ἔξελθε ... εἰς τὰς πλατείας καὶ ῥύμας τῆς πόλεως). Hence Schottroff and Stegemann rightly state that 'the scene of the story is the city' (1986, p. 101). See Rohrbaugh, 1991, for a compelling argument that this story presupposes an ancient city setting.

33 Schottroff and Stegemann, 1986, p. 101. Hamel summarizes some of the reasons for landowners living in cities: 'It is safe to say that those owning most of the land did not cultivate it and that cultivating the land implied absence of significant ownership. In Roman Palestine as in the Hellenistic East in general, landowners acquired status in part by not operating their farms themselves. Important landowners lived in cities distant socially or geographically from their lands' (1990, p. 152). On the deep economic and social divide between urban and rural dwellers see below, p. 91.

34 It is safe to say that peasants were not land buyers, even if they might have been owners of small plots. For the tendency of big landlords to expand and consolidate land holdings see MacMullen, 1974, pp. 3–7; also Hamel, 1990, pp. 151–2.

35 Cf. Jeremias, 1963, p. 177, who calculates that one pair of oxen is needed to work 9 to 9.45 hectares of land. Hence the man in the parable 'possessed at least 45 hectares, and probably much more, and was consequently a large landowner'. White, 1988, relies on Cato (*De Agricultura*) to describe the situation in Italy. A 100-*iugera* (63 acres or 25 hectares) vineyard needed two oxen and three donkeys while a 240-*iugera* (151 acres or 60 hectares) needed three pairs of oxen and four donkeys. Against this picture, too, ten working animals is a purchase of a large landowner. For the sake of contrast one might cite the popular epigram on the suicide of a poor man: 'For Aristides, one heifer and a fleecy sheep were all his wealth. Through them, he drove starvation from the door. Then he lost both: a wolf killed the sheep, pangs of birth the cow; his poverty's consolation perished. He tied a knot against his neck with the strap of his wallet, and died in his misery beside the cabin where no cattle lowed' (*A.P.* 9.150, trans. Gow and Page, 1968, p. 55; cf. variants in *A.P.* 9.149, 9.255).

36 This is the usual differentiation made by commentators. E.g., Marshall, 1978, p. 588: 'All three excuses are concerned with the details of commercial and family

impressions occasionally mislead and they probably do so here. But
to show this will take us on an excursus.

If we take into account Greek and Roman legal and traditional
views on women and marriage,[37] traditions that would have influenced the audition/reading of Luke's parable, the suggestion that
the regrets of the newly-wed were motivated by the desire to forge
'domestic ties' (Marshall, 1978, p. 588) or by the need for 'pleasure'
(Farrar, 1887, p. 298)[38] overlook the extent to which economic
considerations governed the exchange of women. Although it is
doubtful that the archaic notion of purchasing a wife was practised
in the Hellenistic period,[39] the concept of a wife as a possession
(κτῆμα) continued to be current,[40] although some liberalization of

life; and fit in with the teaching of Jesus regarding the danger of letting love of
possessions or domestic ties interfere with total commitment to the call of discipleship.' Occasionally one even finds a commentator almost comically projecting his
ethos of prudery on to 14.20. Thus Farrar suggests that 'the three hindrances are
possessions, wealth, pleasures' (1887, p. 298).

[37] Among the rapidly increasing literature I have relied primarily on Pomeroy, 1976;
1978; den Boer, 1979, pp. 242–71; Keuls, 1985; Foley, 1988; Dickison, 1988;
Treggiari, 1988; a more idyllic picture is drawn by C. Schneider, 1967, vol. I,
pp. 78–116. Versnel, 1987, gives a helpful critical review of scholarly assessments
of women in Greek antiquity and balances the methods of classical scholars with
an anthropological approach. Lefkowitz and Fant, 1982, have collected a vast
number of primary texts related to women in Greek and Roman antiquity.

[38] Neither Greeks nor Romans married for sexual gratification, which was provided
by institutionalized prostitution and concubinage. See Ps-Demosthenes, *Against
Neaera* 59.122 (cited by den Boer, 1979, p. 244): 'Mistresses we keep for our
pleasure, concubines for our day-to-day physical well-being, and wives in order to
beget legitimate children and to have trustworthy guardians of our house-holds.'
A denial of pleasure (ἡδονή) as a motive for marriage is encoded, according to
Plutarch, in one of Solon's marriage laws: 'He [sc. Solon] prescribed that a man
should have intercourse with his wife not less than three times a month, not for the
sake of pleasure (οὐχ ἡδονῆς ἕνεκα), but as cities renew their treaties with each
other from time to time' (Plutarch, *Mor.* 769A). See also Keuls, 1985, p. 99.

[39] The idea of buying a wife with ἕδνα (wedding gifts as bride price) appears in
Homer; see Lacey, 1966; Gould, 1980; and Pomeroy, 1988, p. 1334; and, for an
opposing view, Finley, 1955. Aristotle says 'in the past the Greeks ... used to buy
their wives from each other' (τὰς γυναῖκας ἐωνοῦντο παρ' ἀλλήλων; *Pol.*
1268b.40; cited by Vernant, 1990, p. 271 n. 42). Procne, in Sophocles' lost play
*Tereus*, gives a rare female perspective: '... often I pondered the status of women:
we are nothing. As small girls in our father's house, we live the most delightful life,
because ignorance keeps children happy. But when we come to the age of maturity
and awareness, we are thrust out and bartered away' (Fr. 583; cited by Keuls,
1985, p. 98).

[40] Dionysius of Halicarnassus attributes to Romulus the law of *confarreatio* (on
which see Pomeroy, 1976, p. 152) which 'obliged both the married women, as
having no other refuge, to conform themselves entirely to the temper of their
husbands, and the husbands to rule their wives as necessary and inseparable

women's roles within the family and society took place during this period (Pomeroy, 1976, pp. 120–48). Dowered marriages meant the use of material incentives to transfer women from the tutelage of one male to that of another. Especially among the wealthy élite, primary among motives for marriage was the generation of legitimate sons as heirs to ensure that property remained in the family. Another motive, slightly lesser perhaps, was the attraction of a large dowry (wealth) to which came attached the added benefit of a manager of household chores (labour).[41] Of course, all this does not preclude that once married husband and wife would develop a relationship of friendship and genuine affection,[42] but it is fair to say that acquiring a wife in the first place was governed more by forces that regulated the flow of wealth than by noble fancies for friendship.[43] As Jean-Pierre Vernant puts it, a daughter given in

possessions (κτήματος)' (*Ant. Rom.* 2.25.4; trans. E. Cary, LCL). See Keuls, 1985, pp. 101–2: Women 'were, in fact, as Aristotle defines the slave, a "living piece of property"'. This was aptly symbolized in the capture or abduction ritual that was part of the ancient Greek marriage ceremony, namely the act by the bridegroom of leading the bride χεῖρ ἐπὶ καρπῷ ('hand on wrist') from her paternal home to her new abode. '[The hand-on-wrist motif] may indeed be a device for marking the ceremonial transfer of legal guardianship over the bride from father to son-in-law, and yet the vase painters seem to place their emphasis on the surrender of the bride, and the subordination of her will as κτῆμα, to that of the groom as possessor' (Jenkins, 1983, p. 140; see also Redfield, 1982, p. 192). Note also Countryman, 1988, pp. 147–67, p. 145 on Luke 14.20.

41 These three motives for marriage are listed by Pomeroy, 1988, p. 1335. Cf. Keuls, 1985, p. 101: 'Greek family law ... reveals two profound and abiding concerns: to ensure man's unquestionable paternity of his offspring and to preserve family property.' The motives for Roman marriage were much the same.

42 This ideal is a frequent topic for the Cynics and Stoics in their critique of conventional aristocratic views of marriage (see Diogenes Laertius 7.130–1 for a summary of the views of Diogenes and Zeno); it is best expressed by the first-century Stoic, Musonius Rufus: 'But in marriage there must be above all perfect companionship (πάντως συμβίωσιν) and mutual love of husband and wife ... under all conditions ... Where, then, this love for each other is perfect and the two share it completely, each striving to outdo the other in devotion, the marriage is ideal and worthy of envy, for such a union is beautiful' (XIIIA; trans. C. Lutz, 1947, p. 89; see Klassen, 1984, pp. 185–98, on the 'feminism' of Musonius). Similar views are stated in Plutarch's *Dialogue on Love*. With legal wives, he says, sexual union is 'the beginning of friendship (ἀρχαὶ ... φιλίας), a sharing in great mysteries' (ἱερῶν μεγάλων κοινωνήματα; *Amat.* 769A; see H. Martin, 1978, p. 531).

43 Even once married one should expect that ideals of marital love and mutuality were constrained by codes of patronage and instrumental friendship, the two fundamentals of Mediterranean social ideology that also governed marriage. Thus Versnel, 1987, pp. 75–6: Patronage is 'a very good definition of marriage, and ... the all-pervasive Mediterranean way of thinking in terms of patronage must have left its marks on *this* (sc. marriage) 'friendship' as well ... Marriage is also an 'instrumental friendship' (not necessarily without affectionate elements, of course)

marriage 'fulfills the role of wealth put into circulation' (1990, p. 73).

Given that the association between marriage and property had a long legal and traditional history,[44] when the man in Luke's parable said γυναῖκα ἔγημα ('I have married a wife') we are not unduly subscribing the text in taking it to mean that he was consummating a transfer of ownership, that he was converting an earlier contract (something like the traditional ἐγγύη) he had made with the woman's κύριος into full marriage, 'γάμος being simply *copula carnalis*' (Harrison, 1968, p. 7).[45] The Lukan newly-wed is taking over a woman;[46] he is closing a deal not unlike the men who are finalizing purchases of land and plough animals.

This a harsh reading indeed. Since it also strains against the common view, recently fully documented by Kathleen Corley (1993, pp. 108–9), that '[o]f all the Synoptic Gospels, the Gospel of Luke

in which the husband has the higher status of patron (*kurios*) who is responsible for ... his 'friend' of lesser status ... [T]he partnership of man and woman is a friendship of unequals, a relationship of "benefactor versus beneficiary". This is the language of patronage.' Versnel takes his definition of patronage from Silverman, 1965, p. 176: 'an informal contract between people of unequal status, which places either of them under different mutual obligations'.

[44] This association between women and property is even contained in the term ἐγγύη (first appearing in Homer, *Od.* 8.351) which means both 'marriage' (or a prenuptial contract between a woman's father and the bridegroom) and 'surety'. See Wolff, 1944, pp. 51–3; and Harrison, 1968, pp. 2–9, p. 12: 'In ἐγγύη the contract was between the groom and the woman's κύριος ... [T]here seems no doubt that her κύριος could make a valid contract without her consent'.

[45] Cf. Redfield, 1982, p. 188: '*Gamos* is the name, in its primary significance, not of a ceremony but of the sexual act itself – without which the marriage is not (as we say) consummated, actual.' Similarly Erskine, 1990, p. 26: '*gamein* could be used ... simply for sexual intercourse...[C]ertainly by the Roman period it was just a crude term for sexual intercourse.' Hence Zeno could say (Diogenes Laertius, 7.121) that the philosopher 'will mate ... and make children' (γαμήσειν ... καὶ παιδοποιήσεσθαι) even though Zeno's ideal *Politeia* did not recognize the institution of marriage.

[46] Luke's use of the Attic ἔγημα instead of the Hellenistic ἐγάμησα is so unusual that Kilpatrick, 1967, thought it to be an incorrect reading. Some mss. (D, lat sy) indeed offer the variant γυναῖκα ἔλαβον at Luke 14.20. Although this reading is poorly attested and hence probably an unoriginal harmonization with the usual Lukan λαβεῖν γυναῖκα (20.28,29,31; thus Jülicher, 1910, vol. II, p. 412; Fitzmyer, 1985, p. 1056; *contra* Kilpatrick, 1967, p. 140), it nicely supports my argument. See LSJ, s.v. λαμβάνω, II.1.b, for examples from classical Greek writers (e.g., Herodotus 1.99, 9.108; Xenophon, *Hell.* 4.1,14) for the use of this term in the sense of taking a wife. It might be interesting to conjecture that γυναῖκα λαμβάνειν ('to take a woman') is the contractual counterpart of γυναῖκα ἐκδιδόναι ('to surrender or hand over a woman') Traditionally, ἔκδοσις is a legal term that refers to the formal surrender of property, but it also covered the formal handing-over of the bride (Wolff, 1944, p. 44; see, e.g., Demosthenes 1100.7: τὰς ἐκδόσεις τῶν γυναικῶν; and numerous additional references in Wolff, p. 49).

has always been considered a Gospel for women' (Corley, p. 108), it warrants a brief defence. It should be remembered, first, that Luke's interest in this story is not to focus on the bride (who is not in the picture, in any case), but on the newly-wed, and on him to paint him as a 'typical' man from the ranks of the urban élite. The commodification of women in the marriage image here thus is not to be taken as an indicator of Luke's view of women. Second, as Corley also shows, Luke would not have needed to suppress deep 'feminist' sympathies to exploit the marriage *topos* as a means of characterizing hyper-economic pursuits; he did not have many to suppress; 'of all the Synoptics, Luke is the most concerned to maintain a traditional, Greco-Roman, private role for women' (Corley, p. 109, cf. pp. 144–6).

There is yet another level on which first-century auditors/readers might have seen a firm association between the purchases of land and draft animals and finalizing a marriage procedure. On the metaphorical plane the superiority of men over women and male domination of the female were reinforced by associating women with nature, with fertile fields and receptive furrows, and men with culture, with ploughing the fields and sowing seed in the furrows. Aristotle in *On the Generation of Animals* thought that this distinction was cosmologically grounded and he built his theory on the female role in generation on the notion that a woman is naturally aligned with the earth as female and mother.[47] 'Contemporary popular literature confirms Aristotle's view of conception; woman is the earth, the furrow for a man actively to plow' (Foley, 1988, p. 1306).[48] According to Eva Keuls, the standard Athenian wedding formula asserted that the purpose of marriage was 'for the ploughing of legitimate children' (1985, p. 100). In the Hellenistic period these agricultural metaphors continue to flourish. Soranus, a first-century physician, giving advice on how to prepare a woman for coitus for the purpose of conception, states that 'as the farmer sows

[47] Aristotle, *Gen. An.* 716a5–23. Other relevant excerpts from *Gen. An.* are in Lefkowitz and Fant, 1982, pp. 82–5. See Vernant, 1965, pp. 97–181, for an incisive analysis of the ambiguity that marks the association of woman with nature and earth (outer space), on the one hand, and hearth and home (inner space), on the other. Cf. Gould, 1980, p. 57: 'Like the earth and once-wild animals, they [women] must be tamed and cultivated by men, but their "wildness" will out.'

[48] P. duBois, 1988, has collected numerous references to the metaphorical association between agricultural production and sexual intercourse, i.e. women as fields (ch. 3) and furrows (ch. 4) to be cultivated, plowed and sowed by men.

only after having first cleansed the soil and removed any foreign
material, in the same manner we too advise that insemination for the
production of man should follow after the [female] body has first
been given a rubdown' (*Gynaecology* 1.40.3; translated by Temkin
in Lefkowitz and Fant, 1982, p. 221). Lucretius speaks of 'sowing
the woman's field' and exhorts wives to restrain their buttocks from
undulating when 'the soothing pleasure itself is taken' as this 'turns
the share clean away from the furrow and makes the seed fail of its
place'.[49]

In sum, traditional myths and metaphors, surely well known to
Hellenistic readers, thus generate and enforce the idea that a woman
'is identified with the cultivated land owned by her husband, and
[that] the marriage has the significance of an exercise in ploughing,
with the woman as the furrow' (Vernant, 1990, p. 73).

This identification and its web of signification aid in the association of Luke's newly-wed and his action with those of the rest of
the Lukan trio of refusing dinner guests. It is a trio, to recapitulate,
that is severely marked with an undistractable interest in the acquisition of property. The spare details that the narrative depends on to
create an image of them show them to be men whose energies were
focused on accumulating material wealth. In this they are stereotypes of the attitude and behaviour concerning wealth that marked
the Roman élites generally.[50] The fact that the householder considers these as his table companions is of significance to which it will
be necessary to return.[51]

---

[49] *De rerum natura* 4.1107, 1264, 1272–73. (The movement which Lucretius censures
evidently was used by prostitutes as a contraceptive measure.) For similar metaphors see, e.g., Aeschylus, *Sept.* 753–4; Sophocles, *Ant.* 569; *OT* 1256–57, 1497;
Euripides, *Cyc.* 171, *Phoen.* 18; Plautus, *Asin.* 874; Virgil, *G.* 3.136.

[50] See D'Arms, 1981, esp. ch. 5, on the 'typicality' of a figure represented by
Trimalchio; cf. Mitchell, 1973.

[51] Luke's trio of refusing dinner guests has generated a sizable body of literature. See
Derrett, 1970b; Ballard, 1972; J. Sanders, 1974; Palmer, 1976. The common
tendency is to explain the presence of the trio in Luke's story with reference to the
exemption rules for military duty in Deut. 20.5–7 (cf. *m.Sota* 8.7; Philo, *Virt.* 28
and *De agr.* 148–56). The newly-wed merits an occasional side glance to Herodotus' observation (1.36) that Croesus did not permit his newly-wed son (νεόγαμος)
to go on a hunt (e.g., Farrar, 1887, p. 589). At best the Deuteronomy passage
provides a harmlessly interesting parallel of a similar triad of excuses for not
participating in an activity. I see no reason why the traditional exemptions from
holy war (or a hunt) are useful in explaining the function of the Lukan trio. A call
to holy war or a summons to a hunt do not strike me as analogous to a dinner
invitation. Thus, 'to see Holy War reasons involved in each of the excuses given by
the three [in Luke 14] is eisegetical' (Fitzmyer, 1985, p. 1056). See also the
objections raised by Scott, 1989, pp. 170–1.

## Second invitation: the urban poor

By comparison with all other narrators of the story, Luke shows a heightened interest in characterizing the secondary guests in terms that are heavily loaded with connotations of economic destitution and social marginality.[52] Hence they are not a random lot of folks gathered off the street, as Q, Matthew ('as many as you find . . . both bad and good') and Thomas ('whomever you find') suggest,[53] but specifically the destitute (πτωχοί) and disabled (various ἀδύνατοι).[54] The stereotypical vocabulary of poverty (πτωχοί, ἀναπείροι,

52 This is generally acknowledged and often stressed by commentators. To my knowledge, Linnemann is the only one who denies this. In her view, the guests are 'die ersten besten von der Straße' (as Matthew and *G. Thom.* might support). How does she get around the vocabulary of poverty in 14.21? She erases it, in effect. 'Nicht darauf kommt es dem Hausherrn an, Arme einzuladen, sondern er will in dieser kurzen Zeitspanne schnell [ταχέως!] die nötigen Gäste zusammen haben' (1960, p. 252 and n. 14).

53 In Matthew and *G. Thom.* the servant(s) follow(s) instructions to be indiscriminate in gathering substitute guests. On this point Matthew and *G. Thom.* likely are closest to the Q story. Matthew accentuates the principle of non-selectiveness by adding 'the bad and the good' (πονηρούς τε καὶ ἀγαθούς). All versions suggest that these guests are to be found in the streets, a detail that possibly (but not necessarily) implies that they are poor street people. So Schottroff, 1987, p. 201, commenting on the Q story. If so, she rightly states: 'Lukas hat in Lk 14,21 einen Zug, den er schon [in Q] vorfand, nur verdeutlicht, falls die Formulierung 14,21 auf ihn zurückgeht' (p. 201). *Verdeutlichung* of course is a sign of special interest, of redactional emphasis.

54 The Greek vocabulary for rich and poor constitutes a large web of synonymity, informatively and extensively charted by J. Schmidt, 1886, vol. II, pp. 611–25; vol. IV, pp. 376–451. Here it is enough to draw attention to the difference between πένης and πτωχός. In classical usage especially the πένητες are connected with the idea of labour or toil (πόνος) and thus are the lower class citizens, largely coextensive with ὁ δῆμος ('the people'; small property and shop owners, artisans, fishers, agricultural workers, various wage labourers, etc.), who lived frugally off their labour in contrast to the πλούσιοι who lived luxuriously off their estate. The extreme opposite of the πλούσιοι were the beggarly poor (πτωχοί), the extreme have-nots (οἱ οὐκ ἔχοντες). A concise overview of the widely recognized divisions within Greek urban society into the πλούσιοι, πένητες and πτωχοί is given by Müller, 1976, pp. 20–1. For the most revealing ancient descriptions of the conditions of poverty see e.g. Aristophanes, *Plut.* 535–45; Juvenal, *Sat.* 3.209–11; and the saying describing 'the curses of tragedy' (i.e., the beggarly life) attributed to Diogenes (Diogenes Laertius 6:38): Ἄπολις, ἄοικος, πατρίδος ἐστηρεμένος, πτωχός, πλανήτης, βίον ἔχων τοὐφ᾽ ἡμέραν, 'without city, homeless, deprived of his native land, a beggar, a roamer, living life from day to day'. Essential secondary literature on wealth and poverty: Hemelrijk, 1925; van Manen, 1931; Bolkestein, 1939, pp. 181–99 (largely relying on the dissertations of his students Hemelrijk and van Manen); den Boer, 1979, pp. 151–78; Hands, 1968, pp. 63–76, cf. pp. 77–88; Fuks, 1977; Kloft, 1988a; Hamel, 1990, esp. pp. 164–211 ('vocabulary of poverty' in Greek, Jewish and Christian sources); Bastomsky, 1990;

τυφλοί, χωλοί) used in 14.21 to describe the first set of alternate guests is carried over from 14.13. Although this unfortunate foursome may have been united by the force of cliché (Ernst, 1979, p. 69; cf. Hemelrijk, 1925, pp. 66–90), one should not overlook its significance as a powerful portrait of destitution. Clichés, after all, represent habitual attitudes distilled from long experience. Greek orators often used them because of their proven symbolic value and usefulness for rhetorical purposes (Ober, 1989, p. 44).

Poverty and sickness *de facto* generated and mutually reinforced each other: to be poor often meant a life of ill health due to degenerative diets and living conditions,[55] just as to be ἀδύνατος ('disabled') or ἀσθενής ('feeble') physically or socially[56] was virtually synonymous with a life of poverty. For, to be struck with ἀδυναμία in Luke's Mediterranean world meant to be subject to social discrimination and stigmatization,[57] to be denied a share of

Rosivach, 1991; cf. the relevant articles in *TDNT*: Hauck, 1968; Hauck and Bammel, 1968; Hauck and Kasch, 1968.

[55] E.g., Sophocles, fr. 354 (*TrGF*, Nauck); it is ironic that this association between poverty and illness was occasionally exploited for comical ends at dinner parties (see Athenaeus, *Deipnos.* 10.453a); cf. Diogenes Laertius 6.56 (citing Diogenes of Sinope): 'Being asked why people give to beggars but not philosophers, he said, Because they think they may one day be lame or blind, but never expect that they will turn to philosophy.' See Luke 16.20 for a clear association of poverty and festering sores (πτωχὸς ... εἱλκωμένος). Hamel, 1990, pp. 52–4, has collected the ancient evidence and references to secondary literature on the relationship between poverty, malnutrition, diseases and death. Sippel, 1987, richly documents ancient sources and modern studies in his study of conditions and effects of general malnutrition among the Roman urban *plebs*.

[56] In the ancient sources the rich person is often contrasted with the poor one as πλούσιος vs. ἀσθενής (e.g., Lysias, *Supp.* 433–4), or the poor are described simply as 'the weaker sort' (οἱ ἀσθενέστεροι; Xenophon, *Cyr.* 8.1.30) or as 'the disabled' (οἱ ἀδύνατοι; Herodotus 5.9; cf. Lysias 31.11 where indulgence is urged towards the πένησιν ἢ ἀδυνάτοις τῷ σώματι, 'the poor or physically disabled'). Cf. Diogenes Laertius 6.32: 'The word "disabled" (ἀναπήρους), [Diogenes] said, ought to be applied not to the deaf or blind (κωφοὺς καὶ τυφλούς), but to those who have no wallet (πήρα).' See also 7.105–6 on Zeno's division of things between preferred and rejected classes where one of the lines is drawn between (a) wealth, fame, noble birth, sound mental and moral qualities, bodily health and (b) poverty, ignominy, low birth, mental and moral deficiencies, bodily illness. The δυνατός-ἀδύνατος (powerful, noble, rich vs. weak, of low birth, materially poor) antithesis is especially favoured by Josephus in his characterization of people, as Hamel has shown in detail (1990, pp. 206–9).

[57] Krierer, 1988, pp. 339–47, for a survey of iconographic evidence. 'Menschen von besonders elendem Schicksal und menschenunwürdigem Außenseitertum stellen die zahlreichen Typen der Mißgestalteten, der Buckligen, Zwergwüchsigen oder sonst körperlich und vielleicht auch oft geistig Behinderten, der Kranken der Gesellschaft schlechthin, dar' (p. 341). See also Lorenz, 1988; Graßl, 1988, pp. 35–44, on the 'Lebenschancen' of the ἀδύνατοι in antiquity; Kudlien, 1988; Bolkestein, 1939; and Hands, 1968, for wide-ranging treatments on the topic of the poor and disabled in Greco-Roman society; Uther, 1981, contains an extensive

virtue (ἀρετή),[58] to be barred from important civic institutions,[59] to be excluded from collective forms of social life[60] and, hence, bibliography and citations from ancient sources. The standard work on the life of the blind and attitudes towards them is Esser, 1939, esp. pp. 92–5 on 'Lebensgewohnheit und Lebenslage', pp. 112–8 on attitudes towards and treatment of the blind. Buxton, 1980, and Bernidaki-Aldous, 1990, pp. 11–131, show that blindness is a key metaphor (esp. in Greek myths and Sophoklean dramas) for the defectiveness of humanity, 'the ultimate form of human *pathos* in a culture of light' (p. 119). On Luke's fondness for vocabulary of blindness and sight and its metaphorical value see Hamm, 1986, although he fails to consider blindness/sight as symbolic of social marginalization and integration. This receives scattered attention in Pilch, 1991, but seems still to await a fuller treatment.

58 From Homeric Greece onward the terminology for various classes of people is 'an inextricable mixture of the social and the moral' (Ste. Croix, 1981, p. 279). At the material level social stratification happens along lines of wealth, status (noble birth) and power (e.g., Lucian, *Necyo.* 12: πλούτους καὶ γένη καὶ δυναστείας), but these strata are coordinated with a hierarchy of values and terms of commendation and/or derogation: the aristocratic élite are situated at the top of the *arete*- and *agathos*-standard and often simply called οἱ ἀγαθοί (see Plato, *Rep.* 569a4: οἱ καλοὶ κάγαθοὶ λεγόμενοι) and their way of life ἀρετή, while κακός denigrates the rest of the populace. They are, as Dio of Prusa puts it in his *Euboicus*, 7.126, τοῖς κάκιστα βιωσομένοις, 'those who are to live on the basest plane'. Of the literature on this issue, see esp. Wankel, 1961; also Jaeger, 1945, vol. I, pp. 3–14; Adkins, 1960, pp. 30–60, 153–94; 1972, pp. 10–21; Dover, 1974, pp. 41–5, 69–73; Gouldner, 1965, pp. 12–24, 37 n. 32; Lloyd-Jones, 1990, p. 271. From the vantage point of the 'virtuous' élite the poor often are subjected to slurs and associated with moral and social evils (see Kloft, 1988a, pp. 100–1). See also Welskopf, 1965, pp. 62–3, on the link between élite self-definition and their disdain for the non-élite often expressed in moral and social terms.

59 It is difficult to get a full picture on the regulations governing access to the civic gathering places such as baths, gymnasia, theatres, etc. A first-century BCE inscription from Macedonian Beroia (*SEG* XXVII.261B.26–9; cf. *SEG* XXXII.634), containing the rules for the city's *gymnasion*, lists several categories of people that are to be excluded from admittance, including slaves, freedmen and their sons, those without aptitude for physical exercise (ἀπάλαιστροι), homosexuals, those who make a living by means of ἀγοραίαι τέχνη (presumably street artisans and small vendors), drunks and mentally handicapped (μαινόμενος). We may assume, admittedly with diffidence, that the Beroian law was fairly typical (so Moretti, 1982, pp. 49–55, citing examples of similar practices in other cities). It is noteworthy that all the excluded belonged to social *Randgruppen* (see Weiler, 1988, pp. 19–20, and p. 15 on the Beroia inscription; also Graßl, 1988, pp. 41–2). It is remarkable that the beggarly poor and disabled are not even mentioned in the Beroian gymnasium law. I am inclined to assume that silence here is telling, that is, the πτωχοί *et al.* were so marginal that their exclusion did not need to be stated. It was understood. Similarly Pleket, 1988, p. 272.

60 What Esser says about the blind could be said of the other members of Luke's unfortunate quartet: 'Besuche, Gastmähler, Festlichkeiten, Versammlungen sind seltener im Leben des Blinden. Damit entfällt für ihn ein großes Teil des menschlichen Gemeinschaftsleben' (1939, p. 93). These collective forms of social life, such as dinner parties, should not be understood as simple occasions for amusement or festive frivolity but as essential arenas for securing social advantage (see esp. D'Arms, 1984, pp. 344–8), for 'political manoeuvring' (P. Clark, 1991, p. 32), as indispensable rituals of civic life (Schmitt-Pantel, 1990, pp. 200–7). To be denied access to them effectively meant to be denied a share in citizenship and the 'good life'.

generally to be without leverage in improving one's lot in life.[61]

Luke's choice of vocabulary for identifying the secondary guests makes it entirely unequivocal that they belonged to what a Greek or Roman aristocrat might have called τό ἄπορὸν καὶ ῥυπαρὸν καὶ πάντα ('the indigent and filthy and such'; Dionysius Halicarnassus, *Antiquitates Romanae* 8.71.3), the *misera ac ieiuna plebecula* ('starving, contemptible rabble'; Cicero, *Ad Atticum* 1.16.11). Equally clear is that the first lot of substitute guests is gathered from 'the streets and lanes of the city' (τὰς πλατείας καὶ ῥύμας τῆς πόλεως). The 'city' detail is important, but before stating its significance further it is necessary respectfully to set aside a major commentary tradition.

One of the most stable items of scholarly lore on the Lukan dinner parable relies on the πόλις reference to identify the sorry quartet in 14.21 as marginalized or outcast Jews. Three influential representatives of this view should suffice to illustrate. Adolf Jülicher, in an ironical moment of out-allegorizing Luke's 'half-allegorical narrative', asserts that 'there can be no doubt' about the identity of the urban poor. They are 'the lowliest of God's people, the sick sinners of Luke 5.31–32 to whom Jesus so generously dedicated himself, the spiritual proletariat despised and neglected by official piety' (1910, vol. II, pp. 416–7). Joachim Jeremias also argues that Luke 'read into' the received parable a 'missionary command'. Luke 'may have understood the first invitation to the uninvited, which was confined to those in the city, to signify the publicans and sinners in Israel' (1963, p. 64). T. W. Manson tries to give this view the support of some argumentation:

> The fact that these guests are to be found in the same city as the original guests, suggests that they represent Jews of another class. If the first guests are the righteous Jews, the religious aristocracy, men of the Pharisaic type, these may well be the religious lower classes, the publicans and sinners: Israelites like the Pharisees, but bad Israelites from the Pharisaic standpoint.          (1949, p. 130)

Manson's 'fact' is plainly visible in Luke's text; the originally invited and secondarily invited belong to the same city. But on what evidence should they be identified as Jews? There is none; the

---

[61] Rohrbaugh rightly says of the poor of Luke 14.21: 'These are not the aspiring poor of the city, as anachronistic capitalist readings would have it' (1991, p. 144).

identity of the invited is surmised as a condition ('if'), and the condition is implicitly established by means of an assumed equivalence, 'the πόλις is Israel' (Jeremias, 1963, p. 69). But, as Robert Funk has shown, this equation is not present in Luke. Nor can it be shown to be part of the pre-Lukan parable. Most evidently it is derived from Matthew's banquet parable which clearly has the appearance of an allegory of salvation history (22.7; an oblique reference to Jerusalem; see Funk, 1966, pp. 183–6). Once Matthew's equation becomes operative in the interpretation of Luke's dinner parable, and when this equation is bolstered by the 'from Jerusalem to the ends of the earth' mission scheme of Acts (1.8), a reading of the parable as allegory (though less vitriolic and violent than Matthew's) of salvation history or as Luke's allegory of his own view of early church expansion is almost unavoidable. The dinner story begins to look 'much like the circular and ever-expanding [mission] pattern in Acts' (Scott, 1989, p. 164).[62] Or, as Josef Ernst puts it, the story has become 'interpreted history' (1979, p. 74). It is not that such a reading is self-evidently outrageous, much less impossible; it 'works' well enough to satisfy a large majority of interpreters. Nonetheless, reading Luke's story as a 'missionarische Umbiegung' (Ernst, 1979, p. 73) of an original story depends for its success on a patchwork of hermeneutic cues external to the parable and its episodal context. Without Matthew's equation, city = Israel, the scholarly equation, Luke's city guests = Jews, is arbitrarily suppositional. Similarly, without the ever-expanding mission model of Acts as a pretext it is doubtful that the bald word πόλις in Luke 14.21 could bear the burden of a Christian missionary command to Jews.[63] More importantly, the allegorical reading sponsored by

[62] The 'salvation-historical' interpretation is so common that a roster of representatives is hardly necessary. See, for example, Easton, 1926, p. 230; Creed, 1930, pp. 191–3; Dodd, 1961, p. 91; Vögtle, 1971, pp. 194–6; Marshall, 1978, pp. 586–7; Ernst, 1979, p. 72; Bailey, 1980, pp. 100–12; Horn, 1983, p. 184; Fitzmyer, 1985, pp. 1053–4; Crossan, 1985, pp. 50, 52; most recently, Esler, 1987, p. 186 (surprisingly, since his interest is in Luke's views on the poor); Hintzen, 1991, p. 321; and Gowler, 1991, p. 247 n. 147. Important dissenters include Funk, 1966, pp. 183–5; Hahn, 1970, pp. 71–4; Schottroff, 1987, pp. 207–8; Rohrbaugh, 1991, pp. 137–47, esp. 139; cf. Bossman, 1991, p. 3: 'the story makes no reference to who the invited guests might be'.

[63] It could be argued, I suppose, that the parable as a 'missionary command' (Jeremias) is suggested by the mention of the city + the three invitations, one rejected and the others accepted. It seems, however, that the πόλις is the most crucial element in the 'success' of the allegorical interpretation, because without this word in Luke, Matthew's (implicit) equation of city = Israel could not as easily be transferred to Luke. Of interest is why *G.Thom.*64, following a structure

codes external to the story actually suppresses the thematic forces most obviously at work within the story and its episodal context. These thematic forces, as I have already pointed out, have to do with status definitions, contrastive characterization for the purpose of identifying and commenting on patterns of relations between social equals and opposites and the like. Insofar as the allegorical reading works to camouflage these dynamics it 'works' negatively.

Thus I return to a rather plain reading of the secondarily invited and take them to be the lowest of the *plebs urbana*, presumably the sorriest of those whom Cicero disdainfully calls the 'filth and dregs of the city' (*sordes urbis et faex*; *Ad Atticum* 1.16.11; cited by Ste. Croix, 1981, p. 355; cf. Brunt, 1966, pp. 24–6). The living conditions of these urban poor have been described well by others and thus need here just a summary note.[64] Essentially the utterly poor was one 'having nothing at stake in life' (Lucian, *Cataplus* 15), someone unable to work even at the most menial tasks and thus lacking the three necessary life provisions of food, clothing and shelter (*cibaria, vestitus, habitatio*; *Digesta Iustiniani* 34.1.6; see Kloft, 1988a, p. 83). For food they relied on begging and scavenging for scraps in the market and public places where food was consumed.[65] As for clothing, the typical description has the beggar covered in filthy rags and worn animal skins (Bolkestein, 1939, p. 204; MacMullen, 1971, p. 115). Without money for housing in slum huts or tenements (*insulae*), their home was in the λέσχαι, that is, public arcades, eateries and the like where people met for conversation and to idle

similar to that of the synoptic versions, has never (to my knowledge) been read allegorically either as 'mission history' or as 'salvation history'. A partial answer probably lies in Thomas' use of the story to deny 'buyers and merchants' a place in his group (64.12), but the lack of 'city' in this story may be partly responsible as well.

64  See especially the important article by Rohrbaugh, 1991; cf. Alföldy, 1985, p. 135; MacMullen, 1974, pp. 85–7; and A. Jones, 1947, pp. 268–9, on the 'wretched' living conditions of the urban *plebs*. Esler, 1987, pp. 175–9, provides a reliable summary of relevant social-historical findings by classical scholars.

65  Bolkestein, 1939, p. 209, finds evidence of beggars loitering near temples and altars in the hope of some scraps. The lore surrounding Diogenes is particularly illustrative of the alimentary practices of the beggar. See Diogenes Laertius 6:31 (τροφῇ χρωμένους καὶ ὕδωρ πίνοντας, 'plain fare and water to drink'; 6.46, 58, 61, eating in the marketplace; 6.64, eating in a temple; 6.22, 'he used any place for any purpose, for breakfasting, sleeping, or conversing'; 6.56, begging for food. On begging generally, see the sardonic *chreiai* in 6:49: 'He once begged alms of a statue, and, when asked why he did so, replied, "To get practice in being refused". In asking alms – as he did at first by reason of his poverty – he used this form: "If you have already given to anyone else, give to me also; if not, begin with me"' (trans. Hicks, LCL).

away time (see Acts 17.21),[66] or at the entrances to temples and gymnasia where coming and going crowds could be called upon for handouts.[67] 'The open air is their dwelling, their lodgings are the porticoes and streetcorners and the less frequented parts of the marketplace' (Gregory of Nyssa, *De pauperibus amandis* 1; cited by MacMullen, 1974, p. 87).[68] Even this may be overestimating the freedom of movement of the urban poor and vagrants, given that the spacial and social organization of ancient Mediterranean cities was configured in such a way that the powerful élite occupied the centre while the non-élite lived in more or less outlying sectors separated from each other and from the spatial and political centre by a system of internal walls and carefully monitored traffic control designed to keep people in the spaces appropriate to their social level.[69] Philip Esler's summary of the experience of urban poverty is to the point:

> For them life was a very grim business. Ill-fed, housed in slums or not at all, ravaged by sickness, precluded from all access to social prestige and power over their own destinies, and having virtually no hope of improvement in their conditions, they went through life with little if any confir-

---

66 On the urban 'resting sites' see Oikonomides, 1987; cf. Bolkestein, 1939, p. 204; and LSJ, s.v. λέσχη: 'a place where people gathered for conversation, a favourite resort for idlers and beggars'. Oikonomides cites as 'a sample of the typical information available in the [later] Greek lexica' (p. 30) the entry in Hesychius' dictionary: ΛΕΣΧΗ. ὁμιλία. καὶ ἡ φλυαρία καὶ ὁ δημόσιος τόπος, ἐν ᾧ διέτριβον οἱ πτωχοὶ καὶ διελέγοντο ἀλλήλους· σημαίνει δὲ καὶ κοινὰ δειπνητήρια καὶ τοὺς ἐν αὐτοῖς λόγους. καὶ τοὺς ἀλεεινοὺς τόπους λέσχας καλοῦσιν, 'Lesche: conversation; also talking trash and the public place, where the poor whiled away their time talking with each other. But it also refers to common eating places and the talk in them; they also call the places exposed to the sun *leschai*.' Walcot draws a useful comparison between the ancient urban *leschai* and the coffee-houses as 'the centre of public life' in modern Greek towns and villages (1970, pp. 26–7).

67 Among the best illustrations is Luke's own story in Acts 3.2–10 where a congenital cripple is 'daily' laid at the temple gate 'to ask alms of the people who entered the temple'. Diogenes, the Cynic beggar, is said to have pointed 'to the portico of Zeus and the Hall of Processions, [saying] that the Athenians had provided him with places to live in'. Apparently he wrote to some patron asking him to procure a hut (οἰκίδιον) for him, but when this person was not forthcoming, Diogenes took up his famous residence (οἰκίαν) in a tub (Diogenes Laertius, 6.22–3; cf. 6.43). Cf. Dio, *Or.* 6.14: 'temples and gymnasia' are homes to Diogenes in every city.

68 Esler cites the same passage and adds: 'There is little reason to believe that this would not have been the case in the first century CE throughout the Eastern cities' (1987, p. 178).

69 See Rohrbaugh, 1991, pp. 134–6, esp. the diagram on p. 135; cf. p. 144: Luke is 'deeply conscious of the pattern of the city'. Cadbury already noted that Luke's 'viewpoint is rather urban' (1926, p. 309).

mation that they, as much as the tiny élite who lorded it over them, were creatures with personal dignity and respect, entitled to share in the fruits of the earth.

(1987, p. 179)

Luke's language of poverty to describe the secondary guests as urban *plebs* of the lowest fortunes and his identification of their habitat as 'the narrow streets and alleys along which the poorest of the non-élite lived' (Rohrbaugh, 1991, p. 144) is a socially loaded and a socially locative move. Luke appears not to have interest in the ethnic identity of the poor. Rather, he is after a characterization of an antithesis to the originally invited, all well-to-do urban élite hyperactively engaged in the business of increasing or preserving economic assets and social status. It appears that Luke needed more than just random substitute guests to fill an empty dining room; he wanted them to be unmistakably have-nots (οἱ οὐκ ἔχοντες),[70] to be everything the first guests were not so as to stretch the social distance from the urban 'streets and lanes' to the dining room as far as possible.

The language of invitation, until now either καλεῖν, φωνεῖν (once) or εἰπεῖν ἔρχεσθε (once), becomes noticeably stronger and reinforces the impression of the social gap: εἰσάγαγε ὧδε ('lead them in here'), as if implying that the usual invitation (κλῆσις) would have been regarded as preposterous and likely to be refused on grounds of social propriety.[71] In all, one is inclined to suspect in this exaggeration of contrast not so much a 'salvation-historical' motive as a rhetorical move already familiar to us from 14.12–13.

### Third invitation: para-urban ἐξωπυλεῖτοι

Those who read the parable as an allegory of the command and execution of the early Christian mission see in the clearly redactional supplementary campaign (14.22–3) to gather yet more replacement guests from the 'roads and hedges/walls' (τὰς ὁδοὺς καὶ φραγ-

[70] Cf. Luke 18.24: 'How hard is it for οἱ τὰ χρήματα ἔχοντες [ = πλούσιοι, 18.25] to enter the kingdom of God!'
[71] Against, e.g., Plummer, 1914, p. 362: 'They are not likely to refuse.' Even more off the mark is G. Clark, 1876, p. 335: they 'would gladly and thankfully accept and appreciate the feast'. Jülicher noted that εἰσάγαγε 'die Mitte zwischen dem Bestellen und dem Nötigen innehält', but he did not explain this choice of vocabulary, perhaps because he thought that the invitational language within the parable 'wird dem Evangelisten schwerlich zum Bewusstsein gelangt sein' (1910, vol. II, p. 415).

μούς) an injunction to go on 'a mission beyond the borders of Israel to the Gentiles' (Manson, 1949, p. 130). But here too the equivalencies are weakly conjectural. There is no evidence that the bare image τὰς ὁδοὺς καὶ φραγμούς was ever used as a metaphor for Gentile territory and the people to be found there as Gentiles.[72] Hence the strength of the equation, roads/hedges = Gentiles, and the Gentile mission that it supposedly signifies is entirely derived from the equation, city = Jews, which itself is not computable on the basis of Luke's text. Assuming then that, like the first two invitations, the third one uses spatial language for a socially locative rather than for an ethnic-identifying purpose, the question is who these final guests might be. There are two options, although they may not be exclusive of each other.

That their habitat is outside the walled-in *polis* precincts is at least softly implied in the terms ὁδός and φραγμός.[73] From this it is sometimes suggested that the final guests are country people, the rustic counterparts to the urban *plebs* (Crossan, 1985, p. 45; Blomberg, 1990, p. 234). This suggestion has some attractions when it is set against the background of the city-country polarity that figured so prominently not only in Greco-Roman moral thought and literary traditions, but especially in the social, political and economic anatomy of the Greek city-state and the later Roman administrative patterns in which each πόλις had its own χώρα or *territorium*.[74] Although Greek and Roman writers often idealized

[72] Schottroff, 1987, p. 208. See now the detailed analysis of Luke's understanding of non-urban space by Oakman, 1991. Although Oakman does not specifically refer to Luke 14.23, his study provides no evidence that Luke used any of various designations for rural precincts as metaphors for Gentile territory.

[73] In contrast to the city lanes (14.21), ὁδός suggests a road beyond the city. Φραγμός is the usual term for a contructed hedge or fence surrounding a property, but it may also refer to the fortification surrounging the city (LSJ, s.v. φραγμός).

[74] On the city-country antithesis see A. Jones, 1947, pp. 259–304; Caro Baroja, 1963; MacMullen, 1974, chs. 1–3; Finley, 1973, pp. 123–49; 1977, pp. 325–7; Ste. Croix, 1981, pp. 9–19; the valuable collection of essays in Rich and Wallace-Hadrill, 1991; Oakman, 1991, pp. 152–60; cf. Rohrbaugh, 1991, pp. 129–37. A brief note on a point of method: the idea of 'polarity' (implicitly supposing an interdependence of differences or even antagonisms) and what follows requires acceptance of the view of cities of Greco-Roman antiquity as 'consumer cities', to use Max Weberian terms introduced into the debate by Finley, 1973, pp. 125, 138–9, and 1977, pp. 325–6. That is, cities derived their wealth from rent and taxes collected from the peasant farmers and lived off the agricultural production of these peasants; cities thus were centres of economic exploitation of the countryside. This view dominates scholarship on the ancient city and its *territorium* and is variously represented in the works cited above. A very different model is argued by Engels, 1990. On the basis of a detailed socio-economic analysis of the *polis* and *territorium* of Corinth, he

the rural life as healthy, simple and 'more conducive to virtue than sophistication, city-dwelling, and cosmopolitan luxury',[75] this bucolic ideal is more nostalgic hankering for rustic simplicity or for a golden past on the part of harried urbanites than a real description of the city-country dynamics and peasant life in particular.[76] A. H. M. Jones, among others, has demonstrated convincingly that Mediterranean cities were 'economically parasitic on the countryside. Their incomes consisted in the main of the rents drawn by the urban aristocracy from the peasants ... The wealth of the countryside ... was drained into the towns. The peasants were thus reduced to a very low standard of life' (1947, p. 268).[77] Douglas Oakman's analysis of agrarian economics similarly shows that its basic structure, dictated by urban élite interests, consisted of a 'redistributive network' where goods largely moved one way: 'away from the rural producers to the storehouses of the cities, private estates, temples' (1991, p. 156). The loss of peasant control over land – the chief means of securing economic subsistence and social standing in agrarian societies – through foreclosures on loans[78] secured by land

claims that it and most Mediterranean cities were 'service' centres. 'The classical city was not parasitical, but was maintained to a large extent through the voluntary exchange of the peasant's agricultural surplus for urban goods and services' (p. 128). The 'consumer city' is a modern (Marxist) ideological construct, a 'myth' (pp. 131–42; cf. Dyson, 1979, p. 94, on the distortions resulting from looking at the ancient town-country unit 'from the town outward'). For a detailed critique of Engels that re-asserts the scholarly *status quo* on the ancient town-country relationship see Saller, 1991.

75   Rutherford, 1989, p. 57. *Loci classici* are Hesiod, *Op.* 225–47 (goodness of rural life vs. the evil city); the pastoral *Idylls* of Theocritus and the *Eclogues* and *Georgics* (esp. 2.493–540) of Virgil; Horace, *Od.* 3.6; Seneca, *Ep.* 90; Dio's *Euboicus* (*Or.* 7). On this 'primitivist' ideal see Lovejoy and Boas, 1935, and on bucolic literature, Reitzenstein, 1893, pp. 193–263. The city-country polarity was widely used by moralists and satirists (e.g., Horace, *Sat.* 2.6; *Ep.* 2.2.65–85; Juvenal, *Sat.* 3). Quintilian places first on his list of declamation topics for school-boys the question, 'Is city or country life better?' (*Inst.* 2.4.24). See Braund, 1989.

76   On the ancient longing for the utopian Golden Age often elaborated in a bucolic vision, see Günther and Müller, 1988, pp. 94–9; Müller, 1981, pp. 189–201; Strasburger, 1976, pp. 96–102; cf. Ferguson, 1975.

77   Cf. the graphic description of Wallace-Hadrill: 'The [city-country] relationship is more visible if we picture the tentacles spread out by the Roman town into its hinterland in the form of aqueducts: symbolically siphoning off...the resources of the land into the urban centre, to feed the public baths where the imported water acts as a focus of sociability, and as a symbol of the "washed" and civilised way of life that rejects the stench of the countryman. Implicit in the aqueduct is a dynamic of power, flowing between country and town' (1991, p. x).

78   Loans generally were not obtained at lending institutions. Peasants relied on landowners to borrow money, seed grain and the like. This of course meant entering into a patron-client relationship. On Luke's familiarity with the problem of loans granted by patrons see Moxnes, 1991a, p. 254.

tightened the bonds of peasant dependence on the wealthy élite and contributed to a 'chronic, politically induced poverty of peasant existence' (Oakman, 1991, p. 159). One of the most pernicious effects of the indebtedness-foreclosure cycle was the phenomenon of 'debt bondage' which Ste. Croix has shown to be commonly and widely practised (1981, pp. 136–7, 162–74; cf. Esler, 1987, p. 174). Debt bondage, the result of defaulting on a loan (or even incurring a debt), put the debtor into a contractual situation of servitude to the creditor, i.e., the defaulting debtor was seized as human collateral asset for debt owed. While the most severe forms of debt bondage included incarceration in private estate prisons,[79] it was more likely that the debtor became an *addictus* ('bondsman') 'whom the law orders to be in servitude [*servire*] until he has paid his debt' (Quintilian, *Institutio Oratoria* 3.6.25).[80] This servitude typically amounted to forced labour at the patron-creditor's pleasure; perhaps it meant working on the land the bondsman once owned; or it could mean being transferred 'from the labour of the fields into *urbana servitia*' (Cassiodorus, *Variae* 8.33; cited by Ste. Croix, 1981, p. 169).

Added to the impoverishment of villagers for the benefit of the urban élite was a deep 'cultural cleavage' of sullen unfriendliness or open hostility between urban aristocracy and the rural peasantry.[81] Ramsay MacMullen cites enough evidence to conclude that, on the one side, a 'universal feeling of aloofness and superiority' marked the city-dweller's view of the rustic. 'The peasant was felt to be an unmannerly, ignorant being, in bondage to sordid and wretched labour, and so uncivilized that he could not be called on for the full

---

[79] Luke is familiar with this from the Q material; see 12.58–9 where the prospect of ending up in prison (εἰς φυλακήν) is clearly tied to unpaid debt. See also 6.34 and 7.41–2 where Luke advocates much more generous lending practices. Cf. Lucian, *Catapl.* 15, where the beggar looks forward to life in the underworld because 'there is no dunning of debtors here and no paying of taxes . . . or being thrashed by more powerful people (τῶν δυνατωτέρων). All are at peace, and the tables are turned, for we paupers laugh while the rich are distressed and lament.'

[80] Ste. Croix, 1981, p. 167, cites numerous passages to indicate that the *addictus* was a standard topic for declamation centred on the question whether the *addictus* is free or not and how he differs from the slave (*servus*).

[81] A. Jones, 1947, p. vii: 'The culture which the cities fostered, though geographically spread over a wide area, was limited to the urban upper class. The great mass of the population, the proletariat of the towns, and still more the peasants of the country remained barbarians.' Ste. Croix, 1981, p. 18, cites Babrius (*Fab. Aesop.* 2.6–8) as evidence that the cultural 'contrast between superior city-dweller and unsophisticated countryman could even be projected into the divine sphere'. The simple-minded (εὐηθεῖς) gods 'inhabit the countryside, while those deities who live within the city wall are infallible and have everything under their supervision'.

92    *Aspects of Lukan performance*

duties of a citizen.' On the other side, rural people looked on urbanites as 'baffling, extortionate, arrogant' (1974, pp. 15, 31–2). Each described the other by means of a discourse that depended on manufacturing cultural contrasts and on cultivating a repertoire of terms to emphasize social polarities – all to say that we are what they are not. Mutual stereotyping buttressed the exclusive identities of city and country cultures and solidified the social boundaries between them.[82]

It may be that Luke relied on his readers' familiarity with the prevailing patterns of interaction between urban aristocracy and rural peasantry. He may have expected readers to infer that the final guests were rural have-nots whose presence at a grand banquet of a wealthy city dweller would have been as outlandish as a crowd of beggars and outcasts within the walls but beyond the pale. Identifying the replacement guests as coming from the wrong side not only of one, but of two solidly fixed social boundaries adds to the perception of distance between host and final guests. To return to our earlier language, it is not impossible to interpret the final invitation to people from outside the city as an additional demotional stroke in Luke's pattern of characterization by means of contraries and polarities.

Though not impossible, the theory that the final guests are country peasants has weaknesses. First, rather than living along country roads and hedges, one would expect peasants to live in a village (κώμη; Rohrbaugh, 1991, p. 144), or, less specifically, in the country round about the city (περίχωρος) or even just the country (ἀγρός) or district (χώρα), all spaces that Luke knows how to coordinate quite correctly with the πόλις.[83] Second, Douglas Oakman has shown that despite Luke's 'passing interest in the countryside as an object of evangelization' and his general famili-

[82] For this as a common form of cross-cultural interaction see Al-Azmeh, 1992, p. 3: 'States, civilizations and cultures expend much energy [on the cultivation of contraries] ... in fixing moral boundaries, consolidating their difference from outsiders, and otherwise encircling themselves with [impermeable] frontiers ... Classification in terms of polarity is one of the most elementary forms of collective representation, and one almost universally encountered in cross-cultural discourse.' Al-Azmeh's description of the medieval 'Arab construction of barbarism' is an apt analogue to the ancient Mediterranean urban snobbery towards the ἄγροικος whose low score on the index of urban Hellenic culture qualified her/him as βάρβαρος ('boorish', 'outlandish', in Hellenistic times; see Ste. Croix, 1981, p. 17).
[83] Πόλις/κώμη: 5.17, 8.1, 13.22, 19.28–30, 24.13; πόλις/περίχωρος: 4.31–7, 8.37(?), Acts 14.6; πόλις/ἀγρός: 8.34; πόλις/χώρα: 2.4–8, 21.21; Acts 10.39, 13.14–49, cf. 16.12.

arity with the economic and social conditions of rural life, the gospel writer 'does not seem to take a pro-countryside stance' in a way that represents the real political and economic interests of the peasantry (1991, pp. 170–1). A telling illustration is provided by another Lukan analogy that makes use of a landlord, his farm labourer and conventional dining proprieties to persuade readers towards a thankless and unrewarded servant posture as a matter of duty:

> Will any one of you, who has a servant plowing or keeping sheep, say to him when he has come in from the field (ἀγροῦ), 'Come at once and sit down at table?' Will he not rather say to him, 'Prepare supper for me, and gird yourself and serve me, till I eat and drink; and afterwards you shall eat and drink?' Does he thank the servant because he did what was commanded? So you also, when you have done all that is commanded you, say, 'We are unworthy servants; we have only done what was our duty'. (Luke 17.7–10)[84]

These weaknesses stand in the way of a sure identification of the 'roads and hedges' people as rural peasants.[85] Rather than looking for them far afield, it is worth considering a second option.

It may be that the final guests are drawn from the ranks of those people who lived close to the city precincts because their livelihood depended on the city, but not within the city walls because the nature of their business was too naturally noxious, socially odious or religiously suspect. Cemeteries, for instance, were always located outside the city (C. Schneider, 1967, vol. II, p. 212) and all those engaged in the undertaking business came to be called οἱ ἐξωπυλεῖτοι ('those [who live] outside the gate').[86] Tanners too normally plied

---

[84] See Acts 6.1–6 for another Lukan example of using dinner conventions to reinforce status divisions that follow predictable Greco-Roman lines. Here the preacher (philosopher) does not wait on tables; for this others are elected. Cf. Luke 22.27 for a contradictory example!

[85] Rohrbaugh adds a further objection by invoking the criterion of verisimilitude: 'An already prepared banquet ... would not allow travel to neighboring villages to seek participants' (1991, pp. 144–5). True enough, but why insist on verisimilitude in a fictive story that strains believability at many points? All the actions in the parable, including three trips by the slave, happen after the dinner is prepared (see: ἤδη ἕτοιμά ἐστιν). One must in any case imagine stale *hors d'oeuvres* and cold casseroles by the time the affair actually begins, notwithstanding that the slave is told to 'go quickly' (ἔξελθε ταχέως)!

[86] See the detailed discussion of evidence from papyri and ostraca by Youtie, 1940, pp. 650–7. He establishes convincingly that at least corpse transporters (νεκροτάφοι), embalmers (ἐνταφιασταί), funerary wailers (θρηνηταί) and cemetary guards

their trade outside the city and likely lived there along with drovers, slaughterers and others involved in the less savoury aspects of butchery.[87] Along with these we might expect an assortment of refugee aliens, disenfranchised villagers, run-away slaves, prostitutes, roving beggars and various shunned ill to live on the outside perimeter of the city.[88]

Herbert Youtie points out that the ἐξωπυλεῖτοι were of the lowest social status whose contemporaries called them 'ignoble' (ἄσεμνοι; 1940, p. 656). Ramsay MacMullen places 'the folks beyond the gates' within a constellation of values where social prejudices are aligned with matching places of residence. 'The closer to the heart of the city, the more respectable; the farther away, the more scorned' (1974, p. 71). If the 'roads and hedges' point to a specific but distanced location within the urban system, as Richard Rohrbaugh justifiably insists, the conclusion properly follows that the final guests 'were neither of the city nor of the country. They were afforded neither the protection of the city walls nor attachment to a village. Socially they were isolated from city elite, city non-elite, and villagers alike' (Rohrbaugh, 1991, p. 145).

As for characterization, the outcome is similar to the one we noted in connection with the first option. The final guests are severely distanced from the social orbit of the banquet host. They are from the lowest ranks one could possibly find within the ancient urban environs.

Confirmation and a further underlining stroke is provided by two

(νεκροφύλακες) were among the beyond-the-gate folks, but this designation may have been applied to others as well. Cf. MacMullen, 1974, pp. 71, 175 n. 54.

[87] Note Acts 10.5–6 (a tanner living παρὰ θάλασσαν; see the relevant comment by Cadbury, 1926, pp. 306–7 n. 4). Juvenal lampoons the avaricious entrepreneur who feels 'no disgust at a trade [tannery] that must be banished to the other side of the Tiber ... the smell of gain is good whatever the thing [hides] from which it comes' (*Sat.* 14.201–4). See MacMullen, 1974, pp. 70–1; and Rohrbaugh, 1991, pp. 144–5.

[88] On beggars loitering ἐν ταῖς τριόδοις (at the crossroads) outside the city see Lucian, *Necyo.* 17; *Catapl.* 7; *DMort.* 1.331 (where Menippus looks for his δεῖπνον ἐν τῇ τριόδῳ ῾Εκάτης). See generally also Bolkestein, 1939, p. 209; Luz, 1989, p. 57; and Rohrbaugh, 1991, p. 145. Luke evidently is quite familiar with the general phenomenon. See 18.35 (τυφλός τις ἐκάθητο παρὰ τὴν ὁδὸν ἐπαιτῶν) and 8.27 where Jesus meets a demon-possessed man once from the city (ἐκ τῆς πόλεως) now living not in a house, but in the tombs (ἐν τοῖς μνήμασιν). Cf. Lucian, *Vit. auct.* 9 (satirizing the Cynics by using Diogenes as his mouthpiece): 'Leaving the home of your fathers, you will lodge (οἰκήσεις) in a tomb, in an abandoned watch tower [usually part of city walls], or even an urn (ἢ τάφον ἢ πυργίον ἔρημον ἢ καὶ πίθον).' On the poor and stigmatized ill ('mad' people) living in tombs and funerary urns see Luz, 1989, pp. 55–6.

additional narrative details. The first is the ostensible motive for the final invitation: ἵνα γεμισθῇ μου ὁ οἶκος (14.23; cf. 14.22, ἔτι τόπος ἐστίν). Recalling that the urban poor and sick have already taken their place in the dining room, this detail serves as a notation of the impressive size of the host's facility, itself a sure signal of the man's wealth. Within the context of the invitation to 'the folks beyond the gate', this oblique reminder of who is issuing the invitation insinuatively presses for recognition of the extreme gap between inviter and invited.

Second, and not surprisingly, Luke opts for the most forceful language of invitation of the entire episode at this point.[89] 'Make them enter by force of insistent persuasion' (ἀνάγκασον εἰσελθεῖν).[90] Often this language is simply taken to refer to an 'oriental courtesy', a code of modesty that requires those invited to go through a show of resistance before accepting an invitation.[91] Jülicher too casually thought that the riff-raff ('das scheue Gesindel') hiding in the hedges was 'shy' and needed to be 'encouraged' to come to the feast (1910, vol. II, p. 415).

These views are not so much out of place as they are understated. Although they implicitly understand that the folks beyond the gate will not come voluntarily, much less eagerly, they fail to explain

---

89 Jülicher, 1910, vol. II, p. 415, already noted a 'Steigerung im Modus der Anbietung' within the parable, but he dismissed this as insignificant; the evangelist used this escalating invitational language without 'Bewusstsein'. However, in his subsequent commentary he does acknowledge that each invitation is 'das unter den betreffenden Verhältnissen Geeignete', even if he fails to explain what this might mean. See also G. Clark, 1876, p. 335: 'Notice a gradation in the urgency of the calls. Simply, *say come*, ver. 17; *bring in*, ver. 21; *compel*, ver. 23'.

90 On this see Sutcliffe, 1953, pp. 20–1. Evidently embarrassed by the history of forced conversion tactics (*compelle intrare*; see Norwood, 1953–4) by Christian crusaders, Sutcliffe softens the force of ἀναγκάζω by limiting its meaning to moral persuasion by convincing argument (e.g., Plato, *Gorg.* 472B) that preserves the freedom of the one who is to be compelled. This may be the sense of the term in Luke 14.23, even though it does commonly connote more forceful compulsion, including physical constraint and imprisonment (see LSJ, s.v.). Traditionally, ἀνάγκη was associated with δουλεία. See Thomson, 1938, vol. II, p. 345: 'The ideas of δουλεία and ἀνάγκη are almost inseparable in Greek, the word ἀνάγκη being constantly used to denote both the state of slavery as such [numerous references] and also the torture to which slaves were subjected.' He also points to the Orphic myth where Ἀνάγκη stands over Sisyphus with lash in hand.

91 Jeremias, 1963, p. 177. Similarly, Grundmann, 1961, p. 300; Hahn, 1970, p. 59; Fitzmyer, 1985, p. 1057; and many others. Bailey, 1980, p. 108, elaborates this with reference to modern Mediterranean practices (see Lucian, *Gall.* 9, for shame and honour as factors in invitational protocol). Manson's stress on the 'insistent hospitality' (1949, p. 130) of the host perhaps implies this custom, but is designed to accent the host's magnanimity.

sufficiently why it is precisely to the people along the highways and
hedges that the invitation has to be most aggressive. The forcefulness
of the invitational language indicates that the last guests know that
their social place perforce (ἀνάγκη) of conventional propriety
prohibits dining with people in high places.⁹² An affective posture of
suspicion alone would prevent the poor from going to a rich person's
house for dinner. Their 'negative expectations' (Moxnes, 1991a,
p. 264) of the rich as acting generously only out of self-interest
would cause the poor to suspect hidden motives in a dinner
invitation from a rich townsman. Even if these suspicions should be
overcome, the poor knew what everyone else knew, namely that
dinner invitations normally were issued within the rubric of balanced reciprocity. Under this system, requiring that a gift or favour
be returned in comparable measure, they simply could not afford to
be entertained by the rich.⁹³ Against this background it is not
difficult to account for Luke's forceful language. Bringing the poor
into the rich householder's dining hall would require a counter-
ἀνάγκη in order to break through the social barriers and to
overcome the affective distance between urban outsiders (ἐξωπυλεῖτοι) and élite insiders, to which group the inviting host belongs.⁹⁴

⁹² Rohrbaugh, 1991, p. 145, is, I believe, the first commentator on Luke's dinner
parable to see this. The general principle is stated by Dover, 1974, p. 239: '[A]
certain reluctance on the part of the Greeks to associate with those who may have
incurred the displeasure of the gods ... [namely the poor and the sick] must have
tended to diminish the expectation of the poor and the sick that they would be
treated compassionately, and to increase their desire to hide their misfortune, if
need be, by avoiding contacts.'
⁹³ Neyrey, 1991b, p. 385: 'A person of meager means must decline an invitation from
a wealthy person to dine because this would put the poor man at an enormous
financial obligation to reciprocate with a rich, comparable meal for the wealthy
person.' Cf. the strenuous efforts by someone such as Hippolytus to amend the
patterns of patronage and reciprocity to make it easier for the poor to participate
in the Christian communal meal (Bobertz, 1993).
⁹⁴ There is a mild irony in my (and in Luke's?) use of ἀναγκάζειν here. Dover, 1974,
p. 109, has noted that 'the Greeks used the words "compel" (anankazein) and
"compulsion" (anankē) in speaking of [the] temptation [of the poor to choose
crimes over starvation]'. See, e.g., Isocrates, 17.18; Lysias, 7.13–14. Moreover,
ἀνάγκη is a Stoic *terminus technicus* and, along with δουλεία, an important
antonym of ἐλευθερια. In part, the doctrine of freedom, a pillar of the Stoic social
ideal of ὁμόνοια, was asserted against social structures and relationships where
the few ruled the many and where people found themselves in ἐπιπλοκὰς καὶ
συνδέσεις ἔξωθεν ἀνάγκαις καὶ δόξαις κατεχομένας γίνεσθαι, 'unions and
bonds brought about by external compulsions and opinions' (SVF 3.630). This the
Stoics considered the predicament of the low, common person (φαῦλος) over
against which stands the good person (σπουδαῖος) who οὔτε ἀναγκάζεται ὑπό
τινος οὔτε ἀναγκάζει τινά, 'is neither compelled by anybody nor compels
anyone' (SVF 3.567; both quotations are attributed to Chrysippus; see the detailed

The mode of 'invitation' thus is deeply conscious of the effort that would be necessary for them to meet for dinner. This social awareness evident in the choice of invitational vocabulary indirectly yet unmistakably discloses the distance that separates these two parties. All the narrative clues concerning the last invitation thus cohere. Together they generate maximum distance between the banquet host and the final guests. They do this by demoting the last guests to the lowest social position, while reminding readers of the élite position of the dinner host. The third invitation is a fine final éclat in Luke's strokes of promotion and demotion in the portraiture of the parable's characters.

Before concluding the analysis of Luke's reworking of the dinner story, we need to take up the question that was suggested at the beginning of this section on Luke's redactional tendencies. Is there a purpose that embraces the enlargement of the dinner party and the polarized portraiture of the story's *dramatis personae*? This question of course asks what the story is all about. Though the answer is partly dependent on a clarification of the parable's analogical function in the dinner story as a whole, some directions towards an answer are embedded in the parable itself. In the next chapter I will try to show that Luke's redactional tendencies make for good sense when they are appraised with reference to the householder as the story's primary and pivotal character for whom the bridging of the distance between the urban well-placed and displaced requires nothing less than a 'conversion' of his moral and social values and conduct.

discussion by Erskine, 1990, pp. 52–8). I am not arguing that Luke is alluding to Stoic views on necessities, only suggesting that, like the Stoics, he seems to be aware of social divisions kept intact by 'necessity', a force traditionally akin to 'fate' (Dover, 1974, p. 140 n. 141).

# 6

## THE CONVERSION OF A WEALTHY
## HOUSEHOLDER

The result of Luke's redactional characterization within the parable is, as I suggested in the previous chapter, the creation of status distance between the élite banqueters, including the wealthy host and his upper-crust equals, and the two parties of secondary guests. The point of the story, however, is that this distance, which readers would understand to be created and maintained by Hellenistic social conventions that imposed themselves with a force which we might think of as a kind of cultural ἀνάγκη, is mitigated if not definitively negated by the deliberate and forceful action of the host. The host thus moves to centre stage in the story.

In itself this is not an entirely novel observation. Noticing the householder's paradigmatic importance within the parable is the common stuff of the commentaries where it is suitable for service in a variety of interpretive strategies, whether allegorical, eschatological or, less often, paraenetical. Rarely, however, is the parable deliberately read in its entirety as a story about a *host* who invites guests rather than as a story about *guests* invited by a host. Re-aiming the reading focus more deliberately towards the householder is not an arbitrary, unaccountable matter of preference. On the contrary, it recommends itself from various angles. Focus on the host will enable us to see the coherence and purpose of the Lukan redactional tendencies. The move also follows the patent lead of the narrative itself. Compared to the flatly functional (slave) and contrastively balanced but statically portrayed support characters (various sets of guests), the householder is a most impressively nuanced figure. Not only is he the only constant character in the story, initiating the action and having the last word (14.24), but also the only one who undergoes a dramatic change in social affiliation, implying a prior change of moral and social views. The plot of the story clearly turns on the central character (the householder), thus following a rather stable feature of the compositional pattern in folk tales. As Anna Bihari-Andersson points out, one of the regularities of folk tales is that they focus on a single character as the 'compositional pivot' in accordance with 'the rule of centring around the hero' (1987, p. 94).

Even when the householder is given attention, his role is usually not analysed within the context of Hellenistic 'cultural scripts'[1] that prescribed and proscribed the *propria* of typical dinner hosts from the ranks of the élite. Hence, the question of how evidence of this sort might clarify the actions of the host in the parable remains largely unasked. The few very recent exceptions to the traditional commentary efforts are brief,[2] but important in their attempt to locate Luke's fictional dinner host within the rules of the dining culture of Mediterranean élites, where factors of alimentation and amusement – the convivial celebrations of the good life in an atmosphere of friendliness (φιλοφροσύνη) and casual intimacy (συνήθεια), as Plutarch is wont to put it (e.g., *Pericles*, 7.4–5) – play a secondary even if instrumental role in the competition for positive peer appraisals, the soft currency of honour so essential for maintaining or improving one's position in Luke's culture. What follows solidifies and builds upon these earlier observations on the Lukan host.

The host's role and character in the story becomes visible in a sequence of (1) his quest for honour within the community of the élite, a quest that (2) is denied him by the very people whose approval he desires, which leads him (3) to abandon the circle of the élite and the values and social codes they represent. Each move in this sequence is distinctly profiled; each entails implications for the host's reputation and for who will be the social reference group[3]

---

[1] The phrase is borrowed from Gowler, 1991, p. 15. It refers to the general cultural sensibilities and patterns of social interaction in which a particular text is embedded. These codes may be explicitly alluded to, but more often they are implicitly assumed by the text itself and presumably familiar to and taken for granted by the original readers. They are 'part of the social matrix' (p. 15) that generated the writing and reading of Luke's gospel. Gowler's analysis of the Pharisees in Luke-Acts informatively relies on the 'cultural scripts' of honour/ shame, patron/client, contract/limited good, etc., that cultural anthropological analyses of Mediterranean societies have identified as particularly central.

[2] Scott, 1989, pp. 169, 171–2; Gowler, 1991, pp. 248–50 (containing suggestive categories but not applied to the role of the dinner host); Rohrbaugh, 1991, pp. 141–3. Cf. the sketchy attempt by Bossmann, 1991, p. 3; and the suggestive paragraph by Kloppenborg, 1989, p. 493.

[3] The idea of the reference group is an important concept in social transaction theory. Festinger, for example, argues that people seek to measure themselves, their abilities, merit and status, against a reliable, objective standard. Since such 'objec-

within whose orbit of values he will seek to acquire reputation, self-worth and positive acknowledgment, in short, honour.[4]

## The big dinner and the quest for honour

The preparation-summons (ἐποίει ... ἐκάλεσεν) sequence opens the story. It was likely that this was the opening of the pre-Lukan narrative,[5] and therefore in itself not of great value for disclosing Luke's redactional tendencies. Yet, the fact that it was a mega-banquet prepared for the host's wealthy peers (which is a signal from Luke's hand) implies a measure of self-display designed to

tive, nonsocial means are not available, people evaluate their opinions and abilities by comparison ... with the opinions and abilities of others' (1954, p. 118). The reference group, which may but need not be a membership group, is not selected at random; it consists of people with similar status attributes. In societies where honour is closely linked to status, it follows that a person 'is answerable for his honour only to his social equals, that is to say, to those with whom he can conceptually compete' (Pitt-Rivers, 1977b, p. 31).

[4] That honour and shame were 'pivotal values' in ancient Mediterranean societies is familiar to gospel scholars, much due to Malina's work. See especially 1981, pp. 25–50; and Malina and Neyrey, 1991b; cf. Daube, 1982, pp. 356–7, 359. Two other bodies of literature have contributed to my understanding of the wide diffusion of 'what people will say' (Adkins, 1960, pp. 48–9) as a powerful motivating and controlling force in virtually all domains of Greco-Roman social interaction: (1) from cultural anthropology, Peristiany, 1966; Pitt-Rivers, 1963; 1977b; J. Davis, 1977, pp. 89–101; Abu-Lughod, 1986, esp. pp. 78–117, 186–207; Gouldner, 1965, ch. 2; (2) from classical scholarship, Adkins, 1960, pp. 154–6; Dover, 1974, pp. 226–42; Friedrich, 1977, esp. pp. 290–4; Lloyd-Jones, 1990; Walcot, 1970, ch. 4; 1978, pp. 15–21. The *locus classicus* of the 'human passion for τιμή' is Xenophon, *Hier.* 7.3–4 (see Whitehead, 1983, p. 57); the most concise classical definition of honour (εὐδοξία) and its manifestations (μέρη) is in Aristotle, *Rhet.* 1361a.22–30. Caveat: Herzfeld, 1980, cautions against treating the Mediterranean as a homogeneous, 'discrete cultural zone' and warns against 'massive generalizations' of 'honour' and 'shame' as the 'pivotal' (Malina) concepts in the Mediterranean taxonomy of values. Positively, he argues for the priority of 'ethnographic particularism' (p. 349). This is very sensible, but the ethnographer's methods are not easily applicable to ancient societies and problematic when our primary datum is a written text (Luke) whose particular social setting is unknown us. To locate such a text culturally thus requires some measure of apriorism, that is, to insist on the utility of generalized honour and shame as analytic terms (see J. Davis's defence of the idea of a common circum-Mediterranean culture, 1977, pp. 10–16; cf. Malina and Neyrey, 1991a; Garrett, 1989, pp. 5–9).

[5] See the reconstruction of the received story above. The preparation-summons sequence is a widely diffused literary convention in banquet descriptions. See Lichtenstein, 1968, and the examples from ancient Near Eastern literature cited there. Though typical, this sequence is sometimes reversed; see, e.g., Plutarch, *De garr.* (*Mor.* 511D-E): 'Piso ... invited [Clodius] to dinner and prepared ... a sumptuous banquet'; cf. the ambiguous sequence in *G.Thom.* 64:1, which I noted earlier.

make an impression – not unlike the more explicitly extreme ostentatious dining habits of another well-known Lukan ἄνθρωπός τις (16.19). It is further evident that this is no 'sudden dinner' spontaneously arranged as a casual sympotic respite among friends after a day of work.⁶ This is conveyed by the two-step invitation procedure, which, even if traditional, is clarified and accentuated by Luke.⁷ Though the advance notice-summons pattern is not unusual,⁸ nor the employment of a slave as κλητήρ or *vocator* (summoner) out of the ordinary,⁹ it should be recognized that this manner of invitation is a very formal and ritualized procedure. Contrastively, for a more casual, relatively spontaneous dinner, 'invitations were often given on the same day, and by the host in person, who sought out, in the market-place or the gymnasium, those whom he desired to invite'.¹⁰ This rather casual, impromptu way of getting company for supper is in fact Luke's usual method of narrating how people end up eating together.¹¹ Luke's departure

6  Against Crossan, 1973, p. 73; rightly chided by Rohrbaugh, 1991, p. 141. Crossan takes a different line in 1985, pp. 44–5. Cf. the report of such an informal dinner by Aulus Gellius, *NA* 17.8.1–2: 'The philosopher Taurus at Athens usually entertained us [his students] at dinner at the time of day when evening had already come on; for there that is the time for dining. The entire basis and foundation of the meal usually consisted of one pot of Egyptian beans, to which were added gourds cut in small pieces' (trans. Rolfe, LCL).

7  The two-step invitation, consisting of an advance notice and a summons at the actual dinner hour (14.15, 16), is more clearly evident than in Matthew and Thomas. The fetching of the guests τῇ ὥρᾳ τοῦ δείπνου appears to be a Lukan detail, indicating not only that the writer understood the two-step procedure but that it had to be highlighted in the parable.

8  The two-stage invitation is a well-attested Mediterranean custom (e.g., Esther 5.8, 6.14; Philo, *Opif.* 78; *Lam.R.* 4.2; Str-B, vol. I, p. 880, for other rabbinic examples; Plutarch, *Mor.* 511D-E), practised especially among members of the upper classes. Among modern commentators see especially Bailey, 1980, pp. 94–5.

9  E.g., Plutarch mentions that the host Piso owned a domestic who regularly carried invitations (τὸν εἰωθότα καλεῖν οἰκέτην; *Mor.* 511E). Lucian comically describes the crowd of toadies 'in conference with the dispensers of dinner invitations' (ἐπὶ τὰ δεῖπνα παραγγέλλουσι κοινολογούμενον; *Nigr.* 24). The role of the *vocator* in Roman *convivia* was already noted by Plummer, 1914, p. 360, but is now more fully described (with many textual references) by D'Arms, 1991, pp. 172, 181 nn. 4–8. See also Kim, 1975, p. 397 and n. 6.

10  Becker and Göll, 1866, p. 315. The only reference to warrant this comment is to Plato's *Symposium*. Their notice that 'this free and easy custom' belongs to the Classical period and that 'at a later period greater formality was observed' is inaccurate even as a generalization. Lucian's wealthy host Eucrates, for example, personally delivers a dinner invitation when he met someone (apparently on the street) by a stroke of τύχη (*Gall.* 9); see the next footnote for a profile of Luke's narrations of the invitation.

11  (1) Jesus' encounter with Levi in the tax-office (τελώνιον) results in a great feast (δοχὴν μεγάλην) in Levi's house (5.27–8). Although the story is of Markan origin,

from his usual pattern further underscores the need to take stock of the formal two-step invitation in the parable.

The delay between invitation and summons at dinner time undoubtedly served various purposes (see Rohrbaugh, 1991, p. 141). Practically, the kitchen staff would need to know in advance for how many diners to prepare; the first invitation thus served to generate a guest list in numerical terms (cf. Bailey, 1980, p. 94). For formal banquets, guests needed sufficient time to arrange for suitable apparel and jewellery, for dinner time was show time.[12] Plutarch alludes to both of these reasons in his *Dinner of the Seven Wise Men*: 'Do you not honestly believe that, as some preparation is necessary on the part of the man who is to be host, there should also be some preparation on the part of him who is to be a guest at dinner?' (*Septem sapientium convivium* 147E; cf. Athenaeus, *The Deipnosophists* 521C). In addition, since dinner invitations were dispensed within a cycle of reciprocity that characterized Greco-Roman hospitality (and beneficence generally),[13] offers of hospitality had to be considered carefully for the 'strings attached' to them, for the implied obligations and their cost that came along with accepting the offer.[14]

Luke has heavily edited it in order to make it unambiguous that Levi is the host and that the occasion is a feast (see Steele, 1984, pp. 390–2). There is no invitational language, but the implied scenario is that a chance encounter with an admirer leads to table fellowship. (2) Jesus' participation in two of Luke's Pharisaic *deipna* (7.36–50, 11.37–52) seems to be the result of a spontaneous invitation issued by Pharisees in the crowd of listeners. The episode of 14.1–24 does not begin with an expressed invitation, but it is implied in 14.12. We are not told that the invitation was spontaneous, but neither are we urged to assume it was premeditated and issued in the two-step sequence of 14.16–17. Note (3) the rather casual manner in which Jesus ends up as the guest of Zacchaeus (19.5–7; assuming this story implicitly refers to dinner hospitality, on which see Hamm, 1991, p. 250), and (4) the invitation imposed on Jesus by travellers on the road (Luke 24.28–30).

12  The theatrical dimension of going to dinner is exemplified by Plutarch's host, Periander, who dispatched carriages to fetch his guests at the appointed dinner hour and ceremoniously paraded them through the colonnades into the dining room (*Conv.sept.sap.* [*Mor.*] 146D, 148C). Lucian's description of the hireling with ambitions for upward mobility at the dinner scene in 'great houses' is rhetorically aimed, but nevertheless reveals how important it was to be 'conspicuous' (περί-βλεπτον) among 'men of noble family and high social position' (*De merc.cond.* 9). The linking of dinners/symposia and theatre is not facile. Bek, 1983, p. 101, has shown that even the *triclinium* arrangements emphasized visual access to fellow diners and sympotic entertainment; on the connection between symposia and theatre (and vice versa) see Pellizer, 1990, and C. Jones, 1991.

13  See the discussion of 14.12–14 in ch. 4, pp. 54–61. On the alternation of roles (reciprocity) between guest and host see also the comments by Pitt-Rivers, 1977a, p. 102. Cf. Rohrbaugh, 1991, p. 141: 'Reciprocity in regard to meals was expected in the culture of Luke.'

14  When symposia are subject to the law of reciprocity and when they are, moreover, a primary locale for the social display of self, one can easily imagine the financial

Perhaps the most important purpose of the two-step invitation has been signalled recently by Richard Rohrbaugh. On the basis of the 'nearly complete social stratification of pre-industrial cities' which kept trans-strata social interaction to a minimum, he suggests that 'the time between invitations would allow opportunity for potential guests to find out what the festive occasion might be, who is coming, and whether all had been done appropriately in arranging the dinner. Only then would the discerning guest be comfortable showing up' (1991, p. 141). One might not want to generalize quite so broadly,[15] but the importance of who else might be coming is quite correctly noted. In his *Symposion* Plutarch once more provides the corroborating evidence with the example of Chilon who 'showed most excellent judgment when he received his invitation yesterday, in not agreeing to come until he had learned the name of every person invited' (*Septem sapientium convivium* 148A). The reasons for Chilon's caution are similar to those stated in Plutarch's *Table Talk*, cited in our earlier comments on Luke 14.12–14. That is, nobody wants to come to a dinner unless he can be assured that the other symposiasts are 'the right kind of guest[s]' (*Septem sapientium convivium* 147E; cf. *Quaestiones convivales* 708D, 709A-B), people who move within similar social circles and who therefore share similar views and values. But how Plutarch defines the 'correct dinner companion' (ὀρθὸς σύνδειπνος) need not concern us here, even though this writer must be considered as one of the most important contributors to the Hellenistic definition of the ideal symposiast. The noteworthy point is that within the circles of the cultured élite, invited guests apparently did make it their business to find out who else was on the guest list and then made their decision on whether to accept the offer of table hospitality.

Some inferences may be drawn from the parable's formulaic and formal invitational scheme, even though, unfortunately, it does not specify an exact motive for the dinner, nor give us enough infor-

burden that they represented for the philotimic host, a fact that was a target for the satirists (Hudson, 1989, pp. 81–2, 86). A telling example of this concern for the ancients is found in the repeated discussions of the high price of flute players (standard at cultured tables), to the extent that in classical Athens, at least, their fees were fixed by law, the only evidence of 'wage controls' in antiquity (Starr, 1978, pp. 406–7).

15 The nature of the festive occasion would be specified in the invitation itself (Kim, 1975). That arrangements had been 'done appropriately' would be of little concern if a guest knew the inviting host, although in the case of travelling political dignitaries – Augustus is a luminous example – there are reports of advance scouts being sent to select the wine (Pliny, *N.H.* 14.72; see D'Arms, 1991, p. 174).

mation to identify the host's relative position within the city's upper echelons. If he was a man of low ascribed honour, an errant rich person, who was on a mission to acquire honour with new-found or disreputably earned wealth,[16] someone like Petronius' Trimalchio or the oft-mentioned tax collector Bar Ma'jan of the Palestinian Talmud (*Sanhedrin* 6.23c, *Ḥagiga* 2.77d), the invitation is a token of his aspiration to be acknowledged by and included in the upper social circles.[17] Hellenistic *nouveaux riches* and other toadies trying to slither into the corridors of the establishment through the aristocratic *triclinium* likely were not uncommon figures, if one is allowed to infer this from the fact just such figures show up as targets for satirical ridicule (e.g., Lucian, *Nigrinus* 22). If, on the other hand, and far more likely (see below), the host's social credentials were well intact, the dinner invitation still would be an expected ceremonial replication of his commitment to the values of aristocratic culture.[18] Beyond this, hosting dinner parties was among the most central of means by which the competition for pride of place among equals and the zealous preservation (or enhancement) of honour[19] was carried out in patterns of balanced reci-

---

[16] For the distinction between 'ascribed' and 'acquired' honour, i.e., the difference between honour derived from birth in an aristocratic family and honour actively sought by activities recognized as honourable, see Pitt-Rivers, 1977b, pp. 22–3; Malina and Neyrey, 1991b, pp. 27–9.

[17] The story of Bar Ma'jan is told to illustrate why an errant man received a good burial. The story itself goes thus: 'He never did a meritorious deed in his life. But one time he made a banquet for the councilors of his town but they did not come. He said, Let the poor come and eat the food, so that it not go to waste' (trans. Neusner, *Talmud of the Land of Israel*, vol. xxxi, p. 182). The story is a tricky analogy to the dinner parable, and its utility as 'flood-light' (Jeremias, 1963, p. 179) for illuminating the latter is often overestimated. W. Salm ('Beiträge zur Gleichnisforschung', [Diss., Göttingen, 1953], pp. 144–6; not available to me), cited approvingly by Jeremias, thought that the original (= Jesus') parable was an allusion to the Bar Ma'jan example, but they did not explain how Jesus could be 'making use' (Jeremias, 1963, p. 178) of a story that first appears 'half a millennium' later (Goulder, 1989, p. 592). Further, there is no warrant for using the talmudic story as a basis for identifying the Lukan host as a tax-collector, as Jeremias (p. 179) and many others after him would have it. Nevertheless, Bar Ma'jan justifiably illustrates how a rich person might attempt to use the dinner party as a means of parlaying economic wealth into positive evaluations from those whose opinions are convertible to public honour.

[18] Slater, 1991b, p. 3: 'To go dining [and to give dinners] was to show...that one knew and conformed to the ideals and traditions of a culture ... The ideals of the symposium are cultural ideals, and the well-organized and successful symposium is the vehicle for their expression.'

[19] Rathje argues from archaeological evidence that 'the banquet as the most conspicuous expression of the lifestyle of the aristocracy, be it Greek or Etruscan or Latin, represents the cultural *koine*' (1990, p. 279).

procity,[20] not to speak of the dinner party as an essential forum for furthering ambitions and expanding one's sphere of influence within the 'private space' of the Hellenistic city.[21] In either case, the way the invitation is narrated allows us softly to infer that it signifies an action aimed to secure admiration and respect and thus status and reputation within the conservative social reference group of the wealthy élite.[22] The invitation is a gesture of a desire for affiliation or to remain affiliated. It represents the Lukan host's striving to construct his social biography in terms of allegiance to a particular class of people, the urban élite. As we noted earlier, these élites stood exclusively over against others in the social organization of the city. They wove the fabric of their exclusive 'sociability'[23] in balanced patterns of giving and going to dinners and drinking parties there to preserve or enhance (and occasionally damage!) their public *personae*, which they would gamely negotiate through the maze of manners and cause to effloresce in displays of erudition[24] and other

---

[20] On 'balanced reciprocity', a structure for social exchange and relationships among equals where a gift is always repaid by the recipient, see Moxnes, 1986–7, p. 164; 1989, pp. 127–38; 1991a; 1991b, pp. 64–7; Neyrey, 1991b, pp. 355–6 (sub-section on 'meals and reciprocity'); cf. Pitt-Rivers, 1977a, p. 102.

[21] Jameson, 1990, p. 190, commenting on the sympotic use of the ἀνδρών: '[C]ommon would have been the use of these rooms for the many social contacts between the heads of households, out of the glare of public spaces. Farm and business deals, marriage negotiations, politics on the local level and relating to the numerous cult organizations to which Greek men belonged, would have been carried on by means of hospitality in the private house.' See Pliny, *Ep.* 9.23.4–5, for an example of name-dropping and 'networking' at a *convivium*. On the point generally, see also D'Arms, 1984, pp. 347–8.

[22] In terms of social group formation or maintenance, the conservative function of aristocratic symposia is well known; already in Homeric and classical times the symposium emerged as a formal metaphor for the *polis* insofar as the well-conducted, orderly symposium is a miniature parallel to civic life generally, as seen from the vantage point of the aristocrats. See Levine, 1985; and, on the ideological and practical function of Homer's 'great hall', Wickert-Micknat, 1990, esp. pp. 131–6; cf. Klosinski, 1988, pp. 65–75, where he attends to symposia and their replication and mediation of aristocratic civic ideals. In Hellenistic times, the connections between symposium and civic ideals are probably more complex, but one does not need to read long in Plutarch, for example, to realize that for him the symposium is a symbol of stability and conservation of traditional aristocratic culture in unstable times.

[23] On 'sociability,' the shared ideological and behavioural patterns by which various fraternities and associations achieve their unity, and the symposium see Schmitt-Pantel, 1990, pp. 200–7, 212–3. Cf. Murray, 1982, and M. Miller, 1991.

[24] The popularity of handbooks on manners (see D'Arms, 1990, p. 317) and sympotic miscellanies, such as Plutarch's *Table Talk*, Athenaeus' *Deipnosophists* and Aulus Gellius' *Attic Nights*, indicates the pride taken by the Greco-Roman élite in at least appearing learned. This veneer of erudition in a sympotic context was a common target for the satirists (e.g., Persius, *Sat.* 1). Holford-Strevens' comment on Gellius is apropos: '[T]his social erudition, by now habitual with the Roman élite, enabled the rising rich to display the general education of the gentleman and

often theatrical, ostentatious and agonistic 'rituals of dinner' (Visser, 1991).[25]

## The shame of peer rejection

When the story-teller reports that the invited guests ἀπὸ μιᾶς refused to heed the summons to dinner, readers are to understand that this is a surprising about-face on the guests' previous acceptance (see Jülicher, 1910, vol. II, p. 411). Alfred Plummer's paraphrastic translation of ἀπὸ μιᾶς points out two other features of the refusal that are worth noting: 'it was like a prearranged conspiracy'; there was 'absolute unanimity' (1914, p. 361).[26] A mis-timed, rude refusal, prearranged and unanimously (πάντες) agreed on: these round out the key issues in the sparsely described behaviour of the invited dinner company. Puzzlement over this behaviour is a standard feature in scholarly commentaries; attempted solutions usually focus on the guests and concern themselves with the plausibility of the refusing action and the search for a legitimate cause for the excuses.[27] Jeremias, for example, considered this scenario to be

the orator ... In this satisfied age, the collection of existing knowledge engaged more zeal than the pursuit of new; but the demand for its diffusion that accompanied the greater comfort of the upper class encouraged the writing of handbooks to help their readers shine at cultured tables. One of these was Gellius' *Attic Nights* (1988, p. 6). On the ideal of the *urbanus homo* see the excellent treatment by Ramage, 1973, pp. 111–43; and Quintilian, *Inst.* 6.3.103–12, esp. 105 (quoting Domitius Marsus, *On Urbanity*): 'The *urbanus homo* is one who frequently produces good sayings and responses; who in conversation, social gatherings, dinners, in public meetings, or in all circumstances speaks with wit and appropriateness.'

25 On the agonistic one-upmanship at dinners see, e.g., Lucian, *De merc.cond.* 14–18, 26–30; *Symp.*; Athenaeus, *Deipnos.* Contest, conflict and various discordant behaviour is a *topos* in the literary symposia (J. Martin, 1931, pp. 101–6, 127–39; Paul, 1991, pp. 162–6) and probably reflects the social symposia where, as Macrobius says, 'anger lies in ambush, to take advantage of the merriment' (*Sat.* 7.3.2–3; cited by D'Arms, 1990, p. 318).

26 The occasional claim (e.g., Marshall, 1978, p. 589) that 'the guests acted independently' goes against the sense of ἀπὸ μιᾶς (which Marshall, too, translates as 'unanimously'). Cf. Holtzmann, 1892, p. 241: 'einmüthig ... doch ist nicht etwa an Verabredung zu denken'. Jülicher, 1910, vol. II, p. 411, thinks that 14.18 as a whole implies that the guests must have assembled in one place in order to conspire and then to meet the host's *vocator*. This need not be so; one can hold to the view of a prearranged refusal without linking it to an assembly. But for this one needs to appreciate the nature of communication in ancient 'face-to-face' societies (discussed below, pp. 111–12).

27 One suspects that the frequent attempts to soft-peddle the guests' behaviour as justified, even if poorly judged, are driven by an allegorizing hermeneutic which is itself powered by a theological agenda. The idea of an exclusion from the banquet of the saved, easily generated by reading 14.18 and 14.24 together, lurks as a menacing ghost in the closet of many exegetes.

'absurd in real life' and went on quite correctly to explain the guests' 'mysterious behaviour' as a haughty shunning of the Lukan householder. Falsely, however, he accounts for the snub by claiming that the householder was a socially odious, even if wealthy man, a tax-collector (Jeremias, 1963, pp. 178–9). Luke's story gives no indication that the host is a tax-collector; turning him into one by superimposing on him the (much later) talmudic figure of Bar Ma'jan is a methodologically dissembling manoeuvre that, in the end, is of little help in explaining the bizarre behaviour of the invited guests in Luke's parable.[28] Other commentators attempt to dissolve the absurdity of the scenario by getting the guests off the hook with various excusing moves. Thus, it might be argued, παραιτεῖσθαι does not mean an absolute refusal, but merely an excuse for late arrival.[29] Most commonly the refusals are exonerated on various grounds of 'legitimate' necessity while the excuses are given plausibility with the (misapplied) aid of the Deuteronomistic war exemption rules (see especially Derrett, 1970b, pp. 136–9).

By contrast, one might begin to interpret the behaviour of the invited company by noting that the story does not expressly impute the warrant for their action to the host. The host, when removed from the ignominious shadow of Bar Ma'jan or Lukan publicans for that matter, evidently is not a reprobate; there is nothing obviously wrong with the dinner;[30] the invitations are issued with the proper formality and courtesy that would have permitted the invited folks

---

[28] The talmudic story and Luke's parable differ greatly in the narrational structure of the invitation. In the former it is (implicitly) evident that the town councillors decline the invitation *because* there is something wrong with the host; the missing formal two-step invitation suggests that the refusal followed the initial offer of hospitality. Hence the guests' refusal in the Bar Ma'jan story is an inadequate analogy to the refusal in Luke.

[29] I take παραιτεῖσθαι to mean an absolute refusal to attend the banquet. Linnemann, for example, with obvious theological distaste for the sharpness of the refusal, misreads the action of the guests, claiming that 'die Entschuldigungen der Gäste ... nicht als endgültige Absagen sondern nur als Entschuldigungen für ein späteres Kommen gedacht sind' (1960, p. 250). Similarly, Plummer, 1914, p. 362. Although the late dinner guest is not an unknown literary figure, the language in 14.18 is conventional for expressing one's absolute regrets (Marshall, 1978, p. 588). Since the dining date and hour was normally stated in the initial invitation (Kim, 1975, pp. 392–3; contra Jülicher, 1910, vol. II, p. 410), one would expect guests who had scheduling conflicts to discuss them with the host's κλητήρ at that time.

[30] Rohrbaugh, with whose interpretation of the parable I agree generally, goes beyond the evidence when he claims that '[s]omething is wrong with the supper being offered or the guests would not only appear, social opinion would demand that they do so' (1991, p. 142).

to decline in accordance with social rules designed to preserve the honour of the host and to keep intact the relationship between him and those whom he had invited. All seems to be in line with the regnant cultural script.

It follows that the narrator would have us think that the guests' behaviour, a well-recognized gesture of avoidance and rejection,[31] is puerile, socially improper, an insidious flouting of the code of honour not caused by the host but rather aimed to inflict harm on him. There is something wrong with the invited guests, not the host, the narrator would have us believe. The affection of the reader/ auditor is being managed here (see Linnemann, 1960, p. 254). Sympathies are directed towards the properly acting host in proportion to the antipathies generated by the unwarranted action of the invited guests. Viewed from this angle, the absurdity (Jeremias) of the refusal scene in the banquet story should be appreciated (rather than glossed) as a literary hyperbole, a disengagement of verisimilitude designed to force upon the reader the culpability of the invited and, at the same time, to insist on the innocence and dignity of the host against the stain of shame splashed on him by the rejection of his peers.

The exaggeration is patent in all elements of the refusal scene (14.18–20). All of the 'many' invited accepted the invitation; all agreed to withdraw their acceptance at the dinner hour as if by prior arrangement; all advance alibis which, though dressed in an idiom of respect (ἐρωτῶ σε, ἔχε με παρῃτημένον), do not commend themselves as legitimate excuses but as 'masking devices' (Gilsenan, 1976, p. 198) familiar to Mediterranean ethnographers.[32] The entire scene

---

[31] Bossmann, paying some attention to the rules of Mediterranean social conduct implied in the banquet story, correctly recognizes the guest's refusal as 'normally a sign of avoidance'. But immediately he adds that 'here [the refusals are] apparently innocent of such intentions' (1991, pp. 3–4). We are not let in on why this is apparent to him. Cf. D'Arms, 1990, p. 313: 'Refusal to appear at a former friend's table was an unmistakable sign of fractured friendship.' In the terms of Douglas and Isherwood declining the invitation is a 'refusal to transact, a common, if not world-wide strategy of exclusion' (1978, p. 140; cf. p. 145).

[32] See especially Bailey, 1980, pp. 95–9. In his view, largely driven by observations on modern Middle Eastern codes of behaviour, the excuses are a 'bold-faced lie', 'ludicrous', 'transparent fabrication', etc. Rohrbaugh calls them 'beside the point ... typical diversionary answers of Middle Eastern, honor-shame social interaction' (1991, p. 142). On the idea of deception and honour in ancient Greece see the brief remarks by Adkins, 1960, p. 49, and Friedrich, 1977, pp. 286–7. Modern ethnographers of the Mediterranean have often noted that in honour-shame societies honour is staked upon sincere intentions rather than expressed promises or assurances. Hence if a person's sincere intention was not behind a promise made, it is not dishonourable if the promise turns out to be the lie it ostensibly is.

is an overdrawn literary abstraction from real life. In the real world people undoubtedly did occasionally cancel dinner engagements at inconvenient and potentially embarrassing moments;[33] denials of claim to place at the dining table as a technique of social rejection were probably not uncommon;[34] there surely were some members of the Greco-Roman élite that habitually opted out of the party scene for moral, political or paranoid reasons;[35] but this appears to have been exceptional and idiosyncratic behaviour (Paul, 1991, p. 158) and, as such, hardly comparable to the wholesale, 'class action' rejection of a social equal depicted in Luke 14.18–20.

See Pitt-Rivers, 1977b, pp. 32–4; and the brilliant observations by Gilsenan, 1976, on ulterior motives, deceptive idioms and discourse of suspicion in a Middle Eastern status honour society. Cf. more generally Abu-Lughod, 1986.

[33] Two examples from the literature: Plutarch (*De garr.* [*Mor.*] 502D) tells the story of the *rhetor* Pupius Piso who wanted to honour the magistrate Clodius: 'Piso gave orders that he be invited to dinner and prepared what was, we may suppose, a sumptuous banquet. When the hour came (ἐνστάσης δὲ τῆς ὥρας), the other guests were present, but Clodius was still expected, and Piso repeatedly sent the slave who regularly carried invitations to see if Clodius was approaching.' Clearly agitated, Piso finally asked the slave if the invitation had indeed been delivered. Assured that it had been, he asked, 'Why hasn't he come then?' The slave replied, 'Because he declined' (ὅτι ἠρνήσατο). The story as a whole clearly indicates that Clodius had declined the invitation on getting it; no reason (excuse) is stated. The second example is Lucian's Eucrates who gave a birthday party for his daughter and invited many of his friends. One of them subsequently sent notice that he might be absent due to illness. Both stories, one a singular (perhaps snubbing) refusal, the other a singular notice of regret for a legitimate reason, probably are representative of the grid of invitational conventions. Cf. the anecdote of refusal in Macrobius, *Sat.* 1.2.6–7.

[34] The technique is indirectly visible in the numerous occasions in Luke where Jesus' dining with the socially errant draws a stringent critique (5.30, [Q 7.34–5], 15.1–2, 19.7, cf. Acts 11.1–18; analysis in McMahan, 1987, pp. 113–59), although here table fellowship is clearly a symbol of boundary maintenance between social groups rather than a means of a particular social class excluding one of its members. As an example of the latter, the howling outrage of Hetoemocles the Stoic at having been excluded from the banquet of Aristaenetus in Lucian's *repas ridicule* (*Symp.* 21–7) may reflect the real feeling of injury caused by this type of exclusion.

[35] The prototype of the moral contempt for the drinking-party scene is Socrates; although he is the eminent guest at Agathon's symposium, he goes reluctantly, after refusing the first invitation (Plato, *Symp.* 174A); generally he appears to avoid them (see, in detail, Tecusan, 1990, pp. 238–45). Plutarch, in his *Lives*, offers several examples of notable people refusing to attend symposia: Sertorius avoided them because excessive drinking disagreed with his commitment to simple living (13.2); Pericles consistently declined invitations (μηδένα τῶν φίλων ἐπὶ δεῖπνον ἐλθεῖν). On the one exception (wedding feast of a relative) he left before the libations were poured (i.e., the symposium proper). The reason? He did not want his δόξα (dignity, reputation) and reserve overpowered by wine (7.4–5); Nicias avoided all dinners because he was generally asocial and paranoid of συκοφάντας (5.1). See further Paul, 1991, pp. 158–9.

A reading of the refusal scene as an overblown literary construct, riding on undertonal attributions of foul play on the part of the invited against a fair-playing and honourable associate, probably warns against extracting from it firm conclusions on issues of social formation or group dynamics within the Lukan community. Nonetheless, it may not be a far-fetched speculation to suggest that the narration of the refusal scene, fictive though it is, is partially driven by Luke's knowledge of real peer rejection and dishonour experienced by the urban rich who became members or benefactors of Christian associations. Although there is a tendency to think that strategies of social exclusion are usually employed by the socially central against the socially marginal, this need not always be so, as Mary Douglas has shown. 'Sometimes the person who is to be rejected is not marginal at all ... It is necessary to realize that ... strategies of rejection may sometimes be used against the powerful' (Douglas, 1991, p. 724). Douglas suggests that for such an exclusionary tactic to be successful two things are required: (1) the excluding group must be agreed, that is, there has to be a closing of the ranks against the rejected person; and (2) there has to be a libellous imputation of infamy (1991, pp. 724–5). This twofold technique of rejection functions to 'entrench the hierarchy of social categories and warn well-placed persons against indiscriminate social intercourse' (1991, p. 726). When we look behind the obviously fantastic, wholesale dinner refusal to the general lines of social interaction implicit in it, the peer rejection pattern as described by Douglas is reasonably evident. Thus, first, the notice that 'unanimously all began to make excuses' is an indication of closure of rank against the host.[36] Secondly, the refusal itself is, as we have noted, an insidious defamatory act which, even if entirely unwarranted on the part of the host, would have been sufficient to lower the honour

---

[36] Rohrbaugh, 1991, pp. 143–5, also noticed the issue of not breaking rank, but his explanation of its significance is undecided. On the one hand, he suggests that it simply reflects honour-shame social interaction where 'either all the guests come or none do' (p. 142) because none would want to be seen going to a banquet shunned by important others just as none would want to miss one attended by important others. On this view, each one invited acts independently based upon a calculation of whether the dinner company would be beneficial to his social image. On the other hand, Rohrbaugh seems to suggest that the refusal is a show of solidarity in shunning one of their 'own' for failing to protect 'the system' (the interests and rules of social interaction of the élite; p. 143). The first explanation assumes all kinds of information we simply do not have and, moreover, universalizes ancient 'honour-shame' behaviour that I would regard as atypical. The second explanation comes much closer to my view.

grade of the host in the eyes of those who knew him and thereby seriously impair his ability to maintain a positive social image in the minds of his fellow citizens. Why this should be so would be intuitively understood by Hellenistic readers. Living in what Moses Finley has called a 'face-to-face society',[37] 'a society whose members knew each other intimately and interacted with one another closely' (Ober, 1989, p. 31), they would know that the competition for merit and honour is played out openly before the court of public opinion where 'facts are of much less importance than appearances' (Adkins, 1960, p. 49; cf. Dover, 1974, p. 226), where what 'everyone knows' and says is given greater weight than factual evidence in creating a public estimate of a person's reputation.[38] Readers would bring to their appreciation of the host's predicament the further social knowledge that in a face-to-face urban precinct the host's plans for a large banquet could not have been kept hidden from neighbours and many other households in the city. Numerous 'conduits of gossip' (Ober, 1989, p. 149) and informal networks of information flow guaranteed that nobody, especially not a prominent townsman, had any secrets. Entertainers and prostitutes on the élite banquet circuit would spread 'inside' information. Various other household retainers, even members of households going about their business in the city – shopping, lingering in eateries, barber and perfume shops, visiting gymnasia and theatres – operated flourishing grapevines (see Laurence, 1994; especially Hunter, 1990; cf. Dover, 1988; Adeleye, 1983). Juvenal, for instance, answers with an emphatic 'no' his rhetorical question whether 'a rich man has any secrets'. Among the chiefest of reasons for 'right living', he says, is the need not to provide subjects for 'talk' by the household slaves (Juvenal, *Satire* 9.102–23).

Along these urban 'grapevines' would have sprouted the 'news' that the host's plan for a grand banquet was sabotaged by important abstaining guests. This scandalous turn of events, readers presumably would know, was perfectly programmed to set off the

---

[37] 1985, pp. 17–18. Finley refers to ancient Athens as the model of a face-to-face society. The definition: 'small numbers, concentrated in small residential groupings and living the typically Mediterranean out-of-doors life' (p. 17). Finley's idea has been picked up widely, although he has been criticized for applying it to Athens as a whole, rather than to the urban deme or to the village. See Ober, 1989, pp. 31–3, and the literature cited there; and Hunter, 1990, p. 301.

[38] On the 'everyone knows' *topos* (prevalent among Athenian orators but still in force in later periods; e.g., Juvenal, *Sat.* 9.102–23) as part of a rumour- and gossip-oriented society see Ober, 1989, pp. 149–50.

production of rumour (φήμη) – unfounded half-truths, speculations impugning the host's character and morality, etc. – that would then be launched on the gossip circuit to make sure that 'everyone knew' that there seemed to be something wrong with the host, the facts of the matter aside.[39] The undertow of malice in being made the 'talk' of the town would probably be sufficient to ensure the defamation of the host.[40] In this way, the mere act of snubbing the invitation of the host would have unleashed a chain-reaction process of public humiliation in the form of rumours transmitted along the gossip networks. I am suggesting that all this may be presumed as the kind of social knowledge that was part of the auditory apparatus of Luke's audience. If so, it clarifies the stakes the Lukan host had in the invitations and the social costs for which he was liable upon being shunned by the invited guests.

Why this action of peer exclusion with all its baleful ramifications for the host was set in motion is hidden from us, because we cannot determine the specific motivation of the guests from the narrative.[41] But on the basis of a generalized understanding of the purpose of peer exclusions we may justifiably infer that the motive for the refusal was to apply a punitive measure of disentitlement against someone for espousing views and acting in ways that threatened the values and interests of the élite. Identifying these threatening views and actions more exactly takes us into speculative territory. If we are inclined to go that way and attempt to discern any whispering of fact behind Luke's fiction at this point of the story,[42] one might hear

---

[39] On the 'operation of φήμη' (Hunter, 1990) Aeschines is illustrative: 'Attaching itself to men's life and conduct, talk travels unerringly and spontaneously throughout the city, like a messenger proclaiming to the public at large details of men's private behaviour' (1.127; cited by Hunter, 1990, p. 302).

[40] Rumour and gossip do not have to be intentionally malicious; they could result in welcome notoriety and fame, but judging from the evidence adduced by Hunter, 1990, the ancients were fearful of being the subject of rumours. Hunter herself distills a definition of gossip as 'talk of others – implicit moral judgments – meant to criticize, to scandalize, or to abuse' (p. 300). As I already noted, Juvenal thought it was the worst plight that could attach itself to a rich man, although he may have indulged in hyperbole to serve his satire.

[41] Rightly Gowler, 1991, p. 246 n. 145: 'The motivations behind the three refusals cannot be determined.' This needs to be said against a strong commentary tradition that imputes motives on the basis of the excuses. Yet, precisely the 'cultural scripts' that guide Gowler's interpretation of the dinner parable do help us to identify the action as a technique of peer exclusion which, in turn, rides upon general motives that we can plausibly surmise.

[42] Admittedly, I know of no apparatus for taking reliable soundings of 'real' issues in the Lukan community from a fictional story (14.16–24) embedded in an equally fictional episodal context (14.1–24) itself part of a larger work of literary imagin-

there the bewildered and chagrined murmur of rich 'Lukan' Christians whose association with poor 'Lukan' Christians has earned them all the negative consequences of ostracism from the circle of their ὅμοιοι with whom they once dined and wined for gain in wealth, influence and reputation (cf. Luke 18.23). Richard Rohrbaugh has seen 'the social disaster' that must have troubled the rich with sharp clarity:

> Elite Christians who participated in the socially inclusive Christian community risked being cut off from the prior social networks on which their positions depended ... It is their friendships, their place of residence, their economic survival (and probably health as well), the well-being of their extended families and even the 'system' of the elite that is at stake. (1991, p. 146)[43]

Judging from Luke's implicit insistence on the honourable character of the host, he appears to be deeply sensitive to the painful stresses caused by converting to new social allegiances on the part of the 'good' rich. The rest of the parable may well be Luke's protreptic and rationalizing response to the rejected, dishonoured wealthy person symbolized by the dinner host.

### Rejection of élite sociability

Thus far the story of the wealthy host has been the story of honour sought and honour denied within the ranks of the urban élite. The remainder of the parable (14.21b-24) consists of the defamed host's reaction to his predicament as *persona non grata* within the company

ation (Luke-Acts) of undetermined geographical provenance. Any relationship between Luke's social situation and/or his social ideals and Lukan redaction of the traditional banquet story must in any case be complex. See the soft conclusions drawn on the 'rhetorical situation' of 14.1–24 in ch. 9.

43 According to the logic of the narrative it is obvious that the rich man's association with the poor is the consequence (14.21b), not the cause, of his exclusion from the fraternity of the élite. But this has the look of a fictional inversion of cause and effect – a story-teller of course is free to rearrange sequences and transpose causes and consequences – that may well reflect a process of rationalization within the Lukan community. If the host (= a Lukan patron) is a target of a malicious campaign to dishonour him, so the rationale goes, he is indeed free of blame for the social (and economic?) consequences of his exclusion and therefore not really dishonoured but an honourable victim. Using various expedients to divorce someone's shameful situation from moral blame to save face is a familiar ancient (and modern) tactic. See Dover, 1974, pp. 239–42.

of his ὅμοιοι.[44] The narrated reaction falls into three periods: an expression of anger (14.21b), a turn to a substitute company of guests (14.21c-23) and an *epilogion* (14.24). They shall serve as expedients for my discussion.

Long before Luke wrote his gospel the famous itinerant rhetorician Gorgias put the issue of a stained reputation in intense terms that would have met the assent of people in the first century. 'To good men death is more desirable than a shameful reputation. For one is the end of life, and the other a disease in life.'[45] Gorgias' not uncommon statement reflects the embarrassment and grievous outrage that virtually all Greeks felt in response to an affront against their public reputation (Dover, 1974, p. 237). As we have seen, the host's position is ripe for resentment and the note on his anger, though likely already in the Q *Vorlage*, in the Lukan context is best regarded as a typical response of righteous indignation at being defamed without the warrant of one's actions or intentions.[46] Outrage in the face of insult indeed is demanded by the honour-shame code itself.[47] Resentment is, as Julian Pitt-Rivers remarks, a 'touchstone of honour', an initial step in the effort towards restoring one's integrity whether by demanding an apology or, if that is not forthcoming, by launching various avenging strategies, for 'nobody may harm me with impunity', as a popular aristocratic motto stated.[48] In the context of the reciprocal dining pursuits of the élite,

---

[44] The adverb τότε (14.21b) of course is simply a temporal indicator to advance the narrative, but the charged emotive context (ὀργισθείς) shades it towards signifying a decisive mark in the host's life.

[45] Τοῖς δὲ ἀγαθοῖς ἀνδράσιν αἱρετώτερος θάνατος δόξης αἰσχράς· τὸ μὲν γὰρ τοῦ βίου τέλος, ἡ δὲ τῶι βίωι νόσος (fr. 82B.11a.35.5-7; Diels, 1966, vol. 2, p. 303).

[46] Cf. the reconstruction above. An angry host coheres well with the ideology of later Q (by now conventionally Q², on which see Kloppenborg, 1987, pp. 102-70, 244-5) and is attested also by Matthew, although the latter has a separate need for an irate banquet giver. Since an irritated host is a requirement in the honour-shame logic that partially drives Luke's story, Q delivered a detail that the redactor took over eagerly rather than out of deferent respect for the tradition. In this sense only, I am prepared to consider it as a Lukan detail. A similar view is implied by Rohrbaugh, 1991, p. 141.

[47] Interestingly, Aristotle's definition of anger in *Rhet.* 2.2.1 comes in the context of a discussion on the rhetorical play on emotion (πάθος) to influence someone's judgment, but note how ὀργή itself is defined as the feeling arising from offended honour: anger is 'a longing, accompanied by pain, for a conspicuous (φαινομένης) revenge caused by a conspicuous slight directed without justification towards oneself or one's own'.

[48] Pitt-Rivers, 1977b, pp. 26-7 (the motto is cited by Pitt-Rivers). Resentment and the desire for revenge are closely tied to another honour-linked pair of values,

at almost every turn translated into terms of 'face' saved or lost, anger at having one's invitation rejected or at not receiving an expected invitation is predictable. The irritated host thus is an instance of a commonplace in the narration of snubbed dinner invitations.[49] Not so predictable is how the rich host translates his anger into action. The expected counter-insult, the anticipated righteous display of retaliative bravado that marks the vindication of honour among the Homeric heroes, for example,[50] and that is reflected also in the more familiar Matthean equivalent to Luke's banquet host (Matthew 22.7), is not forthcoming.[51] Instead, the host appears to turn his back not only against the expected vengeance, but against the entire system that governed his original invitation itself. There is a striking analogy here to the flouting of honour-linked expectations John Kloppenborg found in the story of the 'dishonoured master' (Luke 16.1–8) who 'seems to ignore his own honour and his own endangered state. This is tantamount to "laughing" at his own honour and at the honour-shame codes with which the the story [16.1–8a] has operated' (1989, p. 492; cf. Scott, 1989, pp. 173–4, and Rohrbaugh, 1991, p. 145).

courage-cowardice. 'To leave an affront unavenged is to leave one's honour in a state of desecration and this is therefore equivalent to cowardice' (p. 26). See also Friedrich, 1977, p. 293: 'While courage does not presuppose honor, the latter both presupposes and enjoins courage; courage is essential because one cannot be honorable without it.'

49 E.g., Xenophon, *Symp.* 1.7; Plutarch, *De garr.* (*Mor.*) 511D-E; implied in Pliny's effusive excuse letter, *ep.* 9.37; cf. *ep.* 1.15. The obverse case, that is, anger at not receiving an invitation where one thinks it due, is illustrated by Hetoemocles in Lucian's *Symposium*: 'How I feel about dining out, my whole past life can testify; for although every day I am pestered by many men much richer than you [Aristaenetus] are, nevertheless I am never forward about accepting, as I am familiar with the disturbances and riotous doings at dinner-parties. But in your case and yours only I think I have reason to be angry, because you, to whom I have so long ministered indefatigably, did not think fit to number me among your friends: no, I alone do not count with you, and that though I live next door. I am indignant ...' (*Symp.* 22).

50 Friedrich, 1977, p. 294. The Homeric pattern continues to be prevalent in honour societies in the Mediterranean, as the articles in Peristiany, 1966, repeatedly indicate.

51 Scott, 1989, p. 168 (cf. p. 172), suggests that with the second invitations 'the householder avenges his honor by himself rebuffing those who rebuffed him'. But for whom is this action insulting? The originally invited élite would consider it as confirmation of their judgment to shun the host in the first place; they would feel vindicated, not insulted. To be sure, a tone of counter-snub does ring in the turn to the poor, but the sound is that of someone who knows he is no longer wanted among his former peers. He in turn disavows association with them as a way of

We have already described the turn to substitute banquet clientele that Luke has severely characterized as the urban and para-urban poor and disabled. Now we need to return to this action and examine it with reference to the host. How should the second invitation be viewed? An allegorical explanation, whether slanted historically (inaugurating a gentile mission) or eschatologically (a call to table at the heavenly banquet), is to be disavowed.

A second possibility is to interpret the host's action within the rubric of Hellenistic honour-motivated benefaction and in the context of Luke's well-known concern for the disposition of wealth through benevolence and philanthropy. On this view, commonly echoed in recent studies dominated by social-historical interests, the host's reactive invitation might be construed as an act of magnanimous patronage, or as an exemplary shift from the practice of balanced reciprocity, the common mode of exchange among the Hellenistic élite censured by Luke, to that of 'vertical generalized reciprocity, a redistribution from the advantaged to the disadvantaged that expects nothing in return',[52] a mode of exchange that Luke generally favours. This view of the host as benefactor of the poor is not without some credence, for several reasons. (1) It makes some sense against the background of the cultural ideal of the wealthy benefactor (εὐεργέτης) doing good deeds (εὐεργεσία) for public benefit,[53] which may include the sharing of alimentary goods with the poor,[54] and funding voluntary associations.[55] (2) The general cultural ideal of the benefactor is positively embraced by Luke in his dependence on the figure for interpreting Jesus as the

salvaging some face in a disastrous social situation, as Scott seems to understand at other places (pp. 168, 173).
[52] Gowler, 1991, p. 50; similarly Elliott, 1991a, p. 104; 1991b, pp. 236–8; Moxnes, 1989, p. 132; 1991a, p. 265 (householder as a symbol of God as the 'patron of the poor'). Here Moxnes has indulged in a theological abstraction; I am much more attracted to his views stated in 1986–7, p. 162, where he considers the invitation as a 'starting mechanism' of a new social grouping.
[53] For the fullest collection of epigraphic evidence and a broad profile of the figure of the benefactor see Danker, 1982; Mott, 1975, provides a good survey of the idea of benefaction, focusing on the social bonds and obligations between benefactor and beneficiary.
[54] Danker, 1982, pp. 401–2; much additional evidence for food relief provided by individual benefactors (rather than by the state) is gathered and discussed by Mrozek, 1988; see also Fuks, 1979, pp. 60–1.
[55] Danker, 1982, pp. 35, 168. E.g., part of an inscription (*CIG* 2.3067) recording a decree of gratitude to Kraton (a benefactor) states that this is in accord with the guild's practice of honouring 'its benefactors in a manner commensurate with their benefactions' (trans. Danker, 1982, p. 168). See also MacMullan, 1974, p. 78.

benefactor *par excellence*, as Frederick Danker has shown,[56] in opting for the servant-benefactor as a 'model of greatness' among the followers of Jesus,[57] and in his tendency to highlight the merits of wealthy people in terms of their beneficent patronage of the Jesus entourage and the early church.[58] (3) As we have noted, the idea of generous benefaction rather than balanced reciprocity as the principle for determining whom to invite for dinner is an important element in the narrative context of the banquet parable (14.12–13).

(4) The benefactor model appears to overlap with the view which I have represented so far, namely that the story of the householder presupposes familiarity with the social world of the urban élite characterized by the competition for honour. This contest for public recognition was firmly linked to philanthropy by long tradition. One of the traditional marks of a 'good man' was generosity and this was a universally recognized means of earning a good reputation (see Moxnes, 1989, pp. 115–18). Aristotle, for example, had said that τιμὴ δ᾽ ἐστὶ μὲν σημεῖον εὐεργετικῆς δόξης ('honour is a sign of a reputation for doing good'; *Rhethoric* 1361a). David Whitehead and others have shown how the traditional (Homeric) aristocratic φιλοτιμία was later re-aimed to serve the cooperative ideals underlying Athenian democracy: φιλοτιμία thus was harnessed and exploited 'to the profit of the community as a whole' (1983, p. 59).[59] There is no reason to believe that beneficence understood as a

56 Danker, 1982, p. 395; Danker's two commentaries on Luke depend on the benefactor model; see 1988, pp. xv (Jesus as 'Great Benefactor'), 2–10; 1976, pp. 6–17. Note Acts 10:38 where Jesus' career is summarized as διῆλθεν εὐεργετῶν, 'he travelled about doing good'.

57 Lull, 1986. The main part of the essay presents the argument that the term εὐεργετής in Luke 22:25 is not used pejoratively as many, including Danker (1988, p. 348), have thought. It should be noted that the speech about greatness (22.24–30) takes place in the context of another Lukan dinner episode.

58 The following is a partial list: women who provide for Jesus and his followers (4.39, 8.3, 10.38–42); various characters who prepare dinners for Jesus (5.29, 7.36, 11.37, 14.1, 19.1–10, 24.28–30); an anonymous householder provides facilities for the Passover meal (22.9–13); Joseph, a 'good and righteous' member of the βουλή, looks after Jesus' burial in an unused tomb (23.50–3). The Acts are replete with beneficent characters, including those who aid the missionary work of Paul (9.43, 10.6, 16.14, 18.1–4) and converts who merit accolades for their 'good works' (ἔργων ἀγαθῶν) and acts of charity' (Tabitha, 9.36; cf. Cornelius, 10.2,4) and who appear to be wealthy patrons of house-churches (Mary, 12.12–13; an anonymous owner of a three-story facility in Troas, 20.7–9). For a more complete survey of characters as benefactors in Luke-Acts, see Lull, 1986, pp. 304–5.

59 See also Ober, 1989, pp. 240–7, esp. p. 243; and Fuks, 1979. The latter does not link generosity with the pursuit of honour, but provides an excellent survey of well-directed giving by the rich to enhance their social stature and their control of wealth.

'competitive outlay' (Whitehead, 1983) of wealth, that is, as an important honour-linked value,[60] had a diminished currency in Luke's time,[61] for, as Stanislaw Mrozek points out, the later Roman private alimentary charities for the socially disadvantaged (mostly orphans) should be seen in part as a 'Wettbewerb in der Freigebigkeit' (contest in generosity) motivated by 'Ehrgeiz' (greed for honour; 1988, p. 157). When all this is brought to bear on the Lukan householder, a 'clever' figure emerges who raises the stakes in the honour contest after he has lost his initial attempt to maintain or raise his reputation within the orbit of the élite: he is going to earn acclaim by outscoring his peers in generosity.[62] The second set of invitations, understood as a defence of the host's honour, thus would represent another attempt to forge or reinforce his link with the wealthy élite with whom he wants to share a reputation appropriate to such people. In this view, the turn to the poor would amount to a detour on the householder's temporarily blocked path into the circle of his wealthy peers.

Despite the merits of interpreting the householder's turn to the poor as dinner guests with reference to the benefactor model, this model is not wholly satisfactory. When it is further saddled with claims that the beneficent invitations deflect the householder's shame back on his peers, the model breaks down.

First, as already intimated, benevolence by the rich for the profit of the poor normally was conducted with self-referential aims; it was to fulfil the honour-linked requirement of generosity as one way of solidifying the benefactor's position within the stratum of the élite. Notwithstanding the occasional criticism directed against mercenary giving,[63] the prevailing social logic governing beneficence

---

[60] On honour as a motive for benevolence see also Bolkestein, 1939, pp. 18, 152–5 ('φιλοτιμία ist ein Anreiz zum Wohltun und Geben', p. 155); Dover, 1974, p. 231; Hands, 1968, pp. 43, 48 ('the lure of honour remained a powerful and essential motive [for charity well into the Roman period]'), 49–52, 76; the relationship between honour and generosity continues in modern Mediterranean honour societies, as the ethnographers repeatedly note.

[61] Seneca's extensive tome, *On Benefits*, attests to the vitality of issues related to giving and receiving in the first century. Cf. Mott, 1975, pp. 67–9, 72.

[62] This view is most explicitly argued by Bossman, 1991, p. 5: 'The solution [to the problem of having been refused by his peers] was the host's clever strategy of extending the invitation to those that no one else would invite: they would have no excuse, and he would be seen as exceptionally gracious ... The clever host found that [by] including those that others excluded *he was able to achieve greater honor than others who were not so clever as he.*' (emphasis added)

[63] See especially Seneca, *Ben.*; e.g.: 'Let us make our benefits, not investments, but gifts' (1.1.9). 'To seek, not the fruit of benefits, but the mere doing of them ... this

made it virtually impossible to divest even the most magnanimous acts of generosity from the perception that they initiated a mutually obligatory relationship between giver and receiver from which the former expected to profit as much as the latter, not least in the form of public gratitude (χάρις, *gratia*).[64] This meant that beneficiaries were chosen with careful discrimination, lest the donor's outlay of wealth or favours was squandered or led to undesirable social relationships.[65] In practical terms, this meant of course that Hellenistic re-allocative strategies 'made little penetration into the lower classes' (Mott, 1975, p. 72),[66] much less into the urban and para-urban 'rag-tag-and- bobtail' (Dodd, 1961, p. 91) of Luke's parable, because one could not expect to receive from them the proper recompense of public gratitude. All this makes it difficult to understand the second invitations as a benefaction, let alone one that could defend the householder's honour against the suspicions of his peers. They would likely sneer at him further and hurl at him the slogan, 'you have wasted a benefit' (*beneficium perdidisti*; Seneca, *De Beneficiis* 1.10.4).

Second, a good deed by a wealthy man on behalf of the poor should not be confused with an act of social interaction or with a gesture of social identification. While distributing alimentary aid to the poor was well within the range of Hellenistic benefaction, such sharing of wealth did not imply a reorganization or mixing of the social categories. A rich man could then, as now, feed the poor as a token of non-reciprocal generosity, yet keep his social distance by

is the mark of a soul that is truly great and good' (1.1.12). For Seneca the 'chief mark' of a benefit is 'that it carries no thought of a return' (2.31.3); any benefit that carries such a thought is called a loan, a bargaining, an investment and so forth.
[64] To express gratitude for benefits received was more than a necessity of politeness; it was a social duty. For Cicero, for example, 'no duty is more necessary than that of proving one's gratitude' (*Off.* 1.47; cf. Seneca, *Ben.* 2.21.6: 'He who receives a benefit with gratitude repays the first instalment on his debt'). It seems evident from Cicero (*Off.* 42–52) and Seneca that *beneficium-gratia* was a dimension of the patron-client relationship. On χάρις as a public response to wealthy donors see Mott, 1975, pp. 61–3; and Ober, 1989, pp. 226–30.
[65] Cicero probably expresses the typical opinion of wealthy Romans when he says that 'in acts of kindness we should weigh with discrimination the worthiness of the object of our benevolence; we should take into consideration his moral character, his attitude towards us, the intimacy of his relations to us, and our common social ties, as well as the services he has hitherto rendered in our interest' (*Off.* 1.45; trans. Miller, LCL).
[66] Cf. Bolkestein, 1939, p. 107: 'Beistehen soll man – nicht den Armen – sondern den "Guten", nicht so sehr deshalb weil die "Schlechten" es nicht verdienen, sondern weil man nur von guten Menschen Vergeltung der χάρις (freundlichen Hilfe) mit χάρις (Dank, Gegengabe) erwarten kann.'

not entering into the messy mesh of social interaction with them (see Douglas, 1982, p. 117). But this is precisely what the Lukan householder does not do. When he fills his own dining room, i.e., his private space, with people from the despised ranks he goes beyond doing a good deed, although he does that as well, towards initiating social involvement with them.[67] Herein, I would argue, lies the centre of gravity of the second invitations as far as the householder is concerned. Insofar as they initiate a social transaction, the secondary invitations thus function much like the original invitation, although the nature of the intended transaction differs in each case. As the first invitation was an attempt by the householder to cement his links with the society of the élite, so the second offers of hospitality make for the first step in attaching himself to a group extremely opposite to the élite. As the first invitation was aimed to convert commensality into status maintenance/improvement within one grouping, so the subsequent calls are a preliminary indication that the householder has cut his ties with his former friends and thereby forfeited all the advantages and obligations that came with those ties. At the same time, the final invitations are an indication that the host has decided to transfer his social life into an altogether different grouping. Thus the two invitations to the same place and the same banquet are here presented first as a 'fence', a symbol of élite exclusivity, then as a 'bridge', that is, a symbol of the rich householder's conversion to new social loyalties.[68]

We might further clarify what is at issue for the householder in the secondary invitations with reference to categories from cultural

[67] I should stress that I do not intend to deny the beneficent dimension of the householder's turn to the poor, only to argue that seeing this turn within the strictures of the charity model is insufficient. Although 'Almosenfrömmigkeit' is a positive mark of Luke's moral ideal (see Horn, 1983, pp. 54–5, 88–120), the truly paradigmatic πλούσιος goes beyond being full of ἔργων ἀγαθῶν καὶ ἐλεημοσυνῶν (Acts 9.36) to full membership in the Christian fellowship symbolized by the initiation rite of baptism. The Cornelius episode (Acts 10) might in the first place stand as a paradigm of the legitimacy of the Gentile mission, but this wealthy centurion also illustrates Luke's hoped-for response of the rich to the church (Horn, 1983, p. 54). Thus Cornelius is lauded for giving alms generously (ποιῶν ἐλεημοσύνας πολλάς, 10.2, cf. 10.4, 31 [10.35: ἐργαζόμενος δικαιοσύνην = almsgiving?]), but he becomes exemplary because he invited Peter (hungry enough to fall into a swoon!, 10.10) to be his house guest (10.23) and because he undergoes full entry (baptism) into the Christian fellowship (10.47–8).

[68] See Douglas and Isherwood, 1978, pp. 11–12: 'Each free individual is responsible for the exclusiveness of his own home, the allocation of his free time, and hospitality ... Goods are neutral, their uses are social; they can be used as fences or bridges.'

anthropology, namely the terms 'ceremony' and 'ritual'.[69] Prescinding from nuances of definition, ceremonies are marked by a conservative function within a social group; they confirm group values, give shape to interaction among members, 'bolster the boundaries defining a group ... even as they confirm established roles and statuses within the group ... They attend, not to change, but to stability; they are concerned, not with newness, but with continuity' (Neyrey, 1991b, p. 363). Rituals, on the other hand, are markers of status transformation. They may symbolize change of status within the group (e.g., rites of passage), or they may signal a passage from one group to another. Rituals are concerned with discontinuity, with boundary lines that define a group and with crossing those lines (McVann, 1991, pp. 334–6). These distinctions illumine what the sequence of dinner invitations imply for the social self of the host. The first call represents an invitation to a ceremonial meal shared among men of highbrow social positions, while the next calls have all the marks of anticipating a social boundary-crossing ritual meal, one that serves at once to sever the host from his former group and to associate him with a new one, as initiate and initiator/benefactor at once.[70] The difference lies in the convivial assembly which each invitation has in view.

Does the concluding saying (14.24) afford us some confirmation that the banquet parable is the story of the conversion of a dishonoured host? The question is an important test of my reading of the parable and I believe that it is possible to secure an affirmative answer.

It would favour my argument to be able to show that the speaker in 14.24 continues to be the fictional householder. Recalling that he is the 'compositional pivot' (Bihari-Andersson) on which the

---

[69] General definitions are taken from McVann, 1991, pp. 331–41, and Neyrey, 1991b, pp. 362–3; cf. pp. 374–5.

[70] The idea of a meal as a status-transforming ritual is at odds with Neyrey's view that meals in Luke-Acts function as ceremonies. His commitment to 'meals-as-ceremonies' occasionally makes for a strained reading of the evidence where meals function to de-stabilize and realign conventional groupings, values and statuses (see 1991b, pp. 378–9). It is better to relax the view that Lukan meals are ceremonial affairs. Meals are means of fracturing friendship and creating or mending them (Moxnes, 1986–7, p. 162), as was typical in the Hellenistic world (D'Arms, 1990, p. 313). Cf. Sahlins, 1972, p. 215: 'Food dealings are a delicate barometer, a *ritual statement* as it were, of social relations, and food is thus employed instrumentally as a starting, a sustaining, or a destroying mechanism of sociability.' (emphasis added)

parable turns, the declaration, οὐδεὶς τῶν ἀνδρῶν ἐκείνων τῶν κεκλημένων γεύσεται μου τοῦ δείπνου ('none of those invited men will enjoy my banquet'), arguably could then be construed as a self-referential statement, a declarative confession, on the part of the host.

Rather than following the general scholarly consent by reading the final sentence as a minatory saying that asserts the exclusion of the originally invited from the banquet,[71] we could take it to signal the host's final commitment to dissociate himself from his former table fraternity. None of them will enjoy (γεύσεται) table fellowship with him anymore! That is, 'those men', the householder's social equals, will no longer be the reference group to whom he is answerable for his honour and behaviour. Read with reference to the householder, the *epilogion* underscores the interpretation of the parable I have advocated so far: a member of the urban élite severing himself from those who once provided him with his social identity and with whom he once competed for honour and increased status.[72]

But the identity of the speaker (the 'I' of λέγω) is hidden within one of the well-known textual ambiguities in 14.24. The problem is essentially twofold. The first lies in the indeterminable referent of the plural pronoun ὑμῖν. If the saying is part of the fictional householder's *oratio recta* one would expect σοί in agreement with the single slave as the only textually confirmed auditor. A second snag is presented by the λέγω ὑμῖν formula itself, often considered

---

71 This view is almost inevitable when the interpretive focus is on the guests, a commonplace in the scholarly commentaries, rather than on the host. For the view that 14.24 is an exclusionary judgment saying see, among many others, Jülicher, 1910, vol. II, p. 416; Manson, 1949, p. 130; Linnemann, 1960, pp. 249, 255; Jeremias, 1963, pp. 177–8; Hahn, 1970, pp. 59–60; Bailey, 1980, pp. 109–13; Fitzmyer, 1985, pp. 1052–3: 'minatory parable'; Scott, 1989, p. 165; Dschulnigg, 1989, p. 344 n. 29: 'Mit Lk 14,24 wird der exkommunizierende Charakter des Gleichnisses überdeutlich'. Many interpreters sense that this is not an altogether winsome interpretation of 14.24. Why solemnly exclude people who, according to the logic of the narrative, have no intention of being included? Surely, the first-invited would not be insulted, mortified or in any way threatened by the statement of the host. Jeremias articulates the unease of many others: 'A guest who has no intention of coming will not be impressed by the threat that he will not be admitted' (1963, p. 178 n. 23). Yet, he holds to the view that 14.24 is a threat, but in a question-begging way: 'it is only a real threat if it refers to the Messianic banquet' (p. 178).

72 If this view is agreeable, one might note, incidentally, how much the point made in the Lukan *epilogion* differs from the moral drawn from the similar parable in the Gospel of Thomas. In *G.Thom.* 64 rich people (business people and merchants) are explicitly denied a 'place' in the 'Thomas' association. In Luke a rich person who joins the Lukan group gives up his place in the fellowship of the wealthy.

not only as a typically Lukan expression,[73] but, on statistical evidence, also as a lexical 'quotation mark' for the speech of Jesus.[74] Together, these indicators have generated the common view that between 14.23 and 14.24 Luke has attempted to substitute for the voice of the householder that of Jesus (or God), thereby giving a purely fictive story an allegorical bent.[75]

It may indeed well be the case that λέγω refers to several subjects and, hence, that the *epilogion* bestows 'concomitant meanings' on the parable (Funk, 1966, pp. 174–5), but I am reluctant to leap to figurative interpretations without testing the possibility that Luke has attempted to link the final sentence with the preceding speech of the householder to comment on his situation as depicted in the narrative of the parable. A starting point is provided by the overt connection between 14.23, where the householder (here κύριος) obviously speaks, and 14.24. The conjunction γάρ, whether used also to express cause or inference, is a 'function word' whose grammatical role is to provide linkage between the two verses and, by inference, to maintain continuity of speaker (see Funk, 1973, vol. II, pp. 475–526). The previously noted parallelism μου ὁ οἶκος – μου τοῦ δείπνου furthers the impression that the redactor/narrator wanted 14.24 to be considered as a continuation of the householder's speech, that is, as part of the parable itself rather than as an

73 Scott, 1989, p. 257 n. 10; Jeremias, 1963, p. 45; cf. Fitzmyer, 1985, p. 1052.
74 See, in sum, Dawsey, 1986, pp. 16–17; Berger, 1970, pp. 89–91; and Pesce, 1978, pp. 225–32. This view finds additional strength in the observation that κύριος (14.23) in the gospel of Luke predominantly refers either to Jesus or to God (Jeremias, 1963, p. 45; Funk, 1966, p. 174 and n. 54). Indeed, for Dillon, κύριος in 14.22–3 becomes the decisive key for his allegorical interpretation of the parable and all the meal scenes in Luke: 'It is instructive concerning the evangelist's understanding of the meal scenes that in the middle of the sequence in Lk 14, the Lord, who is *table guest* at 14,1 suddenly becomes *host* of the "great banquet," according to 14,22' (1978, p. 202 n. 133).
75 For Jülicher 14.24 ensures that the entire dinner story has 'den Charakter einer Allegorie, deren Hauptbegriffe geistlich verstanden sein wollen'. Hence he postulates that in Luke's view the householder stands for God as the convener of the great banquet (the 'I' of λέγω, based on Rev. 19.17 [τὸ δεῖπνον τὸ μέγα τοῦ θεοῦ]!), that the servant represents Jesus (even though Jülicher recognized that λέγω ὑμῖν is an item 'der geläufigen Sprache' of Jesus!), and that the entire story has to do with deciding 'Einlass und Ausschliessung beim messianischen Mahl' (1910, vol. II, p. 416). I am not convinced that the text is able to propel Jülicher on the long leaps he wants to make. More restrained (and representative of other commentators) is Hahn, 1970, p. 73: '[D]er Hausherr ist in dem ganzen Gleichnis mit Jesus gleichgesetzt, und durch den Mund des irdischen Gastgebers ergeht das Wort des himmlischen Herrn.' But cf. p. 60: 'Vom Zusammenhang her muß es [das redende Subjekt], trotz einer gewissen Verallgemeinerung, der [irdische] Gastgeber sein.'

extrinsically appended application.[76] The textual ambiguities noted above appear to hinder this impression, but there is a way of plausibly accounting for them so that they do not decisively erase it. The case may be put as follows.

In accordance with our reconstruction of the Lukan *Vorlage*, it is exceedingly likely that λέγω ὑμῖν here was already a formula in the final sentence of the parable that the Lukan redactor took over from the Sayings Gospel Q (see ch. 5, p. 72), where, as is typical in this source, the construction probably introduced Jesus' didactic application of the banquet parable for the benefit of the Q audience (hence ὑμῖν).[77] Luke left the formula intact,[78] but transferred it from Jesus to the fictional householder, thereby blurring the referent of ὑμῖν.[79]

Some warrant for this conjecture lies in the fact that Luke operates similarly elsewhere. In the reworking of the Q parable of the talents (Luke 19.11–27),[80] it appears that the original ending, starting with a λέγω ὑμῖν (19.26) of Jesus commenting on a parable, has

---

[76] In agreement with Linnemann, 1960, p. 248: 'Die enge Verbindung von V.24 mit V.23 ... zeigt, daß dieser Vers noch zur Gleichniserzählung gehört.' Pesce agrees and argues that the parallelism 'my house'/'my supper' was generated by the redactional creation of μου ὁ οἶκος to match μου τοῦ δείπνου rather than vice versa. 'È probabile che ... il v.23 sia costruito sul v.24 e non viceversa' (1978, p. 225).

[77] The λέγω ὑμῖν (σοί) formula is frequently associated with the speech of Jesus in Q; its usage there is concorded by Kloppenborg, 1988, p. 237. See the following occurrences in connection with similes and parables (cited according to Lukan versification): [12.37], 12.44, 12.59, 15.7, [15.10], 19.26. Square brackets indicate passages whose inclusion in Q is probable but not totally provable.

[78] It is not surprising that the λέγω ὑμῖν formula is often thought to be a feature of Luke's style, because the evangelist uses it so frequently and because he often drops the ἀμήν (common in Mark and preferred by Matthew) where it occurs in a source (see Scott, 1989, p. 257 nn. 10, 11). This, however, may not be a reliable conclusion. Dawsey finds a much more complex picture. Although Luke does like the expression, it is clear that he 'took over and and emphasized a pattern of speech already associated with Jesus by the tradition' (1986, p. 16). Moreover, although the construction is 'intensively used, [it] does not appear as a hardened formula. Its forms are diverse' (p. 17). Indeed, Dawsey counts seventeen variations of the basic λέγω ὑμῖν, compared to only six forms in Mark (p. 17 n. 7). The fact that Luke does not consistently disavow ἀμὴν λέγω ὑμῖν (keeping it in his parallels to Mark 10.15, 29 and 13.30; even adding it to Mark 6.4!; cf. 12.37 [Q?] and 23.43 [no par.]) indicates Luke's flexibility in the use of the 'I say ...' formula.

[79] It might be noted that the plural pronoun is a problem even for those who suggest that Jesus is speaking in his own voice in 14.24. For, the entire parable is told in response to a remark of a single auditor. Hence the narration commences upon εἶπεν αὐτῷ (14.16; cf. 14.15).

[80] Q provenance is not unequivocally certain and often disputed due to the lack of agreement between Matthew and Luke in substance and story line. See Kloppenborg, 1988, p. 200.

been placed on the lips of the fictional κύριος of the parable.[81] An analogous case of a singular-plural disagreement caused by Lukan redaction of a Q passage containing the (ἀληθῶς) λέγω ὑμῖν formula is in 12.41–5.[82] Here the Q discourse on faithful and unfaithful servants, addressed to 'you' (12.44, ὑμῖν), is prepared by a redactional transition (12.41)[83] consisting of a question posed by an individual (εἶπεν δὲ ὁ Πέτρος). To be sure, Peter asks the question on behalf of ἡμᾶς, 'us' being the other followers, but while this renders the ὑμῖν sensible it remains grammatically licentious, much as in 14.24.

These examples indicate that the textual ambiguities in 14.23–4 are within the range of Luke's (in)capabilities in handling traditional material. They need not stand in the way of our view that Luke has attempted to push 14.24, in Q most probably a true *epilogion*,[84] into the parable and unto the lips of its primary character.

Of course, this view does not entirely solve the problem posed by ὑμῖν. Is it there as the result of an infelicitous attention slip on the part of the redactor?[85] Or has the householder, patently speaking to a single auditor, here taken on an additional voice in order to address an audience outside the parable proper, perhaps the dinner company assembled in the house of the Pharisee or even Luke's real audience? The latter is preferable once we consider that second

81 For 19.26 as the pre-Lukan (Q; om Matthew) ending, see Fitzmyer, 1985, p. 1231. A second ending is introduced by the Lukan πλήν, but even this appears to continue the *oratio recta* of the master in the parable. Cf. the ambiguous identity of 'those standing by' (19.24).

82 On this see the commentary of Pesce, 1978, pp. 228–9. The addition of ἀληθῶς to the basic λέγω ὑμῖν formula is an exclusively Lukan feature (see also 9.27, 21.3), and thus to be considered redactional, as is the ἀμήν in the Matthean parallel.

83 A few authors toy with the possibility that 12:41–42a was in Q, but most recommend Lukan redaction (Kloppenborg, 1988, p. 140).

84 14.23 should probably take its place along Q 11.51b and 13.35b, both using the λέγω ὑμῖν formula, which are widely thought to be commentary sayings added to traditional sayings for a judgmental purpose (see Kloppenborg, 1992b, pp. 14–15).

85 Jülicher thought that Luke did not notice 'den in ὑμῖν liegenden Anstoss' (1910, vol. II. p. 416). Evidently, a few later ms. copyists corrected the singular-plural disagreement, although the variants are not significant enough to make it into the apparatus of Nestlé-Aland, *Novum Testamentum Graece*, 26th edn. Pesce, relying on C. von Tischendorf, *Novum Testamentum Graece* (8th edn; Giesecke & Devrient, Lipsiae, 1869) and H. von Soden, *Die Schriften des Neuen Testaments. Text und Apparat* (Vandenhoeck & Ruprecht, Göttingen, 1913), notes that at 14.16 D, *pc* omit αὐτῷ and a few minor witnesses read αυτοῖς (1978, p. 228 n. 119).

person plurals are popular indicators of extra-narrative or extra-dramatic audience address.[86]

I thus return to affirm the view tentatively embraced earlier. Luke 14.24 is to be considered as the continued speech of the householder. Although there is no need to deny in the saying an exclusionary dimension aimed at the first-invited, I see it in the first place as a self-referential saying. It is a statement by the host about himself, testifying to his decision to relinquish the quest for belonging to the circle of the social élite and, henceforth, to redefine himself in relation to people at the distant opposite end of the social spectrum.[87] The saying thus helps to bring into view a wealthy man who is announcing his 'conversion'.[88] In Lukan terms proximate to our passage, he has 'counted the cost' (Luke 14.28) of his association with the socially marginal and is willing to pay the price even if it is as high as renouncing all he once had (πᾶσιν τοῖς ἑαυτοῦ; Luke 14.33), including his former network of social relations on which he probably depended to secure what he once had (see Rohrbaugh, 1991, p. 145). Whatever the profile and exemplary (parabolic) function of ἄνθρωπός τις in the pre-Lukan story, in the third gospel, whose author shares the prevalent Greco-Roman practice of exemplary characterization, i.e., portraying narrative *dramatis personae* as 'models for imitation',[89] he has been made over into a distinct-

---

[86] Thus Linnemann, 1960, p. 248: 'Meines Erachtens darf man ihn [den Plural in der Anrede v.24] so verstehen, daß sich hier der Hausherr gleichsam an das Publikum wendet und diesem den Sinn und die Absicht der von ihm getroffenen Maßnahmen erläutert – *ein Zug, der in der volkstümlichen Dramatik geläufig ist.*' (emphasis added) For a full treatment of audience address in Greek drama see Bain, 1977; note esp. p. 192: 'Second person plurals and references to ἄνδρες [cf. τῶν ἀνδρῶν in 14.24!] are the obvious pointers to audience address.'

[87] Bacon's argument (1922–3, announcing the still prevalent interpretive view) that the dinner story is a parable of an opportunity lost by the initially intended guests should be adjusted. The opportunity is lost, or, rather, voluntarily declined by the householder. Guests who do not consider attendance at the banquet an opportunity can hardly lose it by not attending.

[88] Cf. Horn, 1983, pp. 184–6: 'Diese Perikope [14.16–24] zeigt, daß Lk die Umkehrungsvorstellung bewußt aufnimmt ... um sie der Paränese zuzuordnen' (p. 184). See also Kloppenborg's article (1989) on the analogous 'conversion' of a wealthy man in Luke 16.1–8.

[89] On the Greco-Roman technique of characterization with the aim of offering positive (or negative) models of attitudes and behaviour to be imitated (or rejected) see Kurz, 1990, esp. pp. 185–8; and Rutherford, 1989, pp. 55–9, with many references to the ancient literature. Kurz does not refer to the householder parable, but the ideal of exemplary portraiture also may have influenced Luke's retelling of received parables. My reading of the householder stands as a case in point; a wider study of how Luke modifies characters in traditional parables in

ively Lukan character who represents the change in attitudes enjoined upon the πλούσιοι by the gospel writer:[90] he has assented to the idea of unrequitable generosity that arguably forms the centre of Luke's economic ethos;[91] he dispenses it without apparently linking it to the honour code of the wealthy élite; neither does he demonstrate this generosity in the distant, socially disengaged manner of the benevolent aristocrat whose magnanimity upholds conventional social boundaries; rather, sympotic generosity is employed as a means towards unconventional social relations and the aristocratic sympotic ideal of τὸ φιλοποίον τῆς τραπέζης (Plutarch, Moralia 612D) is retooled into a mechanism for a social transaction that actually subverts that ideal.

In sum, between the first invitations that signify a wealthy householder's commitment to the social ideals of the élite symbolized by a large banquet, and the final disavowal of these commitments in 14.24, the host appears to have become convinced, in the words of Marcus Aurelius, 'of need for reform and treatment of (his own) character'.[92] He has undergone a Lukan kind of conversion, not-

order to turn them into exemplary embodiments of his ethos would be a profitable undertaking.
90 See esp. Horn's incisive analysis of Luke's ethos ('wirksame Ethos') concerning wealth and its disposition: the core of Luke's 'Gemeindeparänese' consists of a highly valued practical piety ('praktische Frömmigkeit') marked by the readiness to support the needy in terms of ἐλεημοσύνην διδόναι (1983, pp. 35–57). This requirement, coupled with the need to relinquish material holdings, is predominantly ('vorwiegend') enjoined upon the rich by means of positive and negative examples of how wealthy individuals resolve the conflicting demands placed upon them by their wealth and the ethos of renunciation of wealth required by the Lukan community. The types and their responses, Horn argues, are to effect an 'Umdenken' or a change in 'Gesinnung' on the part of the rich, rather than to recommend an ecclesiastical charity 'Programm ... und darin ist er [Luke] Grieche' (p. 53; cf. pp. 242–3).
91 Horn concludes that Acts 20.35 ('Ἰησοῦ ... εἶπεν· μακάριόν ἐστιν μᾶλλον διδόναι ἢ λαμβάνειν) 'den paränetischen Skopos der Predigt des lk Jesus zusammengefaßt hat' (1983, p. 53). The saying itself is a common Greek proverb (numerous citations on p. 52; cf. Barrett, 1985, pp. 686–7), placed in the mouth of Jesus for whom it is otherwise unattested in the Jesus sayings tradition.
92 Meditations 1.7: τοῦ χρῄζειν διορθώσεως καὶ θεραπείας τοῦ ἤθους. Marcus is describing his own conversion to philosophy (see Rutherford, 1989, pp. 103–7). I am attracted to Marcus' words not only because they nicely express the popular Hellenistic concept of the conversion of character (the turn from the pursuit of vices [stereotypically, pleasure, wealth and fame] to the pursuit of virtues; see Nock, 1933, pp. 164–86), neither only because they are terms Luke might have used in a commentary on his own parable, but also because the medical language is a suggestive reminder of the healed dropsy in 14.1–6 whose transformation is the point for which the story of the transformed householder stands as a fictional paradigm (see ch. 8, pp. 174–5).

withstanding the absence of technical conversion language (μετάνοια, ἐπιστροφή and derivatives) in the narrative.[93] To clarify further, it is worth citing Justin Martyr who, though not commenting directly on Luke 14.16–24, apologetically describes the transformation of Christians in terms of a contrast between former and current values and their concomitant social practices in a way that closely resembles the attitudinal turn and the resulting about-face in the social affiliations of the Lukan householder:

> We who [once] valued above any other the way towards wealth and possessions, now transfer what we have into a common lot (εἰς κοινὸν), sharing with everyone who needs; we who [once] hated and destroyed each other and would not make use of the same [table and?][94] hearth (ἑστίας κοινάς) with people not of like kind (οὐχ ὁμοφύλους) because of their different customs, now, since the appearance of Christ, live familiarly together (ὁμοδίαιτοι γινόμενοι).
>
> (*Apology* 1.14.6–8; Otto, vol. II, pp. 45–6; discussion in Riddle, 1938, 142–3)

## Summary

The extended analysis of Luke's performance of the banquet parable now needs a brief recapitulation as a reminder of the main points it won for us.

[93] In Luke 'conversion' is largely understood as a moral 'Gesinnungswandel', as Horn successfully argues (1983, pp. 233–5). See also Michiels who stresses that conversion carries 'un sens principalement morale' (1965, pp. 57–9). E.g., Q's idea of καρποὶ τῆς μετανοίας (3.8) is specified in terms of generosity and economic fair play (3.10–14 = Lukan redaction?); cf. Acts 26.20 (ἄξια τῆς μετανοίας ἔργα πράσσοντας). Horn's remark (1983, p. 233) that the Cornelius story (Acts 10) is a narrative elaboration of Luke's understanding of conversion applies also to Luke 14.16–24. Luke's stress on the moral dimension of conversion corresponds to E. Thompson's observation that μετανοέω in post-classical Greek literature increasingly admits of a change of life's purpose measured in moral terms (1907, pp. 14–16, 28; see also Nock, 1933, pp. 168–9, for a brief description of the analogous Cynic view). For a different view on Lukan conversion see, e.g., Conzelmann, 1961, pp. 99–101; and esp. Haudebert, 1987, p. 366 (summary definition of Luke's concept of conversion): 'inviter les auditeurs à la reconnaissance de Jésus comme Seigneur, de Dieu comme unique et véritable. Elle est éminemment théologale (christologique) avant d'etre morale.'

[94] Otto's text has ἑστίας κοινάς, but he refers to a scribal variant that reads τραπέζας καὶ ἑστίας. Otto's sensible speculation is that the reference to the shared table anticipates the familial sense of togetherness conveyed by ὁμοδίαιτοι in the next clause. In any case, 'hearth' probably should not be restricted to mean

(1) A minimalist, more-or-less agreed on reconstruction of the pre-Lukan banquet story as a comparative guide enabled us to chart the substance and character of Luke's retelling of the story. Although the source problem forbids a recovery of *verbatim* Lukan redaction, general accentuations and tendencies could be identified nevertheless.

(2) Several outstanding features caught our attention: Luke 'escalated' (Crossan) the dinner explicitly (ἐποίει δεῖπνον μέγα, καὶ ἐκάλεσεν πολλούς) and indirectly by telling readers that it took two ingatherings to fill (γεμίζειν) the householder's οἶκος with dinner guests. By implication, but also by means of additional details and general narrative insinuations, the dinner host is portrayed as a member of the wealthy urban élite. We noted again Luke's fondness for extremely contrastive characterization. On the one side, attention to the socially locative ciphers in the three representative excuses of the preferred guests made it evident that they are to be seen as coming from the prosperous stratum of the *polis* going about the business of increasing their wealth; they are to be understood as the householder-host's upper-crust ὅμοιοι. On the opposite side, the description of the secondary guests relies on stereotypical Hellenistic language of poverty and social *Randgruppen* designations to make it sharply clear that the final and actual dinner company consisted of people from the lowest of the low-ranking. They are to be understood as the urban poor and disabled as well as the socially unseemly living on the outside perimeter of the city and hence commonly and pejoratively known as ἐξοπυλεῖτοι. The purpose of this polarized portraiture, we suggest, is to accentuate the spatial, social and moral distance involved in the householder's conversion to new social allegiances. Finally, it was suggested that the aim of these tendencies can be clarified when they are related to the householder as the primary character in the story.

(3) Concerning this interpretation, three strands bear repeating. First: positively, I tried to clarify the features of the story – its accentuated language of wealth and poverty, its characters, their social position relative to each other, the relational dynamics between them, etc. – with reference to common patterns of social interaction in the first century Mediterranean world, to general cultural sensibilities and to Greco-Roman literary *topoi*, in short, to

'fireplace'. Since Homer the hearth symbolized the most intimate inner space of the home; sharing the hearth thus is a metaphor for intimate fellowship which, in Mediterranean terms, certainly included eating together.

the everyday and traditional social knowledge implied in the text and assumed of its first century readers/auditors. Second: negatively, this meant relegating interpretive strategies committed to the Lukan parable as (half) allegory from the position of priority that they have widely enjoyed in the scholarly commentary tradition. Specifically, the mission theory and the eschatological banquet theory, often combined by interpreters, are vulnerable to criticism. Rather than being reliable means of decoding the banquet parable, they strike me as hermeneutic apriorisms, means of encoding the story that depend on a promiscuous combination of an inapt literary analogy (Bar Ma'jan) and stressed equivalencies drawn between narrative *personae* and extra-narrative referents. Third: I tried to shift the analytic spotlight from its common focus on the guests (and the implied issues of inclusion/exclusion) to the host as the story's 'compositional pivot'. The warrant for this may not be obvious, but neither is it an arbitrary move. A measure of encouragement comes from Luke's redactional attribution of the λέγω ὑμῖν saying to the householder as a way of placing attention on him. Furthermore, the host is obviously the primary, constant and most consequential actor in the narrative. To this may be added the more general rule adduced from the construction of folk tales, namely 'the rule of centring around the hero' (Bihari-Andersson, 1987).

(4)   This analytic and interpretive matrix generated a scenario that may be summarized as follows. The opening scene is drawn with a few strokes that rely on and evoke the familiar Hellenistic literary *topos* and social commonplace of the conspicuous dinner as the chief trade mark and locale of exclusive sociability of the rich. The floodlight that illumines the initial action of the householder is powered by currents consisting of cultural ideals, social codes of honour-shame and expected patterns of behaviour that surround the aristocratic big dinner. Readers are to visualize the seemingly honourable host formally inviting his equals to a banquet as a good upper-class man striving to define his social self in terms of allegiance to the circle of the urban élite and their aspirations, values, prejudices and paranoias. The host's plan is denied by those on whom its fruition depend, the refusing invited. An appraisal of the refusal scene with the aid of a generalized understanding of the protocol and social importance of Greco-Roman dinner invitations clarifies the hoped-for guests' action as an unjustified and a malicious (so the narrative would have us believe) effort to damage the householder's reputation and honour and, as the remark on the

conspiratorial unanimity assures us, to deny him a place within their fellowship. The householder predictably becomes angry, having lost both face and family of 'friends' on whom his position, reputation and economic well-being depend. But rather than following the conventional script on reclaiming one's honour by means of avenging strategies, the householder turns his back on his well-placed peers, together with all the moral, social and economic ideals they represent, and starts a new chapter in his social biography. He overcomes the typical aristocratic disdain for the urban vagrants and various socially and morally marginal people, generally presumed ignominious and dishonourable, and 'forces' them across the threshold into his dining room for a meal that is in all respects the anti-type of the banquet envisioned at the outset of the parable. Because the initiative results in a meal in the householder's οἶκος, rather than in a mere giving away of food, it appears as an initiative in group formation, the host being both initiator and most unlikely member, rather than as a mere gesture of generous patronage. A final saying throws further light on the householder's transformed social intentions and the moral 'Gesinnungswandel' (Horn, 1983) presupposed by the change. Straddling the boundary between intra-narrative *oratio recta* and audience address (λέγω ὑμῖν), the saying emphasizes the householder's decision to sever the ties with his former friends. By implication the statement is an expression of loyalty to the dinner group that now surrounds him and, as such, it signals both the completion and the finality of his 'conversion'.

# 7

## FORMS, GENRES AND COMPOSITION

A brief reiteration of the principal points that arose in the examination of the discrete periods of the dinner episode should help us to approach another set of issues. These have have to do with the compositional plan and argumentative logic of the unit in its entirety. The scrutiny of the sub-units, loosely tethered to the poles of form, source and milieu analyses, allows several summary claims that raise the question of the design of the episode as a whole.

### The importance of the forms

As to forms, the episode consists of heterogeneous speech types that in themselves are unremarkable; they are of the stuff common in the gospel literature, including the gospel of Luke. The episode begins with a *chreia* (14.1–6), proceeds through a line-up of sapiential sentences (14.8–10, 12–13), maxims (14.11, 14, 15) and a fictional story about a householder who invited guests (14.16–24), and concludes with an *epilogion* (14.24) that has a narrative function in the householder story but perhaps doubles as a rhetorical conclusion of the whole episode. All this merely states the obvious from the vantage point of a modest familiarity with textbook form criticism. And, for the reader whose percipience is guided primarily by, say, Bultmannian form criticism, neither the identification of the forms nor their sequence is of much significance for the composition of the whole episode. The individual form-critical units are there to be interrogated in isolation from each other, while the explanation of their literary co-existence and sequence tends to abort form-critical considerations altogether.[1] This does not mean, however, that the

---

[1] Bultmann himself demonstrates the virtual uselessness of form criticism for compositional analysis. In his *History of the Synoptic Tradition* each of the sub-units of 14.1–24 is duly classified and analysed separately (pp. 12, 62, 78, 103–4, 175), but the collection itself is composed according to the principle of 'association by

form-critical enterprise ought to be abandoned as a useless taxonomic effort. What it does mean is that attention to forms ought to be contextualized in the rhetoric-influenced literary culture of Luke's time. With the leverage of ancient instructions on rhetoric, we can boost classical New Testament form criticism to the threshold of recognition that Luke 14.1–24 is a composition, perhaps even a narrative argument, rather than a haphazard collage of speech units tenuously held together by the 'situation' and 'catchword' of 'the feast'. I hinted at this in previous chapters. The most oblique hint came as the suggestion that the episode opens with a *chreia*, which, as I will show in the next chapter, in ancient rhetorical treatises was considered to be an important ingredient in persuasive communication in narrative form and, hence, a rather reliable indicator that an argument is being attempted. The remainder of the episode consists of (1) several gnomic sentences and of (2) material that is called παραβολή, though it is not such by any form-critical definition, and (3) of a story that is not called a παραβολή, though it is universally taken to be one in a formal sense. This usage (and non-usage) of the term 'parable', together with the observation that in ancient rhetorical manuals παραβολή refers to one of the proofs (πίστεις) in inductive argumentation, is a second indicator that we are dealing with some kind of persuasive composition. Further, and at this point proleptically (see pp. 145–58 below), analogies and maxims are essential means of elaborating a *chreia* into a narrative argument. Summarily, attention to the formal aspects of the units of Luke 14.1–24 in light of the ancient usage of certain forms already generates the impression of a process of composition, at least insofar as the choice of certain speech forms and their sequence is reckoned as part of the compositional process. Indeed, a rhetoric-informed scanning of the episode as a whole tells that its line-up of forms seems broadly to replicate the pattern of complete argumentation that characterized the ancient speech as taught by the rhetoricians: (1) introduction (προοίμιον, *exordium*), (2) statement of the issue to be argued (διήγησις, *narratio*), (3) proof

catchword' (pp. 325–6), the catchword being 'the feast'. Cf. p. 334, where he remarks on Luke's 'recipe' for composition: 'The feast in 14[ff.] has to serve as the situation for the healing of the dropsical man, for the sayings about order of precedence, the true guests, and for the parable of the great feast.' The phrase 'has to' is revealing. Bultmann clearly is impressed by the artificiality and vacuousness of 'the feast' as an explanation of the literary existence of Luke 14.1–24.

(πίστις, *argumentatio*), (4) conclusion (ἐπίλογος, *peroratio/conclusio*).²

## Measures of compositional activity

The source analysis revealed little that contradicts the impression that the dinner episode owes its shape to more than composition by 'catchword'. On the contrary, some degree of Lukan invention marks all units of the episode. To be sure, in strictly source-critical terms the gospel writer re-uses some material that is pre-Lukan, including, in descending order of certainty, 14.16–24 (Q), 14.11 (Q?) and 14.5 (cf. Matthew 12.11). Yet, as we saw in the case of the banquet story, even re-used material has not been slavishly reproduced, but recast sufficiently to allow us to think of it as a Lukan performance of a traditional 'gist' (Funk, 1992), that is, a Lukan textualization of a story that he knew in general form from an older repertoire. The rest is of indeterminable provenance, either consisting of material that is evidently Lukan though it depends upon familiarity with traditional themes and forms (14.1–6), or of such ordinary stuff (14.8–14) that, if a 'source' is needed to account for it, it makes the idea of 'author' next to meaningless. Episodic introduction (14.1) and transitions (14.7, 15) are demonstrably Lukan.

Previous chapters gave some indications that a 'textbook' source-redaction method of measuring authorial inventiveness and/or indebtedness to sources, though useful to the extent indicated in the previous paragraph, does not give an adequate picture of the tradition-invention ratio in the dinner episode. The method tends to overestimate reliance on sources, even postulating them *ex hypothesi* (e.g., the 'L' source), on the one hand, and to overplay the idea of creative genius at the expense of reliance on sources, on the other. I tried to soften this polarity, which has its roots in the imagination of post-Enlightenment *Quellenforschung* ('scientific' quest for

---

² See the detailed synopsis and explication of the ancient τέχναι in Lausberg, 1960, pp. 150–240 (sections 263–442). Cf. Kennedy, 1963, p. 11; Mack and Robbins, 1989, p. 3 (Robbins), pp. 53–7 (Mack). Robbins, 1994b, pp. 16–22, has criticized this view (which was first presented in Braun, 1993). He argues that Luke 14 is an example of a Theonian rather than a Hermogenean type of *chreia* argument. The latter is modelled on the pattern of the complete argument, while the former is an expansion of the *chreia* 'from the parts' (ἐκ τῶν μερῶν; see Hock and O'Neil, 1986, pp. 106–7, for the text of Theon's instructions), a form of argumentation which does not transpose the *chreia* into a thesis statement to be argued by means of 'proofs', but one that sequentially picks up and expands different (narrative or topical) parts of the *chreia*.

sources) and its inherently anaemic conceptualization of author-ship.[3] Rather than restricting the semantic value of 'source' to its narrow technical meaning of a literary fount flowing into the textual receptacle of a later author,[4] I dilated the term to include in its meaning the larger fund of Greco-Roman *Wiedergebrauchsrede* ('re-usable speech')[5] which Greco-Roman authors recycled in their imitative zeal and patterned modes of communication.[6] This brought into light a less precise, though I hope not a less plausible way of understanding Luke's use of 'sources' in writing the dinner episode. To wit, where Luke appears creative (14.1–6), he is not outrightly inventive, evidently relying on older Jesus traditions for a controversial situation and on a popular Cynic metaphor; where he appears outrightly inventive (14.7–14), he takes up common Greco-Roman sympotic motifs and conventions but manipulates them to reflect a Cynic-like critique of those conventions; where he obviously relies on a written source (14.16–24), he reformulates its text into a better representation of his ideals, but not without the help of the recyclable themes and symbols of the Hellenistic big dinner;

---

[3] This is not intended as an unappreciative 'hit and run' against the *Quellenforschung* model, dominant not only in gospel studies, but also in Classics and in the study of the history and dynamics of literary production generally. That this model has flattened the complex issues revolving around the dialectic between creative genius and dependence on sources (a dependence that itself consists of a gradation from rote recitation to allusion) is perhaps obvious enough not to require argumentation or citation of sources.

[4] Conte (1986, p. 23) appropriately points out that 'source' (and even more the German 'Quelle', one might add) is 'a revealing metaphor of fluidity'. Not only does it evoke the myth of origins as the ideological canopy over the *Quellenforschung* enterprise, but it also is an apt figure for its conception of literary production in terms of a descending flow of genres, forms, themes, techniques, etc., for which authors are seen as conduits.

[5] On *Wiedergebrauchsrede* see Lausberg, 1968, pp. 48–53. To summarize Lausberg's complex discussion, re-usable speech encapsulates the various enduring and versatile idioms, forms, metaphors, etc., that are re-used because they are deeply embedded in and efficient carriers of a culture's traditions and conventions. *Wiedergebrauchsrede* shares in the regularity and formality of religious discourse (e.g., the constancy of recitation of creeds and scriptures) or judicial discourse (bound by the written legal traditions), but 'differs from them by being sub-stantially richer and more varied ... that leaves more scope for the varying effect of the individual' (Conte, 1986, p. 41, nicely capturing Lausberg's sense). Lausberg distinguishes *Wiedergebrauchsrede* from *Verbrauchsrede*, speech that is used up in a particular, momentary situation of everyday life.

[6] Since various oratory and literary activities were built upon a foundation of rhetorical training that itself depended upon repeatable and versatile patterns of constructing arguments, it is not surprising that *Wiedergebrauchsrede* was in fact the bread and butter of oratory and writing of popular literature. See Lausberg, 1968, p. 58, on the re-use of rhetorical patterns in various speech situations and types.

throughout, the episode is unfolded by means of contrasts and polarized comparisons (*synkrisis*), evident not only in the literary antitheses, but also in the rich stock in the entire episode of *synecdoches* (a kind of symbolic 'short-hand')[7] of the rich and poor, the cleavage between them in the stratified urban locale of Luke's world, and the attitudes and conventions that governed their interaction.

This authorial activity resembles the kind that ancient theorists described with (the widely recycled) figure of the author as 'a flitting bee, darting from one source to another, ingesting, digesting, recasting influences in novel and individual configurations'.[8] This image leaves room for a great deal of dependence on tradition for raw material, but nonetheless envisions a real author who blends the 'several flavours [nectars from different flowers] into one delicious compound [honey]' (Seneca, *Epistulae* 84.5). But by what means the blending took place is the question that this figure puts to us.

In sum, the formal observations, the source-critical conclusions and the notice of Luke's indebtedness to the fund of Hellenistic *Wiedergebrauchsrede*, press for the recognition that the dinner episode is a composition in the full meaning of that term. The question that now needs attention is whether the compositional plan of the episode, including the logic of the internal arrangement, can be specified.

## A critique of the symposium hypothesis[9]

It should be said that the way the issue of composition and internal arrangement has been put already, permits me to pass by

---

[7] On συνεκδοχή (*intellectio*) see Quintilian, *Inst.* 8.6.19 and Ps-Cicero, *Rhet. ad Her.* 4.33.44–5: 'Synecdoche occurs when the whole is known from a small part or a part from the whole.' Luke employs the use of trope mainly in the first sense, as in the following examples from *Rhet. ad Her.*: a flute suggests the entire marriage ceremony; luxurious garb the whole world of riches and treasures. See Lausberg,1960, pp. 295–8 (sections 572–7), for varied use.

[8] Hooley, 1990, p. 80, encapsulating the import of the author as a 'bee' found in Lucretius 3.10–12; Horace, *Od.* 4.2.23–8; splendidly elaborated in Seneca, *Ep.* 84.3–8. Much later Macrobius uses the bee figure to describe how he gathered material for his symposium (*Sat. praef.* 5–6). A good indication of how this figure of the writer corresponds to the ideals and educational practices of the Roman period can be obtained in Bonner, 1977, pp. 212–49. Luke's only explicit comment on his use of sources (1.1–4) probably is too aligned with the purposes of the preface to serve as a full and accurate description of his various debts.

[9] This section is a slightly expanded and altered version of Braun, 1992, pp. 73–5, 81–2.

without further comment studies that stress the meal motif as the compositional glue of this episode, or those that comment on 14.1–24 within much broader thematic pursuits, such as Luke's treatment of the Pharisees (see the literature cited on pp. 27–8, 41), views on issues of wealth and poverty,[10] eschatology[11] or the use of meals as a literary motif.[12] All these offer rich fare on the pivotal place of commensality in Luke's gospel, but leave the questions on the compositional logic of 14.1–24 in the realm of the presupposed or on the margin of analysis.

There is, however, one hypothesis that speaks directly to our question and therefore is worthy of consideration. Among those interpreters who have tried to clarify Lukan composition in 14.1–24 with the help of Mediterranean literary forms the 'symposium hypothesis' stands virtually unchallenged, largely due to an influential essay by X. de Meeûs (1961)[13] in which he compares the Lukan

10 Luke's interest in economic issues is well known and the subject of a vast scholarly literature. In addition to scattered citations in earlier chapters, see the extensive bibliographic data (since 1972) in Schreck, 1989, p. 437 n. 206 (names), pp. 456–71 (bibliography).

11 See especially E. Davis, 1967. His diss. uses the Lukan meals as his text base, but his heavy (*a priori*, it seems to me) commitment to the eschatological feast of Jewish apocalyptic theology as the determinative 'background' for the Lukan meal scenes coerces his exegesis and largely neglects the composition of particular scenes. According to Davis, evidently reliant on Conzelmann's views on Lukan eschatological thinking, Luke adapts the Jewish messianic meal tradition to serve his desire to relieve the stress of the delayed *parousia* with an emphasis on the nearness of the kingdom of God, proleptically experienced at the meals of the gathered community (a Lukan 'realization' of the messianic feast) in which the 'righteous' will find their reward. Cf. the similar views of Navone, 1964, pp. 923–4, 926.

12 Most importantly, D. Smith, 1987; cf. Karris, 1985, ch. 4 ('The Theme of Food'). McMahan's fine diss. (1987) belongs in this broad category, although his notion of the 'type-scene' (derived from Robert Alter and owing much to Robert Tannehill and Alan Culpepper) is more an item of narrative strategy (in modern narrative-critical terms) for unfolding plot and characterization than a thematic or compositional category.

13 In the same year (1961) the hypothesis was proposed independently by Grundmann, 1961, pp. 28, 290. Other significant analyses of Luke 14.1–24 as a Hellenistic symposium are Ernst, 1979, (without a reference to de Meeûs); Steele, 1981; 1984, pp. 382–7 (highly dependent on de Meeûs). Cf. Delobel, 1966, pp. 415–75; Aune, 1978, pp. 69–70; Berger, 1984b, pp. 1310–15. The hypothesis has been taken up so widely that it may be taken as a stable commentary tradition; for a partial list of authors see Steele, 1984, p. 379 n. 1, to which may be added as more recent examples Karris, 1985, p. 62; Aune, 1987, p. 122; Sellew, 1987, p. 74; van Tilborg, 1987, pp. 133, 163 n. 2 (cautiously); Kloppenborg, 1992a, pp. 109–10. This list could be extended almost indefinitely if we were to include various thematic studies in Luke, e.g., on the Pharisees, issues related to hospitality, wealth and poverty, and the like. D. Smith's important article, 'Table Fellowship as a Literary Motif' (1987; cf. D. Smith and Taussig, 1990, pp. 54–7), is sometimes

dinner episode with the Greco-Roman *deipnon* or *symposion* writings, a genre that originated with Plato and Xenophon and became a popular form for the literary conveyance of philosophical and didactic discourse until the end of antiquity.[14] According to his analysis, replicated and somewhat refined by E. S. Steele (1981; 1984), Luke 14.1–24 is a deliberate imitation of the classical symposium form, as evidenced by the fact that the passage meets most of the important requirements of this genre. Similar structure (invitation, announcement of an issue for debate [*fait divers*], dialogue in the form of table talk), the presence of typical symposium figures (notable host, chief guest, other invited guests, uninvited [ἄκλητος] guest), and the appearance of regular convivial discussion topics (seating arrangements, appropriate guest lists) constitute the main support pillars for the argument that Luke's compositional plan in 14.1–24 was dictated by the symposium form.

Important ground has been gained by these studies. Luke 14.1–24 clearly emits much conventional clatter of Greco-Romans at dinner. Bringing this episode into proximity to the literary symposia is a gesture that helps to expose the convivial motifs in the episode and invites a reading of it in light of the ancient banquet traditions. Yet, several criticisms rise up against the formulation of the symposium hypothesis and its application to Luke 14.

First, the genre identification of Luke 14.1–24 is overdrawn. Strictly speaking, Hellenistic symposia constitute a macro-genre, writings that in their entirety purport to record the proceedings at dinner or around the mixing bowl. This kind of *symposion* is formally distinct from dining episodes embedded in other macro-

cited in support of the view that Luke 14.1–24 is composed in accordance with the symposium genre, but that ignores his qualifications. He allows that it is 'related to the symposium genre' (p. 614), but stops short of claiming that it *is* a literary symposium. He expressly distinguishes his interest in the Lukan meal 'motif' from de Meeûs, Steele, *et al.* (p. 615 and n. 8).

14 Plutarch, for example, prefaces his own *Quaestiones convivales* ('Table Talk') with the remark that he is following in the footsteps of 'Plato, Xenophon, Aristotle, Speusippus, Epicurus, Prytanis, Hieronymus, and Dio of the Academy, who all deemed it worth the effort to undertake the task of writing down the talk held at a drinking party' (*Mor.* 612D-E). Cf. Philo (*Cont.* 57, 64) for a deliberate effort to portray the meals of the Therapeutae with reference to the Greek symposia. For a more complete chronological list of symposium authors see de Meeûs, 1961, p. 856 n. 49, and Berger, 1984b, p. 1311. The classic study of this genre is J. Martin, 1931, but see also Ullrich, 1908–9; cf. Hirzel, 1895, pp. 1.151–9; Mau, 1901, pp. 1201–8; F. Dupont, 1977. Cf. Aune, 1978, pp. 51–4, 69–78; and, in summary, D. Smith, 1987, pp. 614–17.

genres.[15] Further, even allowing for much variation in the internal features of the literary symposium, Luke's dinner episode lacks several elements so typical that they take on the nature of generic requirements rather than idiosyncratic preferences. Absent, for example, are the ubiquitous characters of medic (ἰατρός)[16] and jester (γελωτοποιός) as well as other constant symposium figures;[17] but for one brief interjection (14.15), the multi-voiced discourse characteristic of the symposia is exchanged for a pronunciatory monologue that silences host and guests alike (14.6);[18] the Lukan diners never rise from their couch for the customary postprandial walk (περίπατος).[19]

Second, even if the symposium hypothesis can accommodate these difficulties, genres are a tricky thing.[20] Though they may share

---

[15] E.g., Trimalchio's *cena* in Petronius' *Satyricon*. J. Martin (1931, p. 291) distinguishes between 'Symposien im literarischen Sinne' and meal stories that are 'unselbständige Einlagen in andere Literaturwerke'. Aune (1978, p. 69) rightly notes that early Christian literature 'contains no examples of the symposium as a literary genre' and that the earliest Christian symposium is the *Banquet of the Ten Virgins* by Methodius of Olympus (late third century CE). 'Gastliche Geselligkeit' (convivial socializing) was so highly valued in Greek and Roman societies that it expressed itself literarily beyond the literary symposia (J. Martin, 1931, p. 291).

[16] Notwithstanding my earlier suggestion (p. 42) that Jesus bears some resemblance to the figure of the philosopher as 'doctor' of the passions. The doctor in the symposia is a medical practitioner.

[17] J. Martin (1931, pp. 33–116) discusses the following 'stehende Figuren': host, jester, uninvited guest, doctor, late guest, weeper, guest with hurt feelings ('der Gekränkte'), drunkard, erotic couple. De Meeûs (1961, p. 856) explains this absenteeism in a way that softens his genre argument: 'L'absence du médecin, d'un grand buveur, ou d'une joueuse de flûte s'explique par la nature du banquet chez le Pharisien: ce n'est pas une beuverie.'

[18] One might note that the absence of the jester and real dialogue makes for a dinner party that hardly meets Plutarch's definition of a *symposion* as 'a sharing of earnest and jest, of words and deeds' (*Quaest. conv.* 708D). The two shared oral activities, eating and talking, were inseparable in the ideals represented by the symposia. The normative aims of the literary symposia thus were to instruct both in cultured behaviour and speech. The conjoining of these two aspects is aptly expressed by Athenaeus whose *deipnosophistae* are at once gastronomes (feasting on food) and logophiles (feeding on a 'feast of words') [*Deipnos.* 354d]; see Jeanneret, 1991, pp. 97–139; and Hock, 1990.

[19] 'Der περίπατος nach dem Mahl ... ist von Xenophon bis zur "Cena Cypriani" ein üblicher Abschluß des Symposions' (Berger, 1984b, p. 1313 n. 304; cf. J. Martin, 1931, pp. 147–8, 211, 317). Luke evidently knows about the περίπατος in connection with a meal (24.13–32) as Aune has pointed out (1978, p. 70). Jesus is on the move right after the dinner (14.25), but the movement here is part of the viatic theme of Luke's central section (in which Jesus is depicted as a wanderer), rather than a postprandial exercise to aid the digestion of dinner ('Verdauungsspaziergang' [Ullrich, 1908–9, p. 2.8]).

[20] See Leitch, 1991, pp. 84–5, 96–8, for a fine discussion of the problems entailed in applying 'genre' as hermeneutic 'instruments to order and control the meaning of literary texts'.

similar formal features and structural elements, they are amenable
to ferrying a variety of authorial aims and able to press a plurality of
demands on the reader. Identification of literary form is not obviously a reliable path to an author's purpose. Plato's *Symposion* may
be an epideictic treatment of Socrates as the the ideal intellectual
and moral person, but this is hardly the unitary tendency and aim of
every exemplar of the genre. To the point, the Cynic anti-
symposia,[21] exemplified by Lucian whose *Symposium or the Lapiths*
is a brawling travesty of its Platonic predecessor,[22] illustrate how
easily possible and effective it is to turn a generic genre against itself
and thereby to lampoon that 'canonical' tradition and to 'explode'
the cultural ideals that lie behind it.[23] The attempt to discern the
purpose of Luke's supper scene through the prism of the Platonic
tradition of symposium writing, which arguably includes Xenophon, Plutarch and Aristeas, i.e., de Meeûs's and Steele's basis of
comparison,[24] thus may be prone to misprision even though it
rightly points interpreters of Luke to the Hellenistic symposium
world as a source of illumination.

A third criticism comes to view when we examine the curious lack
of substantial inferences concerning the internal argumentative
logic of the dinner episode these scholars draw from the claim that

---

[21] The term is Lucian's ('I am anti-banqueting [ἀντισυμποσιάζω] the son of Aristo-
nos' [*Lexiph.* 1]), but used here to refer more generally to the Cynic critique of
Greek symposiastic ideals noted in previous chapters.

[22] See Ullrich, 1908–9, pp. 2.14–56, for a discussion of the Cynic symposia. Lucian's
*Symp.* 'ist ... Platons direkt entgegengesetzt; nicht auf eine Verherrlichung,
sondern auf eine Karikatur von Philosophen ist [es] gerichtet ... Die Satire
Lukians erscheint wie eine Parodie auf das Symposion Platons und auf die
sokratischen Gastmähler überhaupt. Sie greift die gelehrten Syssitien feindselig an
und verfolgt sie mit Spott; sie bedeutet den Umsturz auf diesem Gebiete'
(pp. 2.53–4). Similarly Papst, 1986, pp. 137–41; Jeanneret, 1991, pp. 150–60;
Bracht, 1989, pp. 103–5, 108–9.

[23] Jeanneret offers a particularly incisive explication of Lucian's *Symp.* as the
'exploding' of a tradition. On the literary level, 'heterogeneous gobbets of text,
literary reminiscences, and samples from all genres are juxtaposed without any
hope of integration' and thus the work as a whole seems to aim at the 'disintegra-
tion of a genre' (1991, p. 152). But there is also an ideological explosion. The
'exploded banquet' is a weapon against the 'orthodoxy' represented by the
Platonic symposium tradition and a comic critique of the pretentious social
manners and aspirations of his time (p. 150).

[24] De Meeûs acknowledges the variety of ancient symposia (1961, pp. 856–7 and
n. 49), but in his explication of the Lukan episode he relies exclusively on the
symposia of Plato, Xenophon and Plutarch (pp. 857–68). Steele (1981, p. 59; cf.
1984, p. 380 n. 4) defines the base of comparison more explicitly: 'The texts I have
chosen [as a basis for comparison] ... are Plato and Xenophon's *Symposia* because
of their clarity of form, and the letter of *Aristeas* and Plutarch's *Banquet* for their
temporal proximity to Luke.'

Luke 14.1–24 is an imitation of the classical Greek symposium form. A brief survey of the main proponents of the symposium hypothesis reveals the following. In his commentary on Luke, W. Grundmann labels 14.1–24 'das lukanische Symposion' (1961, p. 290; cf. p. 28), by which he means the literary form exemplified by Plato and Xenophon. But this label appears to be entirely gratuitous, for in the commentary on the episode one finds not a single reference to the Greek symposia. The closest he comes to employing the 'symposium' as an analytic guide is in the remark that the meal is a 'frame' for housing traditional Jesus *logia* that originated in meal situations.[25] X. de Meeûs, though he employs the symposia much more assiduously, similarly stresses genre as a tactic for controlling separate bits of tradition. In his view, Luke's ability to compose a symposium primarily attests to the evangelist's 'talent d'écrivain', the ability to use a generic 'plan préétabli' to homogenize heterogeneous bits of traditional material into a coherent account (p. 869). Beyond this, he toys with the idea that the symposium form conveys Luke's encomiastic intentions concerning Jesus (p. 863). And, based on the observation that Plato's *Symposium* is a dialogue centring on a single theme (*Eros*), de Meeûs looks for the same feature in Luke and suggests that the discourse is on 'humility' (pp. 851, 869–70). The epideictic function of the symposium form is also stressed by E. S. Steele. Supposing that the main function of the classical Hellenistic symposia was to showcase the moral and intellectual superiority of the chief guest(s), he suggests that Luke's option for the symposium genre signifies his intention 'to portray Jesus, much as Plato did Socrates, as the paragon of wisdom and virtue. The Lukan redactor is concerned to show who Jesus is and to evoke a particular response or attitude towards him, a sympathetic hearing' (1981, pp. 186, 192–4). J. Ernst similarly relies on genre to decipher the point of Luke 14.1–24,[26] but does not arrive at Steele's conclusion. According to Ernst, the primary purpose of Luke's choice of genre is not to enrol Jesus in the college of Hellenistic dinner sages (*deipnosophistae*). Rather, Luke relies on the symposium as the literary form best able to reflect the actual context and manner of Christian proclamation; genre thus is a literary replication of the

25 Grundmann, 1961, p. 295: 'das Mahl ist für Lukas ein Rahmen, der eine Reihe von him überlieferten Jesusworten ordnend zusammenfügt, die aus der Mahlsituation stammen'.
26 'Lukas "übernimmt" das literarische Modell des Symposion, weil es für seine Verkündigung in mehrfacher Hinsicht durchsichtig ist' (1979, p. 74).

early Christian community responding to Jesus' invitation to come to dinner (14.17), settling down to eucharistic *Tischgemeinschaft* ('table fellowship') and engaging in Jesus-talk in the form of *Tischgespräche* ('table talk'; pp. 75–6), a practice that Ernst probably quite correctly thought to be patterned after the Hellenistic social symposia.[27] In sum, it is suggested that a comparative reading of Luke's banquet episode shows that it approximates the Hellenistic literary symposia. Herein lies the explanation of Luke's compositional achievement (external and internal unity) and the clue to his ideological claims (Jesus as a mimetic figure) or narrative aims (Christians at table with Jesus as host and teacher). Though none of these insights are incorrect, they are generalizations that do not leave us much the wiser when it comes to specifying precisely how Luke viewed the classical élite symposium traditions.

Fourth, and perhaps most importantly, a genre analysis with its focus on the definition of form is methodologically uninterested and hence in practice sharply adumbrative when it comes to an inner-episodic analysis. By this approach one might recognize the symposium form as a compositional template behind Luke 14.1–24 (Grundmann, de Meeûs) and take this as a general indicator of purpose (Steele, Ernst), yet glide over the logic of the passage's internal rhetoric and blur its distinctive performance and argument in relation to other Lukan dinner episodes.[28]

As an example of the former, I point only to the way that the episodic introduction (14.1–6) is explained according to the symposium hypothesis. According to de Meeûs, followed by Delobel and Steele, this scene functions as a *fait divers*, literally a 'news item', but used as a technical designation for an action or event that initiates the sympotic dialogue.[29] However, this promising notice is not further pressed and hence does not come to fruition despite de Meeûs's claim that he has shed 'a new light on the function of the dropsy episode' (p. 862). Steele strongly implies that the sympotic *fait divers* is strictly an expedient, an innocuous formal convention

---

[27] 'Wir können feststellen, daß die christliche Eucharistiefeier insgesamt in einer vertieften, geläuterten und vergeistigten Gestalt eine Grundstimmung auf sich gezogen hat, die im jüdischen und deutlicher im griechisch-römischen Festmahl "ausgelagert" war und vorzüglich in der Einrichtung des Symposions ihren Niederschlag gefunden hat' (1979, p. 62).

[28] See Steele, 1981, pp. 184–94, for a view of a remarkably unitary redactional aim in Luke 7.36–50, 11.37–54, and 14.1–24.

[29] De Meeûs, 1961, p. 862 (who derives if from Jacques Bompaire, *Lucien écrivain* [1958], p. 308); Delobel, 1966, p. 459; Steele, 1981, pp. 75–9; 1984, pp. 381, 386–7.

that launches the dinner talk, but is otherwise 'usually of an unremarkable or insignificant nature' (1984, p. 381 n. 10; cf. 1981, p. 75 n. 51). Ernst, not familiar with the work of de Meeûs, finds in the symposium figure of the ἄκλητος, who regularly disturbs the dinner ambience and proceedings, an analogy to the dropsical man. But this analogy, unlikely in itself, is gratuitous rather than productive for the interpretation of the scene. In Ernst's view, the exemplary significance of the scene is that it instructs Luke's readers in the ethos of a Christian Sunday ritual ('christliche Sonntagsfeier') against the foil of rabbinic sabbath casuistry (1979, pp. 64–6). Evidently the symposium form here fails to be a useful interpretive guide.

In all, a strictly generic analysis of the composition and aims of Luke 14.1–24 is not quite satisfactory. That Luke knew the literary symposia is hardly questionable, but this particular literature, especially when this is further limited to the classical symposia of Plato and Xenophon and their Hellenistic imitations, does not, in my view, constitute the literary and ideological matrix for Luke's sympotic episode.

In the interest of a more profitable comparative methodology it is best to conceive of the Greco-Roman 'symposium' in broad terms. As a social institution it played an essential role from Homeric times into the late Hellenistic period,[30] replicating and symbolizing civic and cultural ideals, constituting in classical times, at least, 'the heart' of the city in the form of the communal hearth of the *prytaneion*.[31] Not surprisingly, the importance of the symposium exerted an extraordinary influence on Greco-Roman artistic output (see especially Lissarague, 1990; cf. M. Miller, 1991) and literary production, of which the classical symposia-writings are a very small fraction.[32] Clearly, the 'symposium', with its manifold symbols, topics and ideologies, is a trans-generic literary motif and amenable to varied exploitation. As we have seen, the symposium

---

[30] See especially Murray, 1981; 1982; 1983b; F. Dupont, 1977; and the surveys by Fisher, 1988a; 1988b.

[31] Gernet, 1981, p. 314, speaks of 'the prytany with the communal hearth' as the 'heart of the city' 'in a simultaneously religious and political sense'. On the function of the *prytaneion* see the standard work of S. Miller, 1978, pp. 4–24.

[32] To document the full influence of the symposia on literary production would be a large undertaking in its own right. See generally, J. Martin, 1931, p. 291, and more specifically, on poetry: Bielohlawek, 1940; Bowie, 1986; Edmunds, 1987; Giangrande, 1967; Levine, 1985; Reitzenstein, 1893, pp. 3–86 (on skolia and elegies); the articles in Vetta, 1983; on historical writings: Paul, 1991; on satire: Gowers, 1993; Hudson, 1989; Murray, 1985; Shero, 1923.

and banquet of the rich as the primary symbol of the aristocratic configuration of manners and ideals became a favourite target for the Cynic 'anti-sympotic' critique of the rich and their life-styles (see Mack in Mack and Robbins, 1989, p. 48). In Luke 14 we noted the same strategy of using an episode, reminiscent of, perhaps contiguous with, the literary symposia, to counter the sympotic ethos represented by the paradigmatic literary symposia. This suggests at least that Luke's view of the symposia was ambivalent and, therefore, that the attempt to account for the composition of Luke 14 with reference to the classical, aristocratic symposia form is inadequate.

The inability of the 'symposium hypothesis' to account for the internal machinations in the dinner episode puts us in the position of having to consider an alternative solution to the question by what compositional sensibilities the episode was written. The challenge is to outline and apply an analytic model that is historically plausible, that can rationalize the types of literary forms and, as importantly, their sequence, and one that can bring this into coherent alignment with the thematic issues swirling around the contrasted cast of characters and patterns of commensality that we have observed in this episode. If, in the process of taking up this challenge, we can find further support for the working assumptions on Luke as a Hellenistic author and 14.1–24 as a discrete episode, so much the better. My proposal is that the challenge can be met with the thesis that the internal arrangement of Luke 14.1–14 is determined by a creative variation of a standard pattern of ancient argumentation, known as the *chreia* elaboration, and that the force of the argument aims to secure from sympathetic-but-ambivalent πλούσιοι a full commitment to Luke's communal social ideals, symbolized by his utopian *nomoi sympotikoi*, and to compel them to demonstrate this commitment in a manner exemplified by the converted householder. The rest of this study is devoted to explicating this thesis and to arguing in its support.

# 8

## COMPOSITION AS ARGUMENTATION: THE RHETORIC OF LUKE 14

I have pointed out that the dinner episode begins with a unit that falls within the definitional boundaries of a *chreia* and that the remaining parts are of the kind which ancient instructors in the rhetorical arts considered to be essential in constructing a *chreia*-based argument. Before pursuing the intuition that where there is a *chreia* followed by analogies there is probably an argument waiting to be analysed, it is worth noting that the intuition itself has the support of a scholarly tradition, though one neglected until very recently.[1]

### *Chreiai*, parables and arguments

In the second edition (1933) of his *Formgeschichte des Evangeliums* Martin Dibelius introduced a discussion of the Hellenistic *chreiai* and noted their similarity to the gospel units he called 'paradigms' (pp. 149–64). In the context of a notice that Luke seems particularly keen on casting traditional material into a 'chrienartige Fassung' he also observed that this evangelist tended to frame parables with a 'Situationsangabe' reminiscent of the sayings *chreiai*. Among the six parables he cited as examples is 14.16–24 (p. 161). Dibelius oddly offered this only as a bare observation, but one which nonetheless is suggestive for further study.[2]

---

[1] What follows is not intended to be a full review of the evolution of scholarship on *chreiai* in gospel studies. For this see the many writings of Robbins, especially his essay, 'Chreia & pronouncement story in synoptic studies', in Mack and Robbins, 1989; cf. Robbins, 1981; 1988a; 1988b; 1993a; 1994b; Buchanan, 1982. My interest is in tracing the shift from seeing the memorable anecdote as a form-critical unit to the recognition of it as a rhetorical unit that can be elaborated into a narrative argument with the aid of parables, among other things.

[2] It is difficult to imagine that Dibelius was unaware of the implications of his observation for the study of the composition process in the gospels. Although his discussion of the Hellenistic *chreia* relied heavily on exemplars culled from Diogenes Laertius, Philostratus and Lucian's *Demonax*, he appears to have read

In 1949 R. O. P. Taylor published his *Groundwork of the Gospels*, which contains a slim chapter entitled 'Greek Forms of Instruction' (pp. 75–90) in which he set out to correct the German form critics' neglect of 'the careful studies of literary form, which were drawn up for the use of students in the first centuries of our era' (p. 75; cf. R. Taylor, 1943–4).[3] He referred, of course, to the work of the *rhetores graeci*, specifically to the *progymnasmata*,[4] teachers' handbooks outlining 'preliminary exercises' designed to introduce students who had completed basic grammar and literary studies to the fundamentals of rhetoric that they would then put to use in composing speeches and prose.[5] Taylor's reading of the synoptic gospels under the tutelage of the *rhetores* was sweeping and unsystematic, but it was replete with productive insights. From the *progymnasmata* he learnt that they are expositions of methods for making persuasive statements in prose and, therefore, that the interest in the 'forms' (fable, narrative, *chreia*, etc.) discussed in the handbooks is 'not merely literary' (i.e., formal), but much more in their rhetorical usefulness, or as Taylor stressed, their 'necessity' for rhetoric (pp. 75–6).[6] He also pointed out that 'before anything else' the handbooks 'deal with the form of statement which they call the

the *chreia* chapters in the rhetorical handbooks (citing Theon of Alexandria specifically [1933, p. 151 nn. 1, 3]), and there, surely, the various ways of expanding upon a *chreia*, including by the use of analogies.
[3] Taylor's rationale for this move consists of sound presuppositions and logic. The supposition is that the Christian presupposed by the gospel literature is a 'Hellenic citizen'. Like every Hellenic citizen, perhaps even more so, the 'Christian was bound to pursue the art of pleading, both in his own defense and in the work of persuading others ... The Christian had a case to sustain. It was only natural that he should use the methods in vogue. And in the work of the Rhetores, we have an exposition of their methods' (p. 75).
[4] On the origins and history of the *progymnasmata*, a special category of the textbooks on rhetoric, see Hock and O'Neil, 1986, pp. 10–18. The earliest surviving textbook is that of Aelius Theon of Alexandria (late first century CE; complete text, trans. and commentary in Butts, 1986), but according to Theon himself (*Progymn.* 1) he is not the first to compose one. They 'were already a standard part of the educational curriculum of the early Empire' (Hock and O'Neil, 1986, p. 10). Other surviving complete textbooks include those of Hermogenes of Tarsus (second century; text in Rabe, 1913, pp. 1–27; ET in Baldwin, 1928, pp. 23–38); Aphthonius of Antioch (late fourth century; text in Rabe, 1926, pp. 1–51; ET in Nadeau, 1952); Nicolaus of Myra (fifth century; text in Felten, 1913; ET not available).
[5] On the place of the 'preliminary exercises' in the educational curriculum and rhetorical training see Bonner, 1977, pp. 250–76; Marrou, 1964, pp. 173–5; Mack in Mack and Robbins, 1989, pp. 33–5; and scattered comments in the standard analyses of ancient rhetoric by D. L. Clark and Kennedy.
[6] Taylor's term 'literary' is used in the specific sense of literary form (see p. 75). He is obliquely criticizing the form critics' concern over formal definitions. Thus he insistently presses the question of usage rather than that of precision of form.

Chreia' (p. 76).[7] Then, arguing from the stability of the name *chreia* for the brief attributed anecdote in ancient usage, from the name itself (χρεία = 'necessity' or 'usefulness'), and from Theon's statement on the *chreia* as useful *par excellence* (κατ' ἐξοχην),[8] Taylor concluded that this speech form 'was regarded as *the* thing needful' for persuasive communication (p. 77). Finally, for my purpose, the handbooks taught him that the *chreia* proper was a 'fundamental form' (p. 87) that 'was to be used as the basis for other forms', (p. 80) that is, it was to be 'worked out' (pp. 80, 87)[9] by various means into an argument. Taylor was especially taken by the inclusion of παραβολή among these means (pp. 80–1, 88–90),[10] making him not the first modern gospel scholar to recognize that 'parable' was considered as a 'proof' in argumentation, but the first, I believe, to point out that parables were among the proofs in the working out of *chreiai*.[11] Guided by the *progymnasmata*, he sketchily pointed out that the gospels are replete with units that fit the definition of a *chreia* and that these are often connected with parables. Indeed, he went as far as to suggest that in the gospels as a whole, 'we have the contemporary Hellenic treatment of the Chreia implicit in the whole structure of the books' (p. 81).[12]

[7] This is not entirely correct. Only Theon places the *chreia* first in his list of exercises, 'apparently being innovative' in this respect (Hock and O'Neil, 1986, p. 66). Hermogenes and Aphthonius place the *chreia* third, after fable and narrative. For a discussion of the order of the *progymnasmata* in the handbooks see Hock and O'Neil, 1986, pp. 17, 65–6; cf. Butts, 1987, p. 207.

[8] *On the Chreia*, pp. 25–6 (all references to the *chreia* chapters are cited by number, following the numeration of Hock and O'Neil, 1986). Theon's entire sentence states: 'It has the name "chreia" because of its excellence, for more than the other exercises it is useful in many ways for life.'

[9] The *chreia* chapters contain discussions on manipulating this form for argumentative purposes. Taylor cites these passages extensively and though he does not refer explicitly to Hermogenes' pattern of 'working out' (ἐργασία) a *chreia*, evidently he is aware of it, judging from his vocabulary.

[10] Taylor has many fine things to say about the function of 'parables' in Greek and early Christian usage that have yet to find their way into the gospel commentary traditions.

[11] It should be noted that Taylor's view of the connection between *chreia* and parable is somewhat imprecise when he speaks of 'working out a Chreia into a Parable' (p. 80 n. 1).

[12] One might point out that Taylor's suggestions are offered with almost nonchalant assurance, despite the fact that they heavily kick against the sensibilities of the form-critical models of the development of the synoptic traditions that were so in vogue when he wrote. One reason for this, no doubt, is his belief that ancient historical testimony was on his side. This testimony he finds in a statement of Papias concerning Peter, ὃς πρὸς τὰς χρείας ἐποιεῖτο τὰς διδασκαλίας (*ap.* Eusebius, *Hist. Eccl.* 3.34.15; cited by Taylor, pp. 28, 81). He takes this to be authentic testimony, but much more interesting is that he interprets this to say that

The frequent connection between *chreiai* and parables, particularly in the gospel of Luke, was a focal point in an article by
William R. Farmer in 1962. He noticed several units in Luke (and
one in Matthew) that closely resemble each other in the internal
sequence of their arrangement. Taking Luke 15.1–32 and 13.1–9 as
demonstration texts, he showed that they exhibit an identical formal
structure (pp. 305–6). Each is headed by an introductory unit followed by three closely related sayings that make up the rest of the
unit. Of these three sayings the first two are comparatively brief and
closely parallel in structure and content. The third saying in the unit
is in the form of a story (parable) which illustrates the point made in
the preceding saying. Farmer found that this pattern is roughly
replicated also in Luke 12.13–21 and 16.14–15, 19–31, where the
point of introductory sayings is augmented or illustrated by means
of a parable (p. 309). In his accounting for these units in Luke,
Farmer postulated a pre-Lukan source (pp. 303–5),[13] but when he
explained the procedure which probably generated their internal
structure, he appealed to the Hellenistic rhetorical tradition of
citing, paraphrasing, expounding and illustrating a *chreia*
(pp. 307–10, especially p. 308),[14] a tradition in which the argumentative use of parables had a firm place.[15] Farmer thought that
the *chreia*-units he had identified were patterned after the rhetoricians' model by early Christian preachers 'to serve the catechetical
and homiletical [i.e. rhetorical] needs of early Christian communi-

Peter made the Christian teachings into *chreiai*. Cf. the trans. of Kirsopp Lake
(LCL), 'who [i.e. Peter] used to give teaching as necessity demanded'. Quite apart
from the question of whether Peter indeed did it, Papias' phrase admits of Taylor's
interpretation. Papias thus provides very early, external evidence for what the
gospels themselves indicate, namely that the *didaskalia* was most useful for
Christian *paideia* in *chreia* forms, presumably including elaborated ones.

13 Farmer here argues on the basis of linguistic and stylistic peculiarities in Luke
15.1–32 and 13.1–9. He finds further support for his claim 'that there is no
evidence that Luke is responsible for this literary phenomenon of attaching a
parable to a *Chreia*' (p. 309) in Luke 16, where a *chreia*-parable sequence
(16.14–15, 19–21) is apparently interrupted with the insertion of three 'unrelated
sayings' (pp. 309–10). This is not the place for disputing his judgment on Luke 16.
Cf. Berger, 1984a, p. 89, who thinks the entire unit (16.14–31) is an elaborated
('erweiterte') *chreia* to which the verses 16.16–18 contribute argumentatively and
thematically. This still needs to be worked out in greater detail.
14 Farmer cites Quintilian (*Inst.* 1.3.6–9) on the widespread use of the *chreia* in
schools of rhetoric and on their fixed place 'in the educational system of the empire
in the first century' (p. 308 n. 1). His dependence on Dibelius and R.O.P. Taylor is
explicitly acknowledged.
15 E.g., p. 310: '... we should note that the use of a parable to illustrate a saying in a
*Chreia* was one of the prescribed ways in which the rhetoricians were trained to
use *Chreiai* in public speaking'.

ties' (p. 309).[16] He thus provided further support for Taylor's similar ideas and, as importantly, he found Luke to be especially richly loaded with *chreia*-units.

Farmer's identification of the internal structure in Luke 15 and 13.1–9 is illuminating in another regard. Had he worked with a less restricted formal definition of a *chreia*,[17] he probably would have noticed an almost identical internal pattern in 14.1–24, for this unit, too, is organized as a *chreia* plus two relatively brief parallel sayings plus a longer story.[18] The more general phenomenon of expounding on a *chreia* with gnomic material and parables, of which Farmer noted instances in 12.13–21 and 16.14–15, 19–31, also seems to be more widespread in Luke than he recognized. 5.27–39 is an instructive example. Here Luke clearly reworks Markan material (Mark 2.13–22) that is already similarly patterned, but the third evangelist accentuates it by adding to Mark ἔλεγεν δὲ καὶ παραβολήν (5.36) and an *epilogion* (5.39).[19] Further, the Levi episode may be added to 14.1–24, 15.1–32 and 19.1–27 as units that are not only roughly similar *chreia*-units in which parables figure prominently, but all of them are also sympotic episodes, either in theme or setting or

---

[16] It should be said here that since Farmer (incorrectly) thought that the development of a *chreia* into an argument belonged to oral communication, he was theoretically resistant to the idea that this pattern might (also) belong to the level of Lukan redaction, i.e. that *chreia* patterns could be a method of prose composition. Note his statement: 'In Hellenistic literature, outside of these style manuals [*progymnasmata*], *Chreiai* are not developed according to this pattern, since by definition this development was designed to enable a speaker to make more effective use of them in *oral* communication' (p. 309). Every point in this sentence is open to question.

[17] Farmer did not go to the *chreia*-chapters in the *progymnasmata* for his definition; rather, he relied on Dibelius to provide it for him: 'It is a reproduction of a short pointed saying of general significance, originating in a definite person and arising out of a definite situation' (Dibelius, 1933, pp. 152–3; cited by Farmer, p. 307). For a criticism of Dibelius's restrictive definition see Robbins in Mack and Robbins, 1989, p. 13.

[18] The parallelism between 15.1–32 and 14.1–24 actually goes deeper. In both, the two short units after the *chreia* are called παραβολή followed by a gnomic rationale. In both, moreover, the longer final unit is a story about an ἄνθρωπός τις. Much of this has been noted before by Fabris, 1978, p. 132: 'La composizione della nostra sezione [i.e. 14:1–24], data la corrispondenza simmetrica delle prime due piccolo parabole, segue lo schema 2 + 1, cioè due composizione parallele seguite da una terza più ampia'. Cf. p. 138 for a parallel synoptic figure. Fabris notes the parallel structural scheme, but does not pursue the *chreia* pattern as a possible generative model.

[19] If this is correct, Farmer's claim (pp. 309, 310) that Luke cannot be responsible for the phenomenon of parables attached to *chreia* here runs into additional contrary evidence.

both.[20] Not all of this came into Farmer's view, but neither might it have come into ours had he not pointed out what he did see. He has provided additional support for seeing 14.1–24 as a *chreia-argument*.

These three scholars are precursors to a spate of research during the last decade on the *chreia* in Hellenistic education, literature and rhetoric with a view towards understanding the compositional dynamics in the synoptic gospels, in large part consisting of aphoristic and figurative speech units that, in the classic form-critical tradition, were thought to be clustered or sequenced on the principle of formal or thematic likeness rather than arranged according to a discernible logic of argumentation. In Germany, Klaus Berger systematically revised the older form-critical taxonomy of synoptic speech units under the rubric of 'Hellenistische Gattungen im Neuen Testament' (1984b),[21] in which he noted the large number of *chreiai* in the gospels,[22] commented on their usefulness for characterization and deliberative argumentation and recognized that they can be manipulated into 'argumentative Strukturen' (cf. 'erweiterte Chrien') in which an 'Analogiefall' (i.e. parable) may be employed (1984a, pp. 85, 90; cf. 1984b, pp. 1092–110). But because he was heavily committed to the business of classification, he provided little demonstration of how the latter works. Of interest nonetheless is that he is the first to classify the entire unit of Luke 14.1–24 as a *chreia* composition, though he thought it to consist of two unconnected *chreiai*, one of a judicial (14.1–6), the other of a deliberative type (14.7–24) (1984a, p. 91). There is good sense here, even if the idea of two unconnected parts will be shown to be infelicitous.

The general sense that the *chreia* discussions in the Hellenistic handbooks may be helpful in the analysis of synoptic composition was catapulted to a new level by a group of mostly American scholars working on the Chreia Project at the Institute for Antiquity

---

20  Delobel (1966, p. 461 and n. 184) briefly noted that many of Luke's so-called symposia are roughly similar in their internal sequence: (1) Jésus au repas, (2) dispute, (3) réponse, (4) parabole. Of the two other Pharisaic dinners 7.36–50 contains an analogy (7.41–2) but otherwise does not follow the structure identified by Farmer or Delobel. 11.37–54 also uses some figurative material and analogy, but again is structurally different. This does not mean that they are *not chreia-*units. As Mack has shown (Mack and Robbins, 1989, pp. 100–4), 7.36–50 is a very clever *chreia* elaboration.

21  Cf. his *Formgeschichte des Neuen Testaments* (1984), which covers similar ground.

22  See especially 1984a, p. 90, where he calls the *chreiai* 'Grundbausteine der Gattung Evangelium'.

and Christianity (Claremont, CA). Out of the project has come not only a highly useful collection of the *chreia* discussions in the ancient *progymnasmata* (Hock and O'Neil, 1986; cf. Robbins, 1989), carefully contextualized historically and in their contemporary literary and rhetorical setting (Hock in Hock and O'Neil, 1986, pp. 3–60), but also a much more precise understanding of the *chreia*, and the exercises based upon it, as a highly prized and widely used vehicle for developing skills in literary interpretation and composition. Most important for my purpose is Burton Mack's analysis of the rhetoricians' instructions on how to use the *chreia* as a basis for constructing persuasive speech patterns. Hermogenes' influential pattern of elaboration (see pp. 152–8 below), first adduced by Mack as a guide for an analysis of the rhetorical principles at work in Philo's commentary on Genesis 4.2 (*De sacrificiis* 1–10; Mack, 1984, pp. 93–9), shows how a brief *chreia* can be worked out along the lines of what earlier rhetoricians had already described as the 'complete argument'[23] in a series of eight steps that include statements from analogy and example. Mack collaborated with Vernon Robbins to demonstrate that Hermogenes' model elaboration (ἐργασία) is an incisive guide towards the discovery of various argumentative strategies in synoptic passages.[24] Their work, and that of others, has shown that, contrary to what Farmer thought, the *chreia* could be manipulated and elaborated in written form.[25]

[23] See, for example, *Rhet. ad Her.* 2.18.28: 'The most complete and perfect argument ... is that which is comprised of five parts: the Proposition, the Reason, the Proof of the Reason, the Embellishment, and the Résumé' (trans. Caplan, LCL). Cf. 2.29.46 where the idea of 'embellishment' is said to consist of 'similes, examples, amplifications, previous judgments, and the other means which serve to expand and enrich the argument', i.e., a line-up of items that closely resembles those listed in Hermogenes' *chreia* elaboration. See Mack in Mack and Robbins, 1989, pp. 51–7, for the relationship between Hermogenes' pattern and Hellenistic theories of constructing complete arguments.

[24] Mack and Robbins, 1989, ch. 3–7. For a summary see my review of this volume (Braun, 1991). See also Mack, 1988, pp. 186–92 (elaborated *chreiai* in Mark); and 1990, pp. 50–6.

[25] See, in general, Mack in Mack and Robbins, 1989, pp. 63–5 and n. 24. R. Cameron (1990) depends heavily on Mack's exposition of Hermogenes' *chreia* elaboration to demonstrate argumentative composition in Q's redactional (i.e. written) characterization of John and Jesus (Q 7.18–35). Bjorndahl, 1988, pp. 8–26, has convincingly demonstrated composition in accordance with the technique of elaboration in *G.Thom.* 61–7. See also Aune (working without reference to the *chreia* elaboration pattern), 1978, pp. 64–9, where he detects 'wisdom stories' that Plutarch has elaborated in a manner analogous to the *chreia*. See also Robbins, 1981 (on classifying pronouncement stories in Plutarch's *Parallel Lives*); 1991c (rhetorical composition in Plutarch and the gospels); 1993a (progymnastic rhetorical treatment of pre-gospel traditions).

Moreover, they have provided an analytic model that should enable me to test my hunch that Luke 14.1–24 displays deliberate techniques of rhetorical composition.

## Hermogenes on the elaboration of a *chreia*

The clearest pattern of 'working out' (ἐργασία) a *chreia* was developed by Hermogenes of Tarsus (born 161 CE) near the end of the second or the beginning of the third century.[26] This means, of course, Luke could not have had the benefit of Hermogenes' instruction. If we nonetheless use his model as a point of reference in analysing Lukan composition, it is because the elements of what Hermogenes called the ἐργασία exercise had already been established by other rhetoricians by the first century BCE.[27] Hermogenes thus typifies a tradition that can be assumed to have been well established in the educational curriculum and in a wide range of literary practice towards the end of the first century when Luke wrote.[28]

Hermogenes outlines and illustrates *chreia* elaboration as follows:[29]

> But now let us move on to the chief matter, and this is the elaboration (ἐργασία). Accordingly, let the elaboration be as follows: (1) First, an encomium, in a few words, for the one who spoke or acted. Then (2) a paraphrase of the chreia itself; then (3) the rationale. For example:
> *Isocrates said that education's* (τῆς παιδείας) *root is bitter, its fruit is sweet.*

---

[26] For a general discussion of Hermogenes and his *progymnasmata* see Mack and O'Neil in Hock and O'Neil, 1986, pp. 155–63.

[27] See Mack, 1984, p. 86: '[T]he elaboration outline in Hermogenes is an application of discussions of the arrangements of arguments which occur already in authors of the first centuries BCE-CE, i.e., the *Ad Herennium*, Cicero and Quintilian. Cf. *Rhet. ad Her.* 2.18.28, 2.29.46, 4.43.56–44.57; Cicero, *Inv. Rhet.* 1.34.58–35.61, 1.37.67; Quintilian 5.10.1–125. See also Hock and O'Neil, 1986, pp. 162–3; Cameron, 1990, p. 46; D. L. Clark, 1957, p. 179; Kennedy, 1963, p. 270.

[28] Mack, 1990, p. 43, summarily notes that the elaboration pattern which Hermogenes describes so ably and concisely 'became something of a literary convention for the elaboration of maxims, anecdotes, the construction of commentaries, the composition of biographies, and the development of small periods of argumentation even within the genres of wisdom literature and ethical philosophy'.

[29] *On the Chreia*, pp. 30–63; trans. Mack and O'Neil in Hock and O'Neil, 1986, p. 177.

(1) *Praise* (ἔπαινος): 'Isocrates was wise', and you amplify the subject moderately.

(2) Then the *chreia*: 'He said thus and so', and you are not to express it simply but rather by amplifying the presentation (ἑρμηνείαν).

(3) Then the *rationale* (αἰτία): 'For the most important affairs generally succeed because of toil, and once they have succeeded, they bring pleasure'.

(4) Then the statement from the *opposite* (κατὰ τὸ ἐναντίον): 'For ordinary affairs do not need toil, and they have an outcome that is entirely without pleasure; but serious affairs have the opposite outcome'.

(5) Then the statement from *analogy* (ἐκ παραβολῆς): 'For just as it is the lot of farmers to reap their fruits after working with the land, so also is it for those working with words'.

(6) Then the statement from *example* (ἐκ παραδείγματος): 'Demosthenes, after locking himself in a room and toiling long, later reaped his fruits: wreaths and public acclamations' [cf. *On the Crown*, 58].

(7) It is also possible to argue from the statement by an *authority* (ἐκ κρίσεως). For example, Hesiod said [*Op.* 289]: '*In front of virtue gods have ordained sweat*'. And another poet says [Epicharmus, frg. 287]: '*At the price of toil do the gods sell every good to us*'.

(8) At the end you are to add an *exhortation* (παράκλησιν) to the effect that it is necessary to heed the one who has spoken or acted.

A detailed commentary on Hermogenes' pattern is not essential here,[30] but a few remarks should be made to clarify its rhetorical strategy and compositional traits, and to point out its applicability as a general guide on the manner of Luke's composition in 14.1–24.

First, and most obviously, even a brief scanning of the inventory of items in the pattern shows that it depends for its argumentation on material roughly similar in kind and sequence to that found in Luke 14.1–24. Both utilize maxims, pronouncements, contraries,

---

[30] For this see Mack, 1984, pp. 93–9; 1987, pp. 15–28; 1988, pp. 185–6; 1990, pp. 43–7 (in tightly summarized form); Mack in Mack and Robbins, 1989, pp. 57–63. Cf. R. Cameron, 1990, pp. 47–50; Bjorndahl, 1988, pp. 2–5. My own remarks are for the most part culled from these earlier expositions, especially Mack's on whom Cameron and Bjorndahl also depend.

analogies and exempla to construct an argument on an issue embedded in a *chreia*. The extent to and manner in which this is the case in Luke 14 will be detailed below (pp. 162–4).

Second, in order to defuse the possible view that this is due to a coincidentally similar collection of vaguely related gobbets of material, it bears rehearsing Burton Mack's observation that the items in Hermogenes' exercise are not a haphazard collection. On the contrary, his analysis shows that they 'form a set, that each item was chosen with care, and that the resulting composition forms a period of unified discourse' (Mack, 1990, p. 44).[31] The *chreia* chosen for elaboration shrewdly matches a saying on education with a speaker widely recognized as the founder of rhetoric and Hellenistic education,[32] a move that reflects the conventional belief that words (λόγος) should match the speaker's character (ἦθος).[33] The encomiastic word (1), itself expandable to suit the argument or larger narrative aims,[34] serves in place of the standard introduction

[31] See also Mack, 1984, p. 94: 'A study of these discussions [i.e. of the complete argument discussed in *Rhet. ad Her.*, Cicero and Quintilian] shows that the manifold lists of topics and arguments possible had been reduced to a single set of the basic and major types of proofs, arranged in logical order, and correlated with the standard outline of the forensic speech itself. It was the mini-speech outline resulting from these theoretical endeavors which Hermogenes used for the elaboration of the *chreia*.'

[32] Mack, 1984, p. 94; Mack and Robbins, 1989, p. 57. For an expanded treatment of Isocrates' importance see Marrou, 1964, pp. 79–91. The saying itself is widely attested and, though most often understandably attributed to Isocrates, it is sometimes credited to Aristotle, Demosthenes, Cicero *et al.* (see Hock and O'Neil, 1986, pp. 325–6).

[33] Insofar as this belief is conventional, the match would inevitably appeal to the audience and thus constitute a subtle play upon the πάθος of the audience. In rhetorical theory the means by which an audience could be persuaded were discussed under three general categories, in accordance with the understanding that potential for persuasion lay in each component of the communicative triad of speaker-speech-audience (Aristotle, *Rhet.* 1.3.1): (1) ἦθος, a presentation of the speaker's character that favours (can help) the case to be made (see Sattler, 1957); (2) λόγος, the speech or rational arguments by means of the various proofs; (3) πάθος, playing upon the feelings of the audience. This is common knowledge; for a detailed discussion of *ethos* and *pathos* and their complex relationship to rational argument (*logos*) see Wisse, 1989; Mack in Mack and Robbins, 1989, pp. 42–4.

[34] The word of praise in Hermogenes' exercise also seems to allow for the intrusion of an epideictic speech element into the *chreia*–based argument (cf. the panegyric expansion by Aphthonius at this point; Hock and O'Neil, 1986, p. 224). Brief definitions of some technical terms may be useful here. At least since Aristotle ancient rhetoric was generally recognized to fall into three main types (*locus classicus*, Aristotle, *Rhet.* 1.3.3–5; cf. Ps-Cicero, *Rhet. ad Her.* 1.2.2; Cicero, *Inv. Rhet.* 1.5.7, 2.3.12; Diogenes Laertius 7.42 [attributing this division to the Stoics]; synoptic descriptions in Lausberg, 1960, pp. 86–138): (1) ἐπιδεικτικόν (sometimes called ἐγκωμιαστικόν), *demonstrativum*; social *locus* was the public festival or

(*exordium*) of a speech (Mack, 1990, pp. 44–5) and further helps to establish the ἦθος and authority of Isocrates. The 'presentation' (ἑρμηνείαν) of the *chreia* (2) itself, here left in tersely aphoristic form but advisedly a paraphrastic and interpretive move to 'slant' it advantageously for the elaboration to follow,[35] amounts to a 'statement of the case to be argued or the thesis to be defended' in accordance with the requirement of the *narratio* in a standard speech (Mack, 1990, p. 45). Because the statement is not only aphoristic but also metaphorical – the endeavour of παιδεία has something to do with a 'bitter root' and a 'sweet fruit' – its point (issue, thesis) is vague. The rationale (3) thus needs to carry burdens beyond providing 'the "reason" why the chreia is true' (Mack, 1990, p. 45), the normal function of the rationale in the *narratio* of a standard speech. To establish the validity (rationale proper) of the *chreia*, the 'issue' embedded in the latter has to be isolated (an interpretive move) and transposed from its figural mode into a descriptive, thetic statement (an argumentative move) which can be supported with additional arguments (see, in detail, Mack, 1984,

various public ceremonial occasions; its aim was to praise (or blame); its argument was governed by the categories of the noble (or the shameful); its typical form was the *encomium* (on a city, local deity, ruler, etc.) This speech was the least argumentative in that it dealt with issues on which speaker and audience were already in agreement (Mack in Mack and Robbins, 1989, p. 53); epideictic rhetoric thus functions as a 'ritual' celebration of shared beliefs and values (Carter, 1991; see also Sullivan, 1993). (2) συμβουλευτικόν, *deliberativum*; social *locus* was the public assembly; its aim was to exhort or dissuade with respect to decisions on policy, behaviour, etc.; its argument turned on the categories of the expedient/ beneficial or the harmful; its typical form is the political speech. (3) δικανικόν, *iudiciale*; social *locus* was the court; its aim was to accuse or to defend; its argument was governed by the just or the unjust; its typical form was the forensic speech. These distinctions were theoretical. In practical rhetorical situations, including in narrative arguments, these three could be mixed (see Mack in Mack and Robbins, 1989, p. 53). Luke 14.1–24 is a case in point.

35 Hermogenes' exhortation 'not to express it [*chreia*] unadorned (ψιλήν)' should be noted. According to Mack and O'Neil (Hock and O'Neil, 1986, p. 181 n. 12) Hermogenes is here referring to παράφρασις (see item 2 in the introductory paragraph of the exercise), a kind of 'slanted' recitation to enhance the point that will be elaborated. This could be done in various ways, by presenting the saying more loquaciously (cf. Aphthonius; Hock and O'Neil, 1986, p. 226), or by amplifying or expanding moves to accentuate aspects of the situation, circumstances, challenge or characters in order to 'set up' the elaboration to follow. Theon notes that it is possible to expand (ἐπεκτείνειν) a concise *chreia* and to condense (συστέλλειν) an expanded one (*On the Chreia*, Hock and O'Neil, 1986, pp. 193, 309–34). See Hock's discussion of this in Hock and O'Neil, 1986, pp. 40–1 (with illustrations from literary practice; note esp. the two versions of the same *chreia* in Mark 11.15–17 [expanded] and in Luke 19.24–46 [concise]). Cf. Butts, 1987, pp. 209–10.

p. 95; 1987, pp. 23–4). In the interpretive move, the rationale has discovered a fundamental *relationship* between the 'bitter root' and the 'sweet fruit'. Further, it has translated these metaphors into a sequence of toil (πόνος)/success,[36] terms around which the elaboration will turn. Finally, it has exploited contiguous attributes of the metaphor, most likely the vine as a symbol for agriculture, and agriculture as a standard analogy to the process of *paideia*,[37] and combined them under the rubric of 'most important affairs' (τὰ μέγιστα τῶν πραγμάταων). In this way the *chreia* has been restated as a proposition on education as an important undertaking which to pursue is 'bitter' (laborious) but in which to succeed is 'sweet' (pleasure, ἡδονή).[38] As Mack has noted, 'rationale plus chreia actually form a rhetorical syllogism in which the rationale serves as the major premise (Important affairs succeed by toil), the minor premise is left unstated (Education is an important affair), and the chreia established as the conclusion to be supported (Hard work at school will bring success)' (1990, p. 45). The support (the ἐργασία proper, corresponding to the *argumentatio* section of a standard speech outline) begins with a statement from the opposite (4), a dialectical move confirming the stated proposition by showing that the inverse is true as well (ordinary affairs take place without toil and do not lead to pleasure).[39] The analogy (5), an essential means of supporting an argument according to Greek theorists at least since Aristotle and Anaximenes (*Rhetorica ad Alexandrum*), draws

36   This translation is quite plausible, but it is also carefully calculated, because an 'emphasis on the labor or toil requisite for success was axiomatic in the culture' (R. Cameron, 1990, p. 48).
37   Mack, 1984, p. 95. On the analogy of *paideia* to agricultural endeavour see, e.g., Quintilian, *Inst.* 5.11.24 and Seneca, *Ep.* 38.2; and further citations and discussion in Mack, 1988, pp. 159–60; Mack and Robbins, 1989, pp. 155–6; R. Cameron, 1986, pp. 21–3.
38   To posit the reward of education as ἡδονή is clever in itself, for, as Mack has pointed out, pleasure is one of the conventional values used as one of the 'chief ends' (τέλικα κεφάλαια) that determined deliberative argumentation. See n. 34 above for the correlation between the three types of rhetoric and the chief values by which each is guided.
39   See Mack, 1990, pp. 45–6. Behind Hermogenes' particular use of the opposite lies a more general rhetorical principle of championing one's view or case by means of contrasts and against foils of opposing views or cases. Mack reminds us that 'the fundamental principle' of rhetoric was to win a debate against the other side both positively and negatively. Deliberative declamations (such as Luke 14; see Braun, 1992, p. 78) were 'the perfect place for negative contrasts, dissuasions from alternate points of view, charges against those of opposing views, dialectical maneuvers in the interest of verifying the logic of a proposition, censure of the opposite proposition, showing that the opposite case would not make any sense, and so forth' (Mack, 1990, p. 43).

on the familiar world of experience (the natural and the social orders) for a common occurrence or social pattern as an instance of a universal principle (Mack, 1990, p. 46). If the analogy is well chosen, it will imply the same principle that was stated in the proposition. In Hermogenes' case, the analogy is appropriate to the agricultural figures in the *chreia*, confirms its principle (first toil, then reward) with the indisputable observation that working the land precedes reaping the harvest and further explicates and supports the theme of *paideia* in terms of 'working with words'. The support of an example (6), according to the theorists a paradigmatic story drawn from history, in this case, one about the famous orator Demosthenes, not only exemplifies the proposition generally, but also sharpens its focus towards rhetorical education in particular (Mack, 1990, p. 46). The supportive citations (7) serve to show that recognized authorities 'had come to the same conclusion or rendered a similar judgment on the same issue' (Mack, 1990, p. 46).[40] Here they are extremely appropriate and effective. The set of quotations from the revered Hesiod and the comic poet Epicharmus supports the necessity of toil for success, explicitly links the success of education (παιδεία) with the highest ideal (ἀρετή, 'virtue') of Hellenistic παιδεία ('culture') and supports all of this with an appeal to the ordinance of the gods (Mack, 1990, p. 46). This invocation of the authority of canon and deity ends the argument for the truth of Isocrates' statement, leaving only the exhortation (8) to heed it (corresponding to the function of the *epilogos/peroratio* of the standard speech outline). In sum, Hermogenes' elaboration is a tidy, coherent composition, showing skilful techniques of design.[41] It has plausibly interpreted and translated the *chreia* into an arguable proposition on *paideia* as an important activity that requires toil but brings pleasure. All the items in the elaboration, chosen not only for their thematic aptness but, more

---

[40] μαρτύρια τῶν παλαιῶν was a standard item among the argumentative supports (see, e.g., *Rhet. ad Her.* 4.47.54). In Hermogenes the phrase 'it is also possible' suggests that this is optional in the ἐργασία of a *chreia*. Mack and O'Neil toy with the thought that Hermogenes is being innovative here (Hock and O'Neil, 1986, p. 181 n. 14); the 'statement from authority' is a regular feature of the *chreia* elaboration exercises of later *progymnasmata*. We will later note the absence of this item in Luke 14 and speculate there whether this might be due to the fluidity of the elaboration pattern in the first century or whether there may be other reasons for it.

[41] See, in greater detail, Mack's analysis of 'the force of the argument as a whole' (1984, pp. 98–9; cf. 1987, pp. 27–8; 1990, pp. 46–7; Mack and Robbins, 1989, pp. 61–2.

importantly, for their representation of various arenas of 'authority' (the worlds of logical reasoning [contrary], nature and human activity [analogy], history of rhetoric [example], literary and cultural traditions [authoritative judgments], divine order [citations]), aid in the unfolding and supporting of assertion. When one further notes the allusive appeal to important Greek values (the pleasant, good, right, virtuous), 'the entire spectrum of social and cultural convention' (Mack, 1990, p. 47) is marshalled in an '*apologia* for social convention itself' (Mack in Mack and Robbins, 1989, p. 62), using what at first glance appears to be merely a collage of vaguely related small units.

Third, when we turn Luke to 14.1–24, we should not expect to find a mechanical replication of Hermogenes' 'textbook' model, for as Aristotle had pointed out much earlier (*Rhetoric* 3.2.4–5), creativity in the application of technique was a mark of a good rhetor. Improvisation was, after all, as much a literary ideal as imitation (see C. Baldwin, 1928, pp. 13–16). A primary aim of intermediate-level education consisted of developing ideas in rhetorical patterns such as the *chreia* elaboration. This pattern thus 'would have worked its way very deeply into the minds of those being educated' (Bjorndahl, 1988, p. 8) and, by force of a kind of 'second nature', 'could have become simply a way of organizing one's thoughts, a convenient and widely understood framework within which one could make a point' (Bjorndahl, p. 8) even in the composition of a story. All this should be expected to enter into Luke's use of the elaboration pattern.

### Luke's rhetorical invention

The concern that remains is to identify and comment on techniques of argumentative composition in Luke's dinner episode. Luke's story indeed is best understood as a *chreia* that has been expanded into a longer narrative episode along the lines of an Hermogenean type of elaboration.[42] Although this expansion uses

---

[42] Since my argument was first worked out (Braun, 1993), V. Robbins (1994b, pp. 16–22) has challenged the claim that the pattern of argumentation in Luke 14 is best exposed with reference to the Hermogenean ἐργασία, an elaboration pattern that is based on the thesis/proofs logic of the 'complete argument' (see *Rhet. ad Her.* 2.18.28–19.30), i.e., a type of argument 'which places a primary assertion [embedded in a *chreia*] up front and works out the implications of that assertion with a series of succeeding arguments' (Robbins, 1994b, pp. 5–6; cf. ch. 7 n. 2 above). He suggests that Luke 14 is better understood as a Theonian *chreia*

most of the essential items in the standard elaboration pattern, it develops its point (issue/thesis) and invents supporting argument in a manner that differs significantly from Hermogenes' demonstration. It would be useful to gather together the most noticeable differences before I outline the elaboration pattern in Luke 14. As for the 'issue', things are more complex and subtle in Luke, because a judicial question ('Is it lawful?') has to be resolved, and in such a way that the resolution is suitable for redirection towards deliberative pleading for an unconventional dining room ethic which, as we have noted, is itself symbolic of more general patterns of social interaction and values.

In addition, Luke has heavily invested the story with epideictic concerns (Jesus as the author[izer] of an 'anti-sympotic' sympotic sociability). The epideictic agenda is evident in the techniques of vituperative characterization of the Pharisees and in the not so subtle celebration of Jesus' superior perceptive powers and rhetorical skill, in explicit appeals to the epideictic 'chief ends' (τέλικα κεφάλαια)[43] of shame (αἰσχύνη) and honour (δόξα) as motives for behaviour (14.9–10) and in the rhetorically most significant decision to cast Jesus not only as the acting and speaking subject of the *chreia* but also as the one who 'works out' his own *chreia* within the narrative.[44] This option for a strategy of an 'internal' dilation of a *chreia*, a surprising departure from Hermogenes' model, though, as

---

'argument' (ἐπιχείρημα or ἐπιχείρησις rather than ἐργασία, 'elaboration', 'working out'), a manner of dialectically expanding upon (αὔξησις) the parts of a *chreia* that is guided by epideictic interests as its 'major impulse' (Robbins, 1994b, p. 9), interests that Robbins has correctly identified as central in Luke 14. A detailed debate with Robbins is best not undertaken here. Our disagreements are in any case more taxonomic than fundamentally substantial: we agree that Luke 14 is an example of patterned argumentative composition; we agree that there is a pronounced epideictic tone and tactic at work in Luke 14; we similarly see in Luke 14 an argument for a radically adjusted set of social values and practices. On the taxonomic question (Theonian vs. Hermogenean elaboration), the reader is advised that the following analysis of Luke 14 appeals to the Hermogenean model for strategic reasons; it permits me to uncover the internal argumentative dynamics in the dinner episode. The fact that Robbins can look at the same text through a Theonian lens and see in it largely similar dynamics confirms what is fundamentally at stake, namely making a case for persuasive composition in the gospels, a case for which Luke 14 is an important example.

43 The 'final categories' are the general values towards which the various types of speeches (judicial, deliberative, epideictic) were to be aimed. See n. 34 in this chapter and Mack in Mack and Robbins, 1989, p. 38.

44 In Hermogenes' exercise the author of the *chreia* is Isocrates, but he is not given any word in its ἐργασία. The task of interpreting and rationalizing Isocrates' statement is the task of Hermogenes (or his students). Mack and Robbins, 1989, refer to this as an 'external' method of elaboration.

Mack and Robbins have shown, not unusual in Luke and the synoptic *chreiai* generally, 'has the effect of attributing total authority to Jesus' (Mack in Mack and Robbins, 1989, p. 105).[45]

His authoritative *ethos*, assumed by Luke (in this episode) and likely agreed to by his readers, thus lends the whole argument a probability of validity just because Jesus said it, in keeping with the logic of epideictic rhetoric.[46] Epideictic persuasion thus can be expected to carry the argument to a large extent, and certainly to fill the rhetorical gaps in the pattern of establishing an issue and arranging proofs in its support. Naturally, the concentration of authority in Jesus also will have a modifying effect on the arguments from exemplary precedent (παράδειγμα) and authoritative judgment (κρίσις). Neither of these will adduce real exemplary figures from the past (cf. Hermogenes' appeal to Demosthenes) or employ judgments cited from a recognized literary canon (cf. Hermogenes' citations from Hesiod and Epicharmus). Rather, a story (14.16–24) about an anonymous 'someone' (ἄνθρωπός τις) will be introduced to exemplify the point under consideration without, however, relying on the 'authority' inherent in this character to underscore the validity of the exemplary action described in the story.[47]

Similarly, instead of genuine 'scriptural' citations, gnomic utter-

---

[45] Mack and Robbins offer many instructive comments on and examples of 'internal' elaboration of synoptic *chreiai*. This strategy, they plausibly suggest, is linked to the 'authority' issue. Since early Christian societies did not have a long cultural history from which they could draw exemplary paradigms, ancient μαρτυρία, etc., they had to burden a single founder figure with a phenomenal weight of authorizing their claims. See pp. 104–6, 207–8.

[46] See further Carter, 1991, pp. 217–32, for an informative discussion of epideictic speech as a celebration of shared 'extraordinary' knowledge which is not attained by logical cognition nor demonstrated by the formal instruments of logic. A good survey of epideictic theory and practice is in the introduction to *Menander Rhetor* by Russell and Wilson.

[47] This use of a 'general example' instead of a specific, named example coheres with the wider tendency of synoptic authors to avoid references to cultural heroes, whether Jewish or Greek. Mack and Robbins attribute this to the strictures imposed on the Jesus movements that tried to articulate a Christian *paideia* (culture) in contrast to other dominant (Greek and Jewish) cultural traditions. 'A group at pains to distinguish itself from other cultural traditions could not afford to appeal to the history and literature of those cultures to make its novel points' (1989, p. 204). Hence, '[w]here the rhetoric required paradigms, synoptic authors invented a non-specific example . . . It visualized a particular case, but without the usual name, location, and place in the roster of well-known persons . . . Thus, the lack of examples, either from the culture at large or from the group's own tradition, did not prevent the construction of arguments from example. The synoptic authors simply made them up in keeping with the ideals held to be exemplary for the new social movement' (p. 206).

ances (14.11, 14), which help to explicate and rationalize the issue under discussion, seem to be established by a process of analogous reasoning (ἐκ παραβολῆς; 14.8–10, 12–13), but nonetheless give the impression that they simply pronounce claims of whose truth Luke apparently thinks his reader to be already convinced.[48] Another item in Hermogenes' pattern not found in the same way in Luke is the statement from the opposite. In the former, the argument κατὰ τὸ ἐναντίον was in the form of a dialectical inversion of the rationale and hence quite sensibly placed immediately after the rationale. In Luke, the argument from the contrary does not consist of a sharply discrete period in a sequence of proofs, nor is it as clearly dialectical in form. Nonetheless, the category of the opposite is fundamentally important in the construction of the dinner episode. As I have repeatedly noted in previous chapters, the episode is replete with various contrasts, polarities and inversions; in virtually every sentence can be seen elements of Luke's strategy of erecting foils to the ideals he wants to vindicate (see footnote 39 above on this as a general rhetorical technique).

Finally, Hermogenes' prescriptions for an introductory statement of praise and a concluding exhortation are not expressly followed in Luke 14. Although neither needs to be expected in a sub-unit of a larger literary work (see R. Cameron, 1990, pp. 50–1), the element of 'praise' nonetheless is implicitly carried forward from preceding sections of the gospel[49] and an assumed praise of Jesus' *ethos* and authority permeates the entire argument. 14.24 might be seen as a polyfunctional concluding periodization that contains an implicit hortatory appeal.

With these general qualifications in mind, it is possible, first, to outline an argumentative pattern in Luke 14.1–24 and, then, to offer a brief analysis of the argument as a whole.

---

[48] This variation upon the standard use of citations from well-known sages and literary works was probably forced by the set of requirements of Christian social formation referred to in the previous note. See, in sum, Mack and Robbins, 1989, pp. 204–6.

[49] See esp. Talbert, 1980, and McMahan, 1987, pp. 183–213. Robbins (Mack and Robbins, 1989, p. 131) summarizes the technique of establishing the hero's ethos in longer narrative work as it applies to Luke's gospel: 'Once the author has carefully established the ethos of the person in whom he is interested through the standard τόποι ("topics") surrounding his birth, youth, and young adulthood (Luke 1–4:13), the purpose of the person's activity is set forth in a scene that inaugurates his adult career (Luke 4:16–30), then large units of material featuring παραδείγματα ("examples"), ἀπομνημονεύματα ("reminiscences"), and speeches gradually extend and elaborate the issues as the author carries out the overall goals for the account'.

## Outlining the *chreia* pattern

It will be recalled that the *chreia* in Luke 14 is, in Theon's terms, a responsive *chreia* (ἀποκριτικόν) of a mixed (action-saying) type which, moreover, combines features of the interrogative (where the response addresses a specific question) and the non-interrogative (where the response addresses circumstantial affairs) types. The *chreia* thus consists of three essential components: (A) Setting or Situation; (B) Question or Challenge; (C) Response. Each of these components may be amplified to serve the elaboration, as they indeed are in Luke 14, although only the response is technically subject to elaboration proper. In the outline that follows I will break down the text of Luke 14.1–24 into its *chreia* components, briefly indicate how each has been amplified and correlate the appropriate segments of the text with the elaboration pattern, using numbers in parentheses to refer to the items that appear in Hermogenes' model.[50]

COMPONENT A: Setting

Amplification: description of occasion and characters; notice of hostility; challenge obliquely anticipated

> *And it happened, after he* [Jesus] *went into the house of a certain ruler of the Pharisees one Sabbath to eat bread, and they were watching him, that, behold, a certain person with dropsy was before him* (14.1–2).

COMPONENT B: Challenge and Question

Amplification: challenge expressed interrogatively (by the responder on behalf of the challengers)

> *And Jesus replied to the lawyers and Pharisees, saying, 'Is it lawful to heal on the Sabbath or not?'* (14.3).

COMPONENT C: Response

Amplification: description of an action and an extended response to the objection, using the elaboration pattern

---

[50] I am here roughly following Mack's method of outlining the elaboration in Luke 7.36–50. See Mack and Robbins, 1989, pp. 100–1.

(1) *Introduction*: authoritative *ethos* of Jesus indirectly established

> *But they were silent* (14.4a).

(2) *Chreia*: in the form of an action

> *And he took hold of him, cured him, and released him* (14.4).

(3) *Rationale*: interrogative refutation (inference from analogy)

> *And he said to them, 'Who of you, having a son or an ox fallen into a well, will not immediately pull him out on a sabbath day?'* (14.5)

Amplification: quality of the act (*chreia*) implicitly acknowledged; rationale implicitly accepted; additional characterization, negative (Pharisees) and positive (Jesus)

> *And they were powerless to argue against these things* (14.6).

COMPONENT A:Setting

Amplification: description of dining room behaviour

> *And ... directing his attention* (ἐπέχων) *to how they picked out the prime reclining places* (πρωτοκλισίας) *...* (14.7b)

(5) *Analogy*: contains behavioural contrary and inversion of conventional behavioural motive scheme

> *... he told a parable to those invited ... saying to them, 'When you are invited by anyone to a wedding feast, do not recline in the prime reclining places, lest someone ranking higher than you* (ἐντιμότερός σου) *be invited by him; and he who invited you and him will come and say to you, "Give him (your) place," and then you would begin with shame to occupy the lowest place* (τὸν ἔσχατον τόπον). *On the contrary* (ἀλλ'),*when you are invited, go and recline* (ἀνάπεσε) *on the lowest place, so that when your host comes he will say to you, "Friend, ascend higher". And it will be to your honour in the presence of all your reclining company* (συνακειμένων)' (14.7a,c-10).

(7,4) *Judgment* (κρίσις) and *contrary* (reversal)

> *For everyone who exalts himself will be lowered, and he who lowers himself will be exalted* (14.11).

(5)  *Analogy*: contains contrasted hosting rules and inversion of conventional reward scheme

> *And he also said to his host, 'When you prepare a dinner or a banquet, do not call your friends, or your brothers, or your kinsfolk* (συγγενεῖς), *or rich neighbours, lest they invite you in return and this be your repayment. On the contrary* (ἀλλ'), *when you prepare a feast, invite the beggars, the maimed, the lame, the blind, and you will be happy, because they are not able to repay you; for, you will be repaid at the uprising* (τῇ ἀναστάσει) *of the just'* (14.12–14).

COMPONENT B: Challenge/Question

Amplification: issue falsely restated to allow for a clarifying rebuttal by means of a παράδειγμα (example)

> *When someone of the reclining company heard this, he said to him, 'Happy is the one who will eat bread in the kingdom of God'* (14.15).

(6)  *Example*: developed by means of a polarity of socially 'exalted' and socially 'lowered' groups and focusing on an exemplary rich householder for whom a conversion of moral and social values entails a transfer from the first group to the second (see ch. 6)

> *A certain person prepared a banquet and invited many …* [etc] (14.16–24).

(8)  *Conclusion* (embedded in the example story):

> *'For I say to you* (ὑμῖν) *that none of those invited men will enjoy my banquet'* (14.24).

### Explicating the pattern

The outline indicates at a glance that Luke's story has taken up all elements of the elaboration pattern, although not in the sequence prescribed by Hermogenes. Luke briefly describes the setting (A), amplifying it to serve the elaboration to follow. The setting specifies the occasion as a social meal hosted by a ruler and a religious functionary, i.e., a socially élite person, an item of information that will function as a richly suggestive back-drop and as a deposit from which to draw common, and therefore easily understood, images and analogies that can be exploited for deliberation on social and economic themes. That the meal takes place on a sabbath is appropriate to the judicial issue. Readers can be expected to recall that Luke has already infused the sabbath day with special significance; it has repeatedly been a time of contest between Jesus and the Pharisees in which Jesus has emerged victorious as the κύριος τοῦ σαββάτου (6.1–5)[51] and as a champion of a sabbath ethic that stresses 'doing good' (ἀγαθοποίησις), exemplified by relieving people from distress of disease (6.6–11, 13.10–17), over the Pharisees' insistence on marking the sabbath in accordance with the principle of legal correctness (based on a code which Luke does not allow to come into view and which he pejoratively seems to link to κακοποίησις [6.9], hypocrisy and shame [13.15,17]). Mere mention of 'sabbath' thus tacitly guides readers to expect a (rather predictable) challenge in Luke 14, an expectation that is confirmed with the additional narrator's characterizing remark that the Pharisees 'were watching' (ἦσαν παρατηρούμενοι) Jesus with hostile intentions.[52] The introduction of the sick person is required for the ἔξεστιν question, and the fact that the person's sickness is dropsy will be useful for deflecting the judicial controversy on to a deliberative track of argumentation.

The challenge/question (B) is then articulated, though not by the challengers themselves, as one would expect. Rather, the question 'Is it lawful to heal on the sabbath?' is discerned and verbalized (ἀποκριθείς) by Jesus. This is a shrewd rhetorical move. Readers should recognize it as an escalation of an epideictic tactic that Luke has employed earlier to celebrate Jesus' superior perceptive powers and to expose his adversaries as ineffective fools in judicial situations.[53] It also obliquely initializes the motif of silence which will

51 See Robbins's article, 'Plucking Grain on the Sabbath' (Mack and Robbins, 1989, pp. 129–32) for an analysis of Luke 6.1–5 as a *chreia* composition that is abbreviated to 'function as a παράδειγμα ("example") that exhibits Jesus' lordship over the Sabbath' (p. 130). The paradigm is assumed in the rest of Luke's narrative.
52 Παρατηρέω is itself a code word that alludes to and resumes the hostile Pharisaic plot against Jesus. See esp. 6.7: 'On another sabbath, when he went into a synagogue to teach, a man was there whose right hand was withered. And the scribes and Pharisees watched him (παρετηροῦντο) to see if he would heal on the sabbath, so that they might find something with which to accuse him (κατηγορεῖν)'. Cf. 11.53–4, 20.20, 23.2, and the detailed analysis of the plot of suspicion to which Luke 14.1 alludes by McMahan, 1987, pp. 192–8, and the literature cited there.
53 Note the escalation: in 6.2 the Pharisees expressly charge Jesus with doing what is not lawful (οὐκ ἔξεστιν) on the sabbath. However, on another sabbath (6.6–11)

allow Luke to abbreviate the judicial dispute, to settle it quickly in Jesus' favour virtually by default (in a manner reminiscent of the strategy described by Aristotle, *Rhetoric* 3.17.14–15) in order to proceed to the argument that really interests him.[54] After a brief introductory, auxiliary remark (αὔξησις, *amplificatio*, 'amplification') on the silence of the Pharisees (14.4a), an epideictic touch[55] to indicate that Jesus has divined the challenge correctly, the stage is set for the response (*chreia* performance) and its elaboration (C). The *chreia* itself is performed, rather than recited, as a healing of a person suffering from dropsy. Following the performance, an extended discourse, at several crucial points aided by the narrator's amplifying asides, elaborates the *chreia*-action by a process that is entirely inferential and heavily dependent on the topic of contrast and comparison, rationalizing it first in judicial terms, then explicating it deliberatively.

The argumentation begins by proposing a rationale for the sabbath healing by means of an analogy in the form of a rhetorical question, 'Who of you would not immediately pull out a son or an ox that has fallen into a well?' The form (ἐρώτησις, *interrogatio*) expedites the abbreviation of the judicial rhetoric, for it is designed to be answered simply, either with a 'yes' or a 'no',[56] and to humiliate the adversary in a situation of dispute.[57] In this case, if

the Pharisees 'watched him' to see if he would heal someone, but rather than expressing their objection themselves, the narrator states that Jesus 'discerned their objections' (ᾔδει τοὺς διαλογισμοὺς αὐτῶν). In 7.39–40 Jesus refuted (ἀποκριθείς) an objection which a Pharisee mumbled to himself (εἶπεν ἐν ἑαυτῷ). See also 11.38–9 where the 'lord' responds to a Pharisee's unarticulated astonishment at Jesus' table manners. This is the stuff of epideictic (christological) rhetoric; it accentuates the percipience of the master against the foil of foolishness of his Pharisaic adversaries (the only ones called ἄφρονες [fools] in Luke [11.40; by association in 12.20]; see McMahan, 1987, p. 195 and n. 103).

54  Robbins points out in his analysis of the synoptic story of 'Plucking Grain on the Sabbath' (Mack and Robbins, 1989, pp. 112–13) that this narratival tactic leaves the Pharisees extremely vulnerable, for in forensic argumentation a side that speaks first, needs to state its case, produce the law on which the case is based and then apply the law to the case in question. In Luke 14, the opponents speak first (although indirectly), but then forfeit their case by silence (though, in their defence, a silence imposed on them by a heavy-handed narrator).

55  See Kennedy, 1984, p. 75 ('epideictic style tends to amplification'); and Robbins in Mack and Robbins, 1989, p. 162 (citing Kennedy). Amplification can be introduced in all parts of a speech. See, in general, Lausberg, 1960, section 259 (pp. 400–9).

56  The rhetorical question is differentiated from an inquiry (πύσμα, *quaesitum*) that demands a longer reply. See, e.g., Theon, *progymn.* 5: ἡ ἐρώτησις . . . διὰ τοῦ ναὶ ἢ οὒ ἀποκρίνασθαι, τὸ δὲ πύσμα μακροτέραν ἀπαιτεῖ τὴν ἀπόκρισιν. See Lausberg, 1960, sections 767–70, (pp. 379–81).

57  Quintilian, *Inst.* 9.2.7; Lausberg, 1960, p. 397 (section 767): 'Einkleidung der Aussage als Frage geschieht mit dem Ziel der Demütigung der Gegenpartei.'

Jesus (Luke) can gain the Pharisees' assent to the proposition embedded in the rhetorical question (It is permitted to rescue children or livestock from a well on a sabbath) they would by a process of induction (analogy) be pressured to agree that it is similarly permitted to release a sick person from disease on a sabbath.[58] Such agreement would gain Luke (Jesus) even more. If the opponents accept the proposition and agree to the validity of the analogy, they also assume the humiliating position of themselves doubting the intent of the very law which they apparently assume (but do not adduce) in their charge against Jesus.[59]

Although the abbreviated treatment of the sabbath healing question makes for uncertainty, it may also be that the issue is one of 'quality' rather than legality. In this case, the disputing partners would agree on the law, the definition of the terms and intents of the law, and on the fact that it has been broken, but the 'unlawful' action would be justified on other grounds, in Luke 14 presumably on the principle of 'doing good and saving life' (6.9).[60] This second way of defining the issue is obviously advantageous for the rest of the elaboration; an issue of 'quality' signals the priority of beneficence over the binding proprieties of convention (law) thematized in the elaboration. In any case, by the narrator's decree, in the form of an auxiliary comment, the Pharisees 'were powerless to argue against these things' (οὐκ ἴσχυσαν ἀνταποκριθῆναι πρὸς ταῦτα) (14.6), indicating that they have been induced to agree that sabbath healing is sufficiently similar to rescuing children or livestock from a well and therefore within the range of the law's intent (legal question) or justifiable on extra-legal grounds (qualitative question).[61]

58 The rhetoricians recognized induction as an effective technique of establishing a doubtful proposition. Cicero (*Inv. Rhet.* 1.30.51) describes the process succinctly: 'Induction is a form of argument which leads the person with whom one is arguing to give assent to certain undisputed facts; through this assent it wins his approval of a doubtful proposition because this resembles the facts to which he has assented' (trans. Hubbell, LCL). Synopsis in Lausberg, 1960, sections 419–421.
59 The manoeuvre here assumes that the issue (στάσις, in forensic rhetoric) is defined as a 'legal question', that is, as a question which expresses some doubt on the intent of the law to which the objectors apparently appeal. On the various ways of defining *stasis*, see Kennedy, 1984, pp. 18–19; and Robbins in Mack and Robbins, 1989, pp. 108–9, 114. On the 'legal question' Kennedy's definition is appropriate to the text under discussion: 'In a legal question there is an expressed doubt about a law itself, for example about the difference between its wording and intent. The law might prohibit a variety of activities on the Sabbath but not specifically mention healing: "Was it the intent of the law to prevent healing?"'
60 See Kennedy, 1984, p. 19, on the *stasis* of quality.
61 I have translated 14.6 to accentuate its rhetorical nuances as required, I think, by the context. Note the pl. ταῦτα (cf. RSV, 'this'); it suggests that the Pharisees have

The Pharisees thus are caught in a contradiction. Though the humiliated Pharisees are not a pretty sight, in their haplessness they function as a foil (contrary) to help Luke to underscore once more Jesus' rhetorical savvy, to remind his readers that he is the master over the sabbath and to suggest that the 'truth'of the *chreia*-action, though not contrary to the law or its intent, cannot fully be discerned or confirmed strictly by an appeal to law ( = convention). This suggestion makes for an impression that the issue embedded in the healing action is still up for discussion and thus opens the door for the elaboration to veer towards a different course in which another dimension of the *chreia* is pursued: the sabbath healing fades from view and the metaphorical attributes of dropsy and release from it are brought into view.

Once the validity of the *chreia*-action has been vindicated, even approved, however grudgingly, by Jesus' adversaries, it can be used to serve Luke's more pressing desire to craft an advisory rhetoric for his moral and social ideals and the behaviour that corresponds to them. The change of focus is achieved by the narrator's intervention in the form of an auxiliary remark (amplification of setting), or, as Steven Sheeley labels it, a 'contextual aside' (1992, pp. 108–9)[62] which informs readers that Jesus has directed his attention to the dinner guests' posturing for prestigious reclining places (14.7b). This item of information is no mere decorative detail (ἔκφρασις), prized by writers of popular narratives, nor simply a 'catchword' transition to a new period in the episode; it is crucial for the redefining of the issue of the *chreia* and for the advancement of the argument. It links the socially symbolic occasion of an upper-class dinner party (14.1; see ch. 4–6) with a pattern of behaviour that first-century Mediterranean readers in all probability would have recognized as falling within the metaphorical range of the symptoms of dropsy (see ch. 3). Subtly this linkage extracts from the *chreia*, which ostensibly describes strictly a medical operation, the point (issue) that the therapy concerns the cure of a morally malignant character, a point that can be aptly clarified and expanded for

assented to the proposition embedded in the question (14.5) and agreed that it is a valid analogy to sabbath healing.
62 Sheeley's terms and criteria for identifying 'asides' are indebted to modern methods of narrative analysis, but his description of the function of 14.7b is helpful. Noting that 14.7b is the only instance of a 'contextual aside' in Luke's gospel, he describes it as providing 'essential information' without which readers might not be able to infer 'the motivation for his [Jesus'] discourse and the primary point upon which his message turned'.

first-century ears by exploiting familiar dinner-party themes and conventions to develop a contrasting set of *nomoi sympotikoi*, one, corresponding to the values and social sensibilities of a 'dropsical' *ethos*, as a foil for the other, corresponding to the ideology of a transformed *ethos*. In developing this contrast, Jesus, having already appeared as a successful medic and judicial rhetor, will advise and rationalize the conversion from one *ethos* to the other and thus assume also the authority of a 'doctor' (akin to the familiar Hellenistic [Cynic] figure of the moral σοφός) of a 'dropsical' orientation and appear as a deliberative orator.[63] Beyond helping to redefine the issue at stake in the *chreia*, the narrator's amplification of the setting also advances the argumentation, for it expressly generates the analogies that follow (14.7: ἔλεγεν ... παραβολήν, ἐπέψων ... λέγων πρὸς αὐτούς).

The first παραβολή (14.8–10) picks up on the Pharisees' philotimic posturing for the choice couches and uses it to win a general principle (14.11) which is retroflexively operative as premise from which to exhort one pattern of behaviour and excoriate another. Interestingly, the analogy explicates the observed Pharisaic dining room behaviour by extending it diachronically to include a credible set of consequences.[64] In the manner of the analogous case, the Pharisees' striving for prestigious couches could backfire and result in lounging on the least prestigious places and lead to shame (αἰσχύνη), a consequence opposite to the one desired. With one eye towards the ὕψος-ταπεινός maxim and because it is rhetorically useful to him, Luke (Jesus) further extends the social scenario of the parable by suggesting that the inverse of the paradoxical high → low → shame sequence also obtains: low → high → acclaim (δόξα).

---

63 Cf. Hock's notice, 1990, p. 28, unfortunately left undeveloped, that the philosophers' symposia often develop a 'medical ethos'.
64 Cf. Raymond's study of Aristotle's use of analogies to illustrate his own instructions on the use of paradigms and analogies (*Rhet.* 2.20.3–9). 'One aspect of the example that seems to have escaped attention is that every illustration Aristotle gives is diachronic in structure: each one is a story, an event leading to another event, like cause to consequence, not with the inexorable determinism of scientific causality, but in a pattern of probable causality, suggesting that if analogous events were to take place again, analogous consequences would be likely to ensue' (Raymond, 1984, p. 146). Raymond finds here the unarticulated reason for Aristotle's suggestion that examples are best suited to deliberative rhetoric (*Rhet.* 3.17.5). Deliberative rhetoric 'is concerned with the future. Patterns of events – examples in the form of true or at least credible stories – are our best guide to the consequences of decisions facing us in the present "because as a rule the future resembles the past" [Aristotle, *Rhet.* 2.20.8]. Only if the example has a diachronic

While the analogy employs a conceivable dinner-party scenario to illuminate what is at stake in the behaviour of the actual dinner guests, it is of course in the form of a set of injunctions, both negative (do not) and positive (do), which need to be rationalized by suggesting that they represent a concrete enactment of a general truth, or to be 'enforced' by means of an appropriate motive (reward or punishment) clause. The antithetical ὕψος-ταπεινός aphorism, connected to the analogy/injunctions by ὅτι here a 'causal conjunction' (Blass and Debrunner, 1961, section 456.1) which usually introduces a supporting reason (see Kennedy, 1984, pp. 49–50), seems to offer the rationale by restating the reversal instantiated in the parable as a general rule. But since the general rule seems also to be concluded from the concrete example, the analogically clothed injunction and rationale together pose as a kind of tautology, each functioning both as premise and conclusion.

Persuasion, however, does not rest upon flawless logic; it engages in 'probabilistic reasoning' from shared assumptions and accepted premises (Raymond, 1984, pp. 148–9). Such is the case with Luke 14.11. Its 'truth' appears to be assumed by Luke and his readers, presumably because it articulates an ideology that both share and because it is issued as a judgment underwritten by the authoritative *ethos* of Jesus; it thus functions as a rationale for the exhortations by means of an argument ἐκ κρίσεως (judgment, 'statement by an authority').

A few more subtle aspects of the analogy-rationale/judgment complex are worth noting. First, the exemplified injunctions clearly take advantage of a first-century reader's vulnerabilities; any reader would share the general cultural anxieties (shame, loss of face) and aspirations (good reputation) that Luke tags as consequences of the contrasted behavioural options he has identified. That he has further located the possibility of humiliation or recognition in the social locale of the dining room, where the potential for such things was most acute, is a clever and an extremely forceful play on the πάθος of the audience. Second, though clever, this manipulative rhetorical tactic is also conventional. What astonishes is that Luke (like Hermogenes) argues in a recognizably conventional manner for unconventionalities (unlike Hermogenes); he appeals to the standard items on the index of a first-century person's self-interest, fear of shame and desire for honour, to plead for the social applica-

structure does its peculiar applicability to deliberative discourse seem apparent'
(Raymond, 1984, pp. 146–7).

tion of a set of values that his contemporaries would regard as honourable only after a massive redefining of that term. Third, the paradoxical sequences we noted in the exemplary injunctions neatly resemble the paradoxical symptoms of dropsy (wanting that which leads to unwanted ill) and its paradoxical treatment (denying one's wants to get what one wants). *Chreia* and the contraries in the elaboration thus aptly cohere.

The second analogy[65] returns to the dinner party locale to pick up the figure of the host (14.12a) in order to construct a second set of contrary symposium rules around him. Identically constructed, these rules shed further light on the theme of the elaboration, i.e., what the 'cure' of a 'dropsical' character entails. The hosting rules also concretize the general principle of lowliness (and its rather innocuous exemplification in the previous analogy) by advising that the embrace of ταπείνωσις constitutes much more than an attitude of modesty in generalized (pious or moral) terms; rather, it is exemplified in a pattern of commensality (social arrangement)[66] that dissolves the conventional social categories and disengages the rule of balanced reciprocity as the principle that buttressed social boundaries and governed the practice of beneficence. It is becoming much clearer that Jesus extracts from his *chreia* a truth of massive consequences for those (the social élite) whom he wants to persuade; it will require a fundamental revision, indeed, inversion, of all the conceptual and social categories by which they have previously charted the course of their lives. The author of the rhetoric of course knows that he has raised the stakes and therefore introduces a rationale that contributes to the onward move of the argument for the transformation for which he pleads.

Thus the rationale (14.14) expressly works in the idea of compensation and links this to being 'blessed' with a syllogistic sleight-of-hand.[67] We have noted that formally the saying is a beatitude, a speech form that is often interpreted in apocalyptic/eschatological vein. But as Willem Vorster argued, 'one can make a strong case

---

[65] On the possibility of serializing examples in argumentation see Aristotle, *Rhet.* 2.20.9.

[66] It needs to be remembered that in Luke's world commensality expressed ideals and social arrangements of civic life generally, and that general social and moral values were typified and concretely expressed in *nomoi sympotikoi* (see relevant sections in chs. 5 and 6).

[67] Note the multiplication of compensation vocabulary to ensure that this idea receives the proper pause: ἀντικαλέσωσιν, ἀνταπόδομα, ἀνταποδοῦναι, ἀνταποδοθήσεται.

that ... macarisms should be read as wisdom sayings' with a paraenetic intent to declare that 'well-being is connected to conduct' (Vorster, 1990, pp. 47–8). This is the case in Luke 14.14, although it does introduce an eschatological ideal (the authority of a utopian state of affairs; cf. the appeal to the gods in Hermogenes' elaboration) into its argument.[68] The rationale in fact is a miniature, cleverly amplified enthymemic argument in its own right.[69] Like other beatitudes, this one takes 'enthymematic, and thus syllogistic form, and [is] *formally* valid' (Kennedy, 1984, p. 49), even though much of its persuasive potential is staked on premises whose validity is taken for granted.[70] In Luke 14.14, the conclusion is given first (you will be well/blessed), its major premise is unarticulated (rewards generate well-being), and its concrete (minor) premise is expanded into a contrary (the poor *et al.* cannot repay you; you will be repaid at the rise of the just). This makes the enthymeme into a minor rhetorical *tour de force*. Its major premise, functioning as an operative assumption, links a chief Hellenistic social virtue (repayment for kindnesses) to a central value (happiness), which also alludes to one of the τέλικα κεφάλαια of deliberative rhetoric.

When this general assumption, not likely to be disputed by anyone, is concretely specified in the secondary premise, it is cleverly deconstructed and fundamentally redefined. The first part of the applied premise (they cannot repay you) of course requires the conclusion, 'therefore, you will not be happy', which is exactly the logic which guided the wealthy in their practice of channelling their beneficence to those who are able to reciprocate. But by expressly concluding, on the contrary, that happiness comes from not being repaid by those not able (οὐκ ἔχουσιν), the definition of the terms in the general premise are in need of re-examination. That is, since happiness is the result of not being repaid by those who are not able, what is meant by repayment or happiness? Without pursuing this question in detail, it is apparent that the equation happiness =

---

[68] Cf. pp. 59–60 and Braun, 1992, p. 78, on Lucian's similar appeal to the utopian constitution of life in Hades to criticize social practices in real life.

[69] An enthymeme is a rhetorical syllogism that differs from its logical counterpart by omitting one of its premises. See, in detail, Aristotle, *Rhet.* 1.2.10–20 and 2.21–3 (including the discussion of maxims as enthymemes). See Raymond, 1984, pp. 141–4; and the instructive analysis of enthymemic reasoning in synoptic material by Robbins in Mack and Robbins, 1989, pp. 78–80, 120–3; cf. pp. 199–200 (Mack and Robbins).

[70] As Raymond points out (1984, p. 144), enthymemic arguments are really arguments that proceed from premises which are 'accepted by both speaker and audience without being proven', i.e. assumptions.

repayment is being denied in one sense, that is, in the sense of repayment as balanced reciprocity; the foundations of reciprocal economic and social relations are being assaulted here, an impression solidified by the second (positive) part of the stated premise which promises repayment at a time when the 'just', itself a code word for Luke's practical ethic of doing good,[71] will have their day, a proposition which does not deny the importance of rewards for well-being, but either defers them to a future (as suggested by the verb tense) to make room for unrequitable generosity in the present, or suggests that joining the community of the 'just' will bring its own (superior) compensation in the form of well-being which will be found only in that community.[72]

Altogether, 14.14 delivers a strong rationale for the hosting rules exemplified in the instructions to the Pharisaic dinner host. Luke is here at his rhetorical best and most forceful, an indicator that the social and economic advice he delivers is at the heart of his paraenetic aims in the dinner episode, aims, I remind, which are entirely appropriate to the dropsy *chreia* performed in a dinner-party setting.

Luke once more resorts to amplification (14.15), this time permitting one of the assembled dinner guests to misstate the point as it has unfolded in the elaboration (an epideictic touch to show that the Pharisees were not only bad lawyers and inept rhetoricians, but also dense students). This will provide Jesus with an opportunity for a rebuttal that will also serve to clarify the real issue further with an argument ἐκ παραδείγματος.[73] The Pharisee, who, as will be recalled, has already been induced to agree to the validity of the *chreia*, and evidently has listened to the elucidation of its point (ἀκούσας ... ταῦτα), attempts to articulate it as a restatement of the beatitude that served as the rationale for the hosting rules. But while the Pharisee is attracted to the idea of well-being and similarly links this to an eschatological hope (the kingdom of God), he has missed the crucial premise in Jesus' beatitude which sets the conditions for well-being. He thus works with a definition of well-being

---

[71] E.g., Acts 10.35: ἐν παντὶ ἔθνει ὁ φοβούμενος [τὸν θεὸν] καὶ ἐργαζόμενος δικαιοσύνη [= ποιῶν ἐλεημοσύνας πολλάς, 10.2) δεκτὸς αὐτῷ ἐστιν. See further Horn, 1983, pp. 54–5.

[72] The idea of blessedness and related notions of joy and happiness are central values in Luke's gospel. See, e.g., Vorster, 1990, p. 44, and n. 18 (Luke = 'the evangelist of joy').

[73] Cf. ch. 5, pp. 63–4, where I noted the banal ring of this saying and Luke's tendency to use macarisms as a way of expressing ideas he wants to refute.

that Jesus has already criticized. Further, by picking up the same language Luke used to describe the Pharisaic dinner party (φαγεῖν ἄρτον) the Pharisee identifies happiness with a very particular commensality, namely the kind which he is presently enjoying and the kind from which Jesus has tried to dissuade him. When he then projects the Pharisaic dinner party into the divine realm he articulates his desire to prolong the *status quo*, to obtain yet more of that which, in Luke's (Jesus') view, leads not to well-being, but to its opposite. The Pharisee still suffers from 'dropsy'. A *paradeigma* should help to win the point for him.

In Luke's argumentation the so-called 'parable' of the great banquet serves as the proof from exemplary precedent.[74] How aptly the story confirms the elaboration of the *chreia* Luke has advanced thus far need not be belaboured here in detail (see ch. 6). It will be recalled that the story of the householder exemplifies the argument for a transformation of character which the elaboration has taken up as the theme of the *chreia* at all its crucial points. An ostensibly wealthy householder sets out to seek honour (exalt himself in a 'dropsical' manner) by hosting an ostentatious banquet to which he invites many of his wealthy colleagues noted for their ('dropsical') interest in accumulating assets; the result of this quest is not honour, but shame; consequently, the text implies that he undergoes a change of heart ('cure' of his previous 'dropsical' ambitions) and abandons the quest for a reputable place among the social élite, 'lowers' himself, does what is necessary (note ἀνάγκασον [14.23], a primary value governing deliberation!) to become a benefactor to and member of a group of people from the very lowest social rank; he finds this to his taste (γευστός, 14.24; an allusive reference to 'well-being') and declares that he no longer desires the company of his former wealthy colleagues and the 'well-being' that he once thought they would provide.[75]

---

[74] Cf. Aristotle, *Rhet.* 2.20.8–9, on the use and placement of paradigms: '... we must employ examples for demonstrative proofs, for conviction (πίστις) is produced by these ... examples must be used as evidence [for enthymemes if they have been used] and as a kind of epilogue to the enthymemes ... Wherefore also it is necessary to quote a number of examples if they are put first [to function as enthymemes], but one alone is sufficient if they are put last; for even a single trustworthy witness is of use' (trans. Freese, LCL).

[75] Although the paradigm of the householder-host generally fits the plot of the dropsy *chreia* and exemplifies aptly the lesson Luke develops from it in 14.7–14, there is, admittedly, one weak link. In 14.4 the cure of the dropsy was expressly effected by the action of someone else (Jesus). In the case of the householder the 'cure' of his 'dropsical' values (i.e. his conversion) has to be inferred from his

The conclusion to the elaboration is not as sharply focused as Hermogenes suggested to his students. I argued earlier (ch. 6, pp. 121–6) that the epilogue is embedded in the story itself and not an appended παράκλησις as it likely was in the Q version. Since, moreover, 14.1–24 is part of a longer narrative, this does not present a problem; the issues addressed in this episode are indeed further elucidated beyond Luke 14 and therefore do not need a sharp concluding period here. Also, an explicit παράκλησις has been articulated earlier in the form of the exemplary *nomoi sympotikoi*. Should one nonetheless insist, an implicit hortatory appeal does ring in 14.24, for the householder's final declaration represents a paradigmatic witness to the fact that the exhortation to act upon the claims of the *chreia* has been heeded. It may be more than a curiosity to note that the rhetor Jesus heeds his own rhetoric, for Luke 14:1–24 represents the last time that Jesus will dine with the social élite (Pharisees). Henceforth he will find his enjoyment in the convivial company of the despised, sinners and tax collectors (15.1–2, 19.2–10), and among his own followers (22.7–38, 24.28–49). That this leads to his exaltation is amply made clear by Luke; Jesus dies the noble death of a hero and leaves behind a legacy as a mimetic ideal for his followers (see Kloppenborg, 1992a, pp. 109–15).

actions and (implicitly) is the result of his own resolve. This kind of misalignment might be expected. The householder story came to Luke with a rather fixed plot (cf. Matt. 22.1–14, *G.Thom.* 64) which could be adjusted somewhat through narrative embellishment in the manner described in ch. 5, but probably not easily restructured. Some imprecision also inheres in the nature of narrative argumentation itself. Analogies by definition are not samenesses.

# 9

## TOWARDS CLOSURE (AND OPENINGS)

These last few pages finally are an opportunity to step out of the confines of Luke 14. I leave it behind with a few backward glances at Luke's rhetorical achievement, then briefly ponder what this permits us to say about what L. Bitzer (1968) calls the 'rhetorical situation', the real-life situation addressed in Luke's appeal. Finally, as a way of contriving closure and new openings at the same time, I offer several items from a 'wish list' of topics in Lukan studies which are suggested by this study and, I think, worthy of energetic scholarly attention.

### The rhetorical achievement

The dinner episode has shown itself to be the result of a rather sophisticated compositional planning. Its thematic and rhetorical coherence has become evident and, considering all the elements that had to cohere and recalling that the material in the episode was not entirely cut out of whole cloth, this coherence was achieved against demanding odds. Evidently Luke had learnt something about the usefulness of *chreiai* for constructing prose arguments and the dinner episode shows that he could apply his learning with refined skill.

He chose (composed) a *chreia* featuring dropsy as a familiar and highly potent cipher for a range of greedy, gluttonous and hence predatory social behaviours and arrangements that he wanted to excoriate. A cured dropsy would naturally suggest the opposites he wanted to vindicate. The topic of contrast and polarity thus is in place and needs only to be developed and played upon.

The cure itself is the rhetorical aim and the paradoxical nature of the therapy lends itself to pleading in terms of inversions and reversals to convince people that the necessary way to pursue desirable (conventional) ends is by ending the pursuit of (conventional) desires. But how to harness and explicate all this potential with credible and easily understood figures, analogies and examples? A second move would be needed. This consisted in aptly locating the dropsy *chreia* within the setting of an élite dinner party. Itself a miniature representation of more general aristocratic cultural values and patterns of social and economic interaction and, therefore, an oft-used exemplary target for the critique of those values and patterns, the 'big dinner' was replete with easily generated analogies (to supplement the material Luke already had) that could be used advantageously for portraying 'dropsical' characters and behaviour and pleading for their 'cure', using various modes of rhetoric and arranging proofs in a manner that resembles the taught exercise of working out a *chreia*.

## The rhetorical situation

The mixture of rhetorical modes (judicial, epideictic, deliberative) and the primary point of the pleading in 14.1–24 (the transformation of character and reorientation of values) within a dining room setting allow us to draw several soft conclusions on the rhetorical situation (the real-life world) that the writer wanted to influence.[1] What social scenario is envisaged in the dinner episode and who is the target of its rhetoric?

Most generally, the *klinium* setting, though a literary locale not to be converted into an actual historical representation without ado, is not without social-historical significance. In Luke's culture the social *symposia* and *deipna* were regarded as effective symbolic affairs that functioned to introduce participants into an association and to hold up for them its shared values, norms and ideals. Given also the equation between dining room interaction and civic ideals and social relations writ large, Luke's option for the dinner party as the forum in which to present Jesus as a sympotic adviser makes sense as a response to the evangelist's familiarity with social pressures within his circle that surfaced most clearly in dining

---

[1] 'Soft' is, in my view, as firm as one can get in reconstructing a rhetorical situation on the basis of one segment in a larger text. The situation that comes into view in Luke 14.1–24 would need to be tested against the rhetorical situation that is presupposed in Luke's gospel as a whole.

situations and that, therefore, could be addressed most appropriately in terms of *nomoi sympotikoi*.[2]

Extreme characterization to sharpen socio-economic cleavages, the *nomoi sympotikoi* that address the posturing for position (14.8–10) and the problem of social boundaries (14.12–13,14), together with the exemplary point of the householder-host 'parable' suggest an audience that is experimenting with a sociability marked by a mixing of the social categories whose members might have recognized themselves in the stereotypical (to first-century ears) terms which the text uses to describe them, i.e., the poor and powerless (disabled) versus the rich and powerful.

On several counts the rhetoric suggests that it addresses an audience which already has a good measure of commitment to a social arrangement that goes against the grain of well-established social attitudes and practices. We noted that the persuasion in the narrative takes on a pronounced epideictic dimension in the way it assumes and 'applauds' the authority of Jesus. It subordinates the judicial rhetoric to epideictic interests and so takes for granted (rather than *really* demonstrates) his ability to win against his opponents the case for the 'legality' of curing a person afflicated by dropsy. The narrator's decision to step aside in the elaboration of the metaphorical issue embedded in the dropsy cure, letting (with the implied permission of his readers) Jesus talk for him and authoritatively articulate what appear to be agreed on assumptions as rationales for an ideology of 'lowliness' (14.11) with its attendant compensation package in which notions of 'well-being' and 'justice' echo (14.14), sounds of 'enjoyment' ring (14.24), and ambitions surface in terms of 'exaltation' (14.11) and 'rising up' (14.14), suggests that the rhetoric aimed not towards a fundamental restructuring of the audience's views and practices, but towards confirming, legitimizing and celebrating what is already in place.[3] On one level Luke 14.1–24 thus has the sound of a persuasion for the persuaded, the ring of self-congratulatory 'party talk' much as one

---

[2] Cf. the dining room as the 'acid test' of the social experiment for the Corinthian Christians (on which see Gooch, 1993; Klauck, 1982; D. Smith, 1980) and other Jesus associations as well, judging from the meal motifs in their traditions (see Corley, 1993; Mack, 1988, pp. 80–3, 114–20; and on Mark, Klosinski, 1988; cf. on *G. Thom.*, Bjorndahl, 1988, Appendix, pp. 13–15).

[3] See further Robbins's argument that Luke-Acts represents 'a narrative map of territoriality for the development of Christian alliances throughout the eastern Roman Empire' (1991a, p. 203). Cf. Esler's argument (1987, p. 222) that Luke-Acts 'may be described as an exercise in the legitimation of a sectarian movement' for which the association of poor and rich is one of its pressure points.

finds in the epideictic oratory of a modern political or religious convention. One might well imagine that the kind of stuff here textualized once was heard as 'table talk' when Luke's mixed community gathered in the *klinium* for the 'breaking of bread' (κλάσις τοῦ ἄρτου; e.g. Luke 24.35, Acts 2.42–47).

Although the argumentation is predicated on and presumes agreeing applause on the basic level, its deliberative point was aimed towards adjusting particular people, the urban élite, to the ideas and practices that were generally shared by Luke and his audience.[4] The exemplary injunctions, rhetorically sharpened by means of the topic of contrast, but also the paradigm of the householder-host are specifically applicable to the πλούσιοι who may have imperilled the Lukan community's social experiment, tested in the laboratory of the dining room, in a number of ways. One might well imagine, for example, wealthy urban households who, for reasons we cannot pursue here, were attracted to participate in the common life of the local Jesus group, but insisted on special privileges and dues of honour becoming to their rank. They would need to be tuned to the norms of the new community. Others may have found that public identification and association with a group that violated the conventional social codes in significant ways earned them shame and ostracism from the circle of their peers, resulting in losses of income, influence and chances for improving their position (see ch. 6, pp. 106–13). They would need to be dissuaded from second-guessing their decision to join Luke's group and to be reassured that their commitment would pay off.[5] Still others, perhaps living in the discomfort of a double life, secret sympathizers and benefactors in one, committed to the prevailing moral and social terms of reference in the other, would need to be persuaded to make clearer choices. For all these the rhetoric sharply outlines the options, heavy-handedly and unfairly devaluing and maligning one as 'dropsical' and prescribing the other as the panacea, and urges them to calculate the odds – using Luke's measure of course – and throw in their full lot with a group that seems to have had some aspirations of being a 'winner' on the social landscape of Luke's city and beyond (see Robbins, 1991a), aspirations for which fully committed members from the ranks of the wealthy and influential would provide necessary economic means but also political credibility and

---

[4] See Bryant, 1953, p. 413, who summarizes the purpose of rhetoric as 'adjusting ideas to people and ... people to ideas'.
[5] Note Luke 1.4 where ἀσφάλεια is specified as the rhetorical aim of the entire gospel.

clout. At stake appears to be the construction of a Christian culture in which 'the hard facts of patronage' (Brown, 1992, p. 45), so harshly apparent and effective in conventional patterns of commensality, needed to be, if not softened, at least re-aimed to suit and serve that culture (cf. Bobertz's [1993] contiguous analysis of the social dynamics resounding in the *cena dominica* of Hippolytus' *Apostolic Tradition*).

## Openings

If the foregoing analysis of Luke 14 permits us to say this much, it brings us only to additional questions waiting for insistent asking. A rather obvious one is if the confluence of socio-rhetorical dynamics in Luke 14 is more typical than anomalous in Luke-Acts. At its broadest the answer must lie in a detailed socio-rhetorical analysis of the entire Lukan corpus, but much would be gained already in estimating anew the moral discourse, delivered in typical rhetorical patterns, embedded in Luke's central section (the so-called 'travel narrative') and its insistent portrayal of Jesus as an acclaimed wandering sage,[6] who, blending the παρρησία ('outspokenness') of the philosopher (Billault, 1993), the prestige of the rhetor and the flouting social gestures of the Cynic and the (analogous) later Christian monks (see Brown, 1992, pp. 71–8), represents the arguments ἐκ κρίσεως ('from authority') and ἐκ παραδείγματος ('from example') for Luke's Christian *paideia*.

The rhetoric of Luke 14 also raises a cautioning hand in the face of the 'canonical' view that Luke is a gospel for 'the poor' (see, most recently, Baergen, 1993, and the literature reviewed there). Although 'the poor' evidently are near the centre of Luke's beneficient concern, to what extent are they also rhetorical levers, an item of 'symbolic discourse' (Wilder, 1956; cf. Robbins, 1994a), in a 'high stakes' attempt to destabilize, reconfigure and ultimately control the orientation and dispositional patterns of the élite? Lukan 'persuasion' in chapter 14 appears to take its place alongside other harsh (Luke 6.24–7; 12.33; 18.22 [sharpening Mark 10.21]; 14.33) even lethal (Acts 5.1–11) tactics to put the 'great fear' (φόβος μέγας,

---

6 Although Moessner, 1989, has explored the wandering guest motif in this section, his interest in the intertextuality between Deuteronomy and Luke's narrative keeps him from attending to the cultural (de)construction that is at stake. A more fruitful analogue might be found in the orbit of Cynicism where viatic and viandic themes in the service of moralizing discourse are typical (see Moles, 1983).

Acts 5.11) of God into those who might be tempted to withhold a reasonable measure of nonconformity from the totalizing demands of Lukan *paideia*, overseen, as Acts shows, by a centralized and authoritarian kind of proto-bishopry.[7]

Not only does this pose the challenging socio-historical question of how and why Luke's 'persuasion' could possibly have appealed to the urban élite of his time,[8] but it also calls for further theoretical and exegetically applied consideration of the nature of early Christian persuasive discourse and the production of gospels, particularly the complex relationship between 'progymnastic rhetorical composition' (Robbins 1993a), the strategic use of social-definitional vocabulary and tropes (so richly distributed in Luke 14), the 'rhetorical situation' and the deployment of power in social and ideological formation.

[7] This implicitly places my view of the rhetorical tendencies in Luke-Acts on a trajectory of Christian 'rhetoric of empire' that emerges with greater confidence, frankness and clarity in post-Lukan antiquity (see A. Cameron, 1991, and Brown, 1992). Estimating Luke-Acts from the vantage point of these later centuries should prove to be a profitable undertaking, perhaps even a corrective adjustment to the retrospective predispositions of Lukan (and NT) scholarship.

[8] The question invites a coordination of the study of Luke's rhetoric with a socio-historical analysis of the pressure points in the lives of eastern Mediterranean urban élite in the late first and early second centuries. Cf. Plümacher, 1987, who addresses this question in terms of a promise of a new identity ('Identitätsgewinn') for the élite in the face of a fearful dissolution of old social, economic and political certainties ('Identitätsverlust').

# BIBLIOGRAPHY

Abu-Lughod, L. 1986. *Veiled Sentiments: Honor and Poetry in a Beduin Society*, University of California Press, Berkeley and Los Angeles

Adeleye, G. 1983. 'The purpose of the *dokimasia*', *Greek, Roman & Byzantine Studies*, 24, pp. 295–306

Adkins, A. W. H. 1960. *Merit and Responsibility: A Study in Greek Values*, Clarendon Press, Oxford

1972. *Moral Values and Political Behaviour in Ancient Greece: From Homer to the End of the Fifth Century*, Ancient Culture and Society, Chatto & Windus, London

Al-Azmeh, A. 1992. 'Barbarians in Arab eyes', *Past and Present*, 134, pp. 3–18

Alexander, L. C. A. 1986. 'Luke's preface in the context of Greek preface-writing', *Novum Testamentum*, 28, pp. 48–74

1993. *The Preface to Luke's Gospel: Literary Convention and Social Context in Luke 1.1–4 and Acts 1.1*, SNTSMS 78, Cambridge University Press

Alföldy, G. 1985. *The Social History of Rome*, 3rd edn, English trans. D. Braund and F. Pollock, Croom Helm, London

Alpers, P. 1990. 'Theocritean bucolic and Virgilian pastoral', *Arethusa*, 23, pp. 19–47

Anderson, G. 1986. *Philostratus: Biography and Belles Lettres in the Third Century A. D*, Croom Helm, London

Aristophanes. *The Plutus*, in *Aristophanes*, vol. III, LCL, English trans. B. B. Rogers, William Heinemann, London; Harvard University Press, 1924

*Aristotle. The 'Art' of Rhetoric*, LCL, English trans. J. H. Freeze, William Heinemann, London; Cambridge University Press, 1926

Arnal, W. E. 1991. 'IQP Database: Q 14:11', unpubl. paper prepared for the International Q Project

*Athenaeus. The Deipnosophists*, 10 vols. LCL, English trans. C. B. Gulick, William Heinemann, London; Harvard University Press, 1927–41

Aune, D. E. 1978. 'Septem sapientium convivium (Moralia 146B-164D)', in *Plutarch's Ethical Writings and Early Christian Literature*, SCHNT 4, ed. H. D. Betz, E. J. Brill, Leiden, pp. 51–105

1987. *The New Testament in its Literary Environment*, Library of Early Christianity 8, Westminster Press, Philadelphia

Baasland, E. 1986. 'Zum Beispiel der Beispielerzählungen. Zur Formenlehre der Gleichnisse und zur Methodik der Gleichnisauslegung', *Novum Testamentum*, 28, pp. 193–219

Bacon, B. W. 1922–3. 'Two parables of lost opportunity', *Hibbard Journal*, 21, pp. 337–52

Baergen, R. 1993. 'The motif of the renunciation of possessions in the gospel of Luke', *Conrad Grebel Review*, 11, pp. 233–47

(BAGD) Bauer, W. *A Greek–English Lexicon of the New Testament and Other Early Christian Literature*, 2nd edn, trans., rev. and augm. by W. F. Arndt, F. W. Gingrich and F. W. Danker, University of Chicago Press, 1979

Bailey, K. E. 1980. *Through Peasant Eyes: More Lucan Parables, Their Culture and Style*, William B. Eerdman's, Grand Rapids, Michigan

Bain, D. 1977. *Actors & Audience: A Study of Asides and Related Conventions in Greek Drama*, Oxford Classical and Philosophical Monographs, Oxford University Press

Baldwin, B. 1961. 'Lucian as social satirist', *Classical Quarterly*, 11, pp. 199–208

Baldwin, C. S. 1928. *Medieval Rhetoric and Poetic (to 1400) Interpreted from Representative Works*, Macmillan, New York

Ballard, P. 1972. 'Reasons for refusing the great supper', *Journal of Theological Studies*, 23, pp. 341–50

Barr, D. L. and J. L. Wentling 1984. 'The conventions of classical biography and the genre of Luke-Acts', in *Luke-Acts: New Perspectives from the SBL Seminar*, ed. C. H. Talbert, Crossroad, New York, pp. 125–40

Barrett, C. K. 1985. 'Sayings of Jesus in the Acts of the Apostles', in *A cause de l'évangile. Etudes sur les Synoptiques et les Acts offertes au P. Jacques Dupont, O.S.B. à l'occasion de son 70e anniversaire*, Lectio Divina 123, ed. F. Refoulé, Cerf, Saint-André, pp. 681–708

Bartchy, S. S. 1991. 'Community of goods in Acts: idealization or social reality?', in *The Future of Early Christianity: Essays in Honor of Helmut Koester*, ed. B. A. Pearson in collab. with A. T. Kraabel, G. W. E. Nickelsburg and N. R. Petersen, Fortress Press, Minneapolis, pp. 309–18

Bartsch, S. 1989. *Decoding the Ancient Novel: The Reader and the Role of Description in Heliodorus and Achilles Tatius*, Princeton University Press

Bastomsky, S. J. 1990. 'Rich and poor: the great divide in ancient Rome and Victorian England', *Greece and Rome*, 37, pp. 37–43

Beatrice, P. F. 1978. 'Il significato de *Ev.Thom* 64 per la critica letteraria della parabola del banchetto', in J. Dupont, 1978a, pp. 237–77

Beavis, M. A. 1990a. *Mark's Audience: The Literary and Social Setting of Mark 4.11–12*, JSNTSup 33, JSOT Press, Sheffield
1990b. 'Parable and fable', *Catholic Biblical Quarterly*, 52, pp. 473–98

Becker, W. A. and H. Göll 1866. *Charicles: Illustrations of the Private Life of the Ancient Greeks*, 3rd edn. English trans. F. Metcalfe, Longmans, Green, and Co., London

Bek, L. 1983. 'Quaestiones convivales: the idea of the triclinium and the staging of convivial ceremony from Rome to Byzantium', *Analecta Romana Instituti Danici*, 12, pp. 81–107

Berger, K. 1970. *Die Amen-Worte Jesu. Eine Untersuchung zum Problem der Legitimation in apokalyptischer Rede*, BZNW 39, Walter de Gruyter, Berlin

1984a. *Formgeschichte des Neuen Testaments*, Quelle und Meyer, Heidelberg

1984b. 'Hellenistische Gattungen im Neuen Testament', *Aufstieg und Niedergang der römischen Welt*, Vol. II no. 25, 2, ed. H. Temporini and W. Haase, Walter de Gruyter, Berlin, pp. 1031–432

Bernays, J. 1879. *Lucian und die Kyniker, mit einer Übersetzung der Schrift Lucians über das Lebensende des Peregrinus*, Wilhelm Hertz, Berlin

Bernidaki-Aldous, E. A. 1990. *Blindness in a Culture of Light: Especially the Case of Oedipus at Colonus of Sophocles*, American University Studies, ser. XVII/Classical Languages and Literature 8, Peter Lang, New York

Bielohlawek, K. 1940. 'Gastmahls- und Symposienlehren bei griechischen Dichtern', *Wiener Studien*, 58, pp. 11–30

Bihari-Andersson, A. 1987. 'Time and space in Hungarian fairy tales', in *Symbolic Textures: Studies in Cultural Meaning*, Gothenburg Studies in Social Anthropology 10, ed. G. Aijmer, Acta Universitatis Gothoburgensis, Göteborg, pp. 93–117

Billault, A. 1993. 'The rhetoric of a "divine man": Apollonius of Tyana as critic of oratory and as orator according to Philostratus', *Philosophy and Rhetoric*, 26, pp. 227–35

Billerbeck, M. 1979. *Der Kyniker Demetrius. Ein Beitrag zur Geschichte der frühkaiserzeitlichen Popularphilosophie*, Philosophia Antiqua 36, E. J. Brill, Leiden

Bitzer, L. F. 1968. 'The rhetorical situation', *Philosophy and Rhetoric*, 1, pp. 1–14; repr. in *Philosophy and Rhetoric Supplement*, 1992, pp. 1–14

Bjorndahl, S. 1988. 'Thomas 61–67: A chreia elaboration pattern', unpubl. paper presented in the New Testament Seminar, Claremont Graduate School, Claremont, California

Black, M. 1967. *An Aramaic Approach to the Gospels and Acts*, 3rd edn, Clarendon Press, Oxford

(Bl-Dbr) Blass, F. and A. Debrunner 1961. *A Greek Grammar of the New Testament and Other Early Christian Literature*, trans. and rev. of the 19th German edn. incorporating suppl. notes of A. Debrunner by R. W. Funk, University of Chicago Press

Blomberg, C. L. 1990. *Interpreting the Parables*, InterVarsity Press, Downers Grove, Illinois

Bobertz, C. A. 1993. 'The role of patron in the *Cena Dominica* of Hippolytus' *Apostolic Tradition*', *Journal of Theological Studies*, NS 44, pp. 170–84

Boer, W. den 1979. *Private Morality in Greece and Rome: Some Historical Aspects*, Mnemosyne Suppl. 57, E. J. Brill, Leiden

1983. '*Tapeinos* in Pagan and Christian terminology', in *Tria Corda: Scritti in onore di Arnaldo Momigliano*, Biblioteca di Athenaeum 1, ed. E. Gabba, Edizione New Press, Como, pp. 143–62

Bolkestein, H. 1939. *Wohltätigkeit und Armenpflege im vorchristlichen Altertum. Ein Beitrag zum Problem 'Moral und Gesellschaft'*, Oosthoek, Utrecht; repr. Bouma's Boekhuis, Groningen, 1967

Bonner, S. F. 1977. *Education in Ancient Rome: From the Elder Cato to the Younger Pliny*, University of California Press, Berkeley and Los Angeles

Booth, A. 1991. 'The age for reclining and its attendant perils', in Slater, 1991a, pp. 105–20

Bossman, D. M. 1991. 'Values of inclusion and exclusion in Lk 14:23 and Matt 22:11–13', unpubl. paper presented at the SBL Social Sciences and New Testament Section, Kansas City, 1991

Bovon, F. 1979. 'Orientations actuelles des études lucaniennes', *Revue de théologie et de philosophie*, 26, pp. 161–90

Bowersock, G. W. 1969. *Greek Sophists in the Roman Empire*, Clarendon Press, Oxford

Bowie, E. L. 1970. 'Greeks and their past in the second sophistic', *Past and Present*, 46, pp. 3–41
1986. 'Early Greek elegy, symposium and public festival', *Journal of Hellenic Studies*, 106, pp. 13–35

Bracht, B. R. 1989. *Unruly Eloquence: Lucian and the Comedy of Traditions*, Revealing Antiquity 2, Harvard University Press

Braun, W. 1991. Review of B. L. Mack and V.K. Robbins, *Patterns of Persuasion in the Gospels*, Foundations and Facets, Literary Facets, Polebridge Press, 1989, in *Toronto Journal of Theology*, 7/2, pp. 280–2
1992. 'Symposium or anti-symposium? reflections on Luke 14:1–24', in *Scriptures and Cultural Conversations: Essays for Heinz Guenther at 65*, eds. J. S. Kloppenborg and L. E. Vaage (= *Toronto Journal of Theology*, 8/1), pp. 70–84
1993. 'The use of Mediterranean banquet traditions in Luke 14:1–14', Ph.D. Diss., University of Toronto

Braund, S. H. 1989. 'City and country in Roman satire', 128–132 in *Satire and Society in Ancient Rome*, Exeter Studies in History 23, ed. S. H. Braund, Exeter University Press, pp. 23–47, 128–32

Brawley, R. L. 1987. *Luke-Acts and the Jews: Conflict, Apology, and Conciliation*, SBLMS 33, Scholars Press, Atlanta

Breech, J. 1983. *The Silence of Jesus: The Authentic Voice of the Historical Man*, Doubleday Canada, Toronto

Brodie, T. L. 1984. 'Greco-Roman imitation of texts as a partial guide to Luke's use of sources', in *Luke-Acts: New Perspectives from the SBL Seminar*, ed. C. H. Talbert, Crossroad, New York, pp. 17–46

Brown, P. 1992. *Power and Persuasion in Late Antiquity: Towards a Christian Empire*, Curti Lectures, 1988, University of Wisconsin Press, Madison

Brunt, P. A. 1966. 'The Roman mob', *Past and Present*, 35, pp. 3–27

Bryant, D. C. 1953. 'Rhetoric: its function and its scope', *Quarterly Journal of Speech*, 39, pp. 401–24

Buchanan, G. W. 1982. 'Chreias in the New Testament', in *Logia. Les Paroles de Jésus – The Sayings of Jesus. Mémorial Joseph Coppens*, BETL 59, ed. J. Delobel, Uitgeverij Peeters and Leuven University Press, Leuven, pp. 501–5

Bultmann, R. 1964. *The History of the Synoptic Tradition*, English trans. from 2nd German edn by J. Marsh, Basil Blackwell, London

Burke, K. 1945. *A Grammar of Motives*, Prentice-Hall, New York

Busse, U. 1977. *Die Wunder des Propheten Jesus. Die Rezeption, Komposition und Interpretation der Wundertradition im Evangelium des Lukas*, FzB 24, Katholisches Bibelwerk, Würzburg

Butts, J. R. 1986. 'The *progymnasmata* of Theon: a new text with translation and commentary', Ph.D. Diss., Claremont Graduate School, Claremont, California
1987. 'The voyage of discipleship: narrative, chreia, and call story', in *Early Jewish and Christian Exegesis: Studies in Memory of William Hugh Brownlee*, eds. C. A. Evans and W. F. Stinespring, Scholars Press, Atlanta, pp. 199–219
Buxton, R. G. A. 1980. 'Blindness and limits: Sophokles and the logic of myth', *Journal of Hellenic Studies*, 100, pp. 22–37
Cadbury, H. J. 1926. 'Lexical notes on Luke-Acts: III. Luke's interest in lodging', *Journal of Biblical Literature*, 45, pp. 305–22
1927. *The Making of Luke–Acts*, Macmillan, New York, 2nd edn 1958
Cameron, A. 1991. *Christianity and the Rhetoric of Empire: The Development of Christian Discourse*, Sather Classical Lectures 55, University of California Press, Berkeley, Los Angeles and Oxford
Cameron, R. 1986. 'Parable and interpretation in the Gospel of Thomas', *Foundations & Facets Forum*, 2/2, pp. 3–39
1990. '"What have you come out to see?" Characterizations of John and Jesus in the gospels', *Semeia*, 49, pp. 35–69
Caro Baroja, J. 1963. 'The city and the country: reflexions on some ancient commonplaces', English trans. C. Horning, in *Mediterranean Countrymen: Essays in the Social Anthropology of the Mediterranean*, Recherches Méditerranéennes, Études I, ed. J. Pitt-Rivers, Mouton/Maison des sciences de l'homme, Paris, pp. 27–40
Carroll, J. T. 1988. 'Luke's portrayal of the Pharisees', *Catholic Biblical Quarterly*, 50, pp. 604–21
Carter, M. F. 1991. 'The ritual functions of epideictic rhetoric: the case of Socrates' funeral oration', *Rhetorica*, 9, pp. 209–32
Cavallin, C. 1985. '"Bienheureux seras-tu . . . à la résurrection des justes": Le macarisme de Lc 14,14', in *A cause de l'évangile. Etudes sur les Synoptiques et les Acts offertes au P. Jacques Dupont, O.S.B. à l'occasion de son 70e anniversaire*, Lectio Divina 123, ed. F. Refoulé, Cerf, Saint-André, pp. 531–46
*Cicero. De Inventione, De Optima Genere Oratorum, Topica*, LCL, English trans. H. M. Hubbell, William Heinemann, London; Harvard University Press, 1949
*De Officiis*, LCL, English trans. W. Miller, William Heinemann, London; G.P. Putnam's Sons, New York, 1913
*The Letters to His Friends*, LCL, English trans. W. Gg. Williams, William Heinemann, London; Harvard University Press, 1952
Clark, D. L. 1957. *Rhetoric in Greco-Roman Education*, Columbia University Press, New York, 1957
Clark, G. W. 1876. *Notes on the Gospel of Luke: Explanatory and Practical*, American Baptist Publication Society, Philadelphia
Clark, P. A. 1991. 'Tullia and Crassipes', *Phoenix*, 45, pp. 28–38
Conte, G. B. 1986. *The Rhetoric of Imitation: Genre and Poetic Memory in Virgil and Other Latin Poets*, English trans. and ed. with a Foreword by C. Segal, Cornell University Press, Ithaca and London
Conzelmann, H. 1961. *The Theology of St Luke*, English trans. G. Buswell, Harper & Row, New York

Corley, K. E. 1993. *Private Women, Public Meals: Social Conflict in the Synoptic Tradition*, Hendrickson, Peabody, Massachusetts

Countryman, L. W. 1988. *Dirt, Greed, and Sex: Sexual Ethics in the New Testament and their Implications for Today*, Fortress Press, Philadelphia

Creed, J. M. 1930. *The Gospel According to St. Luke*, Macmillan, London

Crossan, J. D. 1971–2. 'Parable and Example in the Teaching of Jesus', *New Testament Studies*, 18, pp. 285–307

1973. *In Parables: The Challenge of the Historical Jesus*, Harper & Row, New York

1985. *Four Other Gospels: Shadows on the Contours of Canon*, Winston Press, Minneapolis

1991. 'Jesus as a Mediterranean Jewish peasant', *The Fourth R*, 4/2, pp. 11–14

Danker, F. W. 1976. *Luke*, Proclamation Commentaries, Fortress Press, Philadelphia

1982. *Benefactor: Epigraphic Study of a Graeco-Roman and New Testament Semantic Field*, Clayton, St Louis

1988. *Jesus and the New Age: A Commentary on St. Luke's Gospel*, 2nd edn, Fortress Press, Philadelphia

D'Arms, J. H. 1981. *Commerce and Social Standing in Ancient Rome*, Harvard University Press

1984. 'Control, companionship, and clientela: some social functions of the Roman communal meal', *Échos du monde classique/Classical Views*, 28, NS 3, pp. 327–48

1990. 'The Roman *convivium* and the idea of equality', in Murray, 1990, pp. 308–20

1991. 'Slaves at Roman convivia', in Slater, 1991a, pp. 171–82

Daube, D. 1982. 'Shame culture in Luke', in *Paul and Paulinism: Essays in Honour of C. K. Barrett*, eds. M. D. Hooker and S. G. Wilson, SPCK, London

Davis, E. C. 1967. 'The significance of the shared meal in Luke-Acts', Th.D. Diss., Southern Baptist Theological Seminary, Louisville, Kentucky

Davis, J. 1977. *People of the Mediterranean: An Essay in Comparative Social Anthropology*, Routledge & Kegan Paul, London

Dawsey, J. M. 1986. *The Lukan Voice: Confusion and Irony in the Gospel of Luke*, Mercer University Press, Macon, Georgia

Delebecque, É. 1976. 'La vivante formule καὶ ἐγένετο', in *Etudes grecques sur l'évangile de Luc*, Belles Lettres, Paris, pp. 123–65

Delobel, J. 1966. 'L'onction par la pécheresse. La composition littéraire de Lc. VII, 36–50', *Ephemerides theologicae lovanienses*, 42, pp. 415–75

Denaux, A. 1989. 'L'hypocrisie des Pharisiens et le dessein de Dieu. Analyse de Lc., XIII, 31–33', in *L'Evangile de Luc – The Gospel of Luke*, rev. and enlarged edn of *L'Evangile de Luc. Problèmes litteraires et théologiques*, BETL 32, ed. F. Neirynck, Leuven University Press and Uitgeverij Peeters, Leuven

Derrett, J. D. M. 1970a. 'The anointing at Bethany and the story of Zacchaeus', in *Law in the New Testament*, Darton, Longman & Todd, London, pp. 266–85

1970b. 'The Parable of the Great Supper', in *Law in the New Testament*, Darton, Longman & Todd, London, pp. 126–55

Dibelius, M. 1933. *Die Formgeschichte des Evangeliums*, 2nd edn, J.C.B. Mohr (Paul Siebeck), Tübingen, English trans. B. L. Woolf, *From Tradition to Gospel*, Charles Scribner's Sons, New York, 1935

Dickison, S. K. 1988. 'Women in Rome', in Grant and Kitzinger, 1988, pp. 1329–32

Diels, H. 1966. *Die Fragmente der Vorsokratiker*, 3 vols., 12th edn, ed. W. Kranz, Weidmann, Dublin and Zürich

Dihle, A. 1957. 'Demut', in *Reallexikon für Antike und Christentum*, vol. III, ed. T. Klausner, E. Dassmann *et al.*, Hiersemann, Stuttgart, pp. 735–78

Dillon, R. J. 1966. 'Towards a tradition-history of the parables of the true Israel', *Biblica*, 47, pp. 1–42

1978. *From Eye-Witnesses to Ministers of the Word: Tradition and Composition in Luke 24*, AnBib 82, Biblical Institute, Rome

*Dio Chrysostom*. 5 vols. LCL, English trans. J. W. Cohoon and H. L. Crosby, William Heinemann, London; G. P. Putnam's Sons, New York, 1932–51

*Diogenes Laertius. Lives of Eminent Philosophers*, 2 vols. LCL, English trans. P. D. Hicks, William Heinemann, London; Harvard University Press, 1972

*Dionysius of Halicarnassus: Roman Antiquities*. 7 vols. LCL, English trans. E. Carey, William Heinemann, London; Harvard University Press, 1937–50

Dodd, C. H. 1961. *The Parables of the Kingdom*, rev. edn. Collins, London

Dormeyer, D. 1974. 'Literarische und theologische Analyse der Parabel Lukas 14, 15–24', *Bibel und Leben*, 15, pp. 206–19

Douglas, M. 1982. 'Food as a system of communication', in *In the Active Voice*, Routledge & Kegan Paul, London, pp. 82–124

1991. 'Witchcraft and leprosy: two strategies of exclusion', *Man*, NS 26, pp. 723–36

Douglas, M. and B. Isherwood 1978. *The World of Goods: Toward an Anthropology of Consumption*, Allen Lane, London

Dover, K. J. 1974. *Greek Popular Morality in the Time of Plato and Aristotle*, Basil Blackwell, London

1988. 'Anecdotes, gossip and scandal', in *The Greeks and Their Legacy: Collected Papers*, vol. II: *Prose Literature, History, Society, Transmission, Influence*, Basil Blackwell, London, pp. 45–52

Downing, G. F. 1982. 'Common ground with paganism in Luke and in Josephus', *New Testament Studies*, 28, pp. 546–59

1984. 'Cynics and Christians', *New Testament Studies*, 30, pp. 584–93

1987. *Jesus and the Threat of Freedom*, Fortress Press, Philadelphia; SCM Press, London

1988 *Christ and the Cynics: Jesus and Other Radical Preachers in First-Century Tradition*, JSOT Manuals 4, JSOT Press, Sheffield

1992. 'The ambiguity of "The Pharisee and the toll-collector" (Luke 18:9–14) in the Greco-Roman world of late antiquity', *Catholic Biblical Quarterly*, 54, pp. 80–99

Dschulnigg, P. 1989. 'Positionen des Gleichnisverständnisses im 20. Jahrhundert', *Theologische Zeitschrift*, 45, pp. 335–51

duBois, P. 1988. *Sowing the Body: Psychoanalysis and Ancient Representations of Women*, Women in Culture and Society, University of Chicago Press

Dudley, D. R. 1937. *A History of Cynicism*, Methuen, London

Dupont, F. 1977. *Le plaisir et la loi: du 'banquet' de Platon au 'satiricon'*, F. Maspero, Paris

Dupont, J. (ed.) 1978a. *La parabola degli invitati al banchetto: Dagli evangelisti a Gesu*, Paideia, Brescia.

Dupont, J. 1978b. 'La parabole des invités au festin dans le ministère de Jésus', *Testi e ricerche du scienze religiose*, 14, pp. 279–329; repr. in J. Dupont, *Etudes sur les évangiles synoptiques*, vol. II, BETL 70B, Uitgeverij Peeters and Leuven University Press, Leuven, 1985, pp. 667–705

Dyson, S. L. 1979. 'New methods & models in the study of Roman town-country systems', *Ancient World*, 2/3, pp. 91–5

Easton, B. S. 1926. *The Gospel According to St. Luke: A Critical and Exegetical Commentary*, T. & T. Clark, Edinburgh

Edmunds, L. 1987. 'Theognis 815–18 and the banquet of Attaginus', *Classical Philology*, 82, pp. 323–5

Egelkraut, H. L. 1976. *Jesus' Mission to Jerusalem: A Redaction-Critical Study of the Travel Narrative in the Gospel of Luke, Lk 9:51–19:48*, Europäische Hochschulschriften 80, Peter Lang, Frankfurt a.M.; Herbert Lang, Bern

Eichholz, G. 1984. *Gleichnisse der Evangelien. Form, Überlieferung, Auslegung*, 4th edn, Neukirchener Verlag, Neukirchen-Vluyn

Elliott, J. H. 1991a. 'Household and meals vs. temple purity: replication patterns in Luke-Acts', *Biblical Theology Bulletin*, 21, pp. 102–9
1991b. 'Temple versus household in Luke-Acts: a contrast in social institutions', in Neyrey, 1991a, pp. 211–40

Engels, D. 1990. *Roman Corinth: An Alternative Model for the Classical City*, University of Chicago Press

*Epictetus. The Discourses as Reported by Arrian, the Manual, and Fragments*, LCL, English trans. W. A. Oldfather, William Heinemann, London; G. P. Putnam's Sons, New York, 1926

Ernst, J. 1979. 'Gastmahlgespräche. LK 14,1–24', in *Die Kirche des Anfangs, Für Heinz Schürmann*, eds. R. Schnackenburg, J. Ernst and J. Wanke, St Benno, Leipzig, pp. 57–78

Erskine, A. 1990. *The Hellenistic Stoa: Political Thought and Action*, Duckworth, London

Esler, P. F. 1987. *Community and Gospel in Luke-Acts: The Social and Political Motivations in Lucan Theology*, SNTSMS 57, Cambridge University Press

Esser, A. A. M. 1939. *Das Antlitz der Blindheit in der Antike. Die kulturellen und medizinhistorischen Ausstrahlungen des Blindenproblems in den antiken Quellen*, Janus Supplement 4, E. J. Brill, Leiden, 2nd edn, 1961

*Eusebius. Ecclesiastical History*, LCL, English trans. K. Lake and J. E. L.

Oulton, William Heinemann, London; G. P. Putnam's Sons, New York, 1926–32
Fabris, R. 1978. 'La parabola degli invitati alla cena. Analisi redazionale de Lc. 14, 16–24', in J. Dupont, 1978a, pp. 127–66
Farmer, W. R. 1962. 'Notes on a literary and form-critical analysis of some of the synoptic material peculiar to Luke', *New Testament Studies*, 8, pp. 301–16
Farrar, F. W. 1887. *The Gospel According to St. Luke with Maps, Notes and Introduction*, Cambridge University Press
Felten, J. (ed.) 1913. *Nicolai Progymnasmata*, Rhetores Graeci 11, Teubner, Leipzig
Ferguson, J. 1975. *Utopias of the Classical World*, Thames and Hudson, London
Festinger, L. 1954. 'A theory of social comparison processes', *Human Relations*, 7, pp. 117–40
Finley, M. I. 1955. 'Marriage, sale and gift in the Homeric world', *Revue internationale des droits de l'antiquité*, 2, pp. 167–94
1973. *The Ancient Economy*, Chatto & Windus, London
1977. 'The ancient city: from Fustel de Coulanges to Max Weber and beyond', *Comparative Studies in Society and History*, 19, pp. 305–27
1985. *Democracy Ancient and Modern*, Mason Welch Gross Lectureship Series, rev. edn, Rutgers University Press, New Brunswick, New Jersey
Fischel, H. A. 1968. 'Studies in cynicism and the ancient Near East: the transformation of a *chria*', in *Religions in Antiquity: Essays in Memory of Erwin Ramsdell Goodenough*, Studies in the History of Religions, Numen Supp. 14, ed. J. Neusner, E. J. Brill, Leiden, pp. 372–411
Fisher, N. R. E. 1988a. 'Greek associations, symposia, and clubs', in Grant and Kitzinger, 1988, pp. 1167–97
1988b. 'Roman associations, dinner parties, and clubs', in Grant and Kitzinger, 1988, pp. 1199–225
Fitzmyer, J. A. 1964. *The Gospel According to Luke*, vol. I, Anchor Bible 28, Doubleday, Garden City
1985. *The Gospel According to Luke*, vol. II, Anchor Bible 28a, Doubleday, Garden City
Flusser, D. 1981. *Die rabbinischen Gleichnisse und der Gleichniserzähler Jesus*, 1. Teil: *Das Wesen der Gleichnisse*, Judaica et Christiana 4, Peter Lang, Bern
Focke, F. 1923. 'Synkrisis', *Hermes*, 59, pp. 327–68
Foley, H. P. 1988. 'Women in Greece', in Grant and Kitzinger, 1988, pp. 1301–17
Frankemölle, H. 1981–2. 'Kommunikatives Handeln in Gleichnissen Jesu. Historisch-kritische und pragmatische Exegese. Eine kritische Sichtung', *New Testament Studies*, 28, pp. 61–90
Friedrich, P. 1977. 'Sanity and the myth of honor: the problem of Achilles', *Ethos*, 5, pp. 281–305
Fuks, A. 1974. 'Patterns and types of social-economic revolution in Greece from the fourth to the second century B.C.', *Ancient Society*, 5, pp. 51–81

1977. 'Plato and the social question: the problem of poverty and riches in the *Republic*', *Ancient Society*, 8, pp. 49–83

1979. 'The sharing of property by the rich with the poor in Greek theory and practice', *Scripta Classica Israelica*, 5 (1979/80), pp. 46–63

Funk, R. W. 1966. *Language, Hermeneutic, and Word of God: The Problem of Language in the New Testament and Contemporary Theology*, Harper & Row, New York

1973. *A Beginning-Intermediate Grammar of Hellenistic Greek*. 3 vols., Scholars Press, Missoula, Montana

1988. *The Poetics of Biblical Narrative*, Foundations & Facets/Literary Facets, Polebridge Press, Sonoma, California

1992. 'The oral repertoire: quoted speech, gist, clichés, and lists', unpubl. paper presented to the Westar Institute Jesus Seminar, Sonoma, California

Gaeta, G. 1978. 'Invitati e commensali al banchetto escatologico. Analisi letteraria della parabola di Luca (14, 16–24)', in J. Dupont, 1978a, pp. 103–25

Garrett, S. R. 1989. *The Demise of the Devil: Magic and the Demonic in Luke's Writings*, Augsburg Fortress Press, Minneapolis

Gellius, Aulus. *The Attic Nights of Aulus Gellius*, LCL, English trans. J. C. Rolfe, William Heinemann, London; Harvard University Press, 1927

Gernet, L. 1981. *The Anthropology of Ancient Greece*, English trans. J. Hamilton and B. Nagy, Johns Hopkins University Press, Baltimore and London

Giangrande, G. 1967. 'Sympotic literature and epigram', in *L'épigramme grecque*, Entretiens sur l'antiquité classique 14, Vandœures, Geneva

Gilsenan, M. 1976. 'Lying, honor, and contradiction', in *Transaction and Meaning: Directions in the Anthropology of Exchange and Social Behavior*, ed. B. Kapferer, Institute for the Study of Human Issues, Philadelphia, pp. 191–219

Glombitza, O. 1962. 'Das grosse Abendmahl (Luk. xiv 12–24)', *Novum Testamentum*, 5, pp. 10–16

*Gnomologium Vaticanum. E Codice Vaticano Graeco 743*, ed. Leo Sternbach, in *Wiener Studien*, 9–11 (1887–9); repr. in *Texte und Kommentare: Altertumswissenschaftliche Reihe 2*, Walter de Gruyter, Berlin, 1963

Gooch, P. D. 1993. *Dangerous Food: I Corinthians 8–10 in its Context*, Wilfrid Laurier University Press, Waterloo, Ontario

Gould, J. 1980. 'Law, custom and myth: aspects of the social position of women in classical Athens', *Journal of Hellenic Studies*, 100, pp. 38–59

Goulder, M. D. 1989. *Luke: A New Paradigm*, 2 vols. JSNTSup 20, JSOT Press, Sheffield

Gouldner, A. W. 1965. *Enter Plato: Classical Greece and the Origins of Social Theory*, Routledge and Kegan Paul, London

Gow, A. S. F. and D. L. Page (eds.) 1968. *The Greek Anthology: The Garland of Philip and some Contemporary Epigrams*, 2 vols. Cambridge University Press

Gowers, E. 1993. *The Loaded Table: Representations of Food in Roman Literature*, Clarendon Press, Oxford

Gowler, D. B. 1991. *Host, Guest, Enemy, and Friend: Portraits of the Pharisees in Luke and Acts*, Emory Studies in Early Christianity 2, Peter Lang, New York

Grant, M. 1980. *Greek and Latin Authors 800 B.C.-A.D. 1000: A Biographical Dictionary*, H. W. Wilson, New York

Grant, M. and R. Kitzinger (eds.) 1988. *Civilization of the Ancient Mediterranean: Greece and Rome*, 3 vols. Charles Scribner's Sons, New York

Graßl, H. 1988. 'Behinderte in der Antike. Bemerkungen zur sozialen Stellung und Integration', in Kloft, 1988b, pp. 35–44

Groningen, B. A. van, 1965. 'General literary tendencies in the second century A.D.', *Mnemosyne*, 18, pp. 41–56

Gruenewald, M. 1961. 'A rabbinic parallel to Luke 14,12', in *Der Friede. Idee und Verwirklichung. Festausgabe für Adolf Leschnitzer*, eds. E. Fromm and H. Herzfeld, Lambert Schneider, Heidelberg

Grundmann, W. 1959. 'Fragen zur Komposition des lukanischen Reiseberichtes', *Zeitschrift für die neutestamentliche Wissenschaft*, 50, pp. 252–70

1961. *Das Evangelium nach Lukas*, ThKNT III, Evangelische Verlagsanstalt, Berlin, 9th edn 1981.

1969. 'ταπεινός, κτλ', TDNT, 8, pp. 1–27

Guenther, H. O. 1989. 'Greek: The home of primitive Christianity', *Toronto Journal of Theology*, 5/2, pp. 247–79

Günther, R. and R. Müller 1988. *Das Goldene Zeitalter: Utopien der hellenistisch-römischen Antike*, W. Kohlhammer, Stuttgart

Haenchen, E. 1965. *Die Apostelgeschichte*, 14th edn, KEK 3, Vandenhoeck & Ruprecht, Göttingen

1968. 'Das Gleichnis vom grossen Mahl', in *Die Bibel und Wir: Gesammelte Aufsätze*, 2. Bd., J. C. B. Mohr (Paul Siebeck), Tübingen, pp. 135–55

Hahn, F. 1970. 'Das Gleichnis von der Einladung zum Festmahl', in *Verborum Veritas. Festschrift für Gustav Stählin zum 70. Geburtstag*, eds. O. Böcher and K. Haacker, Rolf Brockhaus, Wuppertal

Hall, J. 1981. *Lucian's Satire*, Monographs in Classical Studies, Arno, New York

Hamel, G. H. 1990. *Poverty and Charity in Roman Palestine, First Three Centuries C.E.*, University of California Publications: Near Eastern Studies 23, University of California Press, Berkeley, Los Angeles and Oxford

Hamm, D. 1986. 'Sight to the blind: vision as metaphor in Luke', *Biblica*, 67, pp. 457–77.

1991 'Zacchaeus revisited once more: A story of vindication or conversion', *Biblica*, 72, pp. 249–52

Hands, A. R. 1968. *Charities and Social Aid in Greece and Rome*, Aspects of Greek and Roman Life, Thames and Hudson, London; Cornell University Press, Ithaca, New York

Harnack, A. von, 1908. *New Testament Studies, II. The Sayings of Jesus: The Second Source of St. Matthew and St. Luke*, English trans. J. R. Wilkinson, Williams & Norgate, London; G. P. Putnam's Sons, New York

Harrison, A. R. W. 1968. *The Law of Athens: The Family and Property*, Clarendon Press, Oxford

Hauck, F. 1968. 'πένης, πενιχρός', TDNT, 6, pp. 37–40

Hauck, F. and W. Kasch 1968. 'πλοῦτος, πλούσιος, πλουτέω, πλουτίζω', TDNT, 6, pp. 318–32

Hauck, F. and E. Bammel 1968. 'πτωχός, πτωχεία, πτωχεύω', TDNT, 6, pp. 885–915

Haudebert, P. 1987. 'La métanoia, des Septante à Saint Luc', in *La vie de la Parole, de l'Ancien au Nouveau Testament. Etudes d'exégèse et d'hermeneutique bibliques offertes à Pierre Grelot*, ed. H. Cazelles, Desclée, Paris, pp. 355–66

Hemelrijk, J. 1925. Πενία *en* Πλοῦτος, Blikman & Sartorius, Amsterdam; repr. Arno, New York, 1978

Hengel, M. 1979. *Zur urchristlichen Geschichtsschreibung*, Calwer, Stuttgart

Hense, O. 1893. *Die Synkrisis in der antiken Literatur*, Lehmann, Freiburg i.B.

Herman, G. 1987. *Ritualized Friendship and the Greek City*, Cambridge University Press

Herzfeld, M. 1980. 'Honour and shame: problems in the comparative analysis of moral systems', *Man*, NS 15, pp. 339–51

Hintzen, J. 1991. *Verkündigung und Wahrnehmung. Über das Verhältnis von Evangelium und Leser am Beispiel Lk 16, 19–31 im Rahmen des lukanischen Doppelwerkes*, Athenäums Monographien, Theologie 81, Bonner Biblische Beiträge, Anton Hain, Frankfurt a.M.

Hirsch, E. 1941. *Frühgeschichte des Evangeliums*, vol. II: *Die Vorlagen des Lukas und das Sondergut des Matthäus*, J. C. B. Mohr (Paul Siebeck), Tübingen

Hirzel, R. 1895. *Der Dialog. Ein literar-historischer Versuch*, 2 vols., S. Hirzel, Leipzig

Hock, R. F. 1987. 'Lazarus and Micyllus: Greco-Roman backgrounds to Luke 16:19–31', *Journal of Biblical Literature*, 106, pp. 447–63
  1990. 'A dog in a manger: the Cynic Cynulcus among Athenaeus's Deipnosophists', in *Greeks, Romans, and Christians: Essays in Honor of Abraham J. Malherbe*, eds. D. L. Balch, E. Ferguson and W. A. Meeks, Fortress Press, Minneapolis, pp. 20–37

Hock, R. F. and E. N. O'Neil 1986. *The Chreia in Ancient Rhetoric*, vol. I, *The Progymnasmata*, SBLTT 27, Greco-Roman Religion Series 9, Scholars Press, Atlanta

Hoffmann, P. and V. Eid 1975. *Jesus von Nazareth und eine christliche Moral. Sittliche Perspektiven der Verkündigung Jesu*, Herder, Freiburg i.B.

Höistad, R. 1948. *Cynic Hero and Cynic King: Studies in the Cynic Conception of Man*, n.p., Uppsala

Holford-Strevens, L. 1988. *Aulus Gellius*, Duckworth, London

Holtzmann, H. J. 1892. *Hand-Kommentar zum Neuen Testament*, vol. I, *Die Synoptiker. Die Apostelgeschichte*, 2nd edn, Freiburg i.B.

Hooley, D. M. 1990. 'On relations between classical and contemporary imitation theory: some Hellenistic suggestions', *Classical and Modern Literature*, 11, pp. 77–92

Horace. *The Complete Works of Horace (Quintus Horatius Flaccus)*, English trans. in the meters of the originals with notes by C. E. Passage, Frederick Ungar, New York, 1983

Horn, F. W. 1983. *Glaube und Handeln in der Theologie des Lukas*, GThA 26, Vandenhoeck & Ruprecht, Göttingen, 2nd edn 1986

Horsley, G. H. R. 1989. 'The fiction of "Jewish Greek"', in *New Documents Illustrating Early Christianity*, vol. V: *Linguistic Essays*, Australian Ancient History Documentary Research Centre, Macquarie University

Hübner, H. 1973. *Das Gesetz in der synoptischen Tradition. Studien zur These einer progressiven Qumranisierung und Judaisierung innerhalb der synoptischen Tradition*, Luther-Verlag, Witten

Hudson, N. A. 1989. 'Food in Roman satire', in *Satire and Society in Ancient Rome*, Exeter Studies in History 23, ed. S. H. Braund, Exeter University Press, pp. 69–87, 136–9

Hultgren, A. J. 1979. *Jesus and His Adversaries: The Form and Function of the Conflict Stories in the Synoptic Tradition*, Augsburg, Minneapolis

Hunter, V. 1990. 'Gossip and the politics of reputation in classical Athens', *Phoenix*, 44, pp. 299–325

Hunzinger, C.-H. 1960. 'Außersynoptisches Traditionsgut im Thomas-Evangelium', *Theologische Literaturzeitung*, 85, pp. 843–6

Jaeger, W. 1945. *Paideia: The Ideals of Greek Culture*, 3 vols. 2nd edn, English trans. G. Highet, Oxford University Press

Jaher, F. C. 1973. 'Introduction', in *The Rich, the Well Born, and the Powerful: Elites and Upper Classes in History*, ed. F. C. Jaher, University of Illinois Press, Urbana

Jameson, M. 1990. 'Private space and the Greek city', in *The Greek City from Homer to Alexander*, eds. O. Murray and S. Price, Clarendon Press, Oxford

Jeanneret, M. 1991. *A Feast of Words: Banquets and Table Talk in the Renaissance*, English trans. J. Whiteley and E. Hughes, Polity Press, Cambridge

Jenkins, I. 1983. 'Is there life after marriage? A study of the abduction motif in vase paintings of the Athenian wedding ceremony', *Bulletin of the Institute of Classical Studies*, 30, pp. 137–46

Jeremias, J. 1963. *The Parables of Jesus*, rev. edn, English trans. S. H. Hooke, Charles Scribner's Sons, New York
   1980. *Die Sprache des Lukasevangeliums. Redaktion und Tradition im Nicht-Markusstoff des dritten Evangeliums*, KEK Sonderausgabe, Vandenhoeck & Ruprecht, Göttingen

*Joannis Stobaei Anthologium*, vol. III, ed. O. Hense, Weidmann, Berlin, 1884

Johannessohn, M. 1926. 'Das biblische καὶ ἐγένετο und seine Geschichte', *Zeitschrift für die vergleichende Sprachforschung*, 53, pp. 162–212

Johnson, L. T. 1986. *Sharing Possessions: Mandate and Symbol of Faith*, SCM Press, London

Jones, A. H. M. 1947. *Greek City from Alexander to Justinian*, Clarendon Press, Oxford

Jones, C. P. 1971. *Plutarch and Rome*, Clarendon Press, Oxford

1986. *Culture and Society in Lucian*, Harvard University Press, Cambridge (MA) and London

1991. 'Dinner theater', in Slater, 1991a, pp. 185–98

*Josephus.* 9 vols. LCL, English trans. H. St. Thackeray, R. Marcus and L. H. Feldman, William Heinemann, London; Harvard University Press, 1956–65

Jülicher, A. 1910. *Die Gleichnisreden Jesu*, 2 vols. 2nd edn, J. C. B. Mohr (Paul Siebeck), Tübingen; repr. Wissenschaftliche Buchgesellschaft, Darmstadt, 1976

Justin Martyr. *Iustini Philosophi et Martyris: Opera quae Feruntur Omnia*, ed. C. Otto, n.p., 1876; repr. Martin Sändig, Wiesbaden, 1969

*Juvenal. The Satires*, English trans. N. Rudd, with an intro. and notes by W. Barr, Clarendon Press, Oxford, 1991

Kany, R. 1986. 'Der lukanische Bericht von Tod und Auferstehung Jesu aus der Gesicht eines hellenistischen Romanlesers', *Novum Testamentum*, 28, pp. 75–90

Karris, R. J. 1985. *Luke, Artist and Theologian: Luke's Passion Account as Literature*, Paulist Press, New York

Kaser, M. 1980. *Roman Private Law*, 3rd edn, English trans. R. Dannenbring, University of South Africa, Pretoria

Kennedy, G. A. 1963. *The Art of Persuasion in Greece*, Princeton University Press

1972. *The Art of Rhetoric in the Roman World.* Princeton University Press

1984. *New Testament Interpretation Through Rhetorical Criticism*, University of North Carolina Press, Chapel Hill

Keuls, E. C. 1985. *The Reign of the Phallus: Sexual Politics in Ancient Athens*, Harper & Row, New York

Kilpatrick, G. D. 1967. 'The aorist of γαμεῖν in the New Testament', *Journal of Theological Studies*, 18, pp. 139–40

Kim, C.-H. 1975. 'The papyrus invitation', *Journal of Biblical Literature*, 94, pp. 391–402

Kindstrand, J. F. 1976. *Bion of Borysthenes: A Collection of the Fragments with Introduction and Commentary*, AUU/SGU 11, Almqvist & Wiksell International, Stockholm

1986. 'Diogenes Laertius and the *chreia* tradition', *Elenchos*, 7, pp. 217–43

Kissinger, W. S. 1979. *The Parables of Jesus: A History of Interpretation and Bibliography*, ATLA Bibliography Series 4, Scarecrow Press, Metuchen, New Jersey

Klassen, W. 1984. 'Musonius Rufus, Jesus, and Paul: three first-century feminists', in *From Jesus to Paul: Studies in Honour of Francis Wright Beare*, eds. G. P. Richardson and J. C. Hurd, Wilfrid Laurier University Press, Waterloo, Ontario

Klauck, H.-J. 1982. *Herrenmahl und hellenistischer Kult. Eine religionsgeschichtliche Untersuchung zum ersten Korintherbrief*, NTAbh NF 15, Aschendorff, Münster

Klein, H. 1987. *Barmherzigkeit gegenüber den Elenden und Geächteten. Studien zur Botschaft des lukanischen Sonderguts*, Biblisch-Theologische Studien 10, Neukirchener Verlag, Neukirchen-Vluyn

Klinghardt, M. 1988. *Das lukanische Verständnis des Gesetzes nach Her-
kunft, Funktion und seinem Ort in der Geschichte des Urchristentums*,
WUNT 2, Reihe 32, J. C. B. Mohr (Paul Siebeck), Tübingen
Kloft, H. 1988a. 'Gedanken zum Ptochós', in Weiler and Graßl, 1988,
pp. 81–106
Kloft, H. (ed.) 1988b. *Sozialmassnahmen und Fürsorge. Zur Eigenart antiker
Sozialpolitik*, GB Suppl. 3, F. Berger & Söhne, Horn, Austria
Kloppenborg, J. S. 1987. *The Formation of Q: Trajectories in Ancient
Wisdom Collections*, Studies in Antiquity and Christianity, Fortress
Press, Philadelphia
1988. *Q Parallels: Synopsis, Critical Notes & Concordance*, Foundation &
Facets Reference Series, Polebridge Press, Sonoma, California
1989. 'The dishonoured master (Luke 16,1–8a)', *Biblica*, 70, pp. 474–95
1992a. '*Exitus clari viri*: the death of Jesus in Luke', in *Scriptures and
Cultural Conversations: Essays for Heinz Guenther at 65*, eds. J. S.
Kloppenborg and L. E. Vaage (= *Toronto Journal of Theology*, 8/1),
pp. 106–20
1992b. 'The sayings gospel Q: literary and stratigraphic problems', in
*Aufstieg und Niedergang der römischen Welt*, II.25.6, eds. H. Temporini
and W. Haase, Walter de Gruyter, Berlin, 1992; forthcoming (cited
from typescript)
Kloppenborg, J. S., M. W. Meyer, S. J. Patterson and M. G. Steinhauser
1990. *Q-Thomas Reader*, Polebridge Press, Sonoma, California
Klosinski, L. E. 1988. 'The meals in Mark', Ph.D. Diss., Claremont Grad-
uate School, Claremont, California
Klumbies, P.-G. 1989. 'Die Sabbatheilungen Jesu nach Markus und Lukas',
in *Jesu Rede von Gott und ihre Nachgeschichte im frühen Christentum.
Beiträge zur Verkündigung Jesu und zum Kerygma der Kirche*, FS Willi
Marxsen, eds. D.-A. Koch, G. Sellin and A. Lindemann, Gerd Mohn,
Gütersloh, pp. 165–78
Koenig, J. 1985. *New Testament Hospitality: Partnership with Strangers as
Promise and Mission*, Overtures to Biblical Theology 17, Fortress
Press, Philadelphia
Kosch, D. 1989. *Die eschatologische Tora des Menschensohnes. Untersu-
chungen zur Rezeption der Stellung Jesu zur Tora in Q*, NTOA 12,
Freiburg Universitätsverlag; Vandenhoeck & Ruprecht, Güttingen
Krierer, K. R. 1988. 'Mimik als Stigmatisierungsfaktor in Darstellungen
sozialer Randgruppen in der antiken Kunst', in Weiler and Graßl,
1988, pp. 339–48
Kudlien, F. 1988. '"Krankensicherung" in der griechisch-römischen
Antike', in Kloft, 1988b, pp. 75–102
Kurz, W. S. 1980. 'Hellenistic rhetoric in the christological proofs of
Luke-Acts', *Catholic Biblical Quarterly*, 42, pp. 171–95
1990. 'Narrative models for imitation in Luke-Acts', in *Greeks, Romans,
and Christians: Essays in Honor of Abraham J. Malherbe*, eds. D. L.
Balch, E. Ferguson and W. A. Meeks, Fortress Press, Minneapolis
Lacey, W. K. 1966. 'Homeric ἕδνα and Penelope's κύριος', *Journal of
Hellenic Studies*, 86, pp. 55–68
Laurence, R. 1994. 'Rumour and communication in Roman politics',
*Greece and Rome*, 41, pp. 62–74

Lausberg, H. 1960. *Handbuch der literarischen Rhetorik. Eine Grundlegung der Wissenschaft*, 2 vols. Max Huebner, Munich
1968. 'Rhetorik und Dichtung', *Der Deutschunterricht*, 18/6, pp. 47–93
Lefkowitz, M. R. and M. B. Fant 1982. *Women's Lives in Greece and Rome*, Duckworth, London
Leitch, V. B. 1991. '(De)coding (generic) discourse', *Genre*, 14, pp. 83–98
Leivestad, R. 1966. 'ΤΑΠΕΙΝΟΣ-ΤΑΠΕΙΝΟΦΡΩΝ', *Novum Testamentum*, 8, pp. 36–47
Lemico, E. E. 1986. 'The parables of the great supper and the wedding feast: history, redaction and canon', *Horizons in Biblical Theology*, 8, pp. 1–26
Levine, D. B. 1985. 'Symposium and the *polis*', in *Theognis of Megara: Poetry and Polis*, eds. T. J. Figuera and G. Nagy, Johns Hopkins University Press, Baltimore
Lichtenstein, M. 1968. 'The banquet motifs in Keret and in Proverbs 9', *Journal of the Ancient Near Eastern Society of Columbia University*, 1, pp. 19–31
Linnemann, E. 1960. 'Überlegungen zur Parabel vom großen Abendmahl, Lc 14 15–24/Mt 22 1–14', *Zeitschrift für die neutestamentliche Wissenschaft*, 51, pp. 246–55
Lissarrague, F. 1990. *The Aesthetics of the Greek Banquet: Images of Wine and Ritual*, English trans. A. Szegedy-Maszak, Princeton University Press
Lloyd, G. E. R. 1966. *Polarity and Analogy: Two Types of Argumentation in Early Greek Thought*, Cambridge University Press
Lloyd-Jones, H. 1990. 'Honour and shame in ancient Greek culture', in *Greek Comedy, Hellenistic Literature, Greek Religion, and Miscellanea: The Academic Papers of Sir Hugh Lloyd-Jones*, Clarendon Press, Oxford, pp. 253–80; English trans. of 'Ehre und Schande in der griechischen Kultur', *Antike und Abendland*, 33, 1987
Lorenz, T. 1988. 'Verwachsene und Verkrüppelte in der antiken Kunst', in Weiler and Graßl, 1988, pp. 349–68
Lovejoy, A. O. and G. Boas 1935. *Primitivism and Related Ideas in Antiquity*, Johns Hopkins University Press, Baltimore; repr. Octagon Books, New York, 1965
(LSJ) Liddell, H. G. and R. A. Scott 1968. *A Greek-English Lexicon*, rev. and augm. by H. S. Jones *et al.*, Clarendon Press, Oxford
*Lucian*. 8 vols. LCL, English trans. A. M. Harmon *et al.*, William Heinemann, London; Harvard University Press, 1913–67
*Lucretius. De rerum natura*, LCL, English trans. W. H. D. Rouse, William Heinemann, London; Harvard University Press, 1943
Lull, D. J. 1986. 'The servant-benefactor as a model of greatness (Luke 22.24–30)', *Novum Testamentum*, 28, pp. 289–305
Lutz, C. E. 1947. 'Musonius Rufus "The Roman Socrates"', *Yale Classical Studies*, 10, pp. 1–147
Luz, M. 1989. 'A description of the Greek Cynic in the Jerusalem Talmud', *Journal for the Study of Judaism in the Persian, Hellenistic and Roman Period*, 20, pp. 49–60
McCall, M. H. 1969. *Ancient Rhetorical Theories of Simile and Comparison*, Harvard University Press

Mack, B. L. 1984. 'Decoding the Scripture: Philo and the rules of rhetoric', in *Nourished With Peace: Studies in Hellenistic Judaism in Memory of Samuel Sandmel*, Scholars Press Homage Series 9, eds. F. E. Greenspahn, E. Hilgert and B. L. Mack., Scholars Press, Chico, California

1987. 'Anecdotes and arguments: the chreia in antiquity and early Christianity', Institute for Antiquity and Christianity Occasional Papers 10, Institute for Antiquity and Christianity, Claremont, California

1988. *A Myth of Innocence: Mark and Christian Origins*, Fortress Press, Philadelphia

1990. *Rhetoric and the New Testament*, Guides to Biblical Scholarship/ NT Series, Fortress Press, Minneapolis

Mack, B. L. and V. K. Robbins 1989. *Patterns of Persuasion in the Gospels*, Foundations & Facets/Literary Facets, Polebridge Press, Sonoma, California

McMahan, C. T. 1987. 'Meals as type-scenes in the Gospel of Luke', Ph.D. Diss., Southern Baptist Theological Seminary

MacMullen, R. 1971. 'Social history in astrology', *Ancient Society*, 2, pp. 105–16

1974. *Roman Social Relations: 50 B.C. to A.D. 284*, Yale University Press, New Haven and London

Macrobius. *The Saturnalia*. English trans. with intro. and notes by P. V. Davies, Columbia University Press, New York and London, 1969

McVann, M. 1991. 'Rituals of status transformation in Luke-Acts: the case of Jesus the prophet', in Neyrey, 1991a, pp. 333–60

Malherbe, A. J. 1980. 'Medical imagery in the Pastoral Epistles', in *Texts and Testaments: Critical Essays on the Bible and Early Church Fathers. A Volume in Honor of Stuart Dickson Currie*, Trinity University, San Antonio, pp. 19–35; repr. in A. J. Malherbe, *Paul and the Popular Philosophers*, Fortress Press, Minneapolis, 1989

Malina, B. J. 1981. *The New Testament World: Insights from Cultural Anthropology*, John Knox, Atlanta

Malina, B. J. and J. H. Neyrey 1991a. 'First-century personality: dyadic, not individual', in Neyrey, 1991a, pp. 67–96

1991b. 'Honor and shame in Luke-Acts: pivotal values of the Mediterranean world', in Neyrey, 1991a, pp. 25–65

Manen, J. J. van 1931. Πενία *en* Πλοῦτος *in de Periode na Alexander*, N. V. Nauta, Zutphen

Manson, T. W. 1931. *The Teaching of Jesus: Studies of its Form and Content*, Cambridge University Press, 2nd edn, 1939

1949. *The Sayings of Jesus as Recorded in the Gospels According to St. Matthew and St. Luke Arranged with Introduction and Commentary*, SCM Press, London

Marcus Aurelius Antoninus. *The Meditations of Marcus Aurelius Antoninus*, English trans. A. S. L. Farquharson, Oxford University Press, 1944

Marrou, H. I. 1964. *A History of Education in Antiquity*, English trans. G. Lamb from the 3rd French edn (*De la connaissance historique*, Éditions du Seuil, Paris, 1959), New American Library, New York

Marshall, I. H. 1978. *The Gospel of Luke: A Commentary on the Greek Text*, NICNT, Paternoster, Exeter

Martin, H., Jr. 1978. 'Amatorius (Moralia 748E-771E)', in *Plutarch's Ethical Writings and Early Christian Literature*, SCHNT 4, ed. H. D. Betz, E. J. Brill, Leiden

Martin, J. 1931. *Symposion. Die Geschichte einer literarischen Form*, SGKA XVII/1–2, Ferdinand Schönigh, Paderborn; repr. Johnson Reprints, New York, 1968

Mau, A. 1901. 'Convivium, σὺνδειπνον, συμπόσιον', in *Paulys Realencyclopädie der klassischen Altertumswissenschaft*, vol. IV, ed. G. Wissowa, W. Kroll, *et al.*, Metzler, Stuttgart; Druckenmüller, Munich, 4, cols. 1201–8

Mayer, R. 1989. 'Friendship in the satirists', in *Satire and Society in Ancient Rome*, Exeter Studies in History 23, ed. S. H. Braund, Exeter University Press, pp. 5–21, 127–8

Mealand, D. L. 1991. 'Hellenistic historians and the style of Acts', *Zeitschrift für die neutestamentliche Wissenschaft*, 82, pp. 42–66

Meecham, H. G. 1935. *The Letter of Aristeas. A Linguistic Study with Special Reference to the Greek Bible*, Manchester University Press

Meeûs, X. de, 1961. 'Composition de Lc., XIV et genre symposiaque', *Ephemerides theologicae lovanienses*, 37, pp. 847–70

*Menander Rhetor*, ed. with English trans. and commentary by D. A. Russell and N. G. Wilson, Clarendon Press, Oxford, 1981

Michiels, R. 1965. 'La conception lucanienne de la conversion', *Ephemerides theologicae lovanienses*, 41, pp. 42–78

Miller, M. 1991. 'When the old boys met in Athens', *Rotunda*, 24/2, pp. 26–32

Miller, S. G., 1978. *The Prytaneion: Its Function and Architectural Form*, University of California Press, Berkeley, Los Angeles and London

Millet, P. 1989. 'Patronage and its avoidance in ancient Athens', in *Patronage in Ancient Society*, Leicester-Nottingham Studies in Ancient Society 1, ed. A. Wallace-Hadrill, Routledge, London and New York

*The Mishna*. English trans. H. Danby, Oxford University Press, 1933

Mitchell, M. E. 1973. 'The aristocracy of the Roman Republic', in *The Rich, the Well Born, and the Powerful: Elites and Upper Classes in History*, ed. F. C. Jaher, University of Illinois Press, Urbana

Moessner, D. P. 1989. *The Lord of the Banquet: The Literary and Theological Significance of the Lukan Travel Narrative*, Augsburg Fortress Press, Minneapolis

Moles, J. 1983. '"Honestus quam ambitiosius"? An exploration of the Cynic's attitude to moral corruption in his fellow men', *Journal of Hellenic Studies*, 103, pp. 103–23

1985. 'Cynicism in Horace *Epistles* 1', *Proceedings of the Leeds Literary Society*, 5, pp. 33–60

Montefiore, H. W. 1960–1. 'A comparison of the parables of the Gospel According to Thomas and of the Synoptic Gospels', *New Testament Studies*, 7, pp. 220–48

Moretti, L. 1982. 'Sulla legge ginnasiarchica di Berea', *Rivista di filologia e di istruzione classica*, 110, pp. 45–63

Mott, S. C. 1975. 'The power of giving and receiving: reciprocity in Hellenistic benevolence', in *Current Issues in Biblical and Patristic Interpre-*

*tation. Studies in Honor of Merrill C. Tenney*, ed. G. F. Hawthorne, William B. Erdmans, Grand Rapids, Michigan

Moxnes, H. 1986–7. 'Meals and the new community in Luke', *Svensk Exegetisk Årsbok*, 51–52, pp. 158–67

1989. *The Economy of the Kingdom: Social Conflict and Economic Relations in Luke's Gospel*, Overtures to Biblical Theology, Fortress Press, Philadelphia

1991a. 'Patron-client relations and the new community in Luke-Acts', in Neyrey, 1991a, pp. 241–68

1991b. 'Social relations and economic interaction in Luke's gospel: a research report', in *Luke-Acts: Scandinavian Perspectives*, Publications of the Finnish Exegetical Society 54, ed. P. Luomanen, Finnish Exegetical Society, Helsinki; Vandenhoeck & Ruprecht, Göttingen, pp. 58–73

Mrozek, S. 1988. 'Die privaten Alimentarstiftungen in der römischen Kaiserzeit', in Kloft, 1988b, pp. 155–66

Müller, R. 1976. 'Zu einigen Grundzügen der historischen und kulturellen Entwicklung in Griechenland im 5. und 4. Jahrhundert v.u.z.', in *Der Mensch als Mass der Dinge. Studien zum griechischen Menschenbild in der Zeit der Blüte und Krise der Polis*, ed. R. Müller, Akademie-Verlag, Berlin

1981. *Menschenbild und Humanismus der Antike. Studien zur Geschichte der Literatur und Philosophie*, Röderberg, Frankfurt a.M.

1987. *Polis und Res Publica: Studien zum antiken Gesellschafts- und Geschichtsdenken*, Hermann Böhlaus Nachfolger, Weimar

Murray, O. 1981. 'The Greek symposium in history', *Times Literary Supplement*, 6 November, 1981, pp. 1307–8

1982. 'Symposion and Männerbund', *Concilium Eirene*, 16/1, pp. 94–112

1983a. 'The Greek symposion in history', in *Tria Corda: Scritti in onore di Arnaldo Momigliano*, Biblioteca di Athenaeum 1, ed. E. Gabba, Edizione New Press, Como, pp. 257–72

1983b. 'The symposium as social organization', in *The Greek Renaissance of the Eighth Century B.C.: Tradition and Innovation, Proceedings of the Second International Symposium at the Swedish Institute in Athens, 1–5 June, 1981*, Skrifter Utgivna av Svenska Institutet i Athen 4/XXX, ed. R. Hägg, Svenska Institutet i Athen, Stockholm, pp. 195–9

1985. 'Symposium and genre in the poetry of Horace', *Journal of Roman Studies*, 75, pp. 39–50

Murray, O. (ed.) 1990. *Sympotica: A Symposium on the Symposion*, Clarendon Press, Oxford

Nachov, I. 1976. 'Der Mensch in der Philosophie der Kyniker', in *Der Mensch als Mass der Dinge. Studien zum griechischen Menschenbild in der Zeit der Blüte und Krise der Polis*, ed. R. Müller, Akademie-Verlag, Berlin, pp. 361–98

Nadeau, R. E. 1952. 'The *Progymnasmata* of Aphthonius in translation', *Speech Monographs*, 19, pp. 264–85

Nauck, A. (ed.) 1856. *Tragicorum Graecorum Fragmenta*, Teubner, Leipzig

Navone, J. 1964. 'The parable of the banquet', *The Bible Today*, 14, pp. 923–9

Neirynck, F. 1975. 'Jesus and the Sabbath: some observations on Mark II,27', in *Jésus aux origines de la christologie*, BETL 40, ed. J. Dupont, Leuven University Press; J. Duculot, Gembloux, pp. 227–70

(Nestlé-Aland), *Novum Testamentum Graece*, 26th edn, ed. Eberhard Nestlé and Erwin Nestlé with K. Aland *et al.*, Deutsche Bibelstiftung, Stuttgart, 1979

Neyrey, J. H. (ed.) 1991a. *The Social World of Luke-Acts: Models for Interpretation*, Hendrickson, Peabody, Massachusetts
1991b. 'Ceremonies in Luke-Acts: the case of meals and table fellowship', in Neyrey, 1991a, pp. 361–87

Nickelsburg, G. W. E. 1979. 'Riches, the rich and God's judgment in 1 Enoch 92–105 and the gospel according to Luke', *New Testament Studies*, 25, pp. 324–44

Nock, A. D. 1933. *Conversion: The Old and the New in Religion from Alexander the Great to Augustine of Hippo*, Clarendon Press, Oxford

Norwood, F. A. 1953–4. '"Compel them to come in": the history of Luke 14.23', *Religion in Life*, 23, pp. 516–27

Oakman, D. E. 1991. 'The countryside in Luke-Acts', in Neyrey, 1991a, pp. 151–79

Ober, J. 1989. *Mass and Elite in Democratic Athens: Rhetoric, Ideology, and the Power of the People*, Princeton University Press

(OCD) Hammond, N. G. L. and H. H. Scullard 1970. *Oxford Classical Dictionary*, Clarendon Press, Oxford

Oikonomides, A. N. 1987. '"Resting sites" (Λέσχαι) in ancient Athens and Attica', *The Ancient World*, 16, pp. 29–34

O'Neil, E. N. 1978. 'De Cupiditate Divitiarum (Moralia 523C - 528B)', in *Plutarch's Ethical Writings and Early Christian Literature*, SCHNT 4, ed. H. D. Betz, E. J. Brill, Leiden

Ortner, S. B. 1974. 'Is female to male as nature is to culture?', in *Woman, Culture, and Society*, ed. M. Zimbalist Rosaldo and L. Lamphere, Stanford University Press, Stanford

O'Toole, R. F., 1992. 'Some exegetical reflections on Luke 10,13–17', *Biblica*, 73, pp. 84–107

Ovid. *Ovid in Six Volumes*, vol. V, *Fasti*, LCL, English trans. J.G. Frazer, rev. G. P. Goold, William Heinemann, London; Harvard University Press, 1989

Palmer, H. 1976. 'Just married, cannot come', *Novum Testamentum*, 18, pp. 241–57

Papst, W. 1986. 'Zur Satire vom lächerlichen Mahl. Konstanz eines antiken Schemas durch Perspektivenwandel', *Antike und Abendland*, 32, pp. 136–58

Paquet, L. 1975. *Les Cyniques Grecs: Fragments et témoignages*, Collection φ philosophica, Université d'Ottawa, Ottawa

Patterson, S. J. 1988. 'The Gospel of Thomas within the development of early Christianity', Ph.D. Diss., Claremont Graduate School, Claremont, California

Paul, G. 1991. 'Symposia and deipna in Plutarch's Lives and in other historical writings', in Slater, 1991a, pp. 157–69

Pax, E. 1975. 'Der Reiche und der arme Lazarus: Eine Milieustudie', *Studii Biblici Franciscani Liber Annuus*, 25, pp. 254–68

Pellizer, E. 'Outlines of a morphology of sympotic entertainment', English trans. C. McLaughlin, in Murray, 1990, pp. 177–84

Penella, R. J. 1979. *The Letters of Apollonius of Tyana: A Critical Text with Prolegomena, Translation and Commentary*, Mnemosyne Suppl. 56, E. J. Brill, Leiden

Penndorf, J. 1911. *Progymnasmata. Rhetorische Anfangsübungen der alten Griechen und Römer nach den Quellen dargestellt*, Neupert, Plauen i.V.

Peristiany, J. G. 1966. 'Introduction', in *Honour and Shame: The Values of Mediterranean Society*, ed. J. G. Peristiany, University of Chicago Press, pp. 9–18

Persius. *The Satires*, English trans. and notes by J. R. Jenkinson, Aris & Phillips, Warminster, 1980

Pervo, R. I. 1987. *Profit with Delight: The Literary Genre of the Acts of the Apostles*, Fortress Press, Philadelphia

Pesce, M. 1978. 'Ricostruzione dell'archetipo letterario commune a Mt. 22,1–10 e Lc. 14,15–24', in J. Dupont, 1978a, pp. 167–236

*Petronius Arbiter. Satyricon*, LCL, English trans. M. Heseltine, William Heinemann, London; G. P. Putnam's Sons, New York, 1930

*Philo. De Vita Contemplativa*, LCL, English trans. F. H. Colson, William Heinemann, London; Harvard University Press, 1960

*Philostratus. The Life of Apollonius of Tyana*. 2 vols., LCL, English trans. F. C. Conybeare, William Heinemann, London; Harvard University Press, 1912

*Philostratus: and Eunapius: The Lives of the Sophists*, LCL, English trans. W. C. Wright, William Heinemann, London; Harvard University Press, 1922

Pilch, J. J. 1991. 'Sickness and healing in Luke-Acts', in Neyrey, 1991a, pp. 181–209

Pitt-Rivers, J. (ed.) 1963. *Mediterranean Countrymen: Essays in the Social Anthropology of the Mediterranean*, Recherches Méditerranéennes/ Études I, Mouton/Maison des sciences de l'homme, Paris

   1977a. 'The law of hospitality', in J. Pitt-Rivers, 1977b, pp. 94–112; = 'The stranger, the guest and the hostile host: introduction to the study of the laws of hospitality', in *Contributions to Mediterranean Sociology: Mediterranean Rural Communities and Social Change*, Acts of the Mediterranean Sociological Conference, Athens, July 1963, ed. J. G. Peristiany, Mouton, Paris and The Hague, 1968, pp. 13–30

   1977b. *The Fate of Shechem or the Politics of Sex: Essays in the Anthropology of the Mediterranean*, Cambridge Studies in Social Anthropology 19, Cambridge University Press, 1977

*Plato. Symposium*, LCL, English trans. W. R. M. Lamb, William Heinemann, London; Harvard University Press, 1946

Pleket, H. W. 1988. 'Labor and unemployment in the Roman empire: some preliminary remarks', in Weiler and Graßl, 1988, pp. 267–76

*Pliny. Letters, Panegyricus*, 2 vols. LCL, English trans. B. Radice, William Heinemann, London; Harvard University Press, 1969

Plümacher, E. 1972. *Lukas als hellenistischer Schriftsteller. Studien zur Apostelgeschichte*, SUNT 9, Vandenhoeck & Ruprecht, Göttingen

# Bibliography 203

1974. 'Lukas als griechischer Historiker', *Paulys Realencyclopädie der klassischen Altertumswissenschaft*, Suppl. XIV, ed. G. Wissowa, W. Kroll, *et al.*, Metzler, Stuttgart; Druckenmüller, Munich, cols. 253–64

1987. *Identitätsverlust und Identitätsgewinn: Studien zum Verhältnis von kaiserzeitlicher Stadt und frühem Christentum*, Biblisch-Theologische Studien 11, Neukirchener Verlag, Neukirchen-Vluyn

Plummer, A. 1914. *A Critical and Exegetical Commentary on the Gospel According to St. Luke*, ICC, 10th edn. Charles Scribner's Sons, New York

*Plutarch's Lives*, 11 vols. LCL, English trans. B. Perrin *et al.*, William Heinemann, London; Macmillan, New York, 1914–26

*Plutarch's Moralia*, 15 vols. LCL, English trans. F. C. Babbit *et al.*, William Heinemann, London; Harvard University Press, 1927–69

Polag, A. 1979. *Fragmenta Q: Textheft zur Logienquelle*, Neukirchener Verlag, Neukirchen-Vluyn

Pollux. *Onomasticon*, ed. I. Bekker, n.p., Berlin, 1846

*Polybius*. 6 vols. LCL, English trans. W. R. Paton, William Heinemann, London; Harvard University Press, 1922–7

Pomeroy, S. B. 1976. *Goddesses, Whores, Wives, and Slaves: Women in Classical Antiquity*, Schocken Books, New York

1988. 'Greek marriage', in Grant and Kitzinger, 1988, pp. 1333–42

Pöschl, V., H. Gärtner and W. Heyke 1964. *Bibliographie zur antiken Bildersprache*, Bibliothek der klassischen Altertumswissenschaften, NF 1. Reihe, Carl Winter Universitätsverlag, Heidelberg

Quintilian. *The Institutio Oratoria of Quintilian*, LCL, English trans. H. E. Butler, William Heinemann, London, Harvard University Press, 1920–22

Rabe, H. (ed.) 1913. *Hermogenes Opera*, Rhetores Graeci 6, Teubner, Leipzig

1926. *Aphthonii Progymnasmata*, Rhetores Graeci 10, Teubner, Leipzig

Ramage, E. S. 1973. *Urbanitas: Ancient Sophistication and Refinement*, University of Oklahoma Press, Norman

Rathje, A. 1983. 'A banquet service from the Latin city of Ficana', *Analecta Romana Instituti Danici*, 12, pp. 7–29

1990. 'The adoption of the Homeric banquet in central Italy in the orientalizing period', in Murray, 1990, pp. 279–88

Raymond, J. C. 1984. 'Enthymemes, examples, and rhetorical method', in *Essays on Classical Rhetoric and Modern Discourse*, ed. R. J. Connors, L. S. Ede and A. A. Lunsford, Southern Illinois University Press, Carbondale, pp. 140–51

Redfield, J. 1982. 'Notes on the Greek wedding', *Arethusa*, 15, pp. 181–201

Reekmans, T. 1971. 'Juvenal's views on social change', *Ancient Society*, 2, pp. 117–61

Rehrl, S. 1961. *Das Problem der Demut in der profangriechischen Literatur im Vergleich zu Septuaginta und Neuem Testament*, AeC 4, Aschendorff, Münster

Reitzenstein, R. 1893. *Epigramm und Skolion. Ein Beitrag zur Geschichte der alexandrinischen Dichtung*, J. Ricker'sche Buchhandlung, Giessen

# 204    Bibliography

*Rhetorica ad Alexandrum*, LCL. English trans. H. Rackham, rev. edn. William Heinemann, London; Harvard University Press, 1965

*Rhetorica ad Herennium*, LCL, English trans. H. Caplan, William Heinemann, London; Harvard University Press, 1954

Rich, J. and A. Wallace-Hadrill (eds.) 1991. *City and Country in the Ancient World*, Leicester-Nottingham Studies in Ancient Society 2, Routledge, London and New York

Riddle, D. W. 1938. 'Early Christian hospitality: a factor in the gospel transmission', *Journal of Biblical Literature*, 57, pp. 141–54

Robbins, V. K. 1981. 'Classifying pronouncement stories in Plutarch's *Parallel Lives*', *Semeia*, 20, pp. 29–52

1984. *Jesus the Teacher: A Socio-Rhetorical Interpretation of Mark*, Fortress Press, Philadelphia; with new intro., 1992

1988a. 'Pronouncement stories from a rhetorical perspective', *Foundation & Facets Forum*, 4/2, pp. 3–32

1988b. 'The chreia', in *Greco-Roman Literature and the New Testament: Selected Forms and Genres*, Sources for Biblical Study 21, ed. D. E. Aune, Scholars Press, Atlanta, pp. 1–23

1989. *Ancient Quotes and Anecdotes: From Crib to Crypt*, Foundation and Facets Reference Series, ed. V. K. Robbins, Polebridge Press, Sonoma, California

1991a. 'Luke-Acts: a mixed population seeks a home in the Roman empire', in *Images of Empire*, JSOTSup 122, ed. L. Alexander, Sheffield Academic Press, pp. 202–21

1991b. 'The social location of the implied author of Luke-Acts', in Neyrey, 1991a, pp. 305–32

1991c. 'Writing as a rhetorical act in Plutarch and the gospels,' in *Persuasive Artistry: Studies in New Testament Rhetoric in Honor of George A. Kennedy*, ed. D. F. Watson, JSOT Press, Sheffield, pp. 142–68

1993a. 'Progymnastic rhetorical composition and pre-gospel traditions: a new approach', in *The Synoptic Gospels: Source Criticism and the New Literary Criticism*, BETL 110, ed. C. Focant, Uitgeverij Peeters and Leuven University Press, Leuven, pp. 111–47

1993b. 'Rhetoric and culture: exploring types of cultural rhetoric in a text', in *Rhetoric and the New Testament: Essays from the 1992 Heidelberg Conference*, ed. S. E. Porter and T. H. Olbricht, Sheffield Academic Press, pp. 447–67 (cited from typescript)

1994a. 'Socio-rhetorical criticism: Mary, Elizabeth, and the Magnificat as a test case', in *The New Literary Criticism and the New Testament*, eds. E. V. McNight and E. S. Malbon, Sheffield Academic Press; Trinity Press International, Philadelphia, forthcoming (cited from typescript)

1994b. 'The Beelzebul controversy and the great banquet: rhetorical elaboration from "the parts"', forthcoming (cited from typescript)

Rohrbaugh, R. L. 1991. 'The pre-industrial city in Luke-Acts: urban social relations', in Neyrey, 1991a, pp. 125–49

Roloff, J. 1970. *Das Kerygma und der irdische Jesus. Historische Motive in den Jesus-Erzählungen der Evangelien*, Vandenhoeck & Ruprecht, Göttingen

Rosivach, V. J. 1991. 'Some Athenian presuppositions about "the poor"', *Greece and Rome*, 38, pp. 189–98
Russell, D. A. 1983. *Greek Declamation*, Cambridge University Press
Rutherford, R. B., 1989. *The Meditations of Marcus Aurelius: A Study*, Clarendon Press, Oxford
Ste. Croix, G. E. M. 1981. *The Class Struggle in the Ancient Greek World: From the Archaic Age to the Arab Conquest*, Duckworth, London; Cornell University Press, Ithaca, New York
Sahlins, M. D. 1972. *Stone Age Economics*, Aldine-Atherton, Chicago
Saller, R. P. 1991. Review of Donald Engels, *Roman Corinth: An Alternative Model for the Classical City* (University of Chicago Press, 1990), in *Classical Philology*, 86, pp. 351–7
Sanders, J. 1974. 'The ethic of election in Luke's great banquet parable', in *Essays in Old Testament Ethics: J. Philip Hyatt in Memoriam*, ed. J. Crenshaw and J. Willis, Ktav, New York. pp. 245–71
Sanders, J. T. 1987. *The Jews in Luke-Acts*, SCM Press, London
Sato, M. 1988. *Q und Prophetie. Studien zur Gattungs- und Traditionsgeschichte der Quelle Q*, WUNT, 2. Reihe 29, J. C. B. Mohr (Paul Siebeck), Tübingen
Sattler, M. M. 1957. 'Conceptions of *ethos* in ancient rhetoric', *Speech Monographs*, 14, pp. 55–65
Sayre, F. 1948. *The Greek Cynics*, J. H. Furst, Baltimore
Scaglione, A. 1972. *The Classical Theory of Composition from its Origins to the Present: A Historical Survey*, University of North Carolina Press, Chapel Hill
Schenk, W. 1981. *Synopse zur Redenquelle der Evangelien. Q-Synopse und Rekonstruktion in deutscher Übersetzung mit kurzen Erläuterungen*, Patmos, Düsseldorf
Schleiermacher, F. 1825. *A Critical Essay on the Gospel of St. Luke*, English trans. with an intro. by C. Thirlwall, John Taylor, London
Schmidt, J. H. H. 1886. *Synonymik der griechischen Sprache*, 4 vols. Teubner, Leipzig, 1886; repr. Adolf M. Hakkert, Amsterdam, 1969
Schmidt, K. L. 1919. *Der Rahmen der Geschichte Jesu. Literarkritische Untersuchungen zur ältesten Jesusüberlieferung*, n.p., Berlin; repr. Wissenschaftliche Buchgesellschaft, Darmstadt, 1969
Schmitt-Pantel, P. 1990. 'Collective activities and the political in the Greek city', in *The Greek City from Homer to Alexander*, ed. O. Murray and S. Price, Clarendon Press, Oxford
Schneider, C. 1967. *Kulturgeschichte des Hellenismus*, 2 vols. C. H. Beck, Munich
Schneider, G. 1977. *Das Evangelium nach Lukas*, Ökumenischer Taschenbuchkommentar zum Neuen Testament 3/1–2, Gerd Mohn, Gütersloh; Echter Verlag, Würzburg
   1983. 'Jesu überraschende Antworten. Beobachtungen zu den Apophtegmen des dritten Evangeliums', *New Testament Studies*, 29, pp. 321–36; repr. in G. Schneider, *Lukas, Theologe der Heilsgeschichte. Aufsätze zum lukanischen Doppelwerk*, Bonner Biblische Beiträge 59, Peter Hanstein, Königstein/Ts.-Bonn, 1985, pp. 120–35

Schottroff, L. 1978. 'Das Magnificat und die älteste Tradition über Jesus von Nazareth', *Evangelische Theologie*, 38, pp. 298–313
1987. 'Das Gleichnis vom großen Gastmahl in der Logienquelle', *Evangelische Theologie*, 47, pp. 192–211
Schottroff, L. and W. Stegemann 1986. *Jesus and the Hope of the Poor*, English trans. M. J. O'Connell, Orbis, Maryknoll, New York
Schrage, W. 1964. *Das Verhältnis des Thomas-Evangeliums zur synoptischen Tradition und zu den koptischen Evangelienübersetzungen. Zugleich ein Beitrag zur gnostischen Synoptikerdeutung*, BZNW 29, Töpelmann, Berlin
Schreck, C. J. 1989. 'The Nazareth pericope: Luke 4,16–30 in recent study', in *L'Évangile de Luc – The Gospel of Luke*, rev. and enlarged edn of *L'Évangile de Luc. Problèmes littéraires et théologiques*, BETL 32, ed. F. Neirynck, Leuven University Press and Uitgeverij Peeters, Leuven, pp. 399–471
Schulz, S. 1972. *Q. Die Spruchquelle der Evangelisten*, Theologischer Verlag, Zurich
Schürmann, H. 1963. 'Das Thomasevangelium und das lukanische Sondergut', *Biblische Zeitschrift*, 7, pp. 236–60
1968. 'Protolukanische Spracheigentümlichkeiten', in H. Schürmann, *Traditionsgeschichtliche Untersuchungen*, Patmos, Düsseldorf, pp. 209–27
Scott, B. B. 1989. *Hear Then the Parable: A Commentary on the Parables of Jesus*, Augsburg Fortress Press, Minneapolis
Seager, R. 1973. 'Elitism and democracy in classical Athens', in *The Rich, the Well Born, and the Powerful: Elites and Upper Classes in History*, ed. F. C. Jaher, University of Illinois Press, Urbana
1977. '*Amicitia* in Tacitus and Juvenal', *American Journal of Ancient History*, 2, pp. 40–50
(SEG) *Supplementum Epigraphicum Graecum*, ed. J. J. E. Hondius, *et al.*, Sijthoff, Leiden; Gieben, Amsterdam, 1923–
Sellew, P. 1987. 'The last supper discourse in Luke 22:21–38', *Foundations & Facets Forum*, 3/3, pp. 70–95
Sellin, G. 1978. 'Komposition, Quellen und Funktion des lukanischen Reiseberichtes (Lk. IX 51–XIX 28)', *Novum Testamentum*, 20, pp. 100–35
Seneca. *Ad Lucilium Epistulae Morales*, LCL, English trans. R. H. Gummere, William Heinemann, London; G. P. Putnam's Sons, New York, 1920.
*De Consolatione ad Helviam*, in *Seneca: Moral Essays*, vol. II, LCL, English trans. J. W. Basore, William Heinemann, London; G. P. Putnam's Sons, New York, 1932
*De Beneficiis*, in *Seneca: Moral Essays*, vol. III, LCL, English trans. J. W. Basore, William Heinemann, London; Harvard University Press, 1935
*Septuaginta*. Ed. A. Rahlfs, Deutsche Bibelgesellschaft, Stuttgart, 1935
Sevrin, J.-M. 1989. 'Un groupement de trois paraboles contre les richesses dans l'Évangile selon Thomas', in *Les paraboles évangéliques. Perspectives nouvelles*, Lectio Divina 135, ed. J. Delorme, Cerf, Paris, pp. 425–39

Sheeley, S. M. 1992. *Narrative Asides in Luke-Acts*, JSNTSup 72, Sheffield Academic Press

Shero, L. R. 1923. 'The *cena* in Roman satire', *Classical Philology*, 18, pp. 126–43

Sider, J. W. 1981. 'The meaning of *parabole* in the usage of the synoptic evangelists', *Biblica*, 62, pp. 453–70

Silverman, S. F. 1965. 'Patronage and community-nation relationships', *Ethnology* 4, pp. 172–89

Sippel, D. V. 1987. 'Dietary deficiency among the lower classes of late republican and early imperial Rome', *The Ancient World*, 16, pp. 47–54

Slater, W. J. (ed.) 1991a. *Dining in a Classical Context*, University of Michigan, Ann Arbor

1991b. 'Introduction', in Slater, 1991a, pp. 1–5

Smith, C. W. F. 1948. *Jesus of the Parables*, Westminster Press, Philadelphia

Smith, D. E. 1980. 'Social obligation in the context of communal meals: a study of the Christian meal in I Corinthians in comparison with Graeco-Roman communal meals', Ph.D. Diss., Harvard University

1987. 'Table fellowship as a literary motif in the Gospel of Luke', *Journal of Biblical Literature*, 106, pp. 613–38

1991. 'The messianic banquet reconsidered', in *The Future of Early Christianity: Essays in Honor of Helmut Koester*, eds. B. A. Pearson in collab. with A. T. Kraabel, G. W. E. Nickelsburg and N. R. Petersen, Fortress Press, Minneapolis, pp. 64–73

Smith, D. E. and H. E. Taussig 1990. *Many Tables: The Eucharist in the New Testament and Liturgy Today*, SCM Press, London; Trinity Press International, Philadelphia

Solmsen, F. 1941. 'Aristotelian tradition in ancient rhetoric', *American Journal of Philology*, 62, pp. 35–50

Spengel, L. (ed.) 1883–6. *Rhetores Graeci*, 3 vols., Teubner, Leipzig

Starr, C. G. 1978. 'An evening with the flute-girls', *Past and Present*, 33, pp. 401–10.

Steele, E. S. 1981. 'Jesus' table-fellowship with Pharisees: an editorial analysis of Luke 7:36–50, 11:37–54, and 14:1–24', Ph.D. Diss., University of Notre Dame, Indiana

1984. 'Luke 11:37–54: a modified Hellenistic symposium?', *Journal of Biblical Literature*, 103, pp. 379–94

Stöger, A. 1970. 'Sentences sur les repas (Lc 14,1.7–14)', *Assemblées du Seigneur*, 53, pp. 78–88

(Str-B) Strack, H. L. and P. Billerbeck 1978. *Kommentar zum Neuen Testament aus Talmud und Midrash*, 5 vols., 7th edn, C. H. Beck, Munich

Strasburger, H. 1976. *Zum antiken Gesellschaftsideal*, Carl Winter Universitätsverlag, Heidelberg

Streeter, B. H. 1924. *The Four Gospels: A Study of Origins*, Macmillan, London

Sullivan, D. L. 1993. 'The ethos of epideictic encounter', *Philosophy and Rhetoric*, 26, pp. 113–33

Sutcliffe, E. F. 1953. 'Compel them to come in', *Scripture*, 5, pp. 20–1

(SVF) *Stoicorum Veterum Fragmenta*, 3 vols. ed. H. F. von Arnim, Teubner, Leipzig, 1903–5

Talbert, C. H. 1974. *Literary Patterns, Theological Themes, and the Genre of Luke-Acts*, SBLMS 20, Scholars Press, Missoula, Montana

1980 'Prophecies of future greatness: the contribution of Graeco-Roman biographies to an understanding of Luke 1:5–4:15', in *The Divine Helmsman: Studies on God's Control of Human Events Presented to Lou H. Silberman*, eds. J. L. Crenshaw and S. Sandmel, Ktav, New York, pp. 129–41

1989. 'Luke-Acts', in *The New Testament and its Modern Interpreters*, The Bible and its Modern Interpreters 3, eds. E. J. Epp and G. W. MacRae, Fortress Press, Philadelphia; Scholars Press, Atlanta, pp. 297–320

*The Talmud of the Land of Israel*, 35 vols. English trans. J. Neusner, University of Chicago Press, 1983–

Tannehill, R. C. 1975. *The Sword of His Mouth: Forceful and Imaginative Language in Synoptic Sayings*, Semeia Suppl. 1, Fortress Press, Philadelphia; Scholars Press, Missoula, Montana

1986. *The Narrative Unity of Luke Acts: A Literary Interpretation*, vol. I, *The Gospel According to Luke*, Foundations and Facets, Fortress Press, Philadelphia

Taylor, R. O. P. 1943-4. 'Form criticism in the first centuries', *Expository Times*, 55, pp. 218–20

1946. *The Groundwork of the Gospels, With Some Collected Papers*, Basil Blackwell, Oxford

Taylor, V. 1933. *The Formation of the Gospel Tradition*, Macmillan, London

(TDNT) *Theological Dictionary of the New Testament*, 10 vols., ed. G. Kittel, trans. G. W. Bromiley, Erdmans, Grand Rapids, Michigan, 1964–76

Tecusan, M. 1990. '*Logos sympotikos*: patterns of the irrational in philosophical drinking: Plato outside the *Symposium*', in Murray, 1990, pp. 238–60

*Teles (The Cynic Teacher)*, SBLTT 11/Graeco-Roman Religion 3, ed. and trans. E. N. O'Neil, Scholars Press, Missoula, Montana, 1977

Theissen, G. 1974. *Urchristliche Wundergeschichten. Ein Beitrag zur formgeschichtlichen Erforschung der synoptischen Evangelien*, StNT 8, Gerd Mohn, Gütersloh

*Theophrastus. Characters*, LCL, English trans. J. M. Edmonds, William Heinemann, London; Harvard University Press, 1929

Thibeaux, E. R. 1990. 'The narrative rhetoric of Luke 7:36–50: a study of context, text, and interpretation', Ph.D. Diss., Graduate Theological Union, California

Thompson, E. F. 1907. 'ΜΕΤΑΝΟΕΩ and ΜΕΤΑΜΕΛΕΙ in Greek literature until 100 A.D., including discussion of their cognates and of their Hebrew equivalents', Ph.D. Diss., University of Chicago

Thomson, G. 1938. *The Oresteia of Aeschylus*, 2 vols. Cambridge University Press

Tilborg, Sjef van. 1987. 'De parabel van de grote feestmaaltijd (Lc 14,1–24)', in *Parabelverhalen in Lucas: Van Semiotiek naar Pragmatiek*,

Bibliography 209

eds. B. van Iersel *et al.*, TFT-Studies 8, Tilburg University, Tilburg, Netherlands, pp. 133–67
Trautmann, M. 1980. *Zeichenhafte Handlungen Jesu. Ein Beitrag zur Frage nach dem geschichtlichen Jesu*, FzB 37, Echter Verlag, Würzburg
Treggiari, S. 1988. 'Roman marriage', in Grant and Kitzinger, 1988, pp. 1343–54
Trilling, W. 1960. 'Zur Überlieferungsgeschichte des Gleichnisses vom Hochzeitsmahl Mt 22,1–14', *Biblische Zeitschrift*, NF 4, pp. 251–65
Turner, M. M. B. 1982. 'The Sabbath, Sunday, and the law in Luke/Acts', in *From Sabbath to Lord's Day: A Biblical, Historical and Theological Investigation*, ed. D. A. Carson, Zondervan, Grand Rapids, Michigan, pp. 99–157
Ullrich, F. 1908–9. *Entstehung and Entwicklung der Literaturgattung des Symposion*, 2 vols. Stürtz, Würzburg
Uther, H.-J. 1981. *Behinderte in popularen Erzählungen. Studien zur historischen und vergleichenden Erzählforschung*, Suppl. to Fabula, Reihe B/Untersuchungen, Walter de Gruyter, Berlin and New York
Vaage, L. E. 1987. 'The ethos and ethics of an itinerant intelligence', Ph.D. Diss., Claremont Graduate School, Claremont, California
Vernant, J.-P. 1965. *Mythe et pensée chez les grecs. Etudes de psychologie historique*, Les textes à l'appui 13, F. Maspero, Paris
1990. *Myth and Society in Ancient Greece*, English trans. J. Lloyd, Zone Books, New York
Versnel, H. S. 1987. 'Wife and helpmate: women of ancient Athens in anthropological perspective', in *Sexual Asymmetry: Studies in Ancient Society*, eds. J. Blok and P. Mason, J. C. Gieben, Amsterdam, pp. 59–86
Vetta, M. (ed.) 1983. *Poesia e simposio nella Grecia antica. Guida storica e critica*, Universale Laterza 621, Laterza
Vielhauer, P. 1975. *Geschichte der urchristlichen Literatur: Einleitung in das Neue Testament, die Apokryphen und the Apostolischen Väter*, Walter de Gruyter, Berlin
Visser, M. 1991. *The Rituals of Dinner: The Origins, Evolution, Eccentricities and Meaning of Table Manners*, HarperCollins, Toronto
Vögtle, A. 1971. 'Die Einladung zum großen Gastmahl and zum königlichen Hochzeitsmahl. Ein Paradigma für den Wandel des geschichtlichen Verständnishorizonts', in *Das Evangelium und die Evangelien. Beiträge zur evangelischen Forschung*, KBANT, Patmos, Düsseldorf, pp. 171–218
Vorster, W. S. 1990. 'Stoics and early Christians on blessedness', in *Greeks, Romans, and Christians: Essays in Honor of Abraham J. Malherbe*, eds. D. L. Balch, E. Ferguson and W. A. Meeks, Fortress Press, Minneapolis, pp. 38–51
Walcot, P. 1970. *Greek Peasants, Ancient and Modern: A Comparison of Social and Moral Values*, Manchester University Press
1978. *Envy and the Greeks: A Study of Human Behaviour*, Aris & Phillips, Warminster
Wallace-Hadrill, A. 1991. 'Introduction', in Rich and Wallace-Hadrill, 1991, pp. ix–xviii

Wankel, H. 1961. 'Kalos kai Agathos', Diss., Julius-Maximilians-Universität, Würzburg, 1961; repr. Photo-Landa, Frankfurt a.M., 1961
Wechssler, E. 1947. *Hellas im Evangelium*, 2nd edn,. Marion von Schröder, Hamburg
Weder, H. 1978. *Die Gleichnisse Jesu als Metaphern. Traditions- und redaktionsgeschichtliche Analysen und Interpretationen*, FRLANT 120, Vandenhoeck & Ruprecht, Göttingen
Weiler, I. 1988. 'Soziale Randgruppen in der antiken Welt. Einführung und wissenschaftliche Aspekte. Ausgewählte Literatur zur historischen Randgruppenforschung', in Weiler and Graßl, 1988, pp. 11–40
Weiler, I. and H. Graßl (eds.) 1988. *Soziale Randgruppen und Aussenseiter im Altertum. Referate vom Symposion 'Soziale Randgruppen und antike Sozialpolitik' (21. bis 23. September 1987)*, Leykam, Graz
Welskopf, E. C. 1965. 'Elitevorstellungen und Elitebildung in der hellenischen Polis', *Klio*, 43–45, pp. 49–64
Wengst, K. 1987. *Demut. Solidarität der Gedemütigten. Wandlungen eines Begriffes und seines sozialen Bezugs in griechisch-römischer, alttestamentliche-jüdischer und urchristlicher Tradition*, Chr. Kaiser, Munich; English trans. by J. Bowden, *Humility: Solidarity of the Humiliated: The Transformation of an Attitude and its Social Relevance in Graeco-Roman, Old Testament-Jewish and Early Christian Tradition*, Fortress Press, Philadelphia, 1988
Wesseling, B. 1988. 'The audience of the ancient novels', in *Groningen Colloquia on the Novel*, vol. I, ed. H. Hofmann, Egbert Forsten, Groningen
White, K. D. 1988. 'Farming and animal husbandry', in Grant and Kitzinger, 1988, pp. 211–45
Whitehead, D. 1983. 'Competitive outlay and community profit: φιλοτιμία in democratic Athens', *Classica et Mediaevalia*, 34, pp. 55–74
Wickert-Micknat, G. 1990. 'Ursachen, Erscheinungsformen und Aufhebung von Marginalität am Beispiel der homerischen Gesellschaft', *Gymnasium*, 97, pp. 131–44
Wilder, A. N. 1956. 'Scholars, theologians, and ancient rhetoric', *Journal of Biblical Literature*, 75, pp. 1–11
Wilson, S. G. 1983. *Luke and the Law*, SNTSMS 50, Cambridge University Press
Wisse, J. 1989. *Ethos and Pathos from Aristotle to Cicero*, Adolf M. Hakkert, Amsterdam
Wolff, H. J. 1944. 'Marriage law and family organization in ancient Athens: a study on the interrelation of public and private law in the Greek city', *Traditio*, 2, pp. 43–95
*Xenophon*, 7 vols. LCL, English trans. C. L. Brownson, O. J. Todd *et al.* William Heinemann, London; Harvard University Press, 1918–25
York, J. O. 1991. *The Last Shall Be First: The Rhetoric of Reversal in Luke*, JSNTSup 46, JSOT Press, Sheffield
Youtie, H. C. 1940. 'Notes on *O.Mich. I*', *Transactions of the American Philological Association*, 71, pp. 623–59; repr. in *Scriptuinculae I*, Adolf M. Hakkert, Amsterdam, 1973, pp. 63–104

Zeller, D. 1977. *Die weisheitlichen Mahnsprüche bei den Synoptikern*, FzB 17, Echter Verlag, Würzburg

1984. *Kommentar zur Logienquelle*, Stuttgarter Kleiner Kommentar/NT 21, Katholisches Bibelwerk, Stuttgart

# INDICES

## Ancient authors

212

# Indices

213

Methodius of Olympus, 139
Musonius Rufus, 33, 77

Nicolaus of Myra, 11, 146

Ovid, 36, 37

Papias, 147–8
Persius, 39, 105
Petronius Arbiter, 45, 53, 58, 104, 139
Philo, 45, 80, 101, 138, 151
Philostratus, 37–8, 58, 145
Plato, 31, 37, 41, 45, 58, 83, 95, 101,
    109, 138, 140, 141, 143
Plautus, 80
Pliny, 45, 71, 103, 105, 115
Plutarch, 10, 33, 35, 45–6, 55–6, 57, 58,
    71, 76, 77, 99, 100, 101, 102, 103, 105,
    109, 115, 127, 138, 139, 140, 151
Pollux, 50
Polybius, 9, 36, 47
Priscian, 11
Propertius, 50
Ps-Demosthenes, 76
Ps-Longinus, 30, 38

Quintilian, 11, 90, 91, 106, 136, 148,
    152, 154, 156, 166

Sallust, 10
Seneca, 36, 90, 118–19, 136, 156
Sophocles, 31, 76, 80, 82
Soranus, 79–80
Stesichoros, 65
Stobaeus, 33, 34, 35

Tacitus, 56, 66
Teles, 34
Tertullian, 32
Theocritus, 90
Theophrastus, 45
Thomas, Gospel of, 2, 67, 69, 70, 71,
    73, 85–6, 151
Thucydides, 53
Trypho Grammaticus, 11

Virgil, 80, 90

Xenophon, 33, 33–4, 57, 71, 78, 82, 100,
    138, 139, 141, 143

## Modern authors

Abu-Lughod, L., 100, 109
Adeleye, G., 111
Adkins, A. W. H., 83, 100, 108, 111
Al-Azmeh, A., 92
Alexander, L. C. A., 9, 10
Alföldy, G., 52, 53, 86
Alpers, P., 14
Alter, R., 137
Anderson, G., 32
Arnal, W. E., 48
Aune, D. E., 12, 46, 137, 138, 139, 151

Baasland, E., 66
Bacon, B. W., 3, 68, 126
Baergen, R., 180
Bailey, K. E., 85, 95, 101, 102, 108, 122
Bain, D., 63, 126
Baldwin, B., 58, 60
Baldwin, C. S., 10, 146, 158
Ballard, P., 80
Bammel, E., 82
Barr, D. L., 10
Barrett, C. K., 127
Bartchy, S. S., 53
Bartsch, S., 13
Bastomsky, S. J., 81
Beatrice, P. F., 67

Beavis, M. A., 48, 65
Becker, W. A., 101
Bek, L., 102
Berger, K., 65, 66–7, 123, 137, 138, 139,
    148, 150
Bernays, J., 33
Bernidaki-Aldous, E. A., 83
Bielohlawek, K., 143
Bihari-Andersson, A., 99, 121, 130
Billault, A., 180
Billerbeck, M., 33, 36
Bitzer, L. F., 176
Bjorndahl, S., 151, 153, 158, 178
Black, M., 47
Blass, F. and A. Debrunner, 170
Blomberg, C. L., 89
Bobertz, C. A., 31, 96, 180
Boer, W. den, 48, 49, 50, 76, 81
Bolkestein, H., 31, 81, 82, 86, 87, 94,
    118, 119
Bompaire, J., 142
Bonner, S. F., 136, 146
Booth, A., 39
Bossman, D. M., 85, 99, 108, 118
Bovon, F., 9
Bowersock, G. W., 32
Bowie, E. L., 10, 143

## Index of subjects

Printed in the United States
35155LVS00002B/88